C0-AWJ-925

FROM MANAGER TO VISIONARY

M-GEN
Ma908

FROM MANAGER TO VISIONARY

The Secretary-General of the United Nations

Kent J. Kille

BIBLIOTHÈQUES
uO
LIBRARIES

palgrave
macmillan

62933293X

FROM MANAGER TO VISIONARY
© Kent J. Kille, 2006.

All rights reserved. No part of this book may be used or reproduced in any manner whatsoever without written permission except in the case of brief quotations embodied in critical articles or reviews.

First published in 2006 by
PALGRAVE MACMILLAN™
175 Fifth Avenue, New York, N.Y. 10010 and
Houndmills, Basingstoke, Hampshire, England RG21 6XS
Companies and representatives throughout the world.

PALGRAVE MACMILLAN is the global academic imprint of the Palgrave Macmillan division of St. Martin's Press, LLC and of Palgrave Macmillan Ltd. Macmillan® is a registered trademark in the United States, United Kingdom and other countries. Palgrave is a registered trademark in the European Union and other countries.

ISBN-13: 978–1–4039–7104–3
ISBN-10: 1–4039–7104–8

Library of Congress Cataloging-in-Publication Data is available from the Library of Congress.

A catalogue record for this book is available from the British Library.

Design by Newgen Imaging Systems (P) Ltd., Chennai, India.

First edition: December 2006

10 9 8 7 6 5 4 3 2 1

Printed in the United States of America.

JZ
5008
.K55
2006

To my Family
Nicola, Elisabeth, and Charlotte

Contents

LIST OF TABLES

Acknowledgments

I wish to express my gratitude for the training and assistance provided by the professors at The Ohio State University that made this research possible. In particular, Peg Hermann, whose work on political leadership helped to inspire this study and who served as an exceptional mentor; Chad Alger, who first opened my eyes to the world of international organization and provided immeasurable support and inspiration; and Don Sylvan, for his vital critical viewpoint and constructive comments.

My great appreciation to my student research assistants at The College of Wooster—Lisa Basalla, Patrick Bourke, Marina Majdek, Alison Nau, Lara Pfaff, Neha Sahgal, and Margaret Ann Stewart—for their hard work. I especially want to thank Emily Hilty for her essential assistance from book proposal to editorial suggestions and the many details in between that helped to keep this project properly on track. An added thanks to my colleagues in the Department of Political Science at The College of Wooster for putting up with me during the final stages of writing and a particular acknowledgment to Eric Moskowitz for our discussions regarding psychological approaches for studying American presidents.

I thank Mark Kille and Dale Miller for their translation assistance. I am also grateful for the suggestions and comments provided by Roger Scully during our previous collaborative work and Courtney Smith's ideas in regards to the study of Kofi Annan. My thanks to Mark Schafer and Michael Young for their feedback on at-a-distance measurement techniques. My gratitude to the editorial team at Palgrave Macmillan for believing in my work and providing helpful guidance in bringing the project to fruition.

Finally, a special thanks to my family who provided support throughout the process—my mother Carol; my wife Nicola; and my daughters Elisabeth and Charlotte.

CHAPTER 1

Introduction

No matter how dispassionately or scientifically the office of Secretary-General is studied, it still is occupied by a human being with a will. The human qualities of the Secretary-General contribute to his influence. But to determine precisely how much this influence results from personal charm, sensitivity, intelligence, ideological suppleness, mental limitations, neurosis, individual character, or cultural background would require knowledge and research techniques unavailable for this study. It may be possible for future researchers to use psychological and social research methods that may result in a firmer estimate than can be found here.

(Gordenker 1967, 320)

The international community faces a variety of threats to global peace. Since one of the primary objectives of the United Nations is to maintain international peace and security, the organization is highly engaged in trying to overcome such threats. As the chief administrative officer of the United Nations, the Secretary-General has the opportunity to be closely involved in these efforts. Benjamin Rivlin concisely observes, "The United Nations is an integral element in the world system. Within the United Nations, the Secretary-General is the most important figure. Through him and his office pass all the interrelationships represented by the United Nations" (1993, 5). The Secretary-General may play an important role in shaping the peace and security agenda of the United Nations. More directly, office-holders are called upon to assist in resolving breaches of the peace and, at times, use their position to take independent initiatives to become involved in determining what situations require attention and how these threats should be resolved.

Given the centrality of the office, analysts are understandably interested in how Secretaries-General can utilize their position to guide the course of UN activities. In one of the seminal works on the office, Leon Gordenker states, "Even superficial acquaintance with the office of Secretary-General and the work of its holders leads readily to the conclusion that it is a source of influence on the formation of international organization policy. Such a conclusion, however, begs the question of how this influence is exerted, when, and in what circumstances" (1967, xv). Gordenker's question remains relevant today, yet a full understanding of when and how the individual holding such a potentially vital position attempts to influence the path of global events is still lacking.

The proposition at the heart of this study is that, when looking at the leadership provided by a Secretary-General, it is important to recognize how the personal qualities of office-holders guide their political behavior. As Inis Claude argues, "Analysis must go beyond the institution of the Secretary-Generalship to the actual person serving as Secretary-General" (1993, 255). However, despite Claude's call, exploration of the "actual person" in the office has been limited. Although often acknowledged as an important component of studying the Secretary-General, office-holders' personal characteristics have not been systematically considered. While analysts have explored how an office-holder can be influential, the question of *why* particular Secretaries-General choose to act in certain ways in order to exert their influence is often not fully addressed.

The particular focus of the research in this book is on how the leadership style of the individual office-holders affects their actions in the realm of international peace and security. Leadership style is based on the interaction of politically relevant personal characteristics and predisposes leaders to behave in a certain manner. In this manner, leadership style captures how leaders view situations and the way that they are likely to approach their role. Thus, the specific question examined is as follows: how does the leadership style of a Secretary-General affect the way that he or she attempts to influence the manner in which threats to international peace and security are addressed?

Chapter 2 begins the process of answering this question by reviewing the literature on the Secretary-General to determine what leadership styles and related personal characteristics should be examined. The chapter opens by exploring why previous analyses of the Secretary-General have had a relatively limited focus on the personal characteristics of individuals who have held the office. This is often due to an overemphasis on other considerations, such as environmental or organizational factors, that are viewed as limiting the impact of the office. While this study does not seek to disprove the importance of external factors and, in fact, explores the potential interrelation of contextual and personal factors as part of the concluding analysis in chapter 7, it is argued that such approaches have limited understanding of the potential impact of a Secretary-General's personal qualities. Alternatively, other analysts stress the overarching importance of all office-holders in a manner that overlooks individual differences, which once again undermines the examination of personal factors.

However, it is possible to draw across writing on the Secretary-General to detail personal dimensions that have been emphasized. This includes the long-running debate over Secretary-General leadership that revolves around two contrasting styles: bureaucratic manager and visionary activist. Some analysts also call for a more balanced, strategic leadership style that lies between these two extremes. By employing the three leadership style types derived from this debate, this study is able to explore whether these types are analytically useful. Furthermore, careful reading of analyses of the Secretary-General also reveals six personal characteristics—responsivity, belief that can influence, need for relationships, need for recognition, supranationalism, and problem-solving emphasis—which can be interrelated to establish each overarching leadership style.

The lack of understanding regarding the personal qualities of individual Secretaries-General is especially unfortunate in light of advances in scholarship studying other leaders. As detailed in chapter 2, there are scholars who have come to the same conclusion that personal characteristics matter as part of foreign policy analysis, but they have made much greater strides in researching individual differences and considering how these affect political behavior. Such studies can serve as an important source of inspiration for examining the Secretary-General. In particular, this book draws upon the lessons learned from political psychological analyses that employ at-a-distance assessment. Building upon this work demonstrates how it is possible to measure and analyze the leadership styles of Secretaries-General. This is a key step for countering the skepticism of those whose scholarship focuses on the Secretary-Generalship while slighting the relevance of individual traits as well as for providing answers to those who recognize the relevance of personal characteristics, but have been unable to devise measurement schemes to explore these. In addition, this study makes a broader contribution to the study of political leadership by expanding knowledge on leadership into the realm of the United Nations. In this manner it is hoped that this work will serve as another building block in the search for understanding of leadership across different forms of political organization.

Measuring the office-holders' leadership styles provides a better understanding of a series of issues regarding their behavior in office. When faced with a threat to international peace and security, how does a Secretary-General react? Does the office-holder seek to influence how the problem is handled? If so, in what ways? A Secretary-General may or may not seek to be directly involved. Once engaged in handling a threat, office-holders must further decide what degree of involvement should be pursued and how they should try to affect the way that the problem area is addressed. Different Secretaries-General may attempt to influence the way that global tensions are handled in divergent manners. This divergence can be both in terms of the methods employed to become involved and in how these activities are pursued.

In order to closely explore the proposed link between leadership style and political behavior, chapter 3 reviews and organizes the disparate literature on the Secretary-General to construct a coherent behavioral framework. A toolbox analogy is employed to organize the activities of the office in the area of peace and security into three main categories: agenda setting, peaceful settlement of disputes, and UN intervention. Each Secretary-General takes possession of a toolbox that is similarly stocked in terms of these categories, but the way that these tools are used often differs. The argument of this study is that such variation in the way that office-holders employ the avenues for influence reflects the leadership style that they possess. Individual office-holders with dissimilar styles will use this toolbox in distinctively different ways. They will choose to use different types of tools and they will also use similar tools in a divergent manner. Thus, the framework of influential activities is explicitly linked to each leadership style to create a series of behavioral expectations.

Influence can be thought of as a two-step process. What Secretaries-General are like personally will affect what they do and then these efforts can alter the path of the United Nations in handling breaches of the peace. This study is careful to distinguish between attempts to influence and the impact of these actions. The focus of the research is on the first part of this process, the repercussions of leadership style guiding a Secretary-General's behavior, which is not well detailed by others examining the office. Since different individuals act and react in distinct ways, a full understanding of how a Secretary-General could potentially direct the role of the United Nations will not be achieved unless there is better comprehension of how office-holders approach the position. An initial consideration of the potential connection between Secretaries-General with different leadership styles and their impact is incorporated later in the study as part of the analysis that links leadership style and context in the concluding chapter.

The personal characteristics of all seven Secretaries-General are measured using assessment-at-a-distance and the office-holders are categorized according to leadership style at the end of chapter 2. Based on this analysis, Secretaries-General whose coding results indicate that they are representative of the three leadership styles—Dag Hammarskjöld the visionary, Kurt Waldheim the manager, and Kofi Annan the strategist—are selected for behavioral analysis. These three office-holders are examined in the case studies presented in chapters 4–6. Each case study provides information on the office-holder's election, an overview of the leadership style and personal characteristics as discussed by other analysts in order to support the content analysis coding results, and a detailed behavioral analysis organized according to the framework established in chapter 3. This extensive case study material provides important insight into the tenures of three key examples of the Secretary-General and clarifies how office-holders endeavor to address global security.

Chapter 7 presents a comparative analysis across Hammarskjöld, Waldheim, and Annan and discusses the implications of this research. This study demonstrates that a link can be established between different leadership styles and the behavioral variations among holders of the Secretary-Generalship. The results show how office-holders with different leadership styles have sought to influence how threats to international peace and security are handled in a manner congruent with their styles, although a more nuanced understanding of their actions at times requires examining the impact of particular personal characteristics that deviate from the leadership style ideal. In doing so, the study counters doubts regarding personal qualities as an important area of study for understanding the Secretary-General. It also addresses concerns regarding the possibility of measuring and comparing leadership styles and relating these to specific behaviors in a systematic fashion. With the foundation for examining leadership styles well established, the concluding analysis also moves forward to present an initial consideration of how this research could be linked to contextual factors and discusses a range of future research avenues.

CHAPTER 2

The Secretary-Generalship: The Individual Behind the Office

These provisions of the Charter relating to the powers and responsibilities of the Secretary-General leave him much latitude in determining how to exercise his authority, for no constitution, however precise, can or should shape in detail the manner in which an administrative or executive head conducts his office. Much must be left to the manifold qualities of character, mind, and personality which an individual brings to his task.

(Cordier 1961, 3)

INTRODUCTION

To reiterate the question that drove this study, how does the leadership style of a Secretary-General affect the way that he or she attempts to influence the manner in which threats to international peace and security are addressed? A fundamental first step in answering this question is to establish the leadership styles, and the corresponding personal characteristics, for understanding how office-holders might attempt to have influence. The UN Charter outlines the Secretary-Generalship position, but does not shed light on the personal aspects of potential office-holders. C.S.R. Murthy explains how a "cursory reading of the relevant chapter in the Charter shows how ambiguous, if not misleading, the constitutional framework sounds about the nature and scope of the Secretary-General's office. For what is obviously the most important job in the Organization, the Charter does not specify the qualifications of a candidate" (Murthy 1995, 181).

Studies of the Secretary-General are another logical place to look for information about office-holders' personal qualities. However, despite journalistic observations such as "those of us who have been covering the United Nations since its inception tend to recall how earlier Secretaries General saw their role and developed their own style of meeting crises" (Samuels 1979, 3), there has been relatively little effort to carefully address the differences in leadership styles among the Secretaries-General. Many times the oversight is due to the tendency of analysts to focus upon contextual limitations instead of examining the leadership capabilities of office-holders. When the potential importance of personal characteristics is discussed, this is often a secondary consideration relative to environmental factors. Other observers, in their zeal to establish the importance of the office, downplay individual differences by stressing that *every* Secretary-General has played an influential role in international affairs. Overall, the existing descriptions of personal factors are not set out in an explicit or comparable manner. One of the tasks for this study, therefore, is to clarify and structure these efforts to determine what it is about office-holders that should be compared.

The chapter begins by reviewing how the Secretary-General is presented in previous analyses of the office. The three approaches that one finds—dominance of contextual factors where the individual office-holder is largely ignored, the "super Secretary-General syndrome" where the importance of all office-holders is emphasized, and consideration of individual differences—are covered. The discussion then moves into the debate over the type of leadership that a Secretary-General should be prepared to provide the United Nations. The traditional debate over whether organizational heads should posses a managerial or a visionary orientation to leadership is combined with the balanced "strategic" style that many analysts have suggested in order to provide the three ideal leadership style types that are compared in this study. By drawing across previous work on the Secretary-General that discusses personal characteristics it is also established that there are six key personal traits—responsivity, belief that can influence, need for recognition, need for relationships, supranationalism, and problem-solving emphasis—that can be related to each of these leadership styles.

The latter part of this chapter addresses measuring the personal characteristics and leadership styles. This study draws on at-a-distance content analysis techniques initially designed by scholars to study the personal traits of national level leaders that affect foreign policy decision making. Once the measurement procedure has been established, the chapter presents the content analysis results for the personal characteristics, and the corresponding leadership styles, for all seven Secretaries-General who have served the United Nations to date.

These results are compared to demonstrate the variation that exists between these office-holders.

PREDOMINANCE OF ENVIRONMENTAL FACTORS

The literature on the Secretary-General often overlooks or only briefly mentions personal characteristics. As Ian Johnstone notes, "Most scholars who write on the SG consider the political context to be the ultimate determinant of his influence," so they fail to provide a more "nuanced picture" of the office (2003, 454). Such analysis stresses the place of the office relative to environmental or organizational constraints, while downplaying the role played by the Secretary-General and, thereby, largely ignoring personal differences between the office-holders. The office-holder is seen as a secondary concern in comparison to the dynamics of the member-states in the international political environment (e.g., Gordenker 1993; Jackson 1978; and Jakobson 1974). Within the organization itself, the institutional setup or power structure is portrayed as more important than how individuals attempt to work in relation to these constraints (e.g., Franck and Nolte 1993; Gordenker 1993; Jackson 1978; and Kanninen 1995). In such an approach, these factors mean that the activities of the Secretary-General will be inherently limited unless fortuitous circumstances prevail.

THE SUPER SECRETARY-GENERAL SYNDROME

At the opposite end of the spectrum are studies of the Secretary-General where the tendency is to focus on the perceived importance of *all* of the office-holders. In this case, instead of overlooking individual differences by downplaying or ignoring the individual in light of environmental factors, the individual is mentioned, but only in a positive light. This often occurs in discussions of how Secretaries-General have developed the importance of the position over time. This approach is illustrated by statements such as "No incumbent lost an opportunity to interpret his powers under the Charter in an ingenious manner to expand the scope of his activities" (Murthy 1995, 186). Similarly, M. Christiane Bourloyannis claims in an analysis of fact-finding that each Secretary-General "interpreted . . . [his] political functions broadly" and has been "extremely active by interpreting his mandate in very broad terms" (1990, 645, 668). Variation across the office-holders' actions and possible explanations for these differences are largely left aside in favor of sweeping generalizations about the high level of engagement of the office.

In these types of studies individual distinctions may at times be acknowledged, but the author is also usually careful to stress that these differences have not undermined the Secretary-General's efforts on behalf of the United Nations. For example, when discussing the Secretary-General and conflict settlement, Indar Jit Rikhye argues that some of the Secretaries-General have been "more passive" and "their roles have been less dramatic," but that "each has made significant contributions to peace and security" (1991, 72–73). Along similar lines, Diego Cordovez argues, "Personal convictions and temperaments may differ from one individual to another, but every Secretary-General has sought to maximize his commitment to objectivity and to the principles and purposes of the United Nations" (1987, 165).

This study supports a more fine-tuned analysis that questions whether there has really been no significant difference between the Secretaries-General regarding their attempts to have influence. This allows for a closer examination of claims such as the following: "These men had varying personal styles—Lie and Hammarskjöld were as different as mallet and scalpel—yet they all pursued what they believed to be the mandate of the Charter: to be the *independent* and *active* defender of an international perspective" (Franck 1985, 119; Franck's emphasis). Given such an acknowledgment that office-holders possess different leadership styles, it is important to more closely examine the impact on the behavior displayed by the Secretaries-General.

Another issue is that discussions of office-holders are prone to get caught up in how a Secretary-General *should* behave, while glossing over *why* a particular Secretary-General would or would not behave in this manner. In other words, with the focus on how a Secretary-General acts, it is often not clear exactly what personal traits drive this behavior. While studies with an emphasis on structural factors gloss over the potential importance of individual differences, those that focus solely on the behavior of the Secretary-General also miss the personal dimension of what is guiding those actions.

INDIVIDUAL SECRETARY-GENERAL DIFFERENCES

The argument underpinning this study, that personal differences are an important factor for understanding the functioning of the

Secretary-Generalship, is supported by others researching executive heads of international organizations. For example, a study of Commonwealth Secretaries-General finds that "personality and leadership played a crucial role" in the development of the office (Akinrinade 1992, 64). The importance of personal factors has also been explicitly recognized in the work on the UN Secretary-General. For example, Nabil Elarby argues, "The personality and character of each incumbent is reflected in his conceptual reading of the Charter provisions, and in his political judgment and style" (1987, 188). Similarly, longtime Secretariat member Brian Urquhart emphasizes, "The Secretary-General, for all his eminence, in reality enjoys few of the normal attributes of power or authority," so the "strength of his office" relies on the personal character of the individual in office (1972, 18).

However, in many studies of the Secretary-General, even when individual characteristics are discussed they are given perfunctory attention compared to the discussion of organizational or environmental constraints (e.g., Cox 1969; Goodrich 1962; Gordenker 1967, 1972; James 1985, 1993; Nachmias 1993; Skjelsbaek 1991; and Sutterlin 1993, 2003). In this material, the role of an officeholder is given greater consideration compared to the previously referenced work that stressed the sole dominance of environmental factors. However, while the potential importance of personal qualities is indicated, these are not clearly addressed as the emphasis is still on contextual concerns. It is as if it must be acknowledged that a person sits in the office, but the next step of clearly specifying what it is about these individuals that should be compared is rarely taken.

Reflecting this point, a 1969 review of research on the Secretary-General concluded, "The consensus of the authors under review is that while the personal qualities of the officeholders are important, they should be viewed as subsidiary to other variables" (Zacher 1969, 938). More recent work by two scholars who stress a similar perspective, Rivlin (1993, 1995, 1996) and Edward Newman (1998, 2001), illustrate how this statement continues to ring true. Both emphasize the burden of environmental restrictions on the position, but they also recognize that individual differences might be important for how an office-holder will address or work within those bounds. However, exactly what these personal qualities are and what specific behaviors this will in turn lead to are not clarified.

The basic theme of Rivlin's work is that the international environment is a vital area of study for understanding the role of the Secretaries-General because this "establishes the parameters of their behavior" (1993, 13). According to Rivlin, this means that "the prestige, influence, and significance of the office rises and falls with the prestige, influence and significance of the UN as a whole determined by the international political climate at any given moment" (1995, 99–100). However, Rivlin also states that, along with the impact of environmental circumstances, the "office takes on a different cast depending upon . . . the individual occupying it . . . in any particular international political climate" (1993, 6). Later, he asks point blank, "Does the individual occupying the position make any appreciable difference in the role played by the Secretary-General?" The answer is that "the individual's performance also counts" because

> Effectiveness is the combined product of the limitations imposed on the Secretary-General by the nature of the international system and the personal qualities of the office-holder. Surely the differing styles and personalities of each of the six men who have held the position, while not leaving a lasting stamp on the office, in some ways affected their effectiveness in it. (Rivlin 1995, 84)

Therefore, personal characteristics do matter to Rivlin, but compared to the attention he devotes to environmental issues readers are left without a clear understanding of personal differences between office-holders. Exactly what are these "personal qualities" and "styles" that were displayed? How should Secretaries-General with similar leadership styles be expected to behave in the future?

Similarly, Newman recognizes that a Secretary-General's influence is tied to "personality and style" and states "clearly personalities shape political processes and history" (1998, 25–26). However, he also does not closely address what types of personal differences exist and the potential impact that these could have in shaping the behavior of an office-holder. Instead, like Rivlin, Newman stresses the significance of global environmental relations:

> An appreciation of the constraints and opportunities inherent in the changing political environment help to keep this variable in perspective. The personality of the Secretary-General can only take advantage of these opportunities; it cannot create the environmental and constitutional parameters itself. Personality is an interesting—and certainly a popular— explanation for the history of the Office but it is not sufficient. The environmental backdrop is an essential part of the equation. (1998, 27–28)

In the end, despite references to the importance of individual differences alluded to in the text, the office is viewed as an "institutional manifestation" of the cooperative efforts in the international environment (Newman 1998, 7).

In Newman's (2001) research on the Secretary-General's involvement with Cyprus, he once again points to the potential importance of personality as a variable that influences the activities of officeholders in conjunction with environmental factors. Early in the piece he states, "The Cyprus issue is clearly one in which these variables—the Secretary-General's personality, the status of the UN, the position of the great powers towards the Secretary-General and the UN, the complexities of the Cyprus conflict—have interacted over the years, to various effect" (2001, 130). Despite such claims, Newman does not directly study the impact of personality or provide an indication of what this variable entails. Once again, the reader is left wondering about how exactly personal differences can be related to the study of variations in office-holder behavior. If Newman as well as others do not measure personal characteristics and test their relevance and instead spend most of their effort discussing environmental factors, then how can claims that environmental considerations are somehow a more "essential" part of the equation be supported?

Overall, the stress on contextual factors can lead to deterministic accounts that often overlook the potential impact of individual factors. This study does not claim that contextual factors are irrelevant to how the office functions, or that leadership style will necessarily offer a more valid explanation. The goal is not to test the competing effects of these different variables. Instead, this research, based on the assumption that leadership style should also have an impact on a Secretary-General's political behavior, seeks to demonstrate that this premise holds true when studying how an office-holder attempts to have influence over the handling of international peace and security. It is unfortunate that personal traits are often overlooked and understudied in the existing work on the Secretary-General. This study fills this gap and will, hopefully, convince others that this type of research is a worthwhile endeavor by demonstrating how these factors are relevant to how the office functions.

THE DEBATE OVER SECRETARY-GENERAL LEADERSHIP

When considering the type of leadership that a Secretary-General provides, it is possible to tap into a major debate that exists over the handling of the position. Olusola Akinrinade explains the core of this debate: "One of the major issues surrounding the office of the Secretary-General of an international organisation is whether the holder should be a mere administrator or an active diplomatic participant in negotiations on the major issues of the day" (1992, 79). In other words, should the focus of the head of the organization be on the "secretary" or the "general" part of the office's name?

The administrator-activist camps have historically been split. When the League of Nations was being formed "two divergent views on the conception of the Secretary-General appeared. One . . . of a Chancellor as a statesman endowed with political powers and acting as the spokesman of international interests . . . the other view tended to discard the political element and proposed instead a purely administrative conception of the Secretary-General" (Alexandrowicz 1962, 1109–1110). These different role conceptions are often at the heart of analyses of the League of Nations. The League's first Secretary-General, Sir Eric Drummond, possessed an understanding of his role that led him to act as more of a quiet administrator while Albert Thomas, the head of the International Labour Organization during a similar time span, pursued a much more dynamic role. Thus, many have pondered how the League would have operated differently with Thomas at the helm.

This long-running debate over how Secretaries-General should approach their position was also reflected by the delegates at the conference to draft the UN Charter held in San Francisco, where they discussed whether Secretaries-General should view their office as a "humble servant" of the members or as a more "vigorous arm" of the organization (Gordenker 1967, 3). This distinction is illustrated by the competing names for the office that were considered in the process leading up to San Francisco. For example, President Roosevelt felt that "Secretary-General" did not capture the important, independent place that the office-holder should pursue and suggested instead that the head of the United Nations should be referred to as "World's Moderator" (Luard 1994, 105). At one point, the schizophrenic view of the office would have been resolved by having two separate positions: a political executive titled President and an administrative head referred to as Secretary-General, but the two roles remained combined (Schwebel 1952, 18–19). One reason for the lack of Charter clarity regarding the Secretary-Generalship was the inability of the delegates to overcome their disagreement regarding the proper role of an office-holder. As Max Jakobson observes,

> The office of secretary-general has been clouded in ambiguity since its inception. The charter offers no clear guidance, for the founding

fathers of the United Nations were deeply divided over this issue and failed to resolve their differences . . . No real compromise was reached, but instead both concepts were written into the charter. As a result the chapter on the secretary-general turned out to be like a photograph with a double exposure. (1974, 10)

This debate over the proper role for the Secretary-General continues. For example, in a *New York Times* opinion piece, Richard Armitage, the former assistant secretary of Defense for International Security Affairs, states that the "proper relationship" between the United States and the Secretary-General has deviated from the interests of the United States. He argues, for example, that the "Secretary-General should revert to chief clerk," and states that "President Clinton should say yes to American leadership at the U.N. and press for the Secretary-General to concentrate on administrative duties" (1994, A23). Similarly, back before he became the U.S. ambassador to the United Nations, John Bolton disparaged bold moves by an office-holder because of his view that "the fact [is] that the U.N. Charter describes the secretary general as merely a 'chief administrative officer' " (1999, 14). The ongoing difference of opinion regarding the office is hardly an isolated issue among just Americans. Leading up to the opening of the General Assembly in September 2005, the representative from Algeria noted, "You have one side basically saying that the secretary general should be empowered and should have all flexibility as a kind of C.E.O. and the other side saying that it is not ready to give up the prerogative of the General Assembly and would like to keep a close eye on the work of the secretary general" (quoted in Hoge 2005b, A6).

SECRETARIES-GENERAL AS VISIONARIES AND MANAGERS

The discussion of the Secretary-General in the scholarly literature reflects this debate over the merits of office-holders with a managerial leadership style versus visionary leadership style. In this dispute, a visionary Secretary-General is often "not welcome to the bureaucratic purist," who stresses the place of an office-holder as an "administrative servant" (Newman 1998, 204). For example, James Barros contrasts the "Drummond style" of "tact and discretion" with the public political initiative-taking style that he claims was favored by Trygve Lie and Hammarskjöld (1983, 35; 1979, 398–402). Barros argues that the "Hammarskjöld model" has skewed the perception of the office, but this model is embraced by those who want to "escape from the reality" of states dominating international affairs (1983, 34; 1979, 402). Certain Secretaries-General may seek to be more publicly active and influential, but this will only aggravate the member-states. Therefore, Barros believes that office-holders should have a style that predisposes them to handle the office in a quiet, discreet manner.

Similarly, Robert Cox discusses the contrasting "bureaucratic" and "charismatic" styles of leadership (1969, 210). He argues that executive heads with charismatic styles will be generally resisted by member-states and can undermine quiet diplomacy and consensus-building efforts. He does qualify this argument by stating that a more assertive approach is to be avoided unless the opportunity for "rational use of personal initiative" arises (1969, 211). These situations exist when major powers are looking for "verbal leadership" on an accepted course of action that they prefer not to express themselves (1969, 211).

Gordenker presents a comparable dichotomy of "leader" versus a "clerk," arguing that "personal style" will help determine which type of role a Secretary-General will play (1972, 108, 136). He observes that a Secretary-General willing to act as a clerk of the organization will have some chances to make suggestions to member-states because "clerkly functions" provide a "ready-made platform" (1972, 108–109). However, Gordenker notes that if a Secretary-General goes too far and displays an "unaccustomed degree of leadership" then he will likely suffer great backlash from offended member-states (1972, 127).

Although Alan James stresses the impact of the nature of the organization, which is determined by the type of activity that the member-states are willing to allow (1985, 1993), he admits, "This is not to deny that personality affects the way any job is executed, thus each Secretary-General will have his own style" (1993, 37). James makes a distinction between strong and weak styles (1985). He notes that the "colourless," protocol-conscious Waldheim and the "lack-lustre qualities" of the passive U Thant produced similarly unimpressive incumbencies (1985, 42). However, the dynamic and thrustful style of Lie and Hammarskjöld led to their downfall due to the level of state disapproval. Thus, James' argument reflects the notion that a visionary style will be unsuccessful in the end due to the ill will that it brings from the member-states.

THE STRATEGIC STYLE AND UNDERLYING PERSONAL CHARACTERISTICS

Instead of portraying the Secretary-General's role choice as an either-or situation between manager and visionary, many analysts of the

Secretary-General support a more balanced approach. For example, Rivlin argues that the "proper role" for a Secretary-General "lies somewhere in between" a manager and a visionary where the "Secretary-General must lead and take initiatives, but he must do so with caution and restraint" (1993, 5). The leadership style capturing this idea is categorized in this study as the "strategic" style. Unfortunately, such analyses of the Secretary-General do not provide a coherent statement about what personal traits would encourage a strategic approach to the office. This fits with the trend identified earlier that existing descriptions of personal traits of the Secretaries-General are not clearly specified and contain a confusing array of different terminology. However, a survey of the literature does reveal a certain set of personal characteristics that analysts claim are important for an office-holder to possess.[1] Thus, the following discussion draws this material together to provide a more concise presentation of the personal characteristics that interrelate to create a Secretary-General's leadership style. As mentioned earlier, six headings are employed to capture these characteristics: responsivity, belief that can influence, need for relationships, need for recognition, supranationalism, and problem-solving emphasis. These characteristics are summarized in table 2.1.

To begin with, *responsivity* captures the degree to which Secretaries-General are likely to be sensitive to their surroundings and possess the capability to carefully analyze a situation. Many authors stress the need for a Secretary-General with a high degree of responsiveness. For example, Brian Urquhart and Erskine Childers include "analytical capability and insight" as part of their list of "qualities" that are "unquestionably required" for a Secretary-General (1996, 23). This argument that there is need for intellectual acumen and analytical insight is echoed by scholars such as Rivlin (1993) and Claude

Table 2.1   Personal Characteristics Description

Characteristic	Description
Responsivity	Sensitivity to context and analytical capability?
Belief That Can Influence	Perceive self as capable of influencing events?
Need for Recognition	Unwilling to relinquish control and work behind the scenes without credit?
Need for Relationships	Desire to maintain good personal relationships?
Supranationalism	Strong attachment to and desire to defend the United Nations and the organization's values?
Problem-Solving Emphasis	Emphasize completing tasks over interpersonal concerns?

(1993). Others are more specific in tying this analytical capability to an awareness of the types of action that are appropriate given the situational conditions (e.g., Pechota 1972; Ramcharan 1990a; and Rikhye 1991). Overall, there is a clear belief that "the art of peace-making requires flexibility tuned to the complexity of international reality" (Cordovez 1987, 174).

Many observers also agree that *belief that can influence* is an important characteristic. Secretaries-General must not simply perceive themselves as reacting to situations, but as capable of creating initiatives that will have an impact. While Vratislav Pechota does believe that a Secretary-General must be willing to study a situation carefully, he stresses that there must also be a "willingness and determination to use the possibilities of his Office to the full" (1972, 12). Similarly, Kjell Skjelsbaek is careful to note that a Secretary-General should be amenable to following a "pragmatic and practical approach," but should also posses the acumen for taking action (1991, 107). Urquhart and Childers (1996) and Claude (1993) argue that Secretaries-General must be willing to be courageous and inventive in pursuing new ideas. Inventiveness is also a vital part of diplomatic skill for Arthur Rovine (1970) and Oran Young (1967).

Although Secretaries-General who believe themselves capable of influencing events are generally applauded, it is also stressed that office-holders should have a *need for relationships*. For example, Rovine calls for Secretaries-General to be geared toward "maintain[ing] good personal relationships" (1970, 422). A Secretary-General motivated to build positive relationships should be better prepared to cultivate a network of affiliations and to engage other parties in meaningful dialogues. In addition, Secretaries-General should not expect to force their position onto others. Instead, they must be able to accept the fact that there are times that they will need to defer to the wishes of conflicting parties in order to maintain progress toward a solution.

Observers argue that Secretaries-General should also possess a willingness to initiate action in a quiet manner and to relinquish control over situations when necessary. In other words, office-holders should not be motivated by a *need for recognition*. A Secretary-General must be willing to accept the lack of acknowledgment that can be a part of the job. Pechota (1972) notes that the Secretary-General should be prepared to employ many resources without calling for credit for these efforts. Echoing this point, Cordovez stresses, "However instrumental he may have been in working toward a settlement, more often than not the Secretary-General may have to remain without public credit" (1987, 169). Rikhye (1991) argues that the Secretary-General must be willing to maintain quiet diplomatic efforts even if under attack by the general public for failing to take action. Young (1967) suggests that an aspect of successful diplomatic efforts is convincing others to adopt suggestions as if they were their own, so Secretaries-General must be willing to relinquish credit and control over the process when required.

The Secretary-General is often perceived as a defender of the United Nations and the organization's values, so an office-holder is expected to display a high degree of *supranationalism*. Just as nationalism denotes a strong attachment to the nation, supranationalism refers to the desire to maintain a strong position for the international organization. For example, Bertram Ramcharan (1990a) believes that the Secretary-General should be a strong supporter of Charter principles. The Secretary-General should also be prepared to present the United Nations in a positive light and should be willing to act as a spokesperson for multilateral handling of issues (UNA-USA 1986). Barros warns that an "Avenol-type personality," where the office-holder is not committed to the ideals of the organization, is to be avoided (1983, 31).

For the characteristics discussed thus far there has been a clear majority favoring one direction of the characteristic over the other, but for *problem-solving emphasis* there is a division between those who call for the Secretary-General to emphasize completing tasks versus those who believe that there should be more of an emphasis on interpersonal concerns. The UNA-USA (1986) calls for a Secretary-General willing to provide forceful, programmatic leadership and possessing a strong will to manage. However, others refer to the need for tact and discretion (Gordenker 1967) and compassion (Skjelsbaek 1991). Sometimes it appears that a balance between the two aspects of the characteristic is preferable. For example, Ramcharan (1990a) believes that a Secretary-General should be willing to develop policies to handle problems, but should also understand the need to build consensus when handling these issues.

Drawing the six characteristics together, the following strategic leadership style is suggested. Secretaries-General should be supranationalists who are willing to strongly defend the United Nations and inventive individuals who believe that they may be influential, but they must also be responsive to particular situational requirements. In addition, Secretaries-General should have a strong need for relationships, but a low need for recognition. It is less clear how the final component, problem-solving emphasis, should be incorporated into the leadership style, but it can be argued that the Secretary-General needs to balance focusing on completing tasks with tact in relating to others. This composite leadership style reflects a willingness to pro-actively support the United Nations and solve problems alongside an understanding of the requirements of situations and relationships.

COMPARING THE THREE LEADERSHIP STYLES

This study puts forth three ideal leadership style types utilizing the previous work of other writers on the Secretary-General. At opposing ends are the managerial and visionary styles. A third leadership style, the strategic style, falls in between these two. Although Gordenker states, "It does not seem possible to draw up a prescription of personal qualities . . . Rather, the conclusion might be that the work of the office is likely to be conducted with a good deal of personal style" (1972, 135), the argument of this study is that each leadership style represents the interrelation of a particular set of personal characteristics. In other words, to answer Gordenker in his own words, the "personal style" that is displayed depends upon a Secretary-General's "personal qualities."

Thus, all three leadership styles can be captured by looking at variation on the same characteristics used to construct the strategic style. This is a logical step because many of the authors drawn on to formulate the strategic style are, in effect, reflecting on the debate between the managerial and visionary styles since they are calling for a more balanced leader who combines what is perceived to be the best aspects of these two styles. The same characteristics underlie all three styles; the managerial and visionary styles are simply being "deconstructed" into their separate characteristics. This is an important step because it allows for direct comparison across style types. To aid in this comparison, table 2.2 explicitly sets out the degree to which each personal characteristic should be displayed by individuals holding a particular leadership style.

Table 2.2 UN Secretary-General Leadership Style Ideal Types

Characteristic	Managerial	Strategic	Visionary
Responsivity	High	High	Low
Belief That Can Influence	Low	High	High
Need for Recognition	Low	Low	High
Need for Relationships	High	High	Low
Supranationalism	Low	High	High
Problem-Solving Emphasis	Low	Medium	High

By breaking down the leadership styles into personal characteristic components, the similarities and differences of these styles become clear. To express table 2.2 in words, Secretaries-General displaying a managerial style have a limited belief in their ability to have influence, are very responsive to conditions, and are motivated by need for relationships, but they are not motivated by need for recognition. Managers emphasize the needs of others above task completion and do not possess a strong sense of supranationalism. By contrast, a visionary style describes supranationalists who clearly believe in their ability to influence, focus on solving problems over the feelings of others, and desire control over and public acknowledgment of their efforts, but lack responsivity and a need for relationships.

These two styles have clear differences from the strategic style. Claude observes, "Scholars of international organization have also differed among themselves, but have been generally . . . looking with hope and favor upon the Albert Thomas and Dag Hammarskjöld varieties of leadership, featuring the staffer as prime minister rather than as obedient and deferent bureaucrat" (1993, 255–256). This statement is largely supported by the broad survey of the literature, although many analysts are careful to qualify this approach by calling for Secretaries-General to be more responsive to contextual factors, less in need of recognition, displaying a greater need to build relationships, and recognizing the needs and feelings of others more than a visionary style would entail.

It should be noted that, unlike some of the analysts surveyed above, this study does not have preconceived notions as to which style might be the "best" for a Secretary-General, but instead seeks to objectively study the link between leadership style and behavior. The findings will reveal whether the three styles are useful categories for analyzing office-holders' political behavior. In addition, by basing the research around styles that have been used to capture important differences among office-holders in the past, this study is able to examine whether these are the key style types that should be contrasted, or if the styles need to be reconsidered. Thus, in answering the specific research question on the Secretaries-General and their influential activities in the area of international peace and security, this study will also address an important distinction made within the literature on the Secretary-General. The debate over the kind of leadership provided is often framed in terms of the assumed key differences between managers and visionaries, with many analysts synthesizing the two to suggest the need for strategic Secretaries-General. However, are these the styles that really capture the vital differences between Secretaries-General?

Do the Secretaries-General fall along these lines? Does the discussion of Secretary-General styles need to be refined and, if so, in what ways? These are the kinds of additional questions that this study can address.

THE SECRETARY-GENERAL AS AN INDIVIDUAL: MEASURING THE "ELUSIVE QUESTION"

The previous sections of this chapter drew together the existing work on the Secretary-General to present a coherent set of leadership styles and related personal characteristics that can be applied to the substantive issue of how Secretaries-General attempt to exercise influence. However, the issue of measuring the leadership styles must first be addressed. Despite the interest in the Secretary-General's leadership style among some scholars, studying their personal characteristics has remained, according to Newman, "an interesting but elusive question" (1998, 189). As the preceding discussion demonstrated, for some scholars the issue of this "elusive question" does not factor into their research because they are focused on contextual factors or, at the opposite end of the spectrum, they continually stress the importance of the office so variation between individual office-holders is largely overlooked. Other works on the Secretary-General recognize that leadership style can shape the role that office-holders attempt to play. What has largely been lacking in these works, however, is a coherent presentation of the behavioral impact of these styles and how the underlying personal traits could be accurately measured in a comparable manner.

SECRETARY-GENERAL MEASUREMENT FRUSTRATIONS

Newman is not the only one frustrated by the measurement difficulties inherent in analyzing the leadership styles of office-holders. For example, pivotal Secretary-General analysts, such as Leland Goodrich and Gordenker, also consider the possibilities of examining personal characteristics, but they do not envision an avenue of research capable of addressing this dimension. In the quote that opened chapter 1, Gordenker stresses, "It may be possible for future researchers to use psychological and social research methods that may result in a firmer estimate than can be found here" (1967, 320). In his more recent work, Gordenker comments on the continued interest in the personality of the Secretary-General, but critiques how "the vagueness of the term matches some of the speculation about its effects" (2005, 95). Goodrich argues that one major factor "[t]o understand and explain the evolution of the political role of the Secretary-General in the work of the United Nations . . . [is] the personality of the Secretary-General himself," but he feels that "[i]t is too early to evaluate with any confidence the relative importance of the personality factor in the development of the political role of the Secretary-General" (1962, 725, 729–730). As this chapter illustrates, not only are there now more than two Secretaries-General to compare, thus addressing some of Goodrich's concerns, but there are also more advanced research methods to measure these personal characteristics that can counter the perception of their study as untenably vague or elusive.

Demonstrating the capability to measure the personal traits of the Secretaries-General is a vital step. There have been few efforts to measure and compare the personal qualities of UN officials. One such effort examined how the attitudes and values, or "peace cognitions," of UN elites affected their policy preferences for negotiating peaceful solutions (Sylvester 1980). The logic behind such studies is sound: "An uncomplicated rationale underlies this entire approach. If war begins in the minds of men, as the preamble of the UNESCO Charter and Waltz's First Image suggest, it behooves us to map human preferences for peace and to assess factors contributing to differing views" (Sylvester 1980, 306). Unfortunately, while others have discussed personal differences of the Secretaries-General before, they have not followed this rationale to attempt to closely observe and contrast these characteristics. For example, Newman decided that "the personality factor is largely a matter for intuition" (1998, 27). However, in order to answer the questions raised in the debate over leadership styles, it is necessary to move further ahead methodologically to develop measurements that allow for objective analysis.

MEASURING LEADERSHIP STYLE: ASSESSMENT-AT-A-DISTANCE

In developing a scheme for measuring leadership style, this study benefits from an existing body of literature that has explored the relation of personal traits and political behavior. In general, foreign policy analysis has developed around the following core argument:

> To explain and predict the behavior of the human collectives comprising nation-states, IR [international relations] requires a theory of human political choice . . . one area within the study of IR that has

begun to develop such a theoretical perspective is foreign policy analysis (FPA). From its inception, FPA has involved the examination of how foreign policy decisions are made and has assumed that the source of much behavior and most change in international politics is human beings. (Hudson and Vore 1995, 210; see also Hudson 2005, Garrison 2003)

Given the interest in the role of individual leaders in the realm of foreign policy, some foreign policy analysis scholars employ a political psychological approach that seeks to directly tap into how the psychology of individuals may be linked to policy choices (Schafer 2003).[2] As part of this endeavor, scholars have developed methods for measuring leaders' personal characteristics that relate to their political behavior.[3] In a best-case scenario, scholars would be able to directly interview or administer personality tests to political leaders. However, it is difficult to get such direct access to many leaders due to factors such as time constraints on behalf of the leader, a lack of desire by such individuals to have potentially critical personality assessments made public, or even the desire to study deceased leaders.[4]

In particular, scholars responded by developing content analysis assessment-at-a-distance techniques that establish a profile based on what leaders have said.[5] Using content analysis on political leaders' statements, these measurements have been developed and widely tested. Although generally designed for the study of national leaders, these schemes can be adapted for the analysis of leaders of international organizations (Kille and Scully 2003). This helps answer concerns expressed above by some Secretary-General scholars that, despite their interest in individual differences, personal traits are overly difficult to measure.

Others recognize the advantages of examining statements by the Secretaries-General. Many case studies include statements by office-holders to support the analysis. Other work focuses specifically on the office-holder's words, including several edited collections of statements by particular Secretaries-General.[6] As T.S. Settel, who drew together a collection of Hammarskjöld's statements, observes, "It is difficult, perhaps impossible, to arrive at a satisfactory understanding of Hammarskjöld's personality. His most intimate friends differ in their evaluation of his character. One can only approach him through the words he spoke and wrote" (1966, 6). The content analysis in this study, which at times draws material from these useful collections, is simply a more methodologically advanced extension of this logic.

This type of content analysis research allows for systematic and objective examination of international organization leadership. Each

Secretary-General is evaluated along the same characteristics, creating a solid basis for assessment. The results provide for comparison and generalization that one cannot get from case histories. Instead of attempting, for example, to gauge from general descriptions which Secretary-General had the highest need for recognition, quantitative content analysis provides commensurate numerical scores. In addition, while descriptive accounts of a Secretary-General's time in office are often insightful, the content analysis methodology provides an alternative to case histories that is capable of taking a Secretary-General's words by themselves to formulate a profile independent of any bias that could result due to knowledge of their behavior while in office. A further advantage is that inquiry based on content analysis, rather than one based on the personal observations of those close to a Secretary-General, allows for other scholars to replicate the research if they so choose.

LEADERSHIP TRAIT ANALYSIS

As discussed previously, a Secretary-General's leadership style can best be understood by examining the personal characteristics that underlie the style. These personal characteristics can be thought of as the building blocks of a leadership style. The way that the characteristics interrelate establishes a certain mindset, which creates a tendency for a Secretary-General to act in a particular manner. Thus, in order to capture a Secretary-General's leadership style it is necessary to measure the personal characteristics and then construct the overarching leadership style profile.

The particular analytical approach used for this study is adapted from the well-established approach of Margaret Hermann (1974, 1980a, 1980b, 1983, 1984, 1987a, 1987b, 1987c, 1999, 2003a, 2003b, 2003c; Winter et al. 1991, Hermann and Kegley 1995; Kaarbo and Hermann 1998; Hermann et al. 2001).[7] Hermann has devised a detailed at-a-distance content analysis scheme, referred to as leadership trait analysis, to measure leaders' personal characteristics and their corresponding leadership styles. Although her coding measures were initially developed for studying the leadership styles of national leaders, she has used the approach to examine a range of leaders and many of the personal characteristics that she codes reflect the traits derived from the scholarship on the Secretary-General.[8]

In order to determine scores for each personal characteristic, content analysis should be carried out on office-holders' responses to questions that are posed to them in a spontaneous setting where the queries are not provided in advance. For the Secretaries-General, the key source used for such material is their verbatim press conference transcripts, kept as official records by the United Nations, where they had to react to questions posed by the press.[9] Such largely unscripted responses are analyzed because, in comparison to a prepared speech, they are more likely to be spontaneous and, therefore, more revealing of the speaker's true character (Hermann 1980a, 1999, 2003a; Schafer 2000; Schafer and Crichlow 2000; Dille and Young 2000; Dille 2000). This also helps to avoid coding material that is written for the office-holder by others.

The unit of analysis is the answer to one question, not the entire press conference. More than one suitable answer, or "response," may be drawn from a single press conference transcript. A response must be over 100 words to qualify for coding to ensure that there is enough text to reveal clear verbal patterns. At least 50 responses for each Secretary-General were coded, thus guaranteeing a minimum of 5,000 words of coded text for each individual, in order to safeguard against having the results biased by one, or even several, uncharacteristic responses. Similarly, responses were selected across different years and question topics to ensure a range of responses for analysis.

The specific coding rules for each characteristic are summarized in table 2.3. *Responsivity* is measured by relating the levels of conceptual complexity and self-confidence that a Secretary-General possesses. Self-confidence reflects an individual's feeling of self-worth and conviction that they are capable of authoritatively handling people or activities. Conceptual complexity captures the degree to which an individual will seek to differentiate environmental signals. Thus, Secretaries-General with relatively higher self-confidence are more likely to be unresponsive ideologues who want to convince others that their position is correct, whereas office-holders with comparatively higher levels of conceptual complexity will be more responsive to situational cues and will analyze the circumstances to see what behavior best fits with the context (Hermann 1987a, 1999, 2003a).

For both conceptual complexity and *problem-solving emphasis* there are extensive word lists that capture each side of the characteristic (Hermann 1987a). For example, high complexity words include aspects, depends, generally, maybe, and uncertain, along with phrases that are used to illustrate a point by providing examples or to indicate that something is temporary such as "at the moment." Low complexity words include absolutely, continual, entirely, must, only, and sure. Of course, these words or phrases can be reversed by the context. For example, "I am not sure," would be coded as high complexity, not low complexity. For problem-solving emphasis, the contrast is

Table 2.3 Summary of Personal Characteristic Coding Rules

Personal Characteristic	Coding Instructions	Score Used
Responsivity	Relative relation of conceptual complexity to self-confidence	Subtract self-confidence from conceptual complexity, then divide by 2 and add 50
Conceptual Complexity	Focus on particular words that indicate acceptance of ambiguity and flexibility, as opposed to words reflecting a low degree of differentiation and tendency to react unvaryingly	Percentage of words that indicate high complexity
Self-Confidence	Focus on personal pronouns I, me, mine, my, myself: coded for self-confidence if speaker perceives self as the instigator of activity, an authority figure, or a recipient of positive reward	Percentage of self-references meeting criteria
Belief That Can Influence	Focus on verbs (action words): coded for this characteristic in situations where speaker is initiating or planning the action, even if it is a decision not to do action; does not include "feeling," "thinking," "sensory," and "being" verbs	Percentage of verbs meeting criteria
Need for Recognition	Focus on verbs (action words): the conditions coded for recognition are (1) strong, forceful action; (2) giving help or advice when not requested; (3) attempts to control through regulating behavior or seeking information which affects others; (4) attempt to modify others' opinions, where aim is not to reach agreement; (5) attempt to impress through public display; (6) concern for reputation or position	Percentage of verbs meeting criteria

Continued

Table 2.3 Continued

Personal Characteristic	Coding Instructions	Score Used
Need for Relationships	Focus on verbs (action words): the conditions coded for need for relationships are (1) positive feeling for another, desire to be accepted, liked, or forgiven; (2) reaction to disruption of relationship, desire to reach an agreement; (3) companionate activities; (4) nurturing acts	Percentage of verbs meeting criteria
Supranationalism	Focus on noun/noun phrases referring to speaker's or other political units: coded supranationalism if speaker's political unit is identified in a favorable or strong manner or there is the need to maintain honor and identity for the unit; also if other units are viewed unfavorably or as meddlesome	Percentage of references to political units meeting the criteria
Problem-Solving Emphasis	Focus on particular words which stress completing a task or interpersonal concerns	Percentage of task or interpersonal words that are task words

Note: Coding rules based on Hermann (1987a, 1999).

between task-oriented words that relate to undertaking activities and setting or reaching objectives, such as preparation, goal, initiate, work, strive, investigation, problem and achieve, and interpersonal words that capture a concern for other's feelings or needs through positive affect or negative connotation, such as assistance, collaboration, sympathy, understanding, deception, harm, and tension. The final score represents the percentage of time that high complexity words were used relative to the number of low complexity terms and the same holds true for task versus interpersonal words.

Both self-confidence and *supranationalism* explore when the Secretaries-General refer to personal pronouns or to the United Nations or other political units respectively, and whether they do so in a manner that reflects these characteristics. For self-confidence one examines self-references (I, me, mine, my, and myself) for evidence of whether speakers perceive themselves as an instigator of activity, an authority figure, or the recipient of a positive reward. If one of these coding criteria is present then the personal pronoun is identified as self-confidence, but if none of the three criteria are met then it is labeled as not self-confident. Similarly, for supranationalism the coder must identify all references to the United Nations and see whether or not these references are favorable, reflect strength or the need to maintain the honor of the organization. For other organizations and states one examines whether the references to these political actors are unfavorable or accuse them of being meddlesome. Where the United Nations is referred to with positive connotations or other actors are seen in a negative light the reference is coded supranationalism, but where these criteria are not met the remark is coded as nonsupranationalism.

Finally, for *belief that can influence, need for recognition*, and *need for relationships* the coder examines verb phrases where the Secretaries-General or a group they identify with are the subject of the verb. The rough score represents the percentage of the time that these verb phrases indicated the presence of one of these three characteristics. Verb phrases are coded as belief that can influence if they reflect an initiation or planning of action, even if it is a conscious decision not to attempt to influence a situation. A lack of attempts to influence events, which is especially indicated by feeling, thinking, and being verbs, are coded as belief that cannot influence. Need for recognition is indicated by a wide range of criteria that captures the desire to be in control and to receive public credit for one's actions. Need for recognition exists if the verb phrase demonstrates a strong action, giving help when not requested, an attempt to control, impress, or affect others, or a concern for reputation. Need for relationships measures the desire to maintain friendly affiliations by looking for positive feelings for others and a desire to be accepted, reacting with concern when a relationship or agreement is impeded, and companionate or nurturing activities. If these criteria are not met, then the verb phrases are labeled as no need for recognition or no need for relationships respectively.

As indicated previously, the analysis is based on calculating whether a Secretary-General uses a particular word or phrase that illustrates a trait. The focus is not on the overall message that the Secretary-General is trying to impart, but rather on the words and phrases employed in delivering the response to a question. The objective is to infer what their personal characteristics are from what they say. The underlying assumption is that the more often a certain expression is employed, the more that the characteristic(s) related to that phrase are representative of the Secretary-General. Thus, while a particular Secretary-General may employ obfuscating answers at press conferences, such message complexity does not disrupt the interpretation of an individual's character through analysis of the words and phrases that they use to express themselves.

A percentage score for each personal characteristic is tallied for every response.[10] The average result across all of the responses is used to create an overall raw score for each trait. A final standardized score is determined based upon comparison to the base group's scores and standard deviation, in this case the cohort of Secretaries-General, to illustrate how they stand relative to each other. These scores can then be analyzed on a separate basis or combined into the overall leadership styles based on the weighting of characteristics indicated in table 2.2. More specifically, a formula is employed where the "high" characteristics are doubled, the "medium" characteristics are added once, and the "low" characteristics are negatively weighted.

The stage is now set for developing comparable profiles of the office-holders that can be tested in relation to how they behaved in real world situations. The following section presents the coding results from content analysis performed on all seven Secretaries-General: Trygve Lie (from Norway, who served from 1946 to 1953), Dag Hammarskjöld (Sweden, 1953–1961), U Thant (Burma, 1961–1971), Kurt Waldheim (Austria, 1972–1981), Javier Perez de Cuellar (Peru, 1982–1991), Boutros Boutros-Ghali (Egypt, 1992–1996), and Kofi Annan (Ghana, 1997–). While all seven office-holders are coded and discussed in this section, which provides a complete comparable sample for examining the coding results, the case studies that follow in chapters 4–6 will examine only the three

Secretaries-General that best represent the three ideal leadership style types.

THE PERSONAL CHARACTERISTICS OF THE SECRETARIES-GENERAL: CODING RESULTS

Before turning to the overarching leadership style profiles, the separate results for the personal characteristics are detailed. The personal characteristic scores are presented in tables 2.4 and 2.5. When interpreting the scores presented in table 2.5, it should be remembered (as already indicated in the table note) that these standardized scores were computed in comparison to the group of seven Secretaries-General as a whole, using a mean score for the group of 50 and a standard deviation of 10 (Hermann 1987a). A score of 50 represents the mid-range for a characteristic while a score above 60 or below 40 is considered high and low respectively. Scores that are within five points of these high and low marks mean that the Secretaries-General lean toward these tendencies and are labeled medium high and medium low in order to better differentiate the office-holders. Standardized scores are employed because the raw percentages presented in table 2.4, derived using the coding rules described in table 2.3, only present a rough idea of how a Secretary-General stands on the six traits and are relatively meaningless unless they are compared to other leaders. For example, Annan's raw score of 33.74 on need for relationships does not seem that removed from his 38.64 for need for recognition until these raw scores are recalculated relative to the other

Table 2.4 Personal Characteristic Results: Raw Scores

Secretary-General	Responsivity	Belief That Can Influence	Need for Recognition	Need for Relationships	Supra-nationalism	Problem-Solving Emphasis
Lie	39.40	40.53	42.44	15.11	58.07	61.39
Hammarskjöld	46.08	43.06	52.96	5.70	52.31	80.90
Thant	42.55	29.45	34.29	11.70	49.69	75.75
Waldheim	48.11	40.06	54.13	37.38	48.28	66.81
Perez de Cuellar	47.84	38.40	36.35	24.56	51.29	70.10
Boutros-Ghali	45.37	48.55	49.75	14.74	57.15	72.34
Annan	49.65	54.35	38.64	33.74	52.30	64.97

Note: Raw scores represent percentage of the time that the characteristic is displayed when possible, with higher scores indicating that a characteristic is stronger for a Secretary-General. Raw scores are calculated as set out in table 2.3.

Table 2.5 Personal Characteristic Scores: Standardized Scores

Secretary-General	Responsivity	Belief That Can Influence	Need for Recognition	Need for Relationships	Supra-nationalism	Problem-Solving Emphasis
Lie	31.23	47.92	47.83	45.14	65.99	35.52
Hammarskjöld	51.54	51.38	61.75	36.53	48.90	67.16
Thant	40.83	32.74	37.05	42.02	41.13	58.80
Waldheim	57.71	47.27	63.30	65.53	36.95	44.31
Perez de Cuellar	56.89	45.00	39.77	53.79	45.88	49.64
Boutros-Ghali	49.39	58.91	57.50	44.80	63.26	53.28
Annan	62.41	66.85	42.80	62.19	48.87	41.33

Note: Standardized personal characteristic scores are calculated based on the comparison group of all 7 Secretaries-General using a mean of 50 and a standard deviation of 10. Higher scores indicate that a characteristic is stronger for a Secretary-General.

Secretaries-General to reveal that he has a relatively low need for recognition with a standardized score of 42.80, but a high need for relationships with a standardized score of 62.19.

The personal characteristic coding results presented in table 2.5 reveal some interesting differences among the Secretaries-General. Clear variation across all six traits exists, with the predominant scores shifting across different office-holders for the various characteristics. To begin with, for *responsivity* Annan stands out with his 62.41 as the only Secretary-General with a high score on this characteristic. Waldheim and Perez de Cuellar fall behind Annan in the medium high range, while Hammarskjöld and Boutros-Ghali's scores register in the medium range near 50. With no other Secretaries-General possessing less than a medium level score for responsivity, Lie and Thant sit in stark contrast with their low scores. This is especially true for Lie, whose 31.23 for responsivity is the lowest score displayed by any of the office-holders across all six characteristics.

With a 66.85, Annan also has the predominant score on *belief that can influence*, but this time the second highest score, 58.91, belongs to Boutros-Ghali. Hammarskjöld ranks third among the Secretaries-General with a 51.38, while Lie and Waldheim both fall below the 50 point mark with scores of 47.92 and 47.27 respectively. Perez de Cuellar is on the edge of medium low with the exact score of 45.00, while Thant falls well behind the other six office-holders with the low score of 32.74. The scores for *need for recognition* are a different story. Annan does not display a high need for recognition, scoring only a 42.80. Need for recognition is much more prevalent for Waldheim and Hammarskjöld, who both have high scores. Boutros-Ghali is not too far behind, with a medium high score of 57.50. The Secretary-General in fourth place, Lie, is well off this pace, scoring a 47.83. The two remaining office-holders possess a low level of need for recognition. Perez de Cuellar tallies a 39.77 and Thant displays the lowest score overall for this trait with a 37.05.

Waldheim and Annan, who registered a 65.53 and 62.19 respectively, stand above the rest of the group with their high scores for *need for relationships*. No other Secretary-General even scores in the medium high range, with third place belonging to Perez de Cuellar with his score of 53.79. At the opposite end of the spectrum lies Hammarskjöld, who scores a group low 36.53 for this trait. The remaining three office-holders are bunched together in the medium low range. Lie is top of this threesome with a 45.14, followed by Boutros-Ghali's 44.80 and Thant's 42.02. Reversing their ranking on need for relationships, Lie and Boutros-Ghali possess the highest scores on *supranationalism*. Hammarskjöld ranks third and Annan is only .03 behind him in fourth place. The scores drop off from there with Perez de Cuellar barely in the medium range with a 45.88. Thant's score does fall into the medium low range with a 41.13 and Waldheim's result is solidly in the low range with a 36.95.

After a series of low or medium low scores, Thant steps forward with one of the highest results for *problem-solving emphasis*. However, Hammarskjöld's drive to solve problems stands out in relation to the other office-holders. His score of 67.16 is the highest score out of all of the traits across the seven Secretaries-General. No one else comes close to this, with Boutros-Ghali in third place with 53.28 and the fourth place Perez de Cuellar falling around the mean at 49.64. Waldheim and Annan register in the medium low range with 44.31 and 41.33 respectively, while Lie has the lowest score of the group at 35.52.

THE LEADERSHIP STYLES OF THE SECRETARIES-GENERAL: CODING RESULTS

While the previous section discussed the coding results for the personal characteristics of the Secretaries-General, and demonstrated that there are conspicuous differences among the office-holders, at the heart of this study is the question of whether there are significant differences among their overall leadership styles. As set out earlier, the use of styles allows for a better exploration of the interrelation of the personal characteristics and taps into the debate over leadership that is prevalent in the scholarship on the office. Table 2.6 presents the raw style scores, reflecting the weighted pattern of traits presented in table 2.2.[11] Higher scores indicate a more representative style for a Secretary-General. As with the personal traits, for comparability these scores are standardized in relation to the cohort group of all seven Secretaries-General around a mean of 50 with a standard deviation of 10. The standardized scores are presented in table 2.7, with the style that best represents each Secretary-General presented in bold print.

The coding results identify Annan as a strategic Secretary-General. Annan's standardized score of 44.88 for the visionary style is well below 50, indicating that he is unlikely to display behavior consistent with this leadership style. While his mark for the managerial style registers as high with a 61.11, his score for the strategic style at 68.45 is greater than that for managerial style. In fact, looking at the style results for the other six Secretaries-General, Annan is the *only* officeholder to display a strategic style above the high threshold of 60.

Table 2.6 Leadership Style Results: Raw Scores

Secretary-General	Managerial	Strategic	Visionary
Lie	355.48	468.25	518.15
Hammarskjöld	346.93	482.10	570.32
Thant	395.98	435.18	456.59
Waldheim	454.65	495.92	460.41
Perez de Cuellar	441.07	512.98	449.90
Boutros-Ghali	355.44	528.49	571.70
Annan	449.35	579.18	475.10

Note: Raw scores are calculated using characteristic scores presented in table 2.4, and formulas are weighted according to table 2.2, with high characteristics doubled, medium characteristics added once, and low characteristics negatively weighted. Higher scores indicate a more representative style.

Table 2.7 Leadership Style Results: Standardized Scores

Secretary-General	Managerial	Strategic	Visionary
Lie	40.05	42.50	**53.62**
Hammarskjöld	38.13	45.74	**65.21**
Thant	**49.13**	34.77	41.13
Waldheim	**62.29**	48.98	41.90
Perez de Cuellar	**59.25**	52.97	39.77
Boutros-Ghali	40.04	56.59	**64.49**
Annan	61.11	**68.45**	44.88

Note: Standardized leadership style scores are calculated based on the comparison group of all 7 Secretaries-General using a mean of 50 and a standard deviation of 10. Higher scores indicate a more representative style. The scores in bold indicate the most representative style.

Unlike the strategic Annan, the results for Hammarskjöld, Boutros-Ghali, and Lie are highest for the visionary style. For Hammarskjöld, his visionary style tally of 65.21 is not only the foremost out of the seven Secretaries-General, but this is also much higher than his low scores on the other two styles, where he registered a 45.74 for the strategic style and a 38.13 for the managerial style. Thus, the results strongly indicate that Hammarskjöld will be predisposed to provide visionary leadership. Boutros-Ghali's score of 64.49 on the visionary style is nearly as high as Hammarskjöld's and he also possesses a low managerial score of 40.04. Although his score for the strategic style, 56.59, is the second highest out of the seven office-holders, it is only in the medium high range and is outweighed by the much higher visionary score.

The evidence for Lie is not as clear-cut. Out of the three, his highest score is for the visionary style, but it is not an overly high result at 53.62. At this point, the strongest argument that can be made is that Lie should have visionary tendencies and is unlikely to seek to act as a strategist or a manager because his scores on these two styles were a low 42.50 and 40.05 respectively, but his approach to leadership may be more complex than these three types suggest. It should be remembered at this point that the three styles are ideal types drawn from the scholarship on the Secretary-General and the fact that Lie did not code at a high level for any of the three types may indicate the need to consider other style types that might better capture his personal predilections.

The highest style scores for Perez de Cuellar, Waldheim, and Thant are for the managerial style. With a high score of 62.29, the predominant manager of the three appears to be Waldheim. Waldheim's low score of 41.90 precludes him from being considered a visionary and his strategic score of 48.98 falls at the median level. Similarly, Perez de Cuellar shows no predisposition for visionary leadership with the lowest score of the group at 39.77 and his strategic score of 52.97 falls well short of the score of 59.25 that he possesses for the managerial style. Thus, the results indicate that the style that best captures both of these leaders is the managerial style.

Thant's coding results also indicate that, out of the three ideal types being explored, he is most likely to adhere to the managerial style. However, as discussed above in relation to Lie's personal characteristic results, his managerial score of 49.13, while higher in comparison to his low visionary score of 41.13 and the bottom score out of the group for strategic style at 34.77, still does not even reach the average level of 50. Once again, it may be that an alternative style not considered here might be necessary to improve comprehension of the way in which he is likely to approach the duties of the office. That being said, for the most divergent Secretaries-General, Lie and Thant, at a minimum the results do suggest that, whatever the overarching style that better captures their desired approach to the office, Lie is more inclined toward a visionary approach while Thant is more disposed to a managerial leadership style and neither is likely to act as a strategic Secretary-General.

CONCLUSION

Previous work on the Secretary-General has often overlooked or understudied the personal differences between the office-holders, either due to an emphasis on contextual factors or on the vitality of all who have held the office. Personal characteristics have been identified as a potentially important factor in the study of the Secretary-General, but when this recognition has been made these traits have not been closely detailed or examined. Building out of such analyses, however, this study has been able to derive six key personal characteristics that are supported across the literature on the Secretary-General and to connect these to the long-standing debate over leadership style represented by the managerial, visionary, and strategic styles. Explicitly distinguishing the different leadership types and clearly linking these to a comparable set of personal traits allows for clear and direct comparisons between the Secretaries-General.

This chapter has also answered questions regarding the difficulty of measuring such personal dimensions of the Secretaries-General and the content analysis results presented provide important insight into the differences between the office-holders. The analysis clearly demonstrates that the Secretaries-General vary across their personal characteristics and that these traits combine in ways that indicate that they possess different leadership styles. However, the key question remains: can these leadership styles be linked to the political behavior of the Secretaries-General as they make use of their "toolbox" of influential activities in the area of international peace and security? In order to address this question, this study undertakes three detailed case studies that explore the behavioral patterns of Hammarskjöld, Waldheim, and Annan. These three Secretaries-General were chosen because their high scores indicate that they are the most representative of the contrasting styles and should, therefore, display markedly different behavior while in office.

Before undertaking these case studies, it is important to clearly establish the behavioral expectations for each type of Secretary-General. In other words, what are the implications of Hammarskjöld being a visionary leader, Waldheim a manager, and Annan a strategist? In what specific ways should these three Secretaries-General be expected to behave differently? The next chapter sets out a framework of the influential activities available to a Secretary-General and devises a set of behavioral expectations for each leadership style that are then tested in the case studies.

CHAPTER 3

A Secretary-General's
Avenues for Influence

The province of the Secretary-General of the United Nations is something like Woodrow Wilson's concept of the scope of the United States presidential office. It can be as wide and as influential as he wishes and is able to make it. Although in both cases a written instrument sets the formal limits, also in both cases powers can be expanded to include others not clear in the written document.

(Blaisdell 1966, 106)

INTRODUCTION

Now that the three ideal types and specific leadership style results are established, this chapter presents the avenues of influence available to a Secretary-General and links these to behavioral expectations for each of the three leadership styles. As Jonathan Knight argues, it is important to ensure that the "secretary-general's influence relationships are explored within clearly stipulated analytical frameworks" (1970, 597). However, the study of the Secretary-General often lacks such analytical clarity, so this chapter draws across the diverse work on the office to devise a coherent framework for analysis. The chapter begins by describing the different functions available to a Secretary-General that provide opportunities for influence in the area of international peace and security. These activities are organized according to three major categories: agenda setting, peaceful settlement of disputes, and UN intervention. After explaining each category, the activities are related to the three leadership styles in a series of behavioral propositions that serve as the basis for the case studies in chapters 4–6.

THE SECRETARY-GENERAL AS AN INFLUENTIAL ACTOR: THE UN CHARTER AND ITS IMPLICATIONS

While the formal responsibilities set out in the UN Charter provide a "baseline or guide" for understanding an office-holder's capacity for action (Gordenker 1993, 269), on paper a Secretary-General's capabilities appear to be fairly limited. As Cordovez observes, "The text of the Charter is not particularly generous or explicit with regard to all the possible dimensions of the contribution that the Secretary-General might make toward the fulfillment of the ambitious goals of the United Nations in the area of international peace and security" (1987, 163). The key articles in the Charter regarding the activities of the Secretary-General, the text of which are provided in the appendix of this book, are Articles 97 through 101. Article 97 establishes the Secretary-General as the "chief administrative officer" of the United Nations. Article 98 provides the Secretary-General with the ability to attend meetings of other UN organs. In addition, Article 98 instructs the Secretary-General to perform any functions assigned by the other organs and to prepare an annual report for the General Assembly detailing the work undertaken by the United Nations.

Article 101 provides additional responsibilities, giving the Secretary-General control over staff appointments. Article 101 also points to the need for all members of the Secretariat to follow "the highest standards of efficiency, competence, and integrity," while Article 100 emphasizes the independence of the Secretary-General and Secretariat staff from the member-states. Article 99 allows the Secretary-General to bring threats to international peace and security to the attention of the Security Council. Compared to the other articles, Article 99 provides the ability to directly influence UN activities in a manner that the League of Nations Secretary-General lacked. However, as discussed below, the Secretary-General has rarely explicitly invoked Article 99 in the manner set out in the Charter. Finally, along with the General Assembly, Security Council, Economic and Social Council, Trusteeship Council, and International Court of Justice, Article 7 designates the Secretariat as a principal organ, but this status is tempered by decision making being reserved for the other policy-making organs.

Despite the limited powers bestowed by the Charter, analysts note that the Secretary-General is still capable of influencing UN policy. As Urquhart and Childers conclude, "Although the office has little real power, it provides very wide possibilities for excercising influence"

(1990, 22). The Secretary-General has many opportunities to be involved in influencing how decisions are made and implemented. The basic responsibilities set out in the Charter provide an office-holder with more potential than it appears on the surface. Beyond the normal use of the prerogatives afforded by the Charter, there are important possibilities for influence that come from the prominent position of the Secretary-General. Many activities have also developed over time through a broad interpretation of Charter principles. Overall, it is important to recognize the activities as described in the Charter, the "delegated" powers, and the unexpected scope of activities that have developed, the implied "inherent" powers that a Secretary-General might wield (Ratner 1995, 68–71). As Francis Plimpton notes, just as "one doesn't get much of an idea of the Presidency of the United States from reading the Constitution," the Secretary-Generalship should not be judged solely by reading the Charter because "its bony phrases are but a framework skeleton" (1966, 58).

While the Charter provides the legal basis for a Secretary-General's activities, the exact principle that is being employed by an office-holder can at times be difficult to pinpoint (Szasz 1991). For example, Articles 98 and 97 can blur together when considering whether a Secretary-General is performing "functions as are entrusted to him" or following his role as "the chief administrative officer" (Blaisdell 1966, 110). Even more confusingly, Articles 97, 98, and 99 could be used as legal justification for a single function (Pasternack 1994). Thus, the avenues of influence framework that follows is not categorized by the Charter articles, but instead it is organized around the Secretary-General's activities themselves and the legal basis is touched upon where appropriate.

The following discussion outlines the full range of activities through which the Secretary-General can exercise influence in the realm of international peace and security. The analytical framework employed in this study organizes these activities according to the different major functions in which a Secretary-General might be involved: agenda setting, peaceful settlement of disputes, and UN intervention. While any attempt to place a Secretary-General's functions into particular categories carries the risk of artificially dividing the work of an office-holder, it is necessary if a comparative framework is to be established. In the end, analysis requires placing a certain framework judgment onto the activities. The need for this type of approach is echoed by Houshang Ameri: "While it is difficult to compartmentalize the various functions of the Secretariat neatly into . . . categories, nevertheless, an attempt at interpreting them seems to be necessary" (1996, 125). The next section articulates the activities available to a Secretary-General. Each function heading is first briefly described, then the activities are discussed under that heading, and finally how these various activities are linked to influence are addressed. This framework of influential activities is summarized in table 3.1.

Table 3.1   A Secretary-General's Influential Activities

Activity	*Avenue for Influence*	*Mandatory/Voluntary*
Agenda Setting		
Administrative Duties		
● Supervise Reports	Stress viewpoint through wording or content	Mandatory
● Oversee Finances	Emphasize certain areas or programs over others	Mandatory
● Shape Administrative Structure	Alter structure to provides best means of Influence	Voluntary
● Staffing the Secretariat	Independent appointment control can be used to provide conduits of influence	Mandatory
Strategic Political Position		
● Representative in Meetings	Present ideas at meetings; explicitly employ Article 99	Voluntary
● Inherent Strategic Position	Possession of information and consultation provides opportunities to offer advice	Voluntary
Public Pronouncements		
● Annual Report to General Assembly	Report used to express opinions	Mandatory
● Official Representational Activities	Formal statements and representing the organization used to express opinions	Mandatory
● "Unofficial" Representational Activities	Speaking engagements, travel, and media coverage used to express opinions	Voluntary
Peaceful Settlement of Disputes		
Independently Initiated	Direct involvement in monitoring and peacefully settling disputes	Voluntary
Mandated Assignment	Direct involvement in monitoring and peacefully settling disputes	Mandatory
	Shape mission mandate; interpretation of mission mandate	Voluntary
UN Intervention		
Peacekeeping Missions	Administration of mission	Mandatory
	Shape mission mandate; interpretation of mission mandate	Voluntary

A SECRETARY-GENERAL'S INFLUENTIAL ACTIVITIES

AGENDA SETTING

Many of the activities available to a Secretary-General can be geared toward trying to influence the global agenda. For example, office-holders might stress certain problem areas over others or assert how these problems should be handled. They might argue for the importance of the United Nations or their office playing a more meaningful role in managing global security. A Secretary-General has a diverse set of agenda setting methods, but they all capture ways that office-holders can try to convince others that their desired way of handling matters is best. As set out below, office-holders have various opportunities, both private and public, to try to persuade member-state representatives. Secretaries-General may also present their case directly to the general public. In addition, office-holders can shape information, finances, staffing appointments, or the organizational structure to support their position.

ADMINISTRATIVE DUTIES

A Secretary-General is responsible for the day-to-day matters required to keep the United Nations running. The potential avenues of influence available through administrative tasks are important to recognize. As Ameri stresses, "These are, of course, mechanical tasks, but that does not mean that they are not of importance," because, "while the primary tasks of the Secretariat are administrative, there is no doubt room at every level for an intelligent exercise of initiative and influence" (1996, 125, 95). Secretariat officials need not function as powerless bureaucrats, but instead "like national bureaucrats, the Secretariat are able to find many different ways of manipulating and managing the political bodies, persuading them to decide what the Secretariat had decided they should decide" (Luard 1994, 120). As head of the Secretariat, the Secretary-General is well placed to play such a persuasive role. Administrative duties can at times inform important political decisions and a Secretary-General who wants to influence the policy agenda needs to know how to take advantage of such opportunities.

Supervise reports

A major responsibility for the Secretary-General is preparation of reports. Murthy's analysis of the office emphasizes the influential capability of the reporting mechanism because an office-holder can "not only . . . promote certain causes of their choice but also encourage or discourage a particular behaviour pattern of the member states" (1995, 182). As the chief administrative officer supervising the preparation of UN documents, the Secretary-General may try to influence the content of this information, either through the wording of the documents themselves or through the information used in preparing the text. In this manner, office-holders may be able to guide how debate on an issue is carried out. In addition, reporting duties can provide Secretaries-General with "continued visibility" for their office and ideas (Gordenker 2005, 2), which can reinforce public promotion activities discussed below.

Oversee finances

Evan Luard describes preparing the budget as "very much a political act" for the Secretary-General because "though the executive head is supposed to act within the terms of policy guidelines already reached in the political bodies, in practice he enjoys considerable discretion, both in the amount for which he asks, and in its distribution" (Luard 1994, 121). The design of the biennial UN budget is an extended process, with different departments within the Secretariat putting together funding requests, but the Secretary-General can have a vital role in preparing the final budget request as he or she decides what to reject, alter, or support. Although the budget plan must then be approved by the General Assembly, a Secretary-General can set the agenda upon which the delegates debate. The General Assembly may modify these proposals, but, in structuring the budget, the Secretary-General can guide which programs are given prominence and which are downplayed. In addition, once office-holders present their budget proposals they can lobby the General Assembly members to approve their ideas. Overall, as both "originator and lobbyist" for the budget, a Secretary-General may have "major influence on the appropriation and allocation of resources" (Sutterlin 2003, 147), and this distribution of resources can have important policy implications.

Shape the design of the administrative structure

Secretaries-General may seek to bolster their position through restructuring the administrative apparatus. Gordenker notes that the Secretariat structure is often altered to match the "personal style" of a Secretary-General (2005, 94). Accordingly, the Secretariat can be set up to ensure that the Secretary-General is provided with the greatest opportunities to have influence if so desired. Secretaries-General can face major difficulties in this area and may need to lobby strongly to get their proposals put into place. This is largely due to the need for General Assembly authorization on particular bureaucratic structure issues. An office-holder faces certain political restrictions, such as the difficulty achieving approval of resources and restrictions on reallocating posts. Despite this, "the secretary-general *does* have the power to restructure the Secretariat" and "can exert very considerable influence on the decisions of the General Assembly affecting the structure of the Secretariat" (Sutterlin 2003, 143, 145; Sutterlin's emphasis).

Staffing the Secretariat

The ability to appoint Secretariat staff is specified as a separate responsibility under Article 101. There are limits imposed on a Secretary-General's ability to maintain full control over the staffing process, including the need to balance the dual desire for geographical diversity and candidate skills expressed in Article 101. In addition, despite calls by groups such as the Stanley Foundation for "member governments [to] restrain themselves from interfering in the appointment process," (1991, 2) from early on in UN history governments have sought to ensure that individuals from their countries are appointed to particular positions in the hope that their national interests would be represented within the organization. However, it remains true that Secretaries-General can still gain influence through the way that they appoint and administer personnel:

> It must be admitted that the executive heads operate under considerable political and legal restraints and are not omnipotent with regard to appointment and promotion of members of the international civil service . . . [But] [t]he power of appointment belongs to the Secretary-General who, as a matter of law, may intervene in the appointment and promotion process. (Meron 1982, 865–866)

A Secretary-General seeking to be influential will limit national interference and aim to maintain independent control over the staffing process to the greatest degree possible. Secretaries-General with command over the appointment process will have a better chance to place people who are close to them, either personally or in their beliefs, in particular positions to create conduits of influence.

STRATEGIC POLITICAL POSITION

The Secretary-General operates in a strategically advantageous position. Office-holders are both administrators privy to a wealth of information and participants in the political affairs of the United Nations.

Gordenker describes the Secretary-General as "omnipresent" throughout the UN System and explains, "The institutional position of the Secretary-General at the summit of the Secretariat and his steady involvement with the decisional process in the other organs opens the way to both policy and administrative initiatives" (2005, 4; 76). Since Secretaries-General are well placed in the flow of information and activities taking place in the organization, this provides them with opportunities to influence the agenda by serving as an adviser on important issues at both official meetings and more unofficial junctures.

Representative in meetings

An official avenue of influence for Secretaries-General is supported by Article 98, which dictates that they are allowed to act in the capacity of chief administrative officer at all meetings of other primary organs, although, "[m]ercifully, no one has ever insisted that the Secretary General act in *all* meetings of the Assembly and the three Councils— else each incumbent would have long since have suffocated from surfeit of oratory" (Plimpton 1966, 141; Plimpton's emphasis). However, the Secretary-General can take advantage of sitting in on meetings when so desired, which often includes major meetings or special events. As Laszlo Buza stresses, the Secretary-General's presence "does not simply mean a passive attendance at the meetings, but an active co-operation in the deliberations" (1962, 12). Thus, office-holders can use this chance to influence the path of policy within a particular organ by engaging themselves in meeting discussions and passing on their ideas. The opportunity for such participation provides a Secretary-General with direct inroads to the decision-making process.

In addition, the office has developed certain prerogatives to make presentations based on Article 99 responsibilities. The right contained in Article 99 to bring matters that threaten the maintenance of international peace and security to the attention of the Security Council was placed in the Charter to provide an alternative to member-states having to bring complaints forward on their own. Although one might expect that Article 99 would provide the Secretary-General with a key opportunity to influence the agenda of the Security Council, this right has rarely been directly invoked. However, the Secretary-General has also been able to use Article 99 as a basis for making presentations to the Security Council without direct invocation of the article. This is demonstrated in the work of Walter Dorn (1995, 2004), which details the wide range of times where an office-holder alerted the Security Council to an issue of peace and security without formally or explicitly invoking Article 99. More generally, the Secretary-General can propose agenda items and provide views on matters before the Security Council. Beyond the Security Council, despite not being covered by Article 99, arrangements have also been made in respect to the General Assembly's rules of procedure to allow the Secretary-General to place items on the provisional agenda.

Inherent strategic position

More indirect forms of influence also arise from being chief administrative officer. The Secretary-General operates at the intersection of the administrative and political affairs of the United Nations. This position provides office-holders with the opportunity to influence the course of events in both sectors. As touched on earlier, the routine functions that come with being the administrative head of the bureaucracy supply the Secretary-General with a wide range of information and chances for interaction and consultation with other participants at the United Nations. The constant interaction provides openings for an office-holder to offer or to be asked for advice. The likelihood of this occurring is especially bolstered by the knowledge that the Secretary-General is privy to a large flow of information. In the area of international peace and security, Johnstone notes how "the credibility that comes with being an insider to high-level consultations on international crises" provides the Secretary-General with a "tool" that can be used for leverage in interactions with member-state representatives (2003, 453). With multiple venues and situations in which to discuss matters with these representatives at UN headquarters, many opportunities to take advantage of this point of leverage are presented to an office-holder.

Sometimes Secretaries-General are asked to provide their ideas in relation to a particular problem area. Rikhye recognizes this strategic position of the office: "Representatives of countries and heads of states and governments as well as foreign ministers call on the office. The secretary general often meets with distinguished personalities to share their ideas and to consider the degree to which timing is propitious for the de-escalation of specific conflicts" (1991, 64). While in a sense both aspects of the strategic position are mandatory, because every Secretary-General will inherently sit in this position and will be expected to attend meetings, what makes these labeled as voluntary avenues of influence in table 3.1 is that it is up to the office-holder whether or not to try to use their position to influence those with which they come into contact.

PUBLIC PRONOUNCEMENTS

A Secretary-General may also attempt to take advantage of the public aspect of the position. Office-holders have many opportunities, some more formal than others, to try to influence others by publicly expressing their views on issues or calling attention to the activities of their office and the United Nations. As Rivlin explains, "Through his speeches and his annual report on the work of the organization . . . he can use his office as a 'bully pulpit' to inspire, persuade, exhort and cajole" (1995, 100). More broadly, Johnstone emphasizes the role of the Secretary-General in relation to the international legal discourse and argues that, as such, "the voice of the office carries considerable weight" (2003, 442). In addition, by taking steps to make sure that their role is kept visible, Secretaries-General can encourage others to accept their office as a vital part of the international decision-making process that, therefore, should be involved in efforts to maintain peace and security.

Annual report to the General Assembly

The Article 98 responsibility of preparing an annual report detailing the activities of the United Nations can be limited to a straightforward, administrative task. However, the report can be a "document of high significance" (Cordier 1961, 6) because Secretaries-General may take advantage of this opportunity to offer their opinions on how well the United Nations is handling particular issues, detail what problem areas deserve greater or lesser attention, extend concrete proposals, and discuss the role of the Secretary-Generalship and the United Nations in handling international security. Note that before 1978 the primary avenue for this was the introduction, as opposed to later sections that were written up by various departments involved with the issue areas. However, starting in 1978, the latter part of the report was dropped and now the entire report is simply the "introduction" views of the Secretary-General. In either case, "The annual report can be regarded as a tool of influence . . . for placing issues on the agenda; it is in itself a form of intervention in the immediate term and a means of legitimizing ideas or forming norms in the longer term" (Newman 1998, 21).

Although the annual report is technically an internal UN document, the report is widely published and considered beyond the halls of UN headquarters. The member-states certainly take note of the content of the report: "Such reports . . . are read carefully by governments. This has an impact on the governments and has frequently resulted in their taking initiatives or actions in efforts to deal with the issues presented" (Finger and Saltzman 1990, 45). In addition, a Secretary-General's ideas may also be publicized as they are debated in the General Assembly and through media reports.

Official representational activities
There are other official public functions that come with the position
that offer influential opportunities. Secretaries-General are expected
to provide statements representing their office's position regarding
conflicts throughout the world, either through general releases or at
official functions. As the head of the United Nations, the Secretaries-
General are also called on to represent the organization and to preside
over a variety of events. Many such occasions occur outside of UN
headquarters and they travel around the globe accordingly. Office-
holders can take advantage of these official representational functions
to attempt to influence others by offering their advice or opinions.
For example, Cordovez explains that a "well-considered public appeal
by the Secretary-General urging the parties in conflict to take specific
steps may leave parties no choice but to react positively for fear of losing international support" (1987, 172). In addition, while representing the United Nations, the Secretaries-General come into contact
with important decision makers involved in international politics. This
provides them with a chance to try to influence these individuals' policies and encourages the decision makers to turn to the Secretary-
General for assistance.

"Unofficial" representational activities
Secretaries-General can place themselves in the public eye through
involvement in a range of more "unofficial" activities geared toward
getting across their message. While there is some overlap between the
official and unofficial categories, the key difference is that official
avenues for influence come from the office's duties, while the label of
"unofficial" captures independent efforts by Secretaries-General to
express their views. Sometimes a Secretary-General's message is
picked up and made widely available through media coverage. Other
times office-holders must work to ensure that the public is aware of
their ideas or actions. Murthy explains reasons for a direct appeal to
the public:

> Although the Secretary-General is elected by, and is therefore account-
> able to, the member states, his actions are at times aimed at articulating
> the hopes and fears of the peoples of the world. It is not that the
> Secretary-General likes to pit the peoples against their respective gov-
> ernments; but often he found it necessary to influence the member
> governments through the means of educating or aiding the domestic
> opinions of member states. (1995, 186)

A Secretary-General can operate in the public domain in several ways. Office-holders can try to gain attention for their opinions or actions through speaking engagements. Linked to this is the ability to travel and reach out to provide their message. In relation to the media, a Secretary-General may also grant interviews or work to have their ideas publicized. Whether at UN headquarters or traveling abroad, there is always the option of holding public press conferences. Getting one's message out through the press can be important because "[c]reative, carefully timed use of the press can influence the immediate parties as well as policymakers in distant capitals" (Ratner 1995, 78). Office-holders may also write an article or opinion piece for public consumption.

PEACEFUL SETTLEMENT OF DISPUTES

Beyond agenda setting activities, the role of the Secretary-General can extend to more direct involvement in handling threats to international peace and security. As Ameri summarizes, "The political functions of the Secretary-General thus range all the way from that of being a simple observer to that of an intermediary attempting to reconcile the wishes of contending groups in the midst of the Organization, to directing peacekeeping operations" (1996, 137). The next two sections address the peaceful settlement capabilities of the Secretary-General. Then the ways in which an office-holder can be involved in UN interventions are discussed.

INDEPENDENTLY INITIATED

The Secretary-General has the potential to be an independent player in helping to resolve breaches of the peace. This capability is based on the powers conferred by Article 99, which can be interpreted as allowing the Secretary-General to involve the office in a wide range of activities to address disruptions to international peace and security. Paul Tavernier explains that Article 99 "is not merely a simple text on procedure permitting the secretary-general to convoke the meeting of the Security Council. On the contrary, it gives him considerable power" (1993, 170). In fact, the significance of activities based on the extension of Article 99 is hard to overstate:

> The "special right" of the Secretary-General has evolved far beyond original expectations for it as an alternative means for engaging the Security Council in consideration of an international dispute or a situation which could become serious. It has been built up so that now the

chief executive officer has an opportunity to attempt to influence almost any action involving the maintenance of peace and security. Its elaboration and the rationalization to explain its expansion have furnished a firm base for activities by the Secretary-General. (Gordenker 1967, 156–157)

Article 99 provides a Secretary-General with the leeway to voluntarily monitor a conflict and to carry out investigations of problematic situations. If a Secretary-General has the responsibility of alerting the Security Council about threats to international peace and security, then, by extension, an office-holder must maintain a high level of awareness and information about ongoing security issues throughout the world. This logic has led to a broad, and highly significant, interpretation of Article 99 that justifies taking independent initiatives to explore potentially insecure areas in order to ensure that any decision to bring the matter before the Security Council is fully informed. These efforts can take the form of a personal visit because the Secretary-General should not rely on secondhand information in such important and sensitive situations, or the use of personally appointed special representatives.

When a Secretary-General collects information on an unstable area, there is no legal duty to take these details to the Security Council unless the activities are mandated, so that the mission is based on Article 98 and not Article 99 powers (Bourloyannis 1990, 659). If the basis of the discovery is an independent initiative taken under Article 99 authority, the wording of the article does not bind the Secretary-General to present threats to the Security Council. At the San Francisco conference, the delegates debated between "shall bring" and "may bring." When they decided on "may" this solidified Article 99 as a discretionary power (Elarby 1987, 189). Since an office-holder first decides whether an issue is relevant to the Security Council's agenda and, assuming that it is judged to be relevant, then can still conclude whether the situation should be specifically referred to the Security Council, the Secretary-General actually has "double discretion" in the use of Article 99 (Alexandrowitz 1962, 1115).

Article 99 provides Secretaries-General not only with the opportunity to observe conflicts, but also the ability to assist in resolving these situations. By directly monitoring a problem area, office-holders place themselves in an advantageous position to influence how the parties involved in the conflict resolve their differences. The need to find out information about insecure areas allows Secretaries-General to undertake a range of diplomatic consultations under their own initiative so,

"Potentially, the office of secretary-general has always been one which a willing incumbent could use to effect adjustment of international disputes" (Blaisdell 1966, 112). If they are so "willing," the opportunity is present to become engaged as a third party in efforts to settle a conflict. In the end, despite the fact that Article 99 has rarely been directly invoked, this "is not to say that it has not often been employed. The very potential of its use has been an important influence. Its presence itself, without formal invocation, provides the virtually incontrovertible legal justification for a great part of the Secretary-General's political action" (Nayar 1974, 59).

MANDATED ASSIGNMENTS

Many times the Secretary-General does not independently initiate peaceful settlement, but instead is assigned such duties. However, even though the office-holder is given a mandate to carry out, there are still opportunities to have influence. As with independently initiated efforts, Secretaries-General can influence the handling of a conflict through their direct engagement with the protagonists. Even before undertaking such assignments, a Secretary-General may try to guide how the mandate is structured. In this manner, an office-holder could influence the mission profile, thereby setting the parameters of the assignment. In addition, although other organs issue these mandates, the creation of the mission can be at a Secretary-General's insistence that the office be allowed to take action to address a particular problem.

Once an assignment is given, the focus shifts to how the Secretaries-General take advantage of what Steven Ratner refers to as "the critical power to interpret the mandate" (1995, 71). As Ralph Townley explains, "while it is basically the responsibility of members to decide *what* should be done, it is the job of the Secretary-General to decide *how*" (1968, 157; Townley's emphasis). The explicitness of mandates varies and there is often a degree of discretion provided to the Secretaries-General regarding how to carry out their responsibilities. By taking advantage of the latitude in interpreting and carrying out a mandate, Secretaries-General may extend their influence beyond the role of administrator simply carrying out an assignment. For example, Scott Pasternack notes how office-holders can guide the "timing, logistics, and goals of each preparatory mission" when undertaking a fact-finding assignment (1994, 718).

Secretaries-General may seek to use the findings from a mandated mission to their own advantage as well. Observing conflict areas can provide a valuable source of outside information that might be employed to support agenda-influencing efforts. Monitoring missions might also serve as a stepping-stone to broader responsibilities if Secretaries-General seek to stretch the bounds of the assignment. For example, they could move from observation into consultation or mediation with the conflicting parties. In the end, "The assignment of functions to the Secretary-General inevitably involves vesting in him some discretion with regard to the carrying out of his task," so one should expect that the "execution of those tasks involved the exercise of political judgment by the Secretary-General" where the office-holder is so willing (Nayar 1974, 44).

UN INTERVENTION

UN involvement in addressing international security also moves beyond efforts to peacefully settle conflicts to direct intervention through the use of force. Although the Secretary-General plays a more "marginal supporting role" in extensive UN-backed military actions like those in Korea and Iraq (Gordenker 2005, 43), despite specification in the Charter to meet international breaches of the peace with a collective security response such engagements are extremely rare. The general failure to follow these measures led to the creation of peacekeeping as an alternative approach. This organizational development has had a major impact on the Secretary-Generalship as it has provided the office with an "unusually prominent" place in the realm of international security (Shimura 2001, 46), because office-holders have been called on to help devise and run peacekeeping missions. Gordenker emphasizes how peacekeeping greatly extended the Secretary-General's "share in determining the policies of the United Nations in maintaining peace and security" and points to how "these duties have required the use of every means of influence at his command" (1967, 234).

Virtually every step of the peacekeeping process involves opportunities for influence. Newman describes the Secretary-General's involvement in peacekeeping as an "organic relationship" with the deliberative organs because the office can find itself involved in "initiation, formulation . . . and field operation" (1998, 33). Although Secretaries-General are not allowed to independently establish a peacekeeping mission, because these operations depend upon prior authorization, they can be closely involved in discussions about the possibility of creating such a mission. As with mandated peaceful settlement, Secretaries-General may be active in trying to shape the peacekeeping mandates that they will be called on to carry out. Once the mandate is established, the Secretary-General becomes the organizational head of a peacekeeping mission and how office-holders choose to administer peacekeeping operations can greatly enhance or reduce their level of influence. Certain Secretaries-General may seek to make adjustments to ensure that the operation is carried out according to their interpretation of the missions' needs, while other office-holders simply stick to the letter of the mandate.

LINKING THE LEADERSHIP STYLES AND THE AVENUES OF INFLUENCE: BEHAVIORAL EXPECTATIONS

What are the specific differences in political behavior that should be displayed between managers, visionaries, and strategists as they carry out the duties of their office in the realm of international peace and security? With the influential activities of the Secretary-General categorized, this question is addressed by detailing the behavioral variation expected across the three styles in relation to these categories. These expectations are summarized in table 3.2. The case study chapters that follow explore the proposed connections to see if they are supported by concrete examples of Secretaries-General in action.

The wide divergence in behavior between Secretaries-General with a managerial style instead of a visionary style should be displayed across the agenda setting activities. Much of the debate over these two types revolves around the degree to which Secretaries-General should seek to put forward their own ideas versus maintaining a low profile and following the instructions of the member-states. Managers take heed of James' advice that "it behooves the Secretary-General to take great care not to upset his sensitive political masters. He is not an independent international actor, in the sense of being formally free to choose his own policies. And, particularly with respect to political issues, he is a man under authority" (1985, 27). Therefore, managers implement the agenda set by others instead of seeking to set the agenda themselves. They are willing to leave it up to others to identify problems and to determine how these issues should be addressed.

A Secretary-General with a visionary style is much more likely than a manager to try to influence the agenda. Visionaries want to ensure that certain problem areas are given priority status and want their solutions to these problems carried out. Related to the earlier discussion of personal characteristics, visionaries are much less responsive than their complex managerial compatriots. As Michael Young and Mark Schafer explain, "Conceptually complex leaders wanted to check with politically powerful others, to seek information about the

Table 3.2 Leadership Style Behavioral Expectations

Activity	Managerial	Strategic	Visionary
Agenda Setting *Administrative Duties*			
●Supervise Reports	Produce unbiased reports upon request	Produce reports reflecting own views; but not as likely to offer independently when seen as politically disadvantageous	Produce reports reflecting own views
●Oversee Finances	Unbiased design; readily accede to revisions	Involved in budget design; give-and-take over final budget depending on political resistance	Involved in budget design; lobby strongly for not changing
●Shape Administrative Structure	Unlikely to restructure unless told to do so; will alter along guidelines without concern for expanding own influence; will not lobby for particular structure	Likely to restructure, but will back away from areas that are too politically volatile; will try to provide for more influence for own office but not to detriment of politically challenging recalcitrant members; will lobby but be willing to make political sacrifices	Likely to restructure; design structure to provide more influence for own office; will lobby strongly for desired changes
●Staffing the Secretariat	Willing to allow members to influence staffing considerations; will not use staffing appointments to place own people	Flexible in appointment process, willing to make political sacrifices when under pressure; but seek to have influential compatriots put into place when possible	Seek full control over process; use power to place those close to them in positions

Continued

Table 3.2 Continued

Activity	Managerial	Strategic	Visionary
Strategic Political Position			
● Representative in Meetings	Will attend meetings where required under Article 98, but will not act independently to place self in important meetings or express views unless requested to do so; will not employ Article 99 unless asked to do so	Will attend meetings, where will be active in listening to different views and determining what avenues for influence exist; unlikely to employ Article 99 unless asked to do so	Will use authority to attend meetings with the intention of expressing views; most likely to employ Article 99
● Inherent Strategic Position	No attempt to cultivate contacts for influential purposes; may be used by member-states for information that managers possess	Will build relationships, gather information, and use position to get ideas into agenda in a give-and-take process; open to others' needs and ideas	Will attempt to push ideas on those who they come into contact with; seek to use information that they possess to pursue own agenda
Public Pronouncements			
● Annual Report to General Assembly	Make report a straightforward, technical account with limited personal recommendations	Express views regarding conflicts, but in guarded tone and unlikely to take on most politically sensitive conflicts; see as good opportunity to float general ideas for reaction	Express strong views regarding conflicts; stress how issues should be handled and what areas are being ignored that need to be addressed
● Official Representational Activities	Carry out duty in a straightforward manner without seeking to impact on the agenda	Will take advantage of opportunities to express opinions; temper pronouncements according to the situation	Will take advantage of all times and situations to speak out and strongly express views

• Unofficial Representational Activities	Unlikely to undertake many of these activities voluntarily; when speaking maintains a bland message that does not challenge state prerogatives	Seen as good avenue to get message across, but will temper according to audience and sensitivity of topic	will seek out these opportunities to be very vocal in expressing views
Peaceful Settlement of Disputes			
Independently Initiated	Unlikely to undertake such missions; if does become involved will limit forcefulness of the initiative	Will undertake such missions, but only after careful consideration to determine receptiveness to action; will listen to views of combatants in helping them work toward a common understanding and solution	Will seek to undertake such missions based on own authority and will seek to impose a solution
Mandated Assignment	Will not attempt to influence mandate; will follow mandate closely and request clarification if anything unclear	Will probe to determine if input for mandate would be accepted; will use own judgment in interpreting mandate and will seek to test bounds of mandate, although will seek to clarify mission and back away if face backlash over activities	Will attempt to influence mandate and in carrying out will seek to follow own interpretation of mission needs, including moving beyond bounds of mandate where desire
UN Intervention *Peacekeeping Missions*	Will not attempt to influence mandate and will follow mandate closely and request clarification if anything unclear	Will probe to determine if input for mandate would be accepted; will use own judgment in interpreting mandate, although will seek to clarify mission and back away if face backlash over activities	Will attempt to influence mandate and in carrying out will seek to follow own interpretation of mission needs

issue at hand, and to consider a range of alternatives before taking action. Conceptually simple leaders were more single-minded, decisive, and quick to define the situation in terms that fit their predispositions" (1998, 85). In the case of the Secretary-General, visionaries are driven to make sure that the agenda fits their conception.

The strategic style falls in between the managerial and the visionary styles. Strategists seek to be agenda manipulators. Like visionaries, strategists also desire to influence the agenda, but they are much more sensitive to the situational requirements and, therefore, take a more cautious approach to getting their ideas incorporated into the agenda. While strategists are careful to weigh their options relative to the situation, they are quite willing to take advantage of opportunities to play an important role in international affairs. Overall, strategists work hard to balance the different demands of the office. This reflects Luard's prescription for an office-holder, "Either excessive activity or inactivity may be equally criticised. He must be politician, diplomat, and civil servant in one" (1994, 112).

In regards to peaceful settlement of disputes and UN intervention, Secretaries-General with a managerial style perceive their role as implementers of instructions. Managers are involved in these activities when called upon to do so, but they feel increasingly uncomfortable as more independent responsibilities are placed on their office. A managerial Secretary-General is not "likely to forget that in essence the United Nations was a collection of sovereign States. They were the paymasters and he, ultimately, was their piper. He might be allowed or even encouraged to provide appropriate embellishments, but only in keeping with the general tune which they called" (James 1983, 83). By contrast, visionaries welcome the spotlight on their office or the United Nations that these opportunities provide. A strategist is not as likely as a manager to shy away from these activities, but should pursue them in a more sensitive manner than visionaries. In contrast to visionaries, who push their ideas upon conflicting parties, strategists are more likely to recognize, for example, that a "Secretary-General's readiness to provide good offices has to be matched by an equal disposition to withdraw his services whenever he feels that their continuation no longer serves the principles and purposes of the Charter and could be damaging to the status of his office with a view to other peacemaking efforts" (Cordovez 1987, 169). Managers will avoid placing themselves in such politically delicate situations altogether unless instructed to do so.

Overall, managers are constraint respecters, while visionaries are constraint challengers, and strategists are constraint accommodators.

A Secretary-General with a strategic style is keenly aware of the restrictions placed on the office, but tries to find a way to work attentively around these constraints in an effort to have a greater level of influence. Strategists acknowledge that limits on carrying out the duties of their office exist, but perceive these restrictions as something to overcome when possible, not as something to which they should automatically accede. Secretaries-General with a visionary style are not as mindful of such considerations and push hard to be as influential as possible, regardless of barriers placed in their way. At the opposite end of the spectrum, office-holders with a managerial style observe a much more passive role for the office, easily accepting a role as the subordinate servant of the member-states and not taking advantage of the opportunities for independent initiative.

Returning to the toolbox conceptualization discussed earlier, each activity represents a potential influential tool. For each available tool it is important to first examine whether a Secretary-General is likely to use that tool, so activities can be classified as mandatory or voluntary (labeled as such in table 3.1). The more passive managers are unlikely to move beyond a perfunctory use of the tools of influence. They are involved in mandatory activities because they have no option, but they are more likely to shun voluntary opportunities to exert influence. Secretaries-General with a visionary or a strategic style use both mandatory and voluntary tools, although a strategist is more attentive in determining if it is a proper situation to undertake a voluntary activity. An office-holder with a strategic style is likely to use the tools that best fit with the requirements of the situation, while employing these tools in a creative manner to expand their ability to have influence. For the strategic style, Secretaries-General balance the two halves of their demanding position by being involved in a range of activities, but in a responsive manner. By contrast, a Secretary-General with a visionary style is predisposed to use as many tools as possible and to push the parameters of these tools to the extreme in order to gain as much influence as possible without recognizing the danger of "breaking" the tool.

AGENDA SETTING

ADMINISTRATIVE DUTIES

Managerial style
A Secretary-General with a managerial style will perform the full range of mandatory routine duties, but is unlikely to take steps to radically restructure the administrative structure, unless requested to do so.

If managerial Secretaries-General do restructure the Secretariat they will alter the organization along the guidelines provided by others without concern for expanding their own influence and will not lobby for a particular arrangement. Requested reports, along with the budget proposal, should be produced in an unbiased manner with no effort to place their own views into these documents. Managers will allow the political bodies to dictate the guidelines for the budget and readily accept alterations to their proposal. Member-states are able to guide a manager's staffing considerations. Secretariat appointments will likely be made with little consideration over how employee hiring or placement could affect the Secretary-General's capability to use these individuals to further possibilities for influence.

Visionary style
In contrast to managers, visionaries will employ administrative activities to ensure that they have a more influential position within the United Nations. They will seize the chance to safeguard against being relegated to the role of an official carrying out the will of others and instead will take advantage of the process to input their own ideas. However, given the appeal of the routes to influence provided by other tools, routine matters are more likely to be overlooked in light of more direct possibilities to address peace and security. When seeking to use administrative tools to increase their influential capabilities, visionaries will involve themselves in the wording of reports so that they reflect the office-holder's viewpoint. They will be involved in designing and then strongly lobbying for their budget proposals. Visionaries are also likely to alter the administrative structure to better fit their views of a proper organizational setup. They will seek a Secretariat design that provides more influence for their office and will lobby for their desired changes to be approved. They will seek full control over the appointment process and like-minded people who are willing to support the Secretary-General's efforts will be intentionally well placed.

Strategic style
Secretaries-General with a strategic style generally seek to be influential, but they also recognize the need to balance support from the member-states with their efforts. Thus, these individuals are likely to pursue administrative avenues of influence more than office-holders with a managerial style, but they will do so in a more cautious and restrained manner than individuals with a visionary style. Reports and the budget proposal are viewed as useful opportunities since they are

subtle, yet important, tools for influence, but strategists will be less likely to offer their independent views when they feel that it might be politically disadvantageous. For the budget, this means being involved in the design, but undergoing a process of give and take over the final proposals depending on the political resistance that they face over different areas of the budget.

Administrative restructuring and staff appointments will be used to further the base of influence possessed by the Secretary-General to the extent that these activities do not provoke a strong outcry from the member-states. Strategists are likely to attempt to restructure the Secretariat, but they will avoid politically volatile areas. They will seek a more influential place for their office, but not to the detriment of challenging recalcitrant member-states. Similarly, they will lobby for their proposed changes, but they will also be willing to make political sacrifices where necessary. In regards to Secretariat staffing, strategists will be flexible during the appointment process and will give into political pressure, but they will still seek to have influential compatriots put into place when possible.

STRATEGIC POLITICAL POSITION

Managerial style

As a primarily voluntary category of activities, the tools in this section are likely to be underemployed by Secretaries-General with a managerial style. When they do attend required meetings, they will most likely do so in an administrative capacity without adding much of their own input unless requested to do so. Managers should not call a matter to the attention of the Security Council using their Article 99 powers unless they are urged to do so. The inherent strategic position will mostly come into play when others perceive the Secretary-General's position as useful to them and ask for assistance. Most information acquired at the position will be passed along in a neutral manner. Managers will not attempt to cultivate contacts for their own influential purposes.

Visionary style

Visionaries will take every advantage to press their opinion on others, regardless of the appropriateness of their comments or the timing of their intervention. They will use their authority to appear at meetings that they perceive to be important and will attend these meetings with the intention of expressing their views. Out of the three types, visionaries are the most likely to directly invoke Article 99. Unlike managers, they see their strategic position as very useful for expanding their chances for influence. They will attempt to push their ideas on whomever they come into contact with whenever they can and will use the possession of vital information to stress their own agenda.

Strategic style

Given the nature of this style, these Secretaries-General are likely to make use of their strategic political position. By building good relationships and surveying the possibilities for placing their own input into the policy-making process, strategists will use their ability to act as representatives in meetings and their inherent strategic position to their best advantage. They will attend meetings, where they will be less likely to speak up and present their own views than a visionary, but they will be better at listening to different views and determining what openings for influence exist by gathering this information. They are unlikely to use Article 99 unless encouraged by member-states to do so. Through their inherent strategic position, they will work subtly with delegates to try to move their ideas onto the agenda. They seek to learn about others' needs and ideas and will react flexibly to incorporate these points in relation to agenda setting efforts. Thus, sitting at the strategic position, they are actively engaged in both gathering and imparting information.

PUBLIC PRONOUNCEMENTS

Managerial style

All Secretaries-General are expected to write an annual report and to represent the United Nations, but managers are not likely to use these forums to press independent opinions. The annual report should be a straightforward, technical account and personal recommendations will be limited. The ability to use unofficial representational activities for expressing opinions does not have much appeal and will be engaged in sparingly. When managers speak, in official or unofficial settings, they will maintain a bland message that does not challenge state prerogatives.

Visionary style

Public pronouncements are a major set of tools for visionary Secretaries-General. They will actively seek out as much exposure for their ideas and activities in the public domain as possible. The annual report should be a strong statement on how conflicts should be handled, what areas in particular are being ignored that need to be better addressed, and, when discussing the role of the Secretary-General or the United Nations in handling international security more broadly, they will emphasize a more vital role. They will take advantage of all official and unofficial public pronouncement avenues in order to expound on their views regarding global peace and security.

Strategic style

A strategist is more likely to downplay the use of public pronouncements in comparison to a visionary and instead reserve these activities for situations where they appear to be most appropriate. Since the annual report is a mandatory task undertaken each year, these individuals should feel comfortable in using this forum to put forward their own initiatives, but they will do so in more guarded tones and will be unlikely to challenge states on the most politically sensitive conflicts. They will address how issues should be handled, but only to the point where they are within the acceptable range for the member-states and they will not push for the United Nations to get involved in areas where it will face political backlash. They want to get their views across, but do not want to delve into areas of great political controversy, although this is seen as a good opportunity to float ideas regarding the role of the office and United Nations to garner reactions. With representational activities, strategists will seek an influential role, but they will temper pronouncements according to the situation. They should take advantage of interactions to build better relations and should use existing relationships to further their chances for influence. Overall, they try to read the situation to see when a public stance is allowable, or even necessary to get an important point across, as opposed to times when a more restrained approach is called for.

PEACEFUL SETTLEMENT OF DISPUTES

MANAGERIAL STYLE

These activities often involve the Secretary-General telling others how to handle threats to the peace, which goes against a manager's modus operandi of accepting and executing instructions. Compared to Secretaries-General possessing one of the other two leadership styles, there should be a very low use of the right of initiative to intervene because managers will usually wait to be assigned this task. If independently initiated efforts are undertaken, the forcefulness of the effort will be very limited. For mandated missions, managers will not attempt to influence which areas are addressed or how the mandates are worded. Mandates are perceived as something for others to create.

When they receive mandated assignments, managers should stick to closely following their instructions and they will not seek to take advantage of their involvement to influence the path of conflict resolution. These types of leaders are the most likely to simply accept their assignment and work within the specified bounds, seeking clarification from the mandating body when necessary as they carry out their duties. Thus, the level of activity and the degree of influence that these activities provide is dependent on the assigning organs because such individuals are unlikely to attempt to expand their influence beyond what is provided in the mission statement.

VISIONARY STYLE

Out of the three types, visionaries are most likely to encourage a broad interpretation of Article 99 to take center stage in peaceful settlement efforts. Visionaries relish the opportunity to set up their own peaceful settlement missions. While mandated assignments get away from the independent initiative-taking activities associated with Article 99, visionary Secretaries-General are still more than willing to take full advantage of these opportunities. They will seek to push beyond the mission parameters when they do not measure up to the level of influence that they desire. Since visionaries want to make sure that problems are dealt with in a way that fits with their vision for the United Nations, they will encourage the creation of missions to deal with problem areas that they want to address. In addition, they will work to structure the mandate so that they are allowed to handle the problem in the way that they view as best. Whether their involvement is mandatory or voluntary, they will try to push their solution to the conflict on the affected parties. They cherish these opportunities and will seek to involve themselves in insecure areas whenever possible, without being aware of the negative political fallout that this might provoke among countries who see their interests as being challenged.

STRATEGIC STYLE

Secretaries-General with a strategic style will not force the issue in regards to creating a mandated mission. Instead, they will wait until there is a consensus that something needs to be done and then try to build upon this desire to influence how the mission is going to be carried out. In doing so, they will cautiously probe to determine whether the political latitude exists to influence the formation of a mandate. They are much more likely to offer their assistance if it is apparent that their input would be welcomed. Strategists will also engage in independent missions, but these will likely only be initiated if there is a preexisting consensus that this is a good idea or, conversely, if no clear opposition exists to such a mission. Such missions will be undertaken only after careful consideration to ensure that the efforts of the Secretary-General will be supported.

Once involved in peaceful settlement efforts, strategists will carefully probe to see how they can extend their influence. They will build closer ties with the parties involved and will gather as much information as possible that might be useful to provide them with greater leeway at a later point. They recognize that if a more positive environment is established and their role is accepted, then they will be in a better position to present options for settling the parties' differences or to stretch the bounds of the initial mandate that brought them to the situation. Thus, they will back off when faced with political intransigence regarding their efforts, but will seek to continue to build momentum toward settlement as circumstances become more acceptable. They will take the views of the combatants into account as part of working toward a common understanding regarding a solution to the problem, only interjecting their own ideas where appropriate to keep the process moving forward.

UN INTERVENTION

MANAGERIAL STYLE

Since the administration of peacekeeping operations is a mandatory activity, managers do not have a choice as to whether or not to become involved in this activity. However, as with peaceful settlement missions, managers will leave formulating the mandates up to the member-states. In addition, they are unlikely to take advantage of this opportunity for influence by trying to shape how the mission is carried out. Instead, they will follow the guidelines of the mission mandate as closely as possible and seek advice on how to proceed when unexpected circumstances arise. They are more than willing to defer to state authority for forming and managing peacekeeping operations.

VISIONARY STYLE

Despite the potential political pitfalls, visionaries have no such qualms over trying to impose their views on how UN interventions should be carried out. Since peacekeeping missions provide a Secretary-General with a central role in implementing the operations, a visionary will seek to take full advantage of their position. This process starts early with visionaries working to influence the wording of the mandate. When the mission does not match up with their desired approach they will try to restructure activities along the lines they prefer. Overall, visionaries will seek to place a strong personal imprint on the character of peacekeeping operations from the beginning to the end of the mission.

STRATEGIC STYLE

A strategist is primed to take advantage of the crucial role that they can play in shaping peacekeeping activities. As with the peaceful settlement of disputes, strategists will probe for opportunities to guide the development of the mission mandate. However, unlike visionaries, in carrying out missions they will be more aware of the needs and desires of the participants and situational changes. They are careful to heed the warning: "The Secretary-General and those under him must constantly judge the unfolding political scene in the host country and in New York in formulating their approaches" (Ratner 1995, 71). Yet, their approach also differs from Secretaries-General with a managerial style because they are fully willing to take advantage of connections with the countries involved to influence the way that the mission progresses. In addition, they are prepared to independently monitor and handle any changing circumstances. Thus, they will use their own judgment in interpreting the mandate, although they will seek to clarify their mission when it becomes politically difficult and will back down when they face backlash over their activities. Overall, in the peacekeeping realm strategic Secretaries-General will undertake a balanced approach. They will carefully monitor the situation and will aim to make sure that the conflict is primed for intervention before encouraging the use of this tool.

CONCLUSION

As the material in this chapter illustrates, "there are many bases for the Secretary-General to be politically active rather than merely bureaucratically passive" (Szasz 1991, 191). However, not all Secretaries-General choose to take equal advantage of the "bases" of influence. The argument put forth in this study is that this variation is linked to the leadership style of the office-holders. The previous chapter established how the managerial, visionary, and strategic styles represent ideal types of how a Secretary-General is likely to perceive the role as head of the United Nations. Now that these leadership styles have been related to a framework of influential activities to establish a set of behavioral expectations, the stage is set to examine whether or not the proposed connections between style and behavior exist by detailing the tenures of the visionary Hammarskjöld, managerial Waldheim, and strategic Annan.

CHAPTER 4

The Visionary: Dag Hammarskjöld

It took a strong, outstanding personality like that of Hammarskjöld to give to the Secretary-General's office such an impetus . . . by giving life and dynamism to the Secretary-General's office, Hammarskjöld gave by the same token life and impetus to the Organization itself—Mongi Slim, past president of General Assembly.

(Slim 1965, 7)

INTRODUCTION

Looking back at Dag Hammarskjöld's time in office, Larry Trachtenberg asks, "What kind of leader was Dag Hammarskjöld during his tenure as secretary-general? Much has been written about the man and his successes and failures, but little about the type of leader he was or the wellsprings of his leadership" (1982, 613). The content analysis coding results presented in the last chapter, which indicate that Hammarskjöld possessed a visionary leadership style, are the first step toward addressing Trachtenberg's query. This chapter turns to the behavioral side of the equation to explore whether Hammarskjöld's visionary leadership style had an impact on his actions as Secretary-General in the manner expected. As this chapter demonstrates, the visionary style is evident in his behavior while in office. He was notably involved in attempting to influence the handling of peace and security issues as an independent, dynamic Secretary-General who employed the full roster of influential tools in his repertoire.

To support this argument, the chapter first discusses Hammarskjöld's visionary style. The chapter begins with his election, which was based on the misguided managerial expectations of the member-states.

This discussion then turns to his overarching visionary style and the characteristics that make up this style in order to support the content analysis findings. The second part of the chapter discusses his behavior as Secretary-General. Since this section seeks to illustrate how he behaved in a visionary manner, it is preceded by a brief review of what Hammarskjöld's vision entailed so that his attempts to put this into place may be better understood. The behavior section begins with an overview of the general visionary pattern of his political behavior and is followed by a specific analysis of his time in office based on the framework of influential activities that was set out in chapter 3.

HAMMARSKJÖLD: THE MAN BEHIND THE OFFICE

THE ELECTION: A VISIONARY IN MANAGER'S CLOTHING

Hammarskjöld took office in 1953, was re-elected to a second term in 1957, and served until his untimely death in a plane crash in 1961. Before serving as Secretary-General, he had devoted his life to the civil service in his home country Sweden. Hammarskjöld seemed to be an unlikely candidate to become a visionary Secretary-General and he was selected precisely because the great powers did not expect him to act as such. As Jakobson, who later ran for Secretary-General but lost out to Waldheim, details,

> How Hammarskjöld came to be appointed secretary-general in 1952 is a story abounding in irony. He did not seek the office, and those who selected him had no intention of launching him onto a spectacular career. The big powers of the time were tired of the political pretensions of Trygve Lie, the first secretary-general; they wanted a faceless bureaucrat to run the Secretariat, and Dag Hammarskjöld, a neutral civil servant from neutral Sweden seemed perfect for the part. (1998, 75)

As Jakobson indicates, Hammarskjöld did not pursue the Secretary-Generalship. When first informed that he had been chosen to be the second Secretary-General, he thought that the message was an April Fools Day joke. Once he was convinced that the offer was valid, he initially hesitated to accept the position, but quickly decided that this was a task from which he could not turn away.

Very little was known about Hammarskjöld during the selection process. Once his name was suggested, the Americans scrambled to find information and the dossier prepared presented him as "a Swedish civil service aristocrat, gifted administratively, unobtrusive rather than flamboyant, a brilliant technician, an executant rather than a political leader . . . a compromiser rather than a fighter" (Lash 1961, 8). These supposed qualities endeared Hammarskjöld to the member-states that sought a compliant manager and it was widely assumed that he would limit his activities primarily to the administrative realm. This prediction was backed by his predecessor, Lie, who "feared a stagnation in the development of the Office" (Rovine 1970, 274) because he believed that Hammarskjöld would never amount to more than a "clerk" while in office and that the United Nations and its Charter principles would suffer as a result.

However, Hammarskjöld proved both the great powers' hopes and Lie's fears to beincorrect as Thomas Boudreau summarizes below:

> Hammarskjöld's reputation for administrative skill was undoubtedly one of the reasons he was nominated for Secretary-General; the great powers wanted a man who would run the United Nations smoothly, but not "rock the boat." In this regard, Hammarskjöld surprised his great power supporters by asserting, from the very beginning of his service as Secretary-General, an active and independent position for the United Nations. (1991, 39)

Despite his initial surprise with being offered the Secretary-Generalship, Hammarskjöld accepted the challenge and indeed "welcomed the incomparable opportunity that had been given to him to use all of his ability on a much broader stage than before" (Urquhart 1972, 13). As will be shown in the second part of the chapter, Hammarskjöld approached the office with a visionary style that translated into an even stronger, more independent series of actions than the United Nations had experienced under Lie.

HAMMARSKJÖLD'S VISIONARY STYLE

A visionary may not have been what the great powers wanted, but throughout Hammarskjöld's tenure this is exactly who they had as Secretary-General. The member-states should not be criticized too severely for failing to initially realize what they had in Hammarskjöld. Although, "Hammarskjöld's personality and personal style were dominating factors in his conduct of the office" (Urquhart 1983, 140), determining exactly what those personal traits were and how they interacted to guide his political behavior is a complicated matter.

Observers have often commented on the difficulty of understanding the man behind the office, often referring to his "complex personality" (e.g., Bunche 1965, 119; Fosdick 1972, 114; and Thorpe 1969, 45). One of those who worked closely with Hammarskjöld, and within the United Nations for over 40 years, Urquhart claims, "He was the most unusual and striking personality I have encountered in public life" (1987, 126), while another observer simply states, "He is a difficult man to define" (Williams 1958, 22).

In part, this may be due to Hammarskjöld's desire to separate the "private man" from the "international public servant" (Lash 1961, 45). He was generally reserved when dealing with others and could rebuff even those working in close tandem with him if they pursued too high of a level of familiarity (Urquhart 1987; Bunche 1965). The intrigue surrounding his character may also reflect the complexity of his thinking about international affairs, which will be examined more closely below. Despite these expressed difficulties in grasping Hammarskjöld as an individual, this section is able to draw on detailed observations from those who have studied the man and those who knew him personally to piece together a picture of the person behind the office. These accounts support the profile created through the use of content analysis.

There is a definite perception among observers that Hammarskjöld possessed a visionary leadership style. As described by Joseph Lash, Hammarskjöld's style clearly deviated from that of a subservient manager: "Hammarskjöld in practice elected the role of strong leader rather than that of unobtrusive clerk" since he had a "personal proclivity for exercising a strong hand in affairs" (1962, 545). The words most often used to characterize Hammarskjöld are "visionary" and "dynamic," sometimes used together in the same descriptive phrase. He is portrayed as possessing clear ideas regarding international relations and as determined to follow this vision during his time in office. One of his "major traits was the courage to uphold and abide by his principles" (Slim 1965, 3) as he "held cherished views about the need to hold to what would appear to be the 'right' course of action" in his mind (Jordan 1983, 7).

Of course, what Hammarskjöld believed to be "right" was not always accepted, and his visionary approach led to him being "called a 'megalomaniac,' a 'dangerous man out to wreck the United Nations'; and 'idealist' who was 'out of step with reality' " (Kelen 1968, xii). However, he viewed potential constraints on his office not as a limit on what he should try to do, but as obstacles to be challenged and overcome. Thus, for Hammarskjöld, "it was characteristic that he regarded these factors not merely as imposing limits on the use of law, but in a more positive sense as a challenge which called for creative attempts to find new norms and procedures" (Schachter 1962, 7). He believed that he had a personal responsibility to base his actions on his own beliefs regardless of state interests. For Hammarskjöld, the office and the organization was more important than the individual and he was willing to sacrifice himself for the "greater good" if necessary. Quite simply, the vision was more vital than the man and this allowed him to strongly challenge what did not fit with his ideas.

UNDERLYING VISIONARY PERSONAL CHARACTERISTICS

When looking at the separate personal characteristics, problem-solving emphasis and need for relationships are clearly key components of Hammarskjöld's visionary style. His score for problem-solving emphasis is far higher and the score for need for relationships is lower than the other six Secretaries-General. Descriptive accounts of his character also pick out these traits. Hammarskjöld is described as "a man of unbounded energy with a single-minded devotion to his task" (Narasimhan 1988, 279). He showed a "capacity for intense concentration" (Thorpe 1969, 75) that "allowed him to direct all his energies to whatever he was doing and then switch completely to the next task" (Urquhart 1972, 29). This statement really did apply to "whatever" Hammarskjöld turned his attention. He felt that anything worth doing was worth immersing himself in so that it would be completed in an efficient and effective manner. He was not likely to shy away from tackling a challenge or to back down before the proper solution was hit upon. Lester Pearson, the Canadian delegate who served as president of the General Assembly, in response to a question about Hammarskjöld's approach to working, states the following:

> He was not influenced by emotion or by prejudice or by sentiment, but by a cold, yes, cold, intellectual search for a solution. Then having made that approach to a problem, he was a man of terrific energy and determination . . . he was never willing to give up until we had finished that particular job, even if it kept us going all night. (Pearson and Reford 1961, 3)

As Pearson's observation indicates, Hammarskjöld was so focused on handling assignments that he did not show much concern for the feelings of others who lacked his drive. Cordier, who worked closely with Hammarskjöld as his executive assistant, describes one illustrative incident. When a delegate begged off a meeting due to fatigue, Hammarskjöld's response was to stamp "up and down the corridor outside his office repeating, 'Sissy, sissy. The man has to sleep!' " (1967, 17). After all, when asked if he was tired while putting in long hours, Hammarskjöld answered, "That would be frivolous!" (quoted in Urquhart 1983, 134). Equally frivolous were trivial social occasions that would interrupt his work schedule. He hosted small get-togethers with close friends, but generally, "he drove himself like a man possessed, but he would not have been satisfied otherwise . . . His zest for work left little time for formal social gatherings" (Gillett 1970, 99).

Staff members were held to Hammarskjöld's "exacting standards of inexhaustible work" and he became frustrated when these were not met (Heller 2001, 2). No one was spared from Hammarskjöld's drive: "Though a loyal friend, he could be a ruthless taskmaster . . . One could be close to him professionally or intellectually, but the warmth and intimacy of a human relationship escaped him" (Dayal 1976, 303). He never married and indicated that a family should not be subjected to his work schedule. This attitude carried over to those working along with him: "His dedication to work is almost monastic in its concentratedness. He sometimes gives his aides the impression they should not have families because they interfere with getting the job done" (Lash 1961, 208). Subsequently, he stood out as a "man who liked to work by himself, a lone wolf. He was a bachelor and totally dedicated to his job" (Narasimhan 1988, 279).

As this discussion indicates, although imbued with a desire to solve problems, Hammarskjöld displayed little need to build relationships. He did develop some close associations, but he was clearly not motivated by a need for relationships. If anything, the opposite held true. Even those who worked closely with Hammarskjöld found it difficult to relate with the man on a personal basis. Urquhart explains, "Although I worked in Hammarskjold's office for eight years and saw a great deal of him, I never felt I knew him well . . . He did not encourage intimacy or familiarity. Indeed those who attempted it usually suffered painful rebuffs" (1987, 125–126). Ralph Bunche concurs that Hammarskjöld "was a man of great reserve in his personal relations, to the extent even of shyness; he was not easy to know, even for those who worked closely with him" (1965, 120). Others who interacted with Hammarskjöld also reacted to his style: "To many of his UN associates he is an aloof, almost intimidating figure . . . Even high-ranking officials and diplomats find it something of a chore to be with him" as "He cannot bear the idea, as one observer put it, 'of being matey' . . . there is always one part of him withheld" (Lash 1961, 220, 222).

Another distinctive characteristic is Hammarskjöld's high need for recognition, with a coding result second only to Waldheim, although this trait manifests itself in a particular way. Notwithstanding his score on this trait, Hammarskjöld did not possess a self-indulgent need for adulation and, instead, he displayed a "willingness to let others take public credit for work privately done" (Jones 2005, 195). Thus, despite the many opportunities due to "his almost daily increasing power, he did not become vain and full of self-importance" (Thorpe 1969, 80–81). However, he did possess the very strong need for control that is captured by this trait. In other words, he required "recognition" in the sense that he needed to be recognized as being in control. This desire to be in control is reflected in Lash's claim that "He dislikes not being right" (1961, 260). Hammarskjöld believed that there was a correct way to do things and he would get upset if his way was not being followed.

In addition, Urquhart points out a "paradox" of Hammarskjöld's character that ties to his need for recognition. While, as indicated above, Hammarskjöld was "personally modest" he remained "highly ambitious for his office" (1983, 133). He strongly believed that the Secretary-Generalship deserved greater recognition by the international community and close control over UN affairs. While there were those that saw Hammarskjöld as desirous of personal power and recognition, "this was a distinctly minority view." Instead, Hammarskjöld's "patient and persistent efforts to build up the power and authority of his office were not regarded as personal empire-building," but as an extended effort to persuade the world that the Secretary-General was an essential actor on the international stage (Lash 1961, 211).

For supranationalism, Hammarskjöld was unquestionably committed to the ideals of a multilateral world supported by international organizations in general and to the principles of the United Nations in particular. Bunche recognizes Hammarskjöld as a supranationalist who sought "to make the United Nations a dynamic force for peace and human advancement . . . In his conception, the United Nations must play an ever more active role" (1965, 121–122). Hammarskjöld viewed the interests of international organization above those of the individual states. He believed in overcoming national interests and the divisions that these caused and putting in its place a harmonization of interests based on a global understanding. He believed that the United Nations could encourage the member-states to adhere to international principles instead of blindly pursuing their own particular concerns. Thus, the United Nations needed to maintain a strong position in international affairs and "he thought that states had an obligation to use it as much as possible in order to strengthen its effectiveness" (Zacher 1970, 27).

Along with supranationalism, Hammarskjöld also possessed a solid belief in his ability to influence events, scoring third highest among the Secretaries-General. With his "thrustful and imaginative personality" (James 1985, 44) he saw himself as capable of creating inventive initiatives. This belief was reflected in how he viewed the capabilities of his position, "Hammarskjold soon showed that he thought of his office—and of the U.N.—as dynamic instrumentalities capable of energetic initiative and strong action" (Plimpton 1966, 142). Hammarskjöld did not simply perceive himself as capable of taking initiatives, but as adept enough to do so in new and imaginative ways and he is often described possessing a "talent for creative political innovation" (Schachter 1962, 1).

A COMPLEX VISIONARY

For the characteristics reviewed thus far, Hammarskjöld matches up well with the trait pattern of a visionary style. However, an exception can be seen in his coding result for responsivity, which is not as low of a score as one would expect for a visionary Secretary-General. While his score is not overly high for responsivity, only fourth among the seven Secretaries-General, descriptive accounts stress this aspect by consistently referring to him as a very complex, analytical thinker. For example, David Williams notes the analogy: "Hammarskjold's quick and subtle mind functions at a pace that has been compared with a jet plane 'which is gone by the time you hear it' " (1958, 22). The fact that Hammarskjöld's overall responsivity score does not measure up to such descriptions of his intellect is due to the construction of the responsivity measure, which reflects the relation of two separately coded traits—conceptual complexity and self-confidence—that operate at cross-purposes. A highly conceptually complex individual will be more responsive, while a highly self-confident person will be less responsive, and vice versa for both measures. Yet, Hammarskjöld has both the highest score for conceptual complexity *and* for self-confidence among the seven Secretaries-General.

Descriptive accounts support the high scores on both traits. It is difficult to read any account of Hammarskjöld's character without encountering mention of his analytical capability. For example, Lash claims that he had never seen "a mind as superbly gifted at analysis as Hammarskjold's . . . who insists on subjecting all issues, irrespective of their emotional and ideological content, to rigorous intellectual analysis" (1961, 33; 206). In combination with his analytical skill, observers note Hammarskjöld's sense of timing and sensitivity to the situation at hand. For example, Pearson observes, "He was a man of not only great intelligence, but great perceptiveness and sensitivity" (Pearson and Reford 1961, 3).

Urquhart likewise marvels at the level of sensitivity he observed while working with Hammarskjöld over the years (1972, 28). But he also comments on the other side of the responsiveness equation, Hammarskjöld's self-confident nature: "His confidence, sureness of touch, and strength communicated to others the comforting feeling that in any situation he knew what to do and how to do it, where he wanted to go and how to get there" (Urquhart 1972, 30). Others have also noted Hammarskjöld's strong self-confident streak. Rajeshwar Dayal, who headed the Congo peacekeeping operation from 1960 to 1961, observes that an "aura of confidence silhouetted his personality" (1976, 303). Mark Zacher states, "While Hammarskjold had certain reservations about the professional capabilities of some members of the Secretariat, this did not hold true for his evaluation of his own abilities," which was reflected in "his struggle to maintain humility while dealing with people whom he considered of a lesser ability" (1970, 45). This high level of self-confidence can work at cross-purposes with Hammarskjöld's otherwise responsive inclination because it means that he is willing to forge ahead on the basis of his own abilities even where the situation may warrant a different approach.

So what does this mean for Hammarskjöld's overall style? Managers are inclined to accede to contextual necessities, strategists emphasize accommodating constraints while maintaining progress, and vision-aries battle through on the basis of a particular vision. Overall, it is the latter that captures Hammarskjöld the best—albeit in a more sensitive and analytical manner than one would see from an ideal visionary. He was not willing to sacrifice his vision. According to an official from the UN Public Information Department who worked closely with Hammarskjöld, he was aware of the risks involved in following his vision instead of a more politically dictated path, but he believed that the risks were worth the potential benefits (Foote 1962, 18). He had a strategic streak to his style in that he was very open to considering what might be a proper strategy for that circumstance. However, once he had made up his mind about the best way to proceed he was confident enough in his capabilities, as well as wedded to his vision, that he would desire to follow that decision with less regard to the contextual difficulties. As Cordier relates,

> In truth, he had a lightning capacity for gathering and appraisal of facts, for the making and implementation of decisions. I never had the impression that he worried himself into decisions. One could see his brilliant mind at work quickly picking out relevant facts, outlining alternative avenues of action, arriving quickly at a formulation of the policy or decision necessary to the problem. Nor did he worry about a decision after it was made. He frequently indulged in a reasoned self-confidence that the decision taken was the right one. (1967, 6)

In order to capture this personal dynamic, this study refers to Hammarskjöld as a "complex visionary" where his simultaneously strong self-confidence acts to temper his overall level of responsivity. Thus, while Hammarskjöld should carefully consider contextual factors in carrying out his duties, he should also have the confidence in his abilities to take action when he decides that the time is right. Urquhart's description of Hammarskjöld's character captures this understanding well: "Although he was a visionary, Hammarskjold was also a shrewd and prudent leader with very clear ideas of what should and should not be undertaken, what could and could not be done, and whether the essential conditions for useful action were present or not" (1972, x). This notion of Hammarskjöld as a complex visionary is also captured by others using different terminology. For example, he has been referred to as "an intensely practical idealist" (Rusk 1965, 67), "a pragmatist with a vision" (Kelen 1968, 124), and a "realistic idealist" (Miller 1961, 20).

HAMMARSKJÖLD'S VISION

The previous section argued that, despite his unexpectedly high level of responsivity for an otherwise visionary style, Hammarskjöld would be guided by his views on international affairs, so it is important to outline his vision. Analyses of Hammarskjöld stress the centrality of his vision of international relations to his approach. For example, Manuel Fröhlich observes how "both his actions and thoughts as Secretary-General can be seen as the quest for a political philosophy of world organization" (2005b, 131; see also Fröhlich 2005a). Indeed, as Zacher stresses, "Hammarskjold's attachment to these objectives went beyond a mere existential preference for them as a basis for human relationships. They were also a part of his total philosophical outlook on life" (1970, 23).

At the core of Hammarskjöld's vision was his conceptualization of the relation between law and politics, where international law was vital to the construction of a more cooperative international community. He believed not only in international law and a peaceful society in abstract terms, but also in the place of the United Nations in encouraging this process. As such, he had much faith in the Charter principles, which provide a basis to ensure that the common interests of all states—from the greatest powers to the smallest states—are promoted. Thant, reflecting on his predecessor, remembers,

> To him, the provisions of the Charter were so important—almost sacred—that he was willing to forego any temporary advantage that could be gained by following the easier path of expediency. To him, too, the institution, the United Nations Organization and its collective interest, was far more important than the separate interests of the individual Member States. (1965, 39–40)

Thus, Hammarskjöld believed that the Charter and other declarations of international law had to be maintained and a move toward a consensus of global values should continue to develop.

Zacher observes that Hammarskjöld's vision in relation to the United Nations can be organized by two main categories: "the kinds of actions which the Organization could and should undertake to affect particular types of international problems and the institutional developments which could and should be realized in our historical era" (1983, 111–112). For the first category, UN actions, Hammarskjöld wanted the organization to play as influential a role as possible and, accordingly, "held a positive and dynamic concept" of the organization "as an instrument acting independently for the general good" (Heller 2001, 18). Traditional power politics and diplomatic interactions have not provided a peaceful, stable world. The United Nations represented a new, and better, way to organize the interactions of states in a continuous, multilateral fashion and must be at the center of decision making for international affairs.

The role of the Secretary-General follows upon the same logic because "Hammarskjold's conception of his own political role was directly influenced by his view of the role of the United Nations" (Goodrich 1974, 479). Hammarskjöld believed in the importance of remaining a neutral figure, but he also emphasized that the Secretary-General must be prepared to protect the standards of international law. This led to a "conception of his office" based on the "fundamental tenet . . . that the exclusively international responsibility of the

Secretary General implied above all a firm adherence to the principles of the Charter and other standards accepted as binding by Member States" (Schachter 1962, 3). Of course, being neutral and guided by international principles did not mean that the Secretary-General should not be closely involved in international affairs. Quite the opposite held true, for he held a very active view of the Secretary-Generalship, which he believed did not challenge, but was supported by, international principles. Lash explains, "[T]he philosophy of the Charter, as Hammarskjöld construed it, called for a strong Secretary-General. So did the stipulations of the Charter regarding the scope and functions of his office" (1962, 546).

Regarding the second category put forth by Zacher, institutional developments, Hammarskjöld undoubtedly wanted the United Nations to become further developed and placed even more squarely at the center of international cooperation and the advancement of international law and global values. These developments could be linked to the underlying legal standing and accomplishments of the organization, "Hammarskjöld did not take the limits on UN action in his day to be permanent. He looked forward to evolution through 'case law'" (Skidelsky 2005, 383). He also believed that the Secretary-Generalship must develop along with the United Nations. For Hammarskjöld, the Secretary-General should not be held back as a minor part of the UN structure as the office had a vital role to play in international affairs. Zacher explains the overarching connection between the United Nations and the Secretary-General in the development of international organization:

> In order to promote a larger role for the United Nations in world politics, and hence in order to encourage the rule of law, the Secretary-General should seek to become an active agent of the Members in the pursuit of peace, and the Members should support such a role and the unitary character of his office. Such policies support the development of an executive agency in the international community. (1970, 236–237)

In summary, the focus of Hammarskjöld's vision was his belief in the role of international law for creating cooperative international interactions. A strong United Nations and Secretary-Generalship sit at the center of this process. A Secretary-General should actively work to promote the role of the United Nations and to defend the organization's principles as a basis of international legal agreement. The Secretary-General and the United Nations must be capable of addressing current global issues and their efforts will pave the way for further developments that will allow the international community to move beyond competing national concerns and into a world based on collective interests.

While Hammarskjöld possessed a vision of a substantial United Nations, he did recognize that there were limits on the extent of possible development. He once explained that the United Nations was "not created in order to bring us to heaven, but in order to save us from hell" (quoted in Urquhart 1972, 48). In other words, he did not think that the organization would be able to solve all of the world's ills, but he did believe that it was a very necessary player in international politics and needed to continue to be improved and its role increased. He hoped that UN principles and purposes would guide the behavior of states and that international institutions would be used by states to achieve these objectives. To Hammarskjöld, the United Nations and other international organizations were not perfect but "represented indispensable steps along the evolutionary road to that stronger international order he believed must one day be achieved" (Foote 1962, 15). In the review of Hammarskjöld's behavior in the following sections, one can see not only how he behaved in a broadly visionary manner, but also how he took steps to promote his vision.

HAMMARSKJÖLD IN ACTION: VISIONARY BEHAVIOR OVERVIEW

Discussions of Hammarskjöld's time in office often point to how his personal traits were reflected in his political behavior. For example, Foote emphasizes that Hammarskjöld's "qualities of mind and character infused and shaped the approaches to the problems of international relationships and international organization" that he undertook (1962, 14). The visionary set of personal attributes are viewed as connected to the manner in which Hammarskjöld pursued a very active role in addressing disruptions to international peace and security and guided the related expansion of the abilities of the United Nations in general and his office in particular. Indeed, as Urquhart stresses, "It would be hard to overestimate the importance of Hammarskjöld's personality and character on the Office of the Secretary-General and indeed on the development of the Organisation itself during his stewardship" (1983, 137).

As one would expect from a visionary, Hammarskjöld pursued and welcomed opportunities to serve as an influential Secretary-General.

He refused to be bound solely to the administrative side of the position and asserted his independent capabilities. In pursuing an influential presence, he was quite aware of the available activities and recognized the future impact that his actions could have by developing these tools to the fullest. This was possible because Hammarskjöld viewed the responsibilities granted to him by the Charter in a broad fashion where "he rejected 'a restrictive literal interpretation' of the Charter and favored a 'freer interpretation' " (Nayar 1974, 59). This led to a dynamic use of existing tools, as well as the creative formulation of new uses for the Secretary-Generalship and the United Nations. Hammarskjöld did hold a strong belief in properly following international law, but with his "freer interpretation," he was able to build "the few pregnant phrases in the Charter on the Secretary-General's office—and its more numerous silences—into a unique writ in the cause of international peace and security" (Lash 1961, 5).

In carrying out his visionary role, Hammarskjöld came into conflict with the national interests of some of the member-states. However, unlike a manager who bows to the member-states' will or a strategist who works within the boundaries of the acceptable, the visionary Hammarskjöld did not feel like he had to react only in certain circumstances or solely upon request, but instead he "proceeded to put his ideas into practice whenever he felt the situation demanded it" because he felt that the Secretary-General "was best placed to be the spokesman and even the executive" (Urquhart 1972, 259) even if this led to clashes with great powers. As discussed above, Hammarskjöld did have a responsive streak to his character, what this study refers to as a complex visionary style, so he was more aware of the context than a pure visionary. This meant that "he did not fly in the face of politics," but neither did he back down from them. Instead he would find a way to push through his vision and "often, in a remarkable way, [he] bent politics to the objectives he was attempting to realize" (Cordier 1967, 20). Nancy Soderberg discusses how this impacted on his relations with one of the great powers, the United States: "In conducting his duties, Hammarskjöld did not shy away from confronting the US when he deemed it in the interest of the UN and long-term international peace and security," but at the same time as an "astute politician, Hammarskjöld was also ready to give Washington a helping hand at times of distress" (2005, 360).

In acting as he saw fit, regardless of the objections of various member-states, Hammarskjöld was bolstered by the belief that he was endeavoring to carry out his vision for the international arena. Dorothy Jones notes how "the philosophy that guided all of Dag

Hammarskjöld's actions" meant that "[h]is eye was always on the future system of international cooperation toward which, he felt, the present international organization had to evolve if nations and peoples were to survive" (2004, 136). His ventures were, therefore, not designed to simply serve the purposes of the individual member-states, but to support the development of the United Nations. Jean-Marie Guéhenno, Under Secretary-General for Peacekeeping Operations under Annan, emphasizes this point when he observes that Hammarskjöld "saw two possible roles for the United Nations and he devoted himself entirely to what he saw as the proper one" (2005, 181). Along with the United Nations in general, Hammarskjöld was very protective of the rights of his office and put forth an "extraordinary effort to turn the office of secretary-general into an autonomous actor in world politics" (Jakobson 1998, 75). In the process, "He became, perhaps, the most articulate advocate of the Secretary-General's political powers in the history of the United Nations" (Boudreau 1991, 40).

Hammarskjöld worked hard to keep the United Nations at the nexus of resolving international conflicts. He felt that he could neither shirk from his duties in handling present conflicts nor from laying the groundwork for future development of the United Nations. In his mind, these two were often linked: "He believed that every successful cooperative undertaking within the context of the United Nations, even on the most simple of technical matters was another building block in the constitutional development of the Organization" (Zacher 1970, 235). Overall, as one would expect from the Secretary-General with the highest score for the visionary leadership style, Hammarskjöld "provided the most dynamic and striking leadership an international organization had ever had" (Urquhart 1972, 596).

HAMMARSKJÖLD AND INFLUENTIAL ACTIVITIES

With Hammarskjöld's general visionary behavior pattern confirmed, the remainder of the chapter details how his actions across the specific influential activity categories reflect his visionary style. The behavioral expectations for a visionary office-holder established in the previous chapter are revisited, alongside a brief summary description of how Hammarskjöld actually behaved as Secretary-General, in table 4.1.

Table 4.1 Hammarskjöld: Visionary in Action

Activity	Ideal Visionary	Hammarskjöld Behavior
Agenda Setting		
Administrative Duties		
• Supervise Reports	Produce reports reflecting own views	Closely involved in drafting reports so that they carried his views
• Oversee Finances	Involved in budget design; lobby strongly for not changing	Involved in budget process; shaped budgetary priorities in relation to Secretariat and peacekeeping missions and supported these measures despite controversy
• Shape Administrative Structure	Likely to restructure; design structure to provide more influence for own office; will lobby strongly for desired changes	Focused on early in tenure and later against Soviet troika challenge; restructured to match his decision-making approach and to invest his office with more influential position; lobbied hard to GA committee and strongly resisted the troika plan
• Staffing the Secretariat	Seek full control over process; use power to place those close to them in positions	Insisted that he have strong control over staffing; appointed a small circle of handpicked advisers; maintained morale through leading by example
Strategic Political Position		
• Representative in Meetings	Will use authority to attend meetings with the intention of expressing views; most likely to employ Article 99	Closely involved in meetings where openly expressed himself and tried to influence proceedings; referred to as "chief legislator of UN"; sought to

• Inherent Strategic Position	Will attempt to push ideas on those who they come into contact with; seek to use information that they possess to pursue own agenda	hold multilateral meetings within UN so that they can participate; first one to explicitly invoke Article 99 Continual interaction with national delegations; used strategic position to extend influence through middlemen when could not be directly involved
Public Pronouncements		
• Annual Report to General Assembly	Express strong views regarding conflicts; stress how issues should be handled and what areas are being ignored that need to be addressed	Every report seen as seeking to influence the agenda; addressed issues felt strongly about and was working on; also used to expound vision for office and future of UN, despite awareness of political controversy reports would raise
• Official Representational Activities	Will take advantage of all times and situations to speak out and strongly express views	Very engaged in expressing and defending opinions in relation to specific issues as well as vision for office and UN
• "Unofficial" Representational Activities	Will seek out these opportunities to be very vocal in expressing views	Used media to get views across to member-states and general public, although careful not to discuss details that would undermine diplomatic efforts; used speeches to stress views on specific issues as well as vision for office and UN

Continued

Table 4.1 Continued

Activity	Ideal Visionary	Hammarskjöld Behavior
Peaceful Settlement of Disputes		
Independently Initiated	Will seek to undertake such missions based on own authority and will seek to impose a solution	Actively engaged in multiple missions and pushed the boundaries of authority of the office, even when his approach challenged how powerful member-states viewed how best to handle the situation
Mandated Assignment	Will attempt to influence mandate and in carrying out will seek to follow own interpretation of mission needs, including moving beyond bounds of mandate where desire.	Sought to influence mandates; saw mandates as providing not only sound legal backing for actions, but also emphasized independent powers of the office in relation to such missions, including stressing lack of guidance as "vacuum" to be filled, interpreting and stretching bounds of mandates as saw fit, and implementing "Peking Formula"
UN Intervention		
Peacekeeping Missions	Will attempt to influence mandate and in carrying out will seek to follow own interpretation of mission needs	Sought to put strong personal imprint on peacekeeping character; worked to shape mandates and was closely involved in all aspects of operations; ensured that capabilities of mission matched what he wanted to do and carried out as saw fit; also took over existing missions and molded them to his own perspective.

AGENDA SETTING: AGENDA SETTER

Hammarskjöld worked diligently to try to set the agenda. In the administrative realm, he was closely involved in getting his views across through supervising both reports and the budget. In addition, he fought hard to maintain control over staffing the Secretariat and the shape of the administrative structure. He also used his strategic political position to his advantage. As a representative in meetings at the United Nations he openly expressed his views and aimed to influence the proceedings. He further extended his influential efforts through the informal contacts provided from his inherent strategic position. Hammarskjöld's use of public pronouncements was also visionary. Analysts point to his annual reports as important statements on how global security should be handled. He was also very vocal in using his official and unofficial representational activities to get his views across to the member-states and to the general public at large.

ADMINISTRATIVE DUTIES

From early in his career as a Swedish civil servant, Hammarskjöld handled a range of administrative details. However, as one of his university professors observes, "I think he was rather clear in his mind from the beginning to get into administration, but I don't think he wanted to be an administrator. His aim was to get into the layer of civil servants where things are decided" (quoted in Lash 1961, 29). In other words, Hammarskjöld was always involved in the flow of administration, but he was also looking for the avenues of influence that his position could provide. The same held true for his time as the chief administrative officer of the United Nations. Hammarskjöld employed the range of administrative activities not as an end unto themselves, but to bolster his chances of being an influential Secretary-General. Reflecting this study's focus on a Secretary-General's toolbox of influential activities, Lash stresses, "Dag Hammarskjöld's first year as Secretary-General was indeed devoted to administrative responsibilities . . . But from the outset he saw his job as a political one. Administration was only a 'tool' " (1962, 542). In fact, Hammarskjöld displayed an "extraordinary talent for administration" and the capability to shape these administrative duties for his own purposes (Urquhart 1987, 125). His visionary style was reflected in how he sought to mold the functions and structure of the United Nations to his way of operating and control. Supporting this argument, K.P. Saksena stresses that "Hammarskjold's personal traits" were reflected in the way that he "tried to impose his leadership on the UN Secretariat" (1978, 195), while Peter Heller notes, "Hammarskjöld developed his own initiatives to bring personnel, finance, and legal affairs under his more immediate and personal direction" (2001, 25).

Supervise reports

Hammarskjöld put his stamp on all aspects of the United Nations, including rudimentary operations like reports. He liked things done his way, even the formatting of memorandums (Lash 1961, 220). More importantly, Hammarskjöld was closely involved in many of the documents prepared under the auspices of his office. Illustrating his high need for control, he personally drafted most of his reports in order to ensure that the documents "carry his personal accent and distinct policy approach to the matter under review" (Cordier 1961, 5). Trachtenberg recounts how Hammarskjöld understood that reports could be a useful tool to foster his ideas:

> Early in his tenure as Secretary-General, Hammarskjöld came to realize that one of the best means of promoting a particular idea or project was to ensure that the item in question received the widest possible circulation among UN members. The Secretary-General was extremely aware of the importance of regular and detailed reports to the organization as well as the occasional, though usually well-timed statement before one of the principle organs or a committee. In this way, Hammarskjöld was able to present his own philosophies and ideas, and be certain that they would appear in the public record. (1983, 165)

By going into the public record, Hammarskjöld's views would not only have an impact in the present, but they would also continue to be potentially influential well after he had left office. This was part of a pattern of behavior to set out a clear statement of his vision for others to draw upon. Zacher notes that Hammarskjöld "certainly left a more extensive record of his thoughts than any other occupant of the office. He was a man who regarded himself as having a mission . . . and he wanted the imprint of his mission to be recorded not just in his actions but in his own words as well (1983, 111). Given the sheer number of reports put forth by the Secretary-General it is impossible to note, let alone analyze, every one that he prepared. However, the large number and directed use of reports by Hammarskjöld stands out.

For example, Trachtenberg observes that the reports produced during the Suez crisis in 1956 were indicative of Hammarskjöld's "extensive and complex" involvement (1983, 167). This point is reinforced by Cordier, who comments that "at each stage in setting up the Force . . . the General Assembly had before it reports analyzing the problems at hand and suggesting the lines of approach for further action. The Assembly could thus, in each instance, approve the report and give the Secretary-General a mandate to proceed along the lines indicated" (1961, 5). Hammarskjöld followed the same pattern during his later involvement with the Congo, where he produced a prolific level of documents and reports (Trachtenberg 1983, 170). This included a key report issued before the Security Council met in July 1960 to consider the breakdown in the Congo and continued throughout with "extensive personal documentation prepared by the Secretary-General" (Cordier 1961, 5).

Following the United Nations Emergency Force (UNEF) mission, the first UN peacekeeping operation that was set up to address the events in the Suez, Hammarskjöld established a study group to examine the campaign and consider the implications for other such missions. The group spent a year preparing the report, yet when he received it, "Hammarskjold read it politely and then dictated his own version as a report to the General Assembly that set out the principles on which subsequent peace-keeping forces in the Congo and in Cyprus were based" (Urquhart 1972, 228–229). The General Assembly did not endorse the report because some countries felt that Hammarskjöld's conceptualization undermined sovereignty. Undeterred, the report was provided directly to all of the member-states in the hope that his ideas would still have an impact the next time the United Nations was called on to provide troops (Lash 1961, 181).

During the Hungarian crisis in 1956, Hammarskjöld's use of reports led to a clash with the Soviet Union. While limited in what he could do to oppose the move to crush the Hungarian uprising, Hammarskjöld did create an investigatory committee and supported the report that criticized the Soviets' handling of the situation. The Soviets reacted negatively, but Hammarskjöld did not back down. Zacher argues that Hammarskjöld saw this report as a vital statement because "[i]n pursuing such a strategy Hammarskjold was trying to make all Members of the Organization more responsive to general norms of international behavior which are shared by the majority of the membership" (1970, 139). This fits closely with Hammarskjöld's positive vision for global values and the place of the United Nations in international affairs. He did not want to allow the Soviet actions that challenged his vision to occur without comment.

Oversee finances

Hammarskjöld also displayed a visionary approach in his handling of the budget. He was especially involved in the budget during his first year, which raised some controversy among the member-states. In his fashion of taking control and completely engaging with a task, Hammarskjöld "led an intensive survey of the organisation and the budget of the UN and introduced effective reorganisation, streamlining, and cuts in expenditure" (Urquhart 1983, 138). Hammarskjöld wanted the Secretariat to be a more efficient enterprise and, accordingly, he used his guiding influence over the purse strings to enforce this. Urquhart explains, "Hammarskjold had followed a conservative budget policy, first severely cutting the budget and staff and then forcing the Secretariat to absorb new tasks without increasing its size" (1972, 524). His efforts to restructure the Secretariat were geared toward providing him greater leeway in the budgetary process, so the two efforts were mutually reinforcing.

Other major budgetary efforts revolved around the Suez crisis. The funding of UNEF was a contentious issue. This was the first peacekeeping operation, so there were no clear-cut guidelines regarding how the force should be financially supported. Against the wishes of some of the member-states, Hammarskjöld insisted that peacekeeping should be funded in the same manner as the regular UN budget—based on binding financial assessments for each member-state. In the aftermath of the crisis, he also took pride in designing and implementing a budget for clearing the Suez Canal that disproved skepticism that a much larger sum and greater level of outside involvement was needed to accomplish the task (Urquhart 1972, 207).

Shape the administrative structure

As stressed earlier, Hammarskjöld's approach to the United Nations incorporated a strong belief in the importance of an independent civil service and he even "rewrote the staff rules to reflect this principle" (Urquhart 2005, 19). This emphasis on independence was closely tied to his use of the Secretariat as a tool for influence:

> Throughout his tenure Hammarskjold was very concerned with the impact of the Secretariat's character on the Organization's activities and influence in international politics . . . His attitude was that an international civil service, which was loyal solely to the United Nations and which had a unitary executive, was one of the most important and crucial bases of power which the Organization had at its disposal in promoting the resolution of conflicts and building higher forms of international cooperation. (Zacher 1970, 39; 43)

As Dayal expresses, the Secretariat was an "instrument . . . through which he had to work" (1976, 306), so it was important to sharpen this instrument and maintain it in the fashion he desired. Since the Secretariat could serve as a base for his influential ventures, Hammarskjöld made the organization of the administrative structure a priority in his early years in office. In relation to this, Trachtenberg observes, "He concentrated a large part of his energies in this area between 1953 and 1955, appearing on numerous occasions before the Fifth Committee of the General Assembly (Administrative and Budgetary Committee) to put forward his case for re-organization" (1983, 167).

Reflecting his need for personal control, Hammarskjöld began his administrative review effort by closely examining the issue: "He was determined to review the whole operation in person before making detailed changes" (Urquhart 1972, 75), with the goal of structuring the Secretariat so that it would be capable of handling tasks more efficiently. He also organized the administration in a manner that reflected his need for control. He used his power over personnel to place individuals close to him at the top of the Secretariat. Since Hammarskjöld had a difficult time delegating tasks to others, he followed a pattern of surrounding himself at the upper echelon with a core group of collaborators who would try to keep up with him as he pounded away at tasks. In doing so, Hammarskjöld put his own stamp on the Secretariat, ensuring that primary authority rested with his office with the Secretariat "now reorganized around his own formidable capacity for work and insistence on perfection" (Lash 1961, 53). There were doubts expressed from some of the Under Secretaries-General and their home governments, who communicated concerns about Hammarskjöld's high level of personal control over the Secretariat. Hammarskjöld deflected such criticism, arguing that "it was right and proper that he should assume personal responsibility for these important questions" (Urquhart 1972, 81).

In 1960, Hammarskjöld came full circle in defending his beliefs regarding the administrative structure. The Soviet delegation, spearheaded by Nikita Khrushchev, called for a radical restructuring of the Secretariat chain of command. Instead of a single Secretary-General, the Soviets suggested that there should be a "troika" at the head of the United Nations. The three-part executive would be made up of representatives from Western, socialist, and neutral states. Hammarskjöld reacted forcefully against the idea because he viewed it "as a direct challenge to the concept of an independent international civil service" and held firm to his position that there could only be a single officer in charge of the United Nations (Jonah 2005, 170).

Staffing the Secretariat

Hammarskjöld fought to ensure that he had control over the staffing of the Secretariat. Throughout his time in office, he refused to bow to pressure from member-states regarding Secretariat appointments. He inherited anticommunist American pressure in the age of McCarthyism and FBI involvement in UN staffing concerns from Lie. Unwilling to sacrifice his control over the Secretariat to such political demands, he insisted on a "firm stand against the American authorities" (Wallensteen 1995, 12). He ordered the FBI out of UN headquarters and instituted special judicial procedures for potential dismissals in order to protect against demands from the United States that its nationals be terminated for communist beliefs. During his first visit to Washington, in April 1953, he eschewed discussing other topics in order to emphasize the need for an independent Secretariat and the ability to staff his own organization. As Heller observes, he was determined "to ensure that the secretary-general's authority to appoint or dismiss personnel . . . were not invaded" by the Americans (2001, 31). In addition, he clashed with the Soviet Union regarding who was an acceptable Soviet candidate for filling an Assistant Secretary-General position, whereby, "in the end, the Soviet Union accepted the right of the Secretary-General to make his own selections" (Jonah 2005, 167). Zacher argues that because of these actions, "[a]fter 1954 there was very little criticism by the Members of the Secretariat's hiring policies. Hammarskjold had established the power of the Secretary-General over the Secretariat's personnel policies" (1970, 40).

Within the United Nations, Hammarskjöld was equally active in affirming his authority over hiring protocol. Urquhart explains that Hammarskjöld felt the existing regulations "seriously infringed upon his own exclusive responsibility under the Charter for the selection and retention of UN staff" (1972, 62) and he "insisted on his exclusive responsibility for appointments to the Secretariat" (1983, 139). In working to change Secretariat personnel policy, Hammarskjöld asserted the authority of his office in a manner that "enlarged the Secretary-General's power" over staffing matters (Lash 1961, 53). Despite the fact that some members of the Secretariat and member-states were concerned about the new rules, he wanted control over appointment decisions and he pushed his plan through to General Assembly approval.

When Hammarskjöld became Secretary-General, Secretariat members were suffering from low morale. In an unusual personal touch that is widely reported in analyses of Hammarskjöld's tenure, at the beginning of his term he visited throughout UN headquarters to greet and encourage all staff members in their offices. However, reflecting what Heller has described as an "autocratic bureaucratic style" (2001, 26), Hammarskjöld interacted primarily with the upper echelon at UN headquarters and expected loyalty to his office across the Secretariat. As such, little of Hammarskjöld's time in office involved close contact or engagement with most members of the Secretariat. In fact, as Gillett observes, as Hammarskjöld's "work became increasingly diplomatic and confidential and less and less administrative" he became less connected even with many senior officials to the point where "it seemed to make little difference whether he was away or in New York" (1970, 98). At the same time, despite the way that his lack of relationship building and strong task focus was reflected in his interactions—or lack thereof—with staff members, Hammarskjöld was largely able to maintain morale through leading by example.

Summary style comparison for administrative duties
Hammarskjöld seized control of the administrative realm and used the range of duties available to create a more influential position for himself as the head of the United Nations. He dispelled any notions that he would behave as a manager by strongly insisting that he, not the member-states, dictate the structure of the Secretariat and staff hiring practices. This same level of control and determination for doing things his way was displayed in the handling of reports and budgetary matters. Hammarskjöld perceived administrative activities as a stepping-stone to greater influence and acted accordingly. In relation to this, once he had established command over administrative affairs, his primary focus moved into addressing global interactions. Thus, while he did focus on administrative affairs in depth early on, "his interest and immersion in political problems soon began to leave him less and less time for the administrative aspects of his responsibilities and both his attention to and interest in them steadily diminished" (Bunche 1965, 120) and so "[m]any administrative responsibilities were delegated" (Jackson 1957, 441).

STRATEGIC POLITICAL POSITION
The Secretary-General's strategic position was also viewed by Hammarskjöld as a useful tool for influence. He was closely involved in meetings, where he would speak out and try to influence what other organs were considering. He was the first, and one of the only Secretaries-General, to explicitly employ his Article 99 powers, which he used to call the situation in the Congo to the attention of the

Security Council in order to have better control over the timing and content of the deliberations. He appreciated the benefits that his strategic position provided and sought to ensure that other multilateral meetings were held at the United Nations, where his presence would be assured. Even when he could not be directly involved in the decision-making process, he used his inherent strategic position to maintain continual contact with member-state representatives.

Representative in meetings

Hammarskjöld used his official capacity as a representative in meetings to try to influence the proceedings. He was closely involved throughout his tenure in working to shape the legislative agenda and the mandates that dictated his actions. Cordier refers to Hammarskjöld as the "chief legislator" in the United Nations (quoted in Zacher 1970, 50) and recognizes how Hammarskjöld used his position as a tool for influence: "Although his role may be narrowly described as the administrative and executive head of the organization, he has . . . exercised a vital influence in the quasi-legislative processes and results of these organs" (Cordier 1961, 7).

One notable illustration is Hammarskjöld's involvement in both the Security Council and the General Assembly during the Suez crisis in 1956. Before the invasion in October, Hammarskjöld had already been intimately involved in trying to preclude a violent clash over the Suez Canal. He initiated a new use of the Security Council, where the members involved in the crisis met privately in his office. During this meeting he acted as "more catalyst than chaperon, helping by his formulations to crystallize agreements" (Lash 1961, 77). Throughout the meeting he worked to maintain a dialogue between the parties and intervened in the discussions when he thought it was appropriate. Near the end of the talks Hammarskjöld stepped forward and drew up six principles that served as the basis of the resolution (Zacher 1970, 81).

Despite this effort, the Israeli, British, and French forces moved into the Suez area. Hammarskjöld was extremely upset by this, but did not have to carry out his threat to invoke Article 99 because the United States asked for a Security Council meeting first. Still, Hammarskjöld was very much involved in the Security Council deliberations, including the first Security Council meeting on the issue, where "he publicly rebuked" the British and French and "served notice that there were situations in which he felt obliged to enter the political arena as an active participant" (Urquhart 1972, 174). When the deliberations deadlocked in the Security Council, the need for a resolution to address the matter passed to the General Assembly. Hammarskjöld worked in close consultation with General Assembly representatives to convince them that a special session should be convened and then helped to guide through an acceptable resolution.

Hammarskjöld continued this pattern of intervening in meetings and trying to influence the agenda in relation to other breaches of the peace. During the debate over what to do about Lebanon in 1958, he displayed his visionary approach: "The normal thing until then had been for the secretary-general to speak only rarely in the Council, and never before the vote, unless to impart information. Now there were meetings in which he intervened two and three times, and frequently to make a political point" (Ahman 1958, 12). Similarly, when the General Assembly took up the matter, he guided the discussions "in an unusual move" by speaking "immediately after the opening of that meeting in order to head off a long debate between the U.S.A. and the U.S.S.R. and among the various Arab states" (Kenworthy 1988, 61). In handling the Laos situation that began in 1959, Hammarskjöld took the involvement of the Secretary-General in the Security Council a step further. Without explicitly invoking Article 99, he took the "constitutionally risky and unprecedented" (Urquhart 1972, 339) step of asking for the Security Council to be convened to address a provisional agenda regarding Laos, which would include his making a report on the situation. Over the objections of the Soviet delegate, Hammarskjöld created a new tool for his strategic position arsenal. As Boudreau explains, "In a brilliant procedural innovation, Hammarskjöld examined and elaborated upon this discretionary power, thus giving new meaning and scope to the Secretary-General's preventive role under the Charter" (1991, 47).

In 1960, Hammarskjöld was the first Secretary-General to directly invoke the office's Article 99 powers in order to call the Security Council into session to consider the chaos in the Congo following independence from Belgium. According to one UN official, by calling the meeting on his own authority he "would be able to define the issue to the exclusion of certain factors which, if introduced, might make agreement difficult and defeat the possibility of achieving consensus on a firm mandate" (quoted in Zacher 1970, 173). Hammarskjöld worked diligently with the Security Council to set down principles for the operation and to ensure that these formed the basis of the resolutions on the matter (Bring 2003, 506–510). Urquhart notes that his engagement included resisting postponing the mission: "The Council meeting went on through the night, and when delays seemed inevitable it was Hammarskjold who argued for immediate action" (1972, 398). Overall, regarding the Congo affair, "[u]nquestionably, Hammarskjöld dominated the decision-making process, and it was to him that the Council turned to provide the leadership" (Rikhye 1983, 95).

Hammarskjöld demonstrated his desire to maintain a strong position within the United Nations in other situations as well. For example, while the Congo crisis was in full swing, Hammarskjöld also faced a predicament with Cuba at the beginning of 1961. Cuba claimed that there was a pending invasion by the United States, but Hammarskjöld lacked information about the situation due to Soviet anger over his handling of the Congo. He summoned a Soviet aide from a New Year's Eve party and set up a Security Council meeting to be held in several days based on the authority of his office. James Henderson relates how this episode, while relatively minor compared to handling crises like the Congo, was significant because it "provides a good illustration of Hammarskjöld's determination to preserve the authority and dignity of his office" relative to other UN organs (1969, 105).

Hammarskjöld bolstered the usefulness of his strategic position by encouraging the member-states to employ the United Nations for meetings and negotiations. This included the major powers as well, because by bringing "at least some of their top-level negotiations into the UN diplomatic framework . . . gradually the broader system of interests and facilities at the UN could influence their interactions" (Zacher 1983, 124). When Hammarskjöld was unable to get the states to meet within the United Nations, he would try to get them to agree to allow the United Nations to provide conference services for their discussions so that the organization maintained a connection to the events. The handling of disarmament illustrates Hammarskjöld's desire to have international issues related to peace and security addressed within the United Nations. In April 1958, he "took the unprecedented step of making a statement on disarmament in the Security Council" because he wanted to break the Cold War deadlock that was interfering with the capability of the United Nations to address the issue (Urquhart 1972, 318). Hammarskjöld's actions were met by a sharp rebuke from the Soviets, but he did not back down. When the focus of the disarmament discussions shifted outside of the United Nations to the newly created Committee of Ten he still pursued the matter. With the meeting held in Geneva,

> The UN was permitted to supply the housekeeping services and Hammarskjold to submit statements. He invoked this prerogative to

remind the opening session that the four Foreign Ministers in setting up the Committee of Ten explicitly recognized that "ultimate responsibility for disarmament measures rests with the UN" and that the committee's deliberations would prepare the way for discussions in the UN. (Lash 1961, 157)

Inherent strategic position

Hammarskjöld also took advantage of the unofficial avenues for influence that the strategic position as head of the United Nations inherently provides. Unlike the sanctioned meetings discussed above, many of Hammarskjöld's unofficial strategic contacts are harder to track, but Foote stresses their importance:

> Of course, the official records cannot provide a complete record of action by Dag Hammarskjöld as Secretary-General. The personal influence he exercised through his continuous contacts with the Permanent Delegates and his frequent talks and correspondence with virtually all the leaders of government of the Member States in their capitals or at United Nations Headquarters formed a vital part of his total contribution. (1962, 13)

Hammarskjöld did not take particular advantage of the diplomatic social scene, despite the useful contacts that this could provide, because he did not enjoy such situations. Yet, in job-related situations he was very involved in using this tool for influence. As Trachtenberg relates, "Hammarskjöld's informal influence was often evident in corridor diplomacy or behind closed doors" (1982, 614). He used his strategic position to be more involved in the resolution drafting process than his official position allowed, often working via "fire brigades" of smaller and mid-range powers so that, "Ambassadors and Ministers moved in and out of his office with almost conveyor-belt regularity" (Lash 1961, 207; see also Cordier 1961, 6–10).

The member-state representatives were viewed by Hammarskjöld as integral to his efforts to influence peace and security matters. Urquhart explains the significance of these interactions: "Hammarskjold increasingly used the permanent national representatives at UN Headquarters as his collaborators and confidants in the complex operations of his later years—sometimes even to the point where the representatives concerned experienced a conflict of loyalty between the UN and their own governments" (1972, 52). Hammarskjöld's actions during the Suez crisis illustrate this approach. In addition to his official activities, he endeavored to influence the wording of the General Assembly resolution establishing UNEF. The same level of strategic involvement was evident in other crises. For example, during the Lebanese crisis, Hammarskjöld "was very active behind the scenes . . . His office was the center of almost constant consultations with various delegations," where he "used his influence to rally support" for proposals with which he agreed (Miller 1961, 207).

Summary style comparison for strategic political position
Visionaries are the most likely to directly employ Article 99, so it is no surprise that Hammarskjöld is one of the only Secretaries-General ever to do so. Indicative of his visionary nature, he decided to use his Article 99 powers to ensure that he could guide the timing and substance of the Security Council meeting on the violence in the Congo. More generally, he was a forceful presence at meetings, where he used his authority to express his views and to try to influence the proceedings. Hammarskjöld's record is one of continual interaction with delegates at the United Nations, whom he used to get his ideas put into place to the point where some began to question where their loyalty rested, although this consultative process appears to reflect a greater working with others than the ideal visionary expectation of the Secretary-General simply imposing his views.

PUBLIC PRONOUNCEMENTS

Hammarskjöld also employed the influential capabilities of public pronouncements. From annual reports to official statements to interactions with the media, his pronouncements were designed to impart his views to the member-states and the general public at large. His statements not only tackled the issues of the day, but also spoke at a deeper level to his vision for the future. In addition, he traveled extensively in both official and unofficial capacities to ensure that he operated at the forefront of conflicts and had the opportunity to spread his message.

However, the complex part of Hammarskjöld's visionary style also comes to the fore because his use of these activities was much more carefully considered than would be by an ideal visionary. His complex nature led him to consider whether publicity was advantageous or disadvantageous to his particular mission or for the authority of his position and the United Nations in general. In order to fully comprehend Hammarskjöld's use of public pronouncements, one must understand the interrelation of his responsiveness with his drive for completing tasks and supranationalism. Essentially, he did not shirk from the use of public pronouncements, and was especially unwilling to back away if it meant sacrificing his strong supranationalist principles, but he recognized that sometimes a quieter approach was necessary to achieve his purposes. In other words, he was sensitive enough to the context to realize that there were situations where private interactions should take precedence over public statements. At the same time, when he believed that public pronouncements would best suit his goals, even in the face of political roadblocks, he would employ these tools.

Two categories highlight where Hammarskjöld would step up the use of public statements: to defend or promote international principles or to help resolve a breach of peace (Zacher 1970, 122–124). For the latter, he used publicity when he thought the pressure on groups would encourage them to make progress in resolving their differences. However, he was careful to monitor the tone of his messages so that those involved in a conflict would not be discouraged from cooperating with his efforts. Nonetheless, he made sure that his opinion got across to the member-states. This was apparent in his defense of international principles. He recognized that he had to temper his internationalist vision at times and was willing to do so because he saw the future of the United Nations as related to successfully concluding missions. He was willing to sacrifice immediate public recognition if it meant that, over the long term, the effectiveness and the reputation of the organization and the office were improved.

In the end, his public pronouncements reflected "the depth of feeling and concern with which Hammarskjöld approached this task" (Trachtenberg 1983, 167). To help ensure their impact, Hammarskjöld often did not design his messages solely for the public. Although he often felt that the complexity of the ideas he was trying to impart could not be captured in a simple press account, his pronouncements were designed to send important messages to decision makers:

> The transcripts of his press conferences—as, indeed, the texts of his occasional speeches, and the Introductions to his annual reports—were designed to be read and studied in foreign offices and by the diplomatic community generally . . . A Hammarskjold transcript, like a Dead Sea Scroll, is a disappointment if read as an exchange between Hammarskjold and the general public; it is a treasure house of information and insights if read as part of his dialogue with the diplomatic community. (Lash 1961, 192–193)

Annual report to the General Assembly

Analysts often comment on the importance of the annual report for understanding Hammarskjöld's Secretary-Generalship. As Raymond

Fosdick stresses, "To appreciate the quality of Hammarskjold's ideas and leadership one should read his nine annual reports which he filed during his incumbency as Secretary-General" (1972, 110). Hammarskjöld wanted his Introductions to be read and considered as important political statements. He was the first Secretary-General to release the Introduction as a separate document shortly before the General Assembly reconvened for the year. This ensured that the members would have time to look over and reflect on the report during the session. When a reporter commented that the Introduction had turned into Hammarskjöld's own "State of the UN Message," Hammarskjöld expressed his pleasure with the phrase (Trachtenberg 1983, 166).

Hammarskjöld used the annual report to try to shape the handling of topics that he was engaged in at that time. Due to his involvement in administrative reform early on in his career, his first several reports stressed his opinions on the international civil service. For example, in the 1954 report he argued that the Secretary-General needed to have "a large measure of administrative discretion in such measures of internal management as the scheduling of work and the utilization of Secretariat staffing and resources." This pattern continued up to the 1960 report, prepared in the midst of the Congo conflict where "[i]n the introduction to his annual report, Hammarskjold had tried, as usual, to provide an analysis of the current political situation in the UN as a guide for the Assembly's deliberations" (Urquhart 1972, 458).

The annual report was also used to offer Hammarskjöld's views about the future use of the United Nations and his "general philosophical position on many crucial issues of world politics" (Rovine 1970, 276). For example, following the Suez crisis, the 1957 report "was not a review," but a statement regarding UN involvement in the international community that aimed "to weld the United Nations Members into a new sense of solidarity through looking forward to new tasks rather than backward to old issues" (Cordier 1961, 6). Even when he knew that his ideas would be politically controversial, Hammarskjöld was willing to put them in his report. For example, the 1959 report, which came on the heels of his dramatic re-election acceptance speech detailed below, strongly emphasized his views on the office even though "he expected his version of the role of the Secretary-General to be challenged" (Saksena 1978, 196). In the 1960 report—which Theodore Draper describes as a "remarkable self-analysis of Hammarskjold's mind and policy" (1960, 22)—Hammarskjöld codified his views on preventive diplomacy and a UN presence despite great power concern over this emphasis.

In order to ensure that his views were properly expressed, Hammarskjöld was closely involved in writing the Introductions. His final report, prepared for the 1961 General Assembly, took this process to the extreme:

> A document of some eight thousand words that Hammarskjold himself regarded as the final and most complete statement of his position on the controversial issues of the time, was dictated without notes and without a pause, except for one final section, in one Sunday afternoon, and he made virtually no corrections at all to the original transcript. (Urquhart 1972, 31)

As indicated in Urquhart's description of the report, both Hammarskjöld and outside observers stress the importance of the final report as a "testament" of his beliefs—including Annan, who reflects back on the "magisterial work, which reads almost as if he was consciously writing his political testament" (2001, 7). In this report, Hammarskjöld contrasted the place of the United Nations as "static conference machinery" versus as a "dynamic instrument" and, reflecting his vision for international affairs, he emphasized the dynamic instrument approach. In doing so, he used the 1961 report to make an important statement regarding the role of the United Nations as more than a conference of state interests and he hoped that his arguments would influence states to continue to build a stronger and more connected international community.

Official representational activities
Hammarskjöld also used official representational activities in an influential manner. He was impatient with ceremonial activities that kept him from his work, but his need for control shone through nonetheless: "Although he disliked ceremony and pomposity, his position did not always allow him to escape them, and he took the minutest pains to ensure, by personally supervising every detail, the success of formal occasions" (Urquhart 1972, 28). For example, Hammarskjöld insisted on personally choosing the music played at UN concerts, the paintings to hang at UN Headquarters, and on closely reviewing the details of social events held under UN auspices. He put up with such events because he saw them as a potentially important platform for articulating his position on issues and for staking out his vision for the Secretary-Generalship and the United Nations.

As with the annual report, Hammarskjöld was closely involved in writing other public pronouncements. Fosdick describes how

Hammarskjöld "prepared his public addresses with great care" so that "the contents of his addresses showed the wide range and the deep quality of his thinking" (1972, 109). Observers note that the "political Hammarskjöld was not eloquent . . . some of his most significant speeches read like documents" (Kelen 1968, xii), but that was the point. Hammarskjöld did not see himself as playing to an audience, but as imparting important messages about international relations. As Rovine summarizes,

> Hammarskjold's statements and addresses on the United Nations were numerous, in the manner of Trygve Lie, but were often highly elaborate interpretations of the role of world organization and the Office of the Secretary-General. He was not an outstanding speaker, but his addresses were all beautifully written, often by himself, and in some cases were of great significance in terms of postulating new understandings and interpretations of the UN's functions. (1970, 276)

Hammarskjöld used speeches in the principal organs to address particular crises. An illustrative example is his intervention at the beginning of the 1958 General Assembly debate over how to handle ongoing difficulties in the Middle East. Hammarskjöld was faced with British and American demands to address what they saw as Soviet aggression in the Middle East and Soviet insistence that the Assembly tackle the presence of United States troops in Lebanon and the British military presence in Jordan. He wanted the session to focus on peaceful solutions, not aggression. In order to influence the framing of the debate as such, "Hammarskjöld intervened boldly by taking the floor as soon as the Assembly began . . . the way he defined the needs left little doubt about what he thought the answers should be" (Ahman 1958, 12–13).

Upon his re-election in 1957, Hammarskjöld took advantage of the opportunity to speak to the General Assembly. He used the speech to make "an especially strong statement on the way in which he perceived of the Secretary-General's role in political matters" (Trachtenberg 1983, 167). He focused on the need for the Secretary-General to be dynamic and to fill a "vacuum" of inaction by the members (Lash 1962, 550). The key to Hammarskjöld's speech was the way he "forcefully expressed" the "concept of inherent responsibility" for the Secretary-General, which meant that the chief administrative officer had the ability to take initiatives unless explicitly instructed not to by the principal organs (Nayar 1974, 57). In response to the Soviet Union's troika proposal Hammarskjöld also spoke strongly about his office in the General Assembly in order to rebut the idea. The central theme of what has been described as "among the most significant statements ever made by Hammarskjöld" (Kelen 1968, 182) was that he had to resist pressures by great powers and not lose sight of the needs of the small and middle powers. He stressed that, while he might personally consider resigning in the face of such an attack, the prestige of the office was too important for him to sacrifice at the whim of a great power.

Hammarskjöld was also willing to stand up and defend his position in the Security Council. For example, building out of frustration with the invasion of the Suez Canal, he made a statement that was "intended as a challenge or perhaps even a threat to resign" if the integrity of United Nations and his office could not be guaranteed (Rovine 1970, 287). His statement was very notable: "For in one breath he managed not only to state his firm objection to the resort both to force and to the veto by Britain and France, but also to tell them that if they wanted him to go on working for them, they had better not object to his speaking his mind" (Ahman 1958, 11). Similar to his reaction in the General Assembly to the troika proposition, this illustrated how far he was willing to go in making statements that challenged the great powers when he thought that his office was threatened.

"Unofficial" representational activities

One activity Hammarskjöld undertook a great deal, both for official and unofficial functions, was travel. However, he differed from the portrayal of Waldheim (presented in the following chapter) in that he did not take these trips for the popular recognition and indulgence that they could provide. Hammarskjöld did not seek to travel first class: "For his own flights, on UN business, he usually requested tourist-class seats; and in Europe, he ordinarily traveled third class" (Hershey 1961a, 140). Instead, his hectic traveling schedule seems to be at least partially linked to his need to be in control. He displayed a clear preference for being in the heart of breaches of the peace. As Urquhart describes Hammarskjöld's travels,

> Hammarskjold began early on to show a preference for leading his troops from the front . . . He took both political and physical risks in stride if he thought them necessary . . . He was convinced that there was no substitute for direct personal contact with problems and people; as soon as he had settled down in New York, he set out on a concerted program of visits to as many member states and regions of the world as he could fit into the normal requirements of his job. (1972, 33)

When he believed it necessary to increase his chances of resolving a conflict, Hammarskjöld would downplay the press coverage of his trips. For example, for his first major intervention, a trip to China to try to gain the release of captured American pilots, he refused to take any press correspondents with him. However, he did use the press to publicize his trips, especially the deals struck, when he thought that public pressure would serve his cause. For the case of the airmen held in China, Hammarskjöld went public after his visit with a statement urging the United States to accept the Chinese offer to allow the families of the airmen to visit China. Announcing agreements reached with governments so that they were not as likely to violate the accords became a common approach, where he would "send to the headquarters detailed communiqués to be released to the press, which then served to nail down the conferees to agreements reached" (Kelen 1966, 131).

While Hammarskjöld may not have sought out the pomp that could surround his visits, he did appreciate the opportunities that they provided for him to make speeches outside of the official UN context. Urquhart explains that Hammarskjöld "gave many public speeches in an attempt both to improve the public image of the UN and to make his ideas known" because he was "convinced of the importance of mass public opinion as a living force in international affairs" (1972, 84). Hammarskjöld wrote most of his own speeches and, at a minimum, carefully edited each a speech before the presentation. Although this limited the number of speaking engagements that he could accept, he wanted to ensure that his message was properly established so "he spoke only when he could think out and prepare his speeches personally. He disliked oratory and his speeches were never platform performances. They were meant to be pondered and re-read" (Foote 1962, 20).

Hammarskjöld spoke out when he saw his view of the UN's place in handling matters of international peace and security being threatened. A good example of this is the stance that he took on disarmament, despite the protests that arose from the great powers. Hammarskjöld, disparaging much of the propaganda on disarmament employed by the Soviets and Americans, used his speeches to push for real progress in the present and movement toward a goal of total disarmament. His statements regarding disarmament aggravated the great powers and they "severely reprimanded . . . [and] rebuffed" his efforts, yet he "refused to be silenced on the touchy subject. He saw it as his right to intervene in support of the Charter's purposes, and his duty toward nations menaced by nuclear destruction to act as their spokesman" (Kelen 1968, 24).

Beyond reacting to specific issues, Hammarskjöld used speaking occasions to encourage others to follow his vision for the United Nations. Fröhlich argues that Hammarskjöld's speeches provide "major statements on his general philosophy of the United Nations" (2005a, 14; Fröhlich 2005b). While the speeches in this vein are too plentiful to recount, some of his statements were so bold that they have become recognizable just by their names—including his 1959 Copenhagen Speech and 1961 Oxford Speech. In Copenhagen, he built upon a speech that he had made the previous month in Mexico and "talked openly about the need for the Secretary-General to be an independent force in international politics" (Johnson 2003, 94) as well as the United Nations more generally. He contrasted two potential approaches to his office; not taking a stand during conflicts versus stepping forward and acting. He argued strongly for the latter and portrayed the United Nations as a core organization for handling breaches of the peace at a supranational level. He focused on the importance of the international civil service in his Oxford talk, which Urquhart describes as "his last great manifesto . . . It remains to this day the basic tenet on this vital subject (2005, 21). During the "carefully researched speech" (Jonah 2005, 17) he sought to counter the Soviet argument that the Secretariat, including the Secretary-General, could not act as a neutral force because there was no such thing as a neutral person. This claim went against Hammarskjöld's vision for an independent, neutral international Secretariat operating at the heart of developing a more cooperative international environment and he used the speech to strongly back his position.

Interactions with the media are an important aspect of unofficial representational activities and Hammarskjöld "made frequent and skillful use of press conferences" (Heller 2001, 20), yet interviewing Hammarskjöld could be both an enlightening and frustrating experience for reporters. He believed in the necessity of press coverage as "an essential element in making the UN effective and that his relationship with them was crucial to his own performance," but he also recognized that ill-timed publicity could derail diplomatic efforts (Urquhart 1972, 55). Therefore, while Hammarskjöld "developed a constructive rapport with the international media" (Eliasson and Wallensteen 2005, 289), he worked his interactions with the press in a fine-tuned manner. He wanted to use the press as a tool to get his message out on certain issues, but at the same time he did not want to reveal too many details regarding situations that he was not yet prepared to share with the general public. When answering questions in such areas "he was often equivocal and obscure, and that the press found it impossible to pin him down to a clearcut position" (Fosdick 1972, 112).

In addition, while Hammarskjöld wanted to have his vision dispersed through the world community, he believed that news reports were often not the best avenue to pursue this goal because "he was temperamentally and intellectually disposed toward the nuanced statement rather than the simplification or slogan that fitted easily into a headline" (Lash 1961, 190). Efforts by reporters to press him to explain his statements or to delve further on topics that he did not care to enlighten them on rarely paid off. After all, his goal was not to make friends or to worry about the feelings of the press, but to ensure that his point came across on the issues that he wanted to discuss. Therefore, as Cordier observes,

> His press conferences took on the atmosphere of seminars and perceptive correspondents were able to derive from them not many headlines, indeed, but valued interpretations of the Charter, elaborations of the role of the Secretary-General, or amplifications of his views on important current issues. The permanent missions followed them closely and reported them in full to their foreign offices. (1967, 18)

Summary style comparison for public pronouncements

Despite more careful consideration of the use of public pronouncements than one would expect from an ideal visionary due to his complex nature, Hammarskjöld's visionary style is still apparent in his overall behavioral pattern. His forceful annual reports went far beyond straightforward, technical accounts and he was willing to compose such reports despite knowing the political controversy that many of his ideas would raise. He retained a vocal stance in expressing and defending his opinions across official and unofficial venues as well. Although he avoided commenting on certain issues if this could disrupt progress on resolving conflicts, he was more than willing to step forward and speak out even in the face of political intransigence if he believed that what he had to say was important and would point to the correct way to handle matters.

PEACEFUL SETTLEMENT OF DISPUTES: SEIZING THE INITIATIVE

Hammarskjöld was very engaged in the peaceful settlement of disputes throughout his tenure. He was involved in a range of mandated peaceful settlement efforts and he pushed these to the full extent. He often stressed his independent capabilities even when carrying out a mandated mission. In addition, he undertook multiple missions based solely on the independent authority of his office. Despite the controversy that his actions and ideas raised, Hammarskjöld believed that the Secretary-General could not sit idly by waiting for the member-states to overcome their differences. Instead, as discussed earlier, he believed that a Secretary-General should act to fill the vacuum of inaction by states. Based on the Article 99 need to stay informed regarding possible breaches of the peace, Hammarskjöld argued that he needed a UN presence to monitor developments, and would often travel to the site of conflict himself or send a personal representative.

INDEPENDENTLY INITIATED

Hammarskjöld sought to protect the independent prerogatives of his office, and many peaceful settlement efforts were implemented at his initiative. He felt that he had strong backing from the UN Charter to use the authority of his office to undertake such missions without a mandate. When doing so, he was careful to demarcate the basis of his actions. Sydney Bailey explains, "Hammarskjold, from the beginning, distinguished between those specific responsibilities conferred on him by policy-making organs and those general responsibilities which, explicitly or implicitly, attached to the Office of Secretary-General" (1962, 40). In doing so, he displayed a strong proclivity for undertaking independent initiatives. He set out to prove that he was capable of controlling efforts to create a more peaceful world. Peter Wallensteen explains the basis of his efforts: "The precondition for influence was that he could win the confidence of those who had 'real' power. In Hammarskjöld's hands, this could be transformed into strategies of action, which in turn gave 'real' power to him" (1995, 8). In this frequently seen argument, the key to Hammarskjöld's approach was on accomplishing tasks so that his influence could grow with each new success, thus leading to the widely noted phenomenon of a "leave it to Dag" approach that developed among the UN member-states.

The first independent foray into peaceful settlement by Hammarskjöld did not prove to be particularly advantageous for building the confidence of states. In 1954, he had his first clash with a major power when he intervened and attempted to use the United Nations to counter the American-backed toppling of the Guatemalan president, but his efforts failed to have the desired effect. The Guatemala case is not as widely mentioned in the case histories of

Hammarskjöld as his engagement in other peaceful settlement efforts because it was not a success story for the Secretary-General. However, the important issue for this study is whether his leadership style can be linked to political behavior, not the outcome of the case. In this situation, although "he was unsuccessful in doing more than making a protest and infuriating the Government of the United States," he displayed a willingness to challenge a major power over a case of peace and security in a manner that "gave a foretaste" of the approach he employed throughout his tenure (Urquhart 1983, 139). In addition, Hammarskjöld's focus on handling the crisis through the UN Security Council instead of shifting the case to the Organization of American States (OAS) "was consistent with Hammarskjöld's constant efforts to keep the world body in the picture in international political affairs" (Heller 2001, 70).

Hammarskjöld was very involved in Middle East peaceful settlement efforts. While much of his action in this region was mandated, he also used his own initiative to stay in touch with political actors in the region. He perceived the difficulties in the Middle East as an opportunity to be seized and "responded to this challenge with enthusiasm and ingenuity, using the limited resources of the Secretariat to the practical extreme and developing whatever new resources and sources of support that he could find" (Urquhart 1972, 133). His first Middle East mandate, which will be discussed later, came in April 1956, but Hammarskjöld was already active in the region. His private efforts from 1954 to 1955 to serve as a mediator in the Arab-Israeli conflict were not successful, but his perseverance paid off and he was able to initiate talks with Israeli Prime Minister Ben-Gurion and Egyptian President Nasser in January 1956.

Another illustrative case is Hammarskjöld's approach, starting in 1959, to handling the difficulties in Laos, which Urquhart refers to as a "daring and far-sighted plan, designed to develop a UN presence in Southeast Asia as a whole and to transfer to the Secretary-General the main responsibility for the continuing role of the UN in the area" (1972, 348). Without official UN sanction, Hammarskjöld personally visited Laos and left a representative behind to continue to monitor the situation and to gather further information. His intervention was justified according to the Article 99 authority of the Secretary-General to investigate possible breaches of the peace even though "[t]his reasoning caused the Russians to open their eyes like peacocks. They thought it a very dangerous interpretation" (Lash 1961, 204). From the beginning of the conflict he aimed to do what he thought was best to resolve the difficulties instead of reacting to the political interests of the countries involved. For example, he sought to ensure that the UN presence in Laos was not a large committee responsible to the Security Council or General Assembly, but a one-person mission who would report directly to his office. Adding further fuel to the political fire, Hammarskjöld ignored protests regarding his representative and returned to Laos to personally launch the UN presence independent of any Security Council approval. Overall, through his direct and independent intervention, Hammarskjöld demonstrated how willing he was to push the boundaries of what was acceptable for his office.

Across other such cases, Hammarskjöld employed the powers of his office in helping to resolve conflicts. This included his efforts to resolve a border rift between Cambodia and Thailand beginning in 1958. As with Laos, Hammarskjöld stepped in without a formal mandate. Instead of "bringing the dispute to the attention of one or the other political organ of the United Nations" and engaging in "the regular procedure of meetings and debates in public," he took the initiative to appoint a personal representative to assist in resolving the disagreement (Heller 2001, 57). He emphasized that he could establish such a mission when acceded to by member-states involved, even if there was not a UN mandate calling for his engagement. Hammarskjöld also overrode French objections and personally visited Tunisia in 1961 to try to calm tensions caused by clashes with French forces stationed in the country. He was once again in action "moving deftly and confidently behind the scenes to assert the powers of his office to help bring about a solution. The French rebuff did not deter him. He took it for granted that as the executive arm of the UN" he should assert his leadership (Lash 1961, 294). He felt justified in his direct involvement and claimed that he could only properly carry out his Article 99 duties if he was able to personally collect information regarding such a possible threat to international peace and security. His efforts in this case related to his engagement with the Algerian struggle for independence, where he displayed "minimally activist leadership," but this was "still large enough to displease the French" who did not want the Secretary-General to play any part in the conflict (Heller 2001, 78–79).

Hammarskjöld also undertook independent actions to try to shape how the international community handled particular security issues. A good example of this is the way that he positioned himself in the global dialogue on disarmament. He was willing to step up and fight for his vision for disarmament, berating the great powers for their lack of progress and for moving the discussions of the issue outside of the

United Nations. Despite the fact that his initiatives faced great power reluctance, Hammarskjöld "used every possible means at the United Nations' disposal to promote agreements in the arms control and disarmament field" (Zacher 1970, 204). Concrete actions included nonpolitical ways to address disarmament. He called for a technical study of the possibilities for disarmament and played an active role in helping to organize conferences in 1955 and 1958 that brought together scientific experts from both sides of the Cold War divide and led to the development of the International Atomic Energy Agency. He also pushed for greater use of the UN Disarmament Commission, and when this was not successful, he insisted that the 1959 General Assembly agenda include disarmament.

MANDATED ASSIGNMENTS

Hammarskjöld was also involved in several mandated missions. He believed that the mandates could provide a sound legal backing for his activities. However, this did not mean that he was content to sit back and simply follow instructions. Instead, he sought to influence mandated missions at every step. To begin with, as discussed earlier in this chapter, he worked to guide the wording of the mandates, encouraging precisely worded mandates when possible—as long as they reflected the words that he wanted. Once his mission was established, Hammarskjöld carried out mandates to the fullest extent that he saw fit and persevered in fulfilling mandates despite the political roadblocks that he encountered. If the situation required a clarification of his mandate directives, but the members were unable to come to a consensus in order to provide guidance, Hammarskjöld carried out his mission along the lines that he believed were best. As Oscar Schachter summarizes,

> Hammarskjöld observed that in these cases there was a temptation for the Secretary-General to refuse to act until the organs themselves settle the matter. But this "easy refuge" may be incompatible with his responsibility especially in a matter affecting peace and security. The Secretary-General, he declared, cannot lay aside his responsibilities merely because the execution of decisions is likely to be politically controversial. (1983, 47)

Hammarskjöld also stirred up political controversy by insisting on the independent nature of his powers, even when he was acting under a mandate. While his actions were informed by the mandate, he believed that he was justified in acting beyond these instructions based on the authority invested in his office. In addition, he would emphasize his independent capabilities so that they would not be undermined when acting under a mandate. As Lash notes, "In cases where he did act on the basis of a Security Council request, he carefully noted that he would have had the right to act anyway, independently of the Council's request" (1961, 205) and the same held true for missions authorized by the General Assembly.

The manner in which Hammarskjöld handled his mandated visit to China to seek the release of captured American pilots set the tone for his time as Secretary-General. As with many of his mandated activities, he did not see his mission, described as "this labor of Hercules" (Urquhart 1972, 96), as an onerous task, but instead he saw it "as his first real opportunity to make the Organization an effective instrument of peaceful settlement in the Cold War" (Zacher 1970, 60). Hammarskjöld moved beyond the mandate in a very significant manner. He "shrewdly sensed" that China would be unreceptive to the mandate's wording, which harshly condemned the Chinese actions, so he instead contacted the Chinese directly and requested a personal meeting to discuss the release of the airmen based on the authority of this office (Xing 2005, 51).

This radical new approach became known as the "Peking Formula." This is defined by Zacher as follows:

> The essence of this formula was that when a state does not recognize the authority of a resolution of the Security Council or the General Assembly which the Secretary-General has been asked to try to implement, he can request and undertake negotiations under his independent diplomatic powers flowing from the Charter rather than under the authority of the resolution. (1970, 128)

Hammarskjöld's decision to undertake a direct and independent approach to freeing the airmen shocked many of the resolution's sponsors, especially the British and Americans, but he resisted their attempts to change his approach. They were equally unhappy with his actions during the meetings with Chinese leaders, where Hammarskjöld further expanded upon his mandated duties by talking about issues besides the imprisoned airmen. He touched upon a "whole gamut of Far Eastern problems," including Chinese-Taiwanese relations, because "Hammarskjold took the view that if the Secretary-General finds that a situation may become a threat to peace and security, he is entitled to raise the matter with the government involved to ascertain whether it might be possible to take preventive action" (Lash 1961, 61).

In 1960, Hammarskjöld was given a mandate by the Security Council to bring South Africa into line with UN principles by convincing them to start moving away from apartheid and toward a political system based on racial equality. He was willing to take on the difficult task because he saw it as a further stepping stone toward encouraging his vision of the United Nations at the heart of promoting peace. Instead of sidestepping or halfheartedly carrying out his mission, Hammarskjöld "took it on willingly to show that the UN could act and achieve some easing of a situation, even one that to many appeared insoluble" (Lash 1961, 224). The Secretary-General once again eschewed the accusatory mandate that he had been given and used the Peking Formula to gain access to South Africa. Hammarskjöld recognized that the "formula was not merely a face-saving device for reluctant governments; it also provided a means by which the UN, through the physical presence and activities of the Secretary-General, could move into situations where other UN organs would not be acceptable" (Urquhart 1972, 495).

The Middle East is a prime example where, despite his previous independent actions in the region, Hammarskjöld welcomed rather than resented being placed under a specific mandate because he recognized that this would provide him with a stronger legal basis for action. Before the trouble with the Suez boiled over, Hammarskjöld was given a mandate by the Security Council to investigate the tensions in the region. He took this mandate and ran with it, embarking on an extended diplomatic outing where he traveled back and forth between Israel and the Arab countries. As in the China airmen case, although he had been given a specific mandate, he felt that it was proper for him to tackle a range of issues. Newman explains Hammarskjöld's perspective: "On accepting his mandate Hammarskjöld also indicated that, in addition to being an agent of the Council with this specific task, as Secretary-General he had an obligation under the Charter to raise any matter which threatened international peace and security" (1998, 41–42).

While coping with the Suez crisis, as detailed below in the section on UN intervention, Hammarskjöld was also called on to address the Soviet intervention in Hungary. This case highlights his complex visionary nature. The Soviet Union was determined not to allow any UN involvement, but this did not stop the General Assembly from passing a resolution placing the responsibility for doing just that on the shoulders of Hammarskjöld. As highlighted in the public pronouncements section, he did not let the Soviet action go unrecognized. He angered the Soviets by speaking out against the repression, trying to get observers into Hungary, and organizing a special investigatory committee, but his effort still "provides an almost complete contrast" to the handling of the Suez crisis (Heller 2001, 72). He recognized the intransigence of a great power and realized, despite the urging of the General Assembly, that there was no opportunity present for UN engagement. Hammarskjöld was not one to back away from a fight, but, as Goodrich's analysis points out, pressing in this situation might impair his vision for the United Nations: "Hammarskjold was enough of a political realist to recognize that even if he had taken a strong initiative, nothing would have been done and the weakness of the United Nations would only have been further exposed" (1974, 479). In addition, he did not want to push the Soviets on a point that would leave him unable to work with them in the future.

SUMMARY STYLE COMPARISON FOR PEACEFUL SETTLEMENT OF DISPUTES

Peaceful settlement efforts were a central part of Hammarskjöld's influential toolbox. Walter Lippman notes how Hammarskjöld became known for his creative diplomatic efforts: "Never before, and perhaps never again, has any man used the intense art of diplomacy for such unconventional and such novel experiments" (1961, 547). He took liberty with mandated missions and was engaged in a series of independently initiated efforts. While the handling of situations such as Hungary underscores Hammarskjöld's complex nature, for the most part his visionary style shone through as he insisted on stressing the independent nature of his office, even when operating on a mandated mission, and refused to bend to political pressure to change his approach.

UN INTERVENTION: AT THE FOREFRONT

Hammarskjöld's name will forever be linked with the concept of peacekeeping due to his visionary role in working to create, implement, and set the protocol for the first major peacekeeping operations. Although Secretaries-General cannot establish a peacekeeping mission on their own authority, they can try to shape the mandate and take full advantage of the assignment to play an influential role in handling the serious breaches of security that require UN forces to intervene. In Hammarskjöld's case, he was closely involved across all possible avenues of influence that peacekeeping mandates provide:

> He concerned himself with every detail and supervised every discussion in deciding their organization and operations. He personally negotiated operational arrangements for the peacekeeping forces with the host governments. In fact, there was hardly an aspect of these operations that did not carry a Hammarskjöld mark. (Rikhye 1983, 78)

Under Hammarskjöld's guidance, three major operations were established. First, UNEF was implemented in 1956 on the heels of the Suez invasion by Israel, France, and the United Kingdom and ran until the operation was terminated under Thant in 1967. Second, Hammarskjöld was further involved in the Middle East with the United Nations Observation Group in Lebanon (UNOGIL), which began and ended in 1958. This mission was established during a time of violence within Lebanon and was instructed to determine whether outside forces were infiltrating the country. Third, in 1960 Hammarskjöld helped to create and guide the UN intervention in the Congo—Opération des Nations Unies au Congo (ONUC)—to address the violence that broke out in the newly independent country.

For all three of these missions, Hammarskjöld performed in a visionary manner. Indicative of this was a letter he wrote to a friend about the Congo in 1961: "I have had to choose between the risk that the organization would break down and die out of inertia and inability and the risk that it might break up and die because I overstretched its possibilities" (quoted in Jakobson 1974, 11). As a visionary, he chose the latter. His role in peacekeeping can hardly be overstated. He was at the center of the creation of UNEF and was just as intimately involved in the design and implementation of the other peacekeeping operations. In doing so, Hammarskjöld became a guiding force for the concept of peacekeeping and the principles he established remain a lasting legacy.

At the same time, Hammarskjöld behaved as a complex visionary focused on the long-term capabilities of his office and the United Nations. While approaching the projects according to his vision for how they should be carried out, Hammarskjöld was careful to nurture the peacekeeping tool because a

> UN peace-keeping force is a delicate organism requiring special circumstances for its functioning and survival. Its evolution into something more desirable and versatile will inevitably be a long process, a process that Hammarskjold was determined should not be ended

prematurely by overenthusiasm, overexploitation, or misunderstanding of the nature of the problems involved. (Urquhart 1972, 230)

This meant that he would not expand a mission just for the sake of having a larger presence. Instead, as will be shown in the case of UNOGIL, Hammarskjöld insisted on carrying out the operation in a manner that he believed best fit the circumstances. Thus, he was complex enough to recognize situational requirements, but he also maintained his visionary stance of insisting on doing things his way—even in the face of political criticism and pressure. He was willing to place himself in the center of the storm that arose over peacekeeping, even though he recognized that "he was risking his future efficacy as Secretary-General, since he might make a decision regarding a force which would seriously alienate important Members" because "[w]hile he was aware of these risks, he also felt that his role in these operations was important to the Organization's ability to promote international peace" (Zacher 1970, 181). In this manner, Hammarskjöld's visionary handling of peacekeeping often brought about much controversy.

Hammarskjöld began his strong engagement with UN intervention through his management of existing operations. Although started under Lie, Hammarskjöld moved to put his stamp on both the United Nations Truce Supervision Operation (UNTSO) and United Nations Military Observer Groups in India and Pakistan (UNMOGIP). UNMOGIP monitors the ongoing tensions over Kashmir, while UNTSO operates in the Middle East and assists with helping to maintain peaceful relations between Israel and the surrounding Arab countries. After taking office, "Hammarskjold had taken a firm hold of UNTSO," including appointing General Burns as chief of the operation, and together the two "acted energetically" in 1955 in employing the operation to counter possible military action (Lash 1961, 68). Besides his commitment to UNTSO, he also worked to strengthen the operations of UNMOGIP (Bunche 1965, 122).

Hammarskjöld's visionary role with peacekeeping came to the fore through his close involvement with the UNEF operation. As set out in the previous section, Hammarskjöld had already been very diplomatically active, but UNEF is viewed as a watershed event in his tenure. This point is emphasized by Josef Kunz: "Dag Hammarskjöld's role as a diplomatic negotiator could already be seen in his mission to Peiping in 1954 and to the Middle East in 1956. But in the Suez crisis of 1956 his position was truly dominating" (1958, 301). Despite the previous forays with UNTSO and UNMOGIP, UNEF is widely considered to be the first full peacekeeping operation established by the United Nations. As such, there was little to guide the creation of the mission, and Hammarskjöld took advantage to step to the forefront of shaping the operation. The peacekeeping action was initially proposed by Pearson and Hammarskjöld hesitated at first, but "he quickly grasped the legal and practical implications of a peacekeeping force suggested by Canada and was able to turn an idea into an action programme in record time" (Odio-Benito 2005, 258).

Despite the enormous complexities of establishing such an operation, Hammarskjöld immersed himself in the conceptualization and implementation of UNEF. Although he got very little sleep, especially in the early days of the mission, Hammarskjöld remained energized by the challenge of the task and devoted his unflagging energy to the operation. He welcomed the challenge of the assignment and "viewed UNEF as a fascinating experiment" (Miller 1961, 123) for handling breaches of the peace that could serve as a base for a strong UN role in future conflicts. To ensure that the mission was properly carried out, he was involved in all details, even when faced with politically difficult decisions. Rovine describes the course of action: "He was the focal point for the process of international bargaining that went on throughout the period of crisis and was able to press particular positions and formulations not altogether pleasing to any of the parties" (1970, 294).

Hammarskjöld was also at the center of the creation and functioning of UNOGIL. The mission was formally proposed by Sweden, but Hammarskjöld was behind the scenes recommending that the Swedes take this action. With his knowledge of how the mandate was being shaped, Hammarskjöld went ahead and prepared the force before the resolution asking him to do so had been approved (Curtis 1964, 746). Once UNOGIL was established, Hammarskjöld continued to be closely involved in running the operation. Displaying his need to control, Hammarskjöld traveled to Lebanon in the midst of the crisis to ensure that the mission was correctly set up. Even when not on site, he continued to maintain a high level of involvement over the operation. Urquhart details one example:

> He asked the Observation Group for an immediate further report on its work and organization that would explain its significance in the present situation. He himself provided an outline of the kind of report he would like to receive, including a suggestion to increase the number of observers and possibly add a quota of noncommissioned personnel to be used for ground reconnaissance work. The Group duly submitted a report along these lines. (1972, 283)

In his handling of UNOGIL, Hammarskjöld "unmistakably challenged United States policy" (Gordenker 2005, 78) as he resisted pressure from the Americans and Lebanese to expand the mission from an observation unit into a broader fighting force. In Hammarskjöld's view, inserting troops would exacerbate rather than improve the situation. He refused to back away from his position and openly defended his views that peaceful resolution was more likely once it became clear that there would be no outside military intervention. He went as far as to claim that he would be unwilling to carry out a mandate that moved beyond his understanding of the needs of the situation, noting "that if a proposal for a UN force in Lebanon were to be put to the Security Council or the General Assembly and if the Secretary-General were to be asked to execute such a decision, he would be compelled to state that in the present circumstances he could not accept such a mandate" (Urquhart 1972, 272). When the United States unilaterally placed their own troops in Lebanon, Hammarskjöld still refused to budge and instead "made clear his narrow and cautious interpretation of the resolution" that the UN observers and the U.S. military were operating separately (Curtis 1964, 742).

Following the insertion of American troops into Lebanon, Hammarskjöld did feel that the observer group should be expanded. While this brought him closer in line with the American and Lebanese position, he now found himself having to override Soviet objections. The Soviet Union was set against expanding the size of the mission and vetoed a Japanese resolution along these lines. However, Hammarskjöld was undeterred and pushed ahead in "an exercise in liberal construction of the Secretary-General's powers that left the strict constructionists breathless" (Lash 1961, 119). Instead of waiting for the paralyzed Security Council to work out their disagreements, he interpreted the situation as a vacuum in need of action and he proceeded to enlarge UNOGIL as if the resolution had passed. According to Hammarskjöld, the principle to act when explicit instructions were not forthcoming had been set with his statement in October 1956 regarding the Suez crisis and his re-election speech in 1957, which had not been questioned by the member-states at the time (Henderson 1969, 60).

The final peacekeeping operation established during Hammarskjöld's tenure turned out to be the most controversial. ONUC was a complex undertaking, both in terms of the scale of the problem and the intricacy of the internal Congolese political situation. However, as in the other cases of UN intervention, Hammarskjöld embraced the challenge as an opportunity to further UN engagement in handling international peace and security. The United Nations may not have become involved in the Congo without Hammarskjöld's machinations. He was enmeshed in the case well before he had been given a formal mandate. Before the situation exploded, Hammarskjöld sent a personal representative and instructed him to explain to the Congolese how they should phrase their request for assistance to ensure his ability to guide the UN response, including making sure that the message was directly addressed to him and not one of the principal organs (Rikhye 1993, 5–6). As the situation threatened to spiral out of control, as discussed earlier, Hammarskjöld became the first Secretary-General to explicitly employ Article 99 to call the Security Council together to discuss the breach of the peace.

Hammarskjöld's close involvement did not end with the invocation of Article 99. Boudreau explains, "[T]here is no spirit of Article 99 that can justify executive action by the Secretary-General especially after the Article is invoked. Yet, this is exactly what Hammarskjöld claimed in the Congo crisis, giving the constitutional meaning of Article 99 a broader and more controversial scope" (Boudreau 1991, 41). He worked to keep the Security Council meeting moving and once the members finally adjourned in the middle of the night, having established the mandate for ONUC, Hammarskjöld immediately started planning the operation's details. In line with his temperament, he moved to get the ONUC forces in place quickly and he was occupied with the "conception, planning, organization" of ONUC to ensure a "vigorous pursuit of his objectives" (Rikhye 1983, 96).

Once ONUC was established, Hammarskjöld was closely involved in handling operational details. Dayal notes Hammarskjöld's connection to the mission: "I was both surprised and impressed by the amount of time the Secretary-General was devoting to the Congo problem in the midst of his other heavy duties" (1976, 11). An illustrative example is his role in getting Belgian troops, which were supporting Katangese separatism, out of the region. Hammarskjöld faced the precarious circular logic that the Belgians would not pull out until ONUC was in place, but UN troops could not move into Katanga due to the threat of forceful resistance. In a move that "was typical of the risks he took in this entire controversy" (Draper 1960, 11), Hammarskjöld decided to escort a contingent of Swedish peacekeepers by plane into Katanga and refused to land unless the troops were allowed to arrive with him. He argued that any risk was justified by the pressing need to get troops into Katanga. In the end, his "daring and unprecedented" maneuver paid off and the UN force was established in Katanga (Urquhart 1972, 427).

Hammarskjöld faced criticism of his handling of ONUC from different countries, as well as factions within the Congo, which were all looking out for their own interests. Dayal quickly discovered that the Secretary-General and his staff were buffeted from all sides: "As the harassed Special Representative noted in his second report, 'almost every significant measure taken by ONUC, in the impartial fulfillment of its mandate, has been interpreted by one faction or another as directed against itself' " (Hoffman 1962, 339). Hammarskjöld came under fire from both Cold War blocs and he frustrated the great powers by declining to bend to their political dictates. The Soviet Union was particularly disgruntled. Eric Stein explains the Soviet stance:

> The Government of the Soviet Union has claimed, in connection with the United Nations activities in the Congo, that Secretary General Hammarskjold and his staff have taken upon themselves functions which are outside their competence and within the exclusive competence of the political organs of the United Nations, and that they have acted arbitrarily and not impartially. (1962, 9)

The Soviets became so angered that, as discussed earlier, they called for Hammarskjöld's resignation and proposed that a leadership troika be established in his place, but he "refused to be intimidated" and continued to decline to "give the Soviets special privileges" (Draper 1960, 31).

Hammarskjöld also had to cope with multiple complaints from the very people that he was trying to help, the Congolese. Since the Congo had just achieved independence, he had to deal with an inexperienced group of government officials. Having called for UN assistance, the officials' impression "seemed to be that the United Nations would quickly respond with everything that was wanted and needed and that the United Nations personnel, military and civilian alike, would be constantly at the bidding of Congolese government officials . . . Congolese officials holding such views have naturally suffered profound disillusionment" (Bunche 1965, 124). Hammarskjöld had several run-ins with Prime Minister Lumumba in particular and their clashing "negotiating styles" were rapidly apparent (Rikhye 1993, 22). Lumumba wanted to control the UN forces for his own purposes, but Hammarskjöld insisted that this could not occur. In one instance, he "resisted having ONUC coerce Katanga militarily on behalf of Lumumba's regime. He felt such a role would destroy any sense of the United Nations' political neutrality—Hammarskjöld's central diplomatic ideal" (Dobbins et al. 2005, 14).

Despite complaints from a variety of political actors, Hammarskjöld remained thoroughly involved in the functioning of ONUC. He saw the Congo as an opportunity to move the international community closer to his vision for an active United Nations at the heart of managing international peace and security. As Dayal recalls, "He told me that the task of the United Nations in the Congo was unique in the experience of the Organization both in regard to its character and magnitude. A new course in international cooperation was being charted that would expand the frontiers of the Organization's responsibilities and functions and greatly stimulate its future growth" (1976, 11–12). Hammarskjöld was willing to go to any length to protect this vision when he saw it threatened, including returning to the Congo again in September 1961 to meet personally with the leader of Katanga. He felt that the situation was getting out of control and was threatening the status of the United Nations. On route to the meeting, Hammarskjöld's plane went down and, although he was thrown clear of the wreckage, he died at the site (see Gavshon 1962; Gibbs 1993; Henderson 1969; Norden 1965; Rösiö 1993 and Wallensteen 1995 for competing interpretations of the reasons for the crash). In the end, "Dag Hammarskjöld initiated the Congo operation in midsummer of 1960, encouraged it to become the biggest of all United Nations operations to date, and gave his major attention to it through many tense and unpleasant months until, in September, 1961, he gave his life while serving it" (Bunche 1965, 119).

SUMMARY STYLE COMPARISON FOR UN INTERVENTION

That Hammarskjöld lost his life performing functions related to peacekeeping is indicative of his devotion to the United Nations and its efforts at resolving breaches of the peace through intervention with force. Through each stage of the peacekeeping process, Hammarskjöld was closely involved in guiding peacekeeping missions. He worked with the member-states to develop the mandates and monitored each mission to make sure that they were carried out in the manner that he desired. His complex nature was once again in effect in the way that he monitored and analyzed the conflict areas. However, despite the political aggravation that it caused among some of the member-states, Hammarskjöld refused to back down from how he thought the existing peacekeeping operations should be run and reinforced his vision for the path that the United Nations should play in enforcing peace in the future.

CONCLUSION

The review of Hammarskjöld's tenure supports the coding results that indicated he would behave as a visionary Secretary-General. Across the variety of tools at his disposal, Hammarskjöld performed as an active Secretary-General who sought to influence the handling of global peace and security. He possessed a clear vision of a world based on collective interests grounded in international law. He believed that the United Nations and the Secretary-Generalship have central roles to play in handling disruptions of peace and that they serve as an important base for developing a more cooperative international arena for the future. Throughout his time in office, his actions reflected this vision.

Due to his high level of conceptual complexity Hammarskjöld did deviate somewhat from the ideal visionary style, both in terms of his personal characteristics and subsequent behavior as Secretary-General. While his overall level of responsivity was tempered by his equally high self-confidence, he was more responsive to contextual cues than one would expect from a visionary. Yet, a visionary approach to handling the office does predominate. He was proactive in deciding when the time was right to do what he wanted, maintained his vision throughout, and refused to sacrifice his ideals for political expediency.

Hammarskjöld's overarching visionary approach was demonstrated from the beginning of his tenure when he stepped forward and took control of administrative affairs. He insisted that his office, not the member-states, had power over Secretariat staffing. He also focused early efforts on restructuring the Secretariat to emphasize its independence and to match his own decision-making approach. In doing so, he invested more authority in his office and was able to place the people that he wanted close to him at the upper levels of the organization. Later in his tenure, when faced with the Soviet troika proposal, he reacted vociferously against this challenge to the authority of the Secretary-Generalship. He was closely involved in drafting a large number of reports, thus ensuring that his views were being expressed. He shaped budgetary priorities for the organization and continued to be at the forefront of financial matters for peacekeeping missions, although it is also true that Hammarskjöld largely left administrative concerns behind as he became more focused on international diplomatic efforts.

The strategic political position within the United Nations was fully taken advantage of by Hammarskjöld. He was actively engaged in official meetings. He openly expressed his opinions and tried to influence proceedings to the point that he has been referred to as the "chief legislator" in the United Nations at that time. As part of maintaining this avenue of influence, he sought to keep certain meetings, most notably disarmament talks, within the confines of the United Nations. He became the first Secretary-General to directly invoke Article 99, largely to ensure that he would have greater control over the Security Council meeting about the Congo. When he could not be directly involved in influencing matters, he employed informal influential channels. He maintained continual interaction with permanent mission members to the point where some members began to express a conflict of loyalty between the United Nations and their home governments, and he used these middlemen to influence the drafting of resolutions; although in this process he seemed to work in conjunction with others instead of simply forcing his ideas.

The use of public pronouncements was intentionally limited by Hammarskjöld when he thought that the work of the United Nations might be damaged, but he did maintain a strong presence and level of pressure through his use of public pronouncement activities. All of his annual reports were seen as seeking to influence the agenda. Despite being aware of the political controversy that some of his views would raise, he used his introductory thoughts to address issues that he felt strongly about and was working on at the time, as well as to expound a broader vision for the Secretary-Generalship and the United Nations. He did not particularly enjoy the pomp that attended some official functions, but he did take advantage of these situations to be very vocal in expressing and defending his opinions in relation to specific issues and his general vision for global affairs. He traveled extensively to personally monitor missions, gather information, and meet directly with those involved, and he used the opportunities for speeches to make his ideas known to the public. Although he shied away from unnecessary publicity, he did use the media to get his views across to states and the general public. He guided and controlled questions at his press conferences to ensure that the focus was placed on the message that he wanted to impart. When he traveled, he would limit media coverage when he thought that it would impede his mission, but he did use the press to promote the purpose of his trips and to publicize the results.

Hammarskjöld possessed a very liberal interpretation of the capabilities of his office for peacefully settling disputes. For mandated missions, he often inserted himself into the process at the early stages to try to influence the mandate. In carrying out his assignments, he perceived a lack of guidance not as an indicator to pull back from his duties but as a vacuum that he needed to fill with his own ideas. When he believed that the phrasing of the mandate was improper, as in the China airmen and South Africa apartheid cases, he skirted the mandate and undertook trips to these areas based on his own authority under what has been termed the Peking Formula. He sought to carry out the mandates as he saw fit, often moving beyond the bounds of the mandate, and, although he backed away from the challenge presented by the Soviet intervention in Hungary, rarely bent to political pressure to alter his approach. He also undertook multiple missions based solely on his own authority. In doing so, he was willing to challenge the member-states and push for his views over how breaches of the peace should be handled.

Hammarskjöld's role in the realm of UN intervention is well documented. He was at the forefront of peacekeeping operations and sought to put a personal imprint on their character. Existing missions were molded to his perspective and he worked to shape the mandates of new operations. He was closely involved in all aspects of carrying out the missions to ensure that the operations matched what he wanted to do. As the interventions in Lebanon and the Congo especially illustrate, he continued to organize the UN missions as he saw fit despite alternative plans and criticisms from member-states. In the end, despite the intentions of the Security Council members to replace Lie with a compliant manager, in Hammarskjöld they selected a Secretary-General who proved to be a visionary head of the United Nations. The next chapter turns to a profile of Waldheim, whose tenure as a managerial Secretary-General provides a clear contrast to the visionary Hammarskjöld.

CHAPTER 5

The Manager: Kurt Waldheim

He was reluctant to assert his office or even run the risk of courting superpower disapproval. Thus, it is not surprising that his ten-year tenure in office was characterized by a lack of constitutional innovations, especially in the realm of international peace and security.

(Boudreau 1991, 77–78)

INTRODUCTION

In contrast to the visionary Hammarskjöld, the content analysis coding results presented in chapter 2 indicate that Kurt Waldheim possesses a managerial leadership style. The analysis of his political behavior as Secretary-General in this chapter strongly supports this categorization. Just as Hammarskjöld predominantly executed his duties in a visionary manner, Waldheim's actions in regards to international peace and security closely reflected the behavioral expectations that were established for the managerial style.

The chapter begins by discussing Waldheim's electoral drive and related willingness to meet state expectations. This is followed by a brief discussion of revelations concerning his Nazi links during World War II and whether this needs to be taken into account to explain how he operated as Secretary-General. The following section draws on observations of Waldheim's character to support the assertion that he possesses a managerial style and the corresponding personal traits. The chapter then provides a general overview of his managerial actions and concludes with a detailed analysis of his time in office based on the behavioral categories set out in chapter 3.

WALDHEIM: BACKGROUND AND STYLE OVERVIEW

THE ELECTION: MANAGERIAL EXPECTATIONS AND REALIZATIONS

With the memory of the visionary Hammarskjöld still fresh, many of the member-states focused on selecting a manager during the 1971 election. This worked against one of the front-runners for the office, Max Jakobson of Finland. Jakobson and Waldheim were perceived as possessing very different ideas regarding how to approach the office. Reflecting on his failed bid for the office, Jakobson recalls, "My concept of the role of the Secretary-General displeased everyone, in fact. I was in favor of stronger powers for him and a more interventionist attitude when a crisis arose" (quoted in Cohen and Rosenzweig 1987, 120). In sharp contrast, as Waldheim arduously pursued the Secretary-Generalship, he made it clear that he believed in a managerial role for the office. None of the other candidates debated were able to make it through the Security Council gauntlet: "Before they considered him [Waldheim], they had rejected a half-dozen rivals, ostensibly stronger men who, in the course of their diplomatic careers, had threatened or offended one or another of them . . . Finally, he emerged as the lowest common denominator among the electing powers" (Viorst 1972, 40).

Waldheim always had his eye on attaining a high-status office. When he failed in his first bid for the Austrian presidency in early 1971, he quickly turned his "ambition for higher office" to the United Nations and "did not hold back" in his pursuit of the Secretary-Generalship (Ryan 2001, 6). Despite becoming Austria's foreign minister in 1968, he was not satisfied:

> A less ambitious man might have regarded his rise to the top of the foreign ministry as the culmination of a glorious career. Not Kurt Waldheim. He had his eye on even higher peaks. It was looking increasingly likely that U Thant would be retiring as UN secretary-general when his term ended in 1971. Waldheim intended to be ready to take advantage of the opening if and when he did. (Herzstein 1988, 221–222)

To ensure that the office would be his, Waldheim courted the full range of member-states, endearing himself to the great powers of the Security Council while also making strong overtures to the smaller countries. Waldheim had set the groundwork for his election triumph well before 1971. During the time he spent representing Austria at the United Nations in the 1950s and 1960s, he carefully built relationships with representatives from other delegations and called on these connections when his chance arrived.

Upon Waldheim's selection, one Secretariat member stated hopefully, "They said Dag Hammarskjöld was nothing but a glorified clerk when he took over. One can always hope that Waldheim will turn out to be an equally pleasant surprise" (quoted in *Newsweek* 1972, 24). However, a UN diplomat was closer to the truth when he argued that Waldheim would be unwilling to provide dynamic leadership, "Do you know that story about what happened to the girl with thick black stockings? Nothing happened—and that's what's going to happen to the United Nations" (quoted in *New York Times* 1971, 10). In the case of Waldheim, the managerial expectations of the selecting countries were fully realized.

As the end of his first term neared, Waldheim keenly sought to remain in office. He built his successful campaign around a managerial record and a continued cultivation of relationships with member-state representatives. Notwithstanding claims that he "lacked dignity" (Nossiter 1981, 5) for doing so, in 1981 Waldheim pressed to become the first Secretary-General to serve a third term. There were no signs from the majority of the great powers that they would object:

> It appears that the Reagan Administration, Brezhnev, Thatcher, and the French government were content to have a plodding bureaucrat who would not take initiatives that might disturb them . . . Despite his lackluster performance in his ten years as secretary-general, none of the permanent members expressed dissatisfaction with him . . . with the major powers more concerned that a secretary general might create problems for them than that he might be too cautious, a tireless, careful bureaucrat like Waldheim was quite acceptable. (Finger and Saltzman 1990, 79–81)

Unfortunately for Waldheim, China vetoed his candidacy. China did not appear to have had any reservations regarding his performance in office, but instead acted on the belief that it was time for a Secretary-General from the third world.

THE IMPACT OF WALDHEIM'S NAZI BACKGROUND?

Searching for interesting anecdotes on the new Secretary-General, the *New York Times* found that Waldheim was generally so discreet that acquaintances did not have any to offer and acknowledged that "the fact that there are none is the most telling characteristic" (1971, 10). Similarly indicative of Waldheim's managerial style was the relatively limited public or scholarly attention paid to him compared to the visionary Hammarskjöld. This changed when information regarding Waldheim's Nazi involvement came to light when he again pursued, and this time won, the Austrian presidency in 1986. Following the disclosures, there was a flurry of publications on Waldheim that, while often pursuing his Nazi past, also provide useful insight into his time as Secretary-General. Ironically, the same drive to hold a political office that led Waldheim to downplay his capabilities and to acquiesce to state needs, which resulted in little initial coverage of his efforts at the United Nations, also led him to seek the Austrian presidency despite having already achieved the Secretary-Generalship. This resulted in an increased level of scrutiny that brought his past to light. Thus, in a sense, "He became a victim of his insatiable ambition" (Finger and Saltzman 1990, 83).

Much has been made of the fact that Waldheim was apparently a willing participant in the Nazi war effort once the Germans moved into Austria in 1938. He joined the National Socialist German Students League that year and later served as an active member of the German armed forces. The question of his participation, albeit apparently tangentially, in the atrocities committed during World War II is compounded by Waldheim intentionally misleading those inquiring about his wartime record. This background raises serious issues about Waldheim's character. However, when placing Waldheim under intense scrutiny most conclude, as Robert Herzstein expresses, "I discovered a man who was not evil but merely ambitious and clever" (1988, 23). In fact, Waldheim's Nazi past appears to reveal more about this overriding ambitious nature than a desire to support the Nazi agenda. Urquhart stresses this point, arguing, "Waldheim, it has now become clear, lied for nearly forty years about his war record, presumably believing that the truth would stand in the way of his relentless pursuit of public position and office" (1987, 227). In other words, Waldheim recognized what he had to do to ensure that his career path was not interrupted and followed the demands of the power that had control over his destiny—a theme that this chapter will return to multiple times to highlight his managerial willingness to please in order to obtain and retain his position as Secretary-General.

Studies of Waldheim's past have largely concluded that rumors of countries, such as the Soviet Union, using knowledge about his past to blackmail or unduly pressure him to act in their countries' interests do not appear to have a factual base. Reacting to these claims, Seymour

Maxwell Finger and Arnold Saltzman, based on extensive interviews, found, "The consensus was that he took great pains not to antagonize the Soviets but that he was just as anxious to please the United States" (1990, 55). Similarly, a senior UN official claims, "On the political level, Kurt Waldheim did not particularly favor the Soviet Union during his two terms of office. He was above all a careerist who was ready to do anything to take care of his future" (quoted in Cohen and Rosenzweig 1987, 129). In the end, as this chapter illustrates, Waldheim equally sought to meet to all member-states' concerns.

WALDHEIM'S HIGH PROFILE MANAGERIAL STYLE

Descriptions of Waldheim habitually allude to his managerial style. For example, William Jackson describes Waldheim as possessing "the orientation of the passive conciliator" (1978, 240). An oft-quoted passage reads, "Waldheim was an energetic, ambitious mediocrity . . . he lacked the qualities of vision, integrity, inspiration, and leadership" (Urquhart 1987, 228). However, just as Hammarskjöld deviated from the ideal visionary style due to his complex nature, Waldheim's score on need for recognition, the highest of all seven Secretaries-General, is unusual for a manager. Although for the other personal traits Waldheim matches with the managerial style expectations, his high need for recognition leads to referring to him as a "high profile manager."

Emphasizing Waldheim's high profile nature, when serving under him in the Secretariat, Urquhart observes, "We used to speculate on just how far Waldheim would go to get publicity" because he had a "need for constant public recognition" (1987, 228, 283). Waldheim's desire for publicity connected with his drive, described earlier in this chapter, to achieve a position of prestige. This point is reinforced by Bernard Cohen and Luc Rosenzweig, who titled a section of their book on Waldheim "Portrait of a Lover of Power" (1987, 133), and Richard Holbrooke's observation, "He didn't care about anything except his own political position" (quoted in Fasulo 2004, 30). Once he had achieved the Secretary-Generalship, and the recognition that the office inherently provided, Waldheim did not want to let it go. Unlike Thant, who had to be convinced to stay on for a second term and refused to even consider a third, Waldheim had achieved his goal and reveled in holding the office:

> Waldheim loved being the UN secretary-general, though he called it "the toughest job in the world." He adored the spectacular view from

his palatial office atop the UN building on Manhattan's East Side. He enjoyed the formal ceremonies during which he bestowed or received decorations. He relished the fact that wherever he went (except for Iran), he was greeted with the respect befitting the world's leading diplomat. (Herzstein 1988, 230)

In fact, when it was time for Waldheim to hand over the office, Perez de Cuellar was forced to live in a hotel for several weeks until Waldheim finally moved out of the Secretary-General's official residence (Urquhart 1987, 334). Therefore, although Waldheim had an unusually high need for recognition for a manager, this need was directed toward continual re-election efforts, thereby reinforcing the managerial style instead of challenging it as one might otherwise expect.

For the other five personal characteristics, Waldheim holds true to managerial form. He possesses a low sense of supranationalism, with his score coming in last of all the Secretaries-General. According to U.S. Assistant Secretary of State Joseph Sisco, "He did not have a strong independent commitment to the institution *per se* as a Dag Hammarskjöld—a sharp contrast" (quoted in Meisler 1995b, 195). It is true that, from the earliest days of Austria's ties to the United Nations in the 1950s, Waldheim was involved with the organization. However, this was not linked to an underlying belief in the importance of the United Nations and its principles. Similarly, his desire to hold public office led him to focus on the United Nations as a likely target not because he was committed to supranational ideals, but simply because the Secretary-Generalship was a prestigious position that he thought he could achieve. As Urquhart stresses, "He seemed to be a man without real substance, quality, or character, swept along by an insatiable thirst for public office . . . [which] showed an astonishing lack both of self-respect and of concern for the reputation of the United Nations" (1987, 268, 331). While Waldheim was occasionally willing to vigorously defend the United Nations, this was more out of an isomorphic relationship with the organization where he was protecting his own position rather than that of the reputation of the organization.

Waldheim also does not have a strong belief in his ability to be influential, with his score on this trait ranking fifth of the seven Secretaries-General. Anthony Astrachan echoes the thoughts of many others when he observes "Waldheim's sense of the limits of his powers" (1974, 13). Waldheim believed that he should defer to the states over the handling of international affairs. He thought that his office and the United Nations were ineffective as independent actors in comparison to the member-states. As Jackson observes,

> Waldheim has frankly conceded that the U.N. cannot play an effective conflict management role in the absence of positive political coopera-tion among the members. He has tended to stress the limits of the ability of the U.N. to maintain international peace and the primary importance of diplomacy among the principal actors in the system. (1978, 240)

Waldheim possesses a high level of responsivity, with his score on this trait falling only behind Annan. The combination of high need for recognition and responsivity is captured by Finger: "He had an enor-mous ego. He wanted to be recognized as a world leader. At the same time, he had this caution which enabled him to accede to the wishes of the powerful" (quoted in Cohen and Rosenzweig 1987, 133). Waldheim is often described as "too passive and responsive, the typical faceless diplomat" (James 1983, 84) and *Los Angeles Times* reporter Don Shannon recalls, "The press used to call him 'The Headwaiter' . . . He always stood there as if he were wringing his hands on a towel, asking what he could do for the powerful countries" (quoted in Meisler 1995b, 195).

The high level of responsivity is also reflected in Waldheim's ability to consider multiple angles of complicated issues. He is noted for his meticulous attention to detail and his desire to carefully examine situ-ations to consider all potential repercussions before action is taken. Although Waldheim "was ready to accept ideas and suggestions and follow them up," when the time came to make a policy decision, "[w]orking with Waldheim could be a grind because he insisted on going over and over the smallest details . . . This was partly due to his innate dislike for coming down firmly on one side or the other" (Urquhart 1987, 229). After all, choosing a side opened him up to criticism from those opposed to the stance. Although Waldheim claimed after leaving office, "I am convinced that the Secretary-General must do two basic things . . . he must be responsive to the apprehensions, aspirations and sensitivities of all the member states . . . The Secretary-General is also the custodian of the idea of world community which is set forth in the United Nations Charter" (1983, 21), it was the responsive aspect of the position that was strongly displayed in his character.

As a further indication of his high level of responsivity, even when Waldheim chose a position there was no guarantee that he could not be readily swayed to change his mind. Shirley Hazzard (1990, 58) and Stanley Meisler (1995b, 195) both note Waldheim's "pliancy," with Meisler referring to this as Waldheim's "hallmark." Given this inclination, the member-states that wanted Waldheim to follow their desires had to be careful to ensure that he maintained his focus on what they wanted. In an interview with United States permanent representative Donald McHenry, Finger and Saltzman found, "He said that Waldheim would whisper 'I'm for you' in order to get along with everybody and tended to bend to pressure. Consequently, McHenry had felt the need to keep the heat on Waldheim when U.S. interests were involved" (1990, 64).

Waldheim also has a remarkably high need for relationships, with his score for this trait surpassing all other office-holders. He demonstrates a great desire to be accepted and is geared toward carefully cultivating relationships. Hazzard details how his "appeasement of member governments—which was eager and obsessive" quickly became recognized in United Nations circles (1990, 77), while Newman observes Waldheim's concentration on "attempting to avoid confrontation and win friends" (1998, 53). Waldheim is focused on working hard at his job. James Ryan notes that Waldheim is a "self-described workaholic" who possesses a "belief in the efficacy of personal hard work" (2001, 16). However, while Finger and Saltzman echo this sentiment, describing Waldheim as "[c]ertainly hard working, tenacious . . . and possessed of uncommon stamina," they simultaneously recognize that this was "driven more by laser-beam ambition than by dedication to principles" (1990, 17).

More importantly, any drive to complete tasks is dwarfed by Waldheim's desire to respond to the needs of others, as indicated by a relatively low score on problem-solving emphasis that only comes ahead of Lie and Annan. He believes in an approach that allows him to be open to the feelings of others instead of pushing for solutions to problems. Finger and Saltzman stress Waldheim's often-noted "desire to please" (1990, 86). In the end, Waldheim was much more focused on taking care of the needs of others than carrying out tasks.

WALDHEIM IN ACTION: MANAGERIAL BEHAVIOR OVERVIEW

Finger and Saltzman ask the question "Who Is Kurt Waldheim?" as the title of their opening chapter (1990, 1) and their answer can be seen in the title of the book *Bending With the Winds: Kurt Waldheim and the United Nations*. Similarly, one receives a quick sense of the perception of Waldheim simply by perusing the descriptive section and article headings employed by those discussing the fourth Secretary-General. A sampling to illustrate this point includes section headings "Kurt Waldheim: 'Caretaker' Secretary-General" (Boudreau 1991, 76) and "Waldheim: Self-Described Pragmatist" (Nachmias 1993, 121), while article titles include "Waldheim: Learning the Uses of Limited Power" (Astrachan 1974) and "Kurt Waldheim: Diplomats' Diplomat" (James 1983). These titles alone suggest that Waldheim fits the managerial mode of behavior established by his leadership style profile. More concrete support for this assertion rapidly becomes available as one moves into the descriptive accounts of his time in office. For the question "who is Kurt Waldheim?" the evidence presented in this chapter clearly supports the answer that he is a manager.

In introducing Waldheim upon his election, the *New York Times* wrote, "The words often used to describe the 53-year-old Austrian— and they are often used together—are 'correct' and 'diplomat.' Even during his two years as Austria's Foreign Minister, he has appeared to see his function as that of carrying out policy rather than making it" (1971, 10). This pattern held throughout his time at the United Nations. Peter Baehr and Gordenker explain that "Waldheim dealt with the great powers with much caution" and in comparison to other Secretaries-General behaved in a "more circumspect and less influential" manner (1994, 31). Generally, Waldheim did not indicate that he possessed ideas of his own that he sought to implement, so his tenure was guided by others giving him proposals and then encouraging him in that direction.

For some commentators, the way that his leadership style predisposed Waldheim to act as a manager is viewed in a negative light. Newman's claim that "his personal idiosyncrasies, and his approach to a number of issues, have left a particularly negative impression of his incumbency" is an understatement (1998, 52). For example, Finger and Saltzman conclude, "Kurt Waldheim's performance as secretary general might best be described as uneven and unspectacular" (1990, 85), while Hazzard adds even more derisively, "Uninspired, officious, and essentially trivial, Waldheim was proof against every occasion of a larger kind" (1990, 73). Others perceive the role that Waldheim played in a more positive manner. One proponent is James, who believes that his "disposition and approach . . . were very suitable for the job" (1983, 81). Connor Cruise O'Brien applauds Waldheim in an article titled "The Very Model of a Secretary-General" (1986). Upset that the Chinese vetoed Waldheim's efforts for a third term, he argues, "With Waldheim you knew where you were; with Waldheim there would be no surprises," and he clearly favors Waldheim's "discretion" over Hammarskjöld's activism (quoted in Hazzard 1990, 103–104).

The intention of this study is not to debate the relative merits of Waldheim as Secretary-General. As the discussion in chapter 2 highlighted, there has historically been a split between individuals who prefer managers versus those who support visionaries. Those who desire a manager applaud Waldheim as Secretary-General, while others deride his performance and pine for another Hammarskjöld to step forth. The key point to take away from this debate related to the proper role of the Secretary-General for the purposes of this study is that, like his approach to the office or not, all observers have agreed that Waldheim fit the managerial mode of behavior.

WALDHEIM AND INFLUENTIAL ACTIVITIES

Now that Waldheim's general managerial behavioral pattern has been established, the analysis turns to how his actions in relation to the specific opportunities for influence set out in chapter 3 reflect his managerial style. The following discussion is summarized in table 5.1. The side-by-side comparison of behavioral expectations along with Waldheim's behavior as Secretary-General demonstrates how well these match overall.

AGENDA SETTING: AGENDA IMPLEMENTER

For the first category, agenda setting, Waldheim displays a clear tendency to behave as a manager across the range of available activities. He carried out the mandatory administrative duties of supervising reports, overseeing the budget, and staffing the Secretariat, but he infrequently acted upon the influential potential of these activities. Although he was involved somewhat in voluntarily restructuring the Secretariat, he rarely employed this prerogative to push for a particular agenda. The primary focus for Waldheim was on meeting the needs and desires of the member-states, even when this ran counter to the interests of the UN administration as a whole.

Similarly, Waldheim deferred to the member-states when serving as a representative at meetings and did not use his inherent strategic political position to try to influence others. In the final subcategory, public pronouncements, his annual reports were presented in a straightforward fashion that did not push ideas for how international

Activity	Ideal Manager	Waldheim Behavior
Agenda Setting		
Administrative Duties		
●Supervise Reports	Produce unbiased reports upon request	Did not use reports to provide ideas; maintained a cautious, noncritical tone in wording
●Oversee Finances	Unbiased design; readily accede to revisions	Generally showed little concern or understanding of budgetary matters; an initial fiscal reform effort, but more focused on own lavish expenditures
●Shape Administrative Structure	Unlikely to restructure unless told to do so; will alter along guidelines without concern for expanding own influence; will not lobby for particular structure	Little emphasis on restructuring possibilities beyond an initial limited focus on upper level of the Secretariat; political expediency determined structural moves
●Staffing the Secretariat	Willing to allow members to influence staffing considerations; will not use staffing appointments to place own people	Allowed states to dictate appointments, unwilling to make appointments that he wanted due to fear of political backlash; ignored Secretariat concerns and damaged morale; allowed Secretariat to expand when cuts were needed to provide more positions to meet member-state demands
Strategic Political Position		
●Representative in Meetings	Will attend meetings where required under Article 98, but will not act independently to place self in important meetings or express views unless requested to do so; will not employ Article 99 unless asked to do so	Little evidence to suggest that did anything but defer to member-states at meetings; more than willing to work under authority of other UN organs; did employ Article 99 but many questions regarding the independence of use

Continued

Table 5.1 Continued

Activity	Ideal Manager	Waldheim Behavior
• Inherent Strategic Position	No attempt to cultivate contacts for influential purposes; may be used by member-states for information that managers possess	Many meetings held, but did not actively seek to influence agenda; state representatives saw chance to influence him and gather info, not vice versa
Public Pronouncements		
• Annual Report to General Assembly	Make report a straightforward, technical account with limited personal recommendations	Did not use report to push for greater say in how international peace and security should be handled
• Official Representational Activities	Carry out duty in a straightforward manner without seeking to impact on the agenda	High profile, but low key; statements designed to avoid confrontation and backed away from statements that met with resistance; much travel but unclear whether that was used to attempt to influence, more likely guided by re-election effort and appreciation of public recognition
• "Unofficial" Representational Activities	Unlikely to undertake many of these activities voluntarily; when speaking maintains a bland message that does not challenge state prerogatives	Was eager for publicity and concerned for image, but no real message was imparted

Peaceful Settlement of Disputes

●Independently Initiated	Unlikely to undertake such missions; if does become involved will limit forcefulness of the initiative	Was actively involved in some independent efforts; but careful not to overstep limits regarding acceptable action or where he should be involved
●Mandated Assignment	Will not attempt to influence mandate; will follow mandate closely and request clarification if anything unclear	Followed belief that his office should mainly get involved at request of conflicting parties or UN organs and should closely follow mandated instructions
UN Intervention		
●Peacekeeping Missions	Will not attempt to influence mandate and will follow mandate closely and request clarification if anything unclear	Not involved in shaping mission mandates; in carrying out mandates sought to closely cater to views of member-states

peace and security should be addressed. While Waldheim did operate in a more high profile fashion than one would expect from an ideal manager for official and unofficial representational activities, the lack of an influential message in these pronouncements reflected his managerial style.

ADMINISTRATIVE DUTIES

Waldheim is generally considered an "appalling administrator" (UN expert quoted in Cohen and Rosenzweig 1987, 131) who displayed a limited desire to focus on administrative affairs. There is no evidence to suggest that he sought to use reports or the budget in an influential manner. In addition, he did not use structural or personnel issues to provide himself with greater chances to influence policy, but instead to curry favor with the member-states responsible for his re-election.

Supervise reports

Waldheim's managerial approach is evident in the first area of administrative duties, supervising reports. Research did not uncover any evidence to suggest that he involved himself in guiding the content of reports for influential purposes. The general impression of Waldheim's actions in this area is that he displayed a lack of interest in overseeing the report mechanism in a manner that would allow him to impart his own ideas. In addition, the text of the reports reinforced his managerial approach: "His reports accurately reflect his public life; he writes like a cautious man, and one is struck by his labored attempts to soften harsh criticism and judgment through qualifying words and phrases" (Ryan 2001, 16). Thus, when requested to produce reports, he produced straightforward accounts that did not seek to influence the debate at hand and steered clear of controversial wording.

Oversee finances

Ryan (2001, 21–24) emphasizes Waldheim's fiscal reform efforts to address the UN financial crisis that he inherited upon taking office, but across his tenure he generally showed limited concern for budgetary issues. Finger and Saltzman note, "He had little interest in or understanding of these areas [administration and finance]. George Sadler relates how he would provide Waldheim with a statement on program budgeting and explain it carefully, but it appeared to roll right off the secretary general's back" (1990, 76). While Waldheim called for the United Nations to undertake greater budgetary constraint, he did not work to guide the budgetary priorities. In addition, despite his own calls for UN fiscal responsibility, Waldheim often indulged himself while in office. For example, he carried out a costly decoration of the Secretary-General's official residence, kept expensive gifts for himself, and coveted a private plane. His lavish approach to the office did not go unnoticed: "Waldheim's predecessors were satisfied, without any harm being done to the job, with much more modest lifestyles . . . The Director of Finance at the United Nations still blushes with shame when he is reminded of it" (UN official quoted in Cohen and Rosenzweig 1987, 137).

Shape the administrative structure

Austrian representatives at the United Nations claimed that Waldheim "would give priority to a basic reorganization of the United Nations Secretariat" (Tanner 1971, 11), but he failed to address structural problems or to cultivate the Secretariat as a base for influence. His structural moves were designed not to increase his chances to influence policy, but to maintain member-state support. He did focus some initial effort on reorganizing the top positions closest to his office, but Ryan cites this as a missed opportunity to put an innovative administrative team in place because, instead, "Waldheim's appointments followed political lines that reflected the relative strengths of the great powers and voting blocs" (2001, 24). Later in his tenure, Waldheim was called on by the General Assembly to create a special Secretariat unit to address Palestinian rights. Waldheim would ordinarily avoid such a divisive topic, but he was required to address the situation due to the General Assembly request. However, he placed the unit "under the supervision of William Buffum, an American" in order to send "a signal to Washington that Waldheim himself did not want the unit to run amuck," thus ensuring that the Americans would not turn against him when he ran for re-election (Finger and Salzman 1990, 51).

Waldheim's behavior toward the Secretariat did not enhance his ability to use the administrative structure to support his position. His primary focus on remaining in office led him to largely ignore or mistreat lower-ranking Secretariat members, as they would not play a role in his re-election chances. Thomas Keel, an American labor negotiator hired by the UN staff union in the late 1970s, observes, "Waldheim would be a better international mediator if he'd eschew the role of ayatolla toward his own staff" (quoted in Finger and Saltzman 1990, 74). He rarely bothered to visit the lower floors of UN headquarters, reserving an elevator for his own use so that he could quickly reach his office without interacting with others, and generally "behaved like a creep" in relations with his staff (UN official quoted in Cohen and Rosenzweig 1987, 134). Waldheim's approach led to "corruption and demoralisation within the Secretariat" (Luard 1994, 112) and undermined the possible use of the Secretariat as a base for influence.

Staffing the Secretariat

Waldheim's power over appointments was not directed at placing people close to him in important positions, but as a method to seek member-state support. Instead of standing firm against pressure from governments to provide jobs for their nationals, he quickly gave in to such demands as he "tended to use them as a way of ingratiating himself with governments, like a politician building support through patronage" (Finger and Saltzman 1990, 73). For example, Waldheim once complained that he needed "a deputy of his own choosing," but was unwilling to request this because his choice would be a fellow West European and he thought that he could not resist pressures from the member-states for the Secretariat positions to reflect a particular regional balance (Buckley 1974, 109). The way that Waldheim distributed Secretariat positions based on political pressure instead of staff capabilities further damaged morale. In addition, relating to the administrative structure, he increased the number of positions in order to meet member-state demands for their nationals to be appointed, which led to a dangerously overstaffed Secretariat at a time when cuts were required.

Summary style comparison for administrative duties

Across all four administrative duties categories, Waldheim's behavior meshed closely with the managerial leadership style expectations. He did not attempt to insert his own views while supervising reports or overseeing the financial plan for the United Nations. Except for limited engagement in shifting senior positions, he also demonstrated little desire to undertake an organizational restructuring and political demands played a much greater part in determining the Secretariat setup as well as staff appointments.

STRATEGIC POLITICAL POSITION

Secretaries-General can use their influential strategic political position in two ways. First, they have their official duties of attending meetings. Here it is possible for Secretaries-General to offer up their ideas regarding how global security should be addressed. Second, since they operate at the nexus of administrative and political affairs, Secretaries-General have the opportunity to gather information and use informal contacts to stress their ideas. However, Waldheim did not take advantage of either of these opportunities for influence and instead allowed the member-states and their representatives at UN headquarters to dictate the agenda.

Representative in meetings

As chief administrative officer, Waldheim had the privilege of attending a range of UN meetings. However, there is little evidence to suggest that he pursued this as an avenue for influence. Instead of working to set the agenda or to frame how problems should be addressed, he deferred authority to the member-states. In relation to the Security Council, for example, Jackson observes, "Waldheim has interposed no objections to Soviet and French views expressed repeatedly in the Security Council that the Secretary-General work under the supervision of the Council in matters related to peace and security" (1978, 240). He did indicate concern with the Security Council moving into more secretive and informal consultations, claiming that this removed the educational function that more open meetings provided. However, related to the earlier discussion of Waldheim tying his own fate to that of the United Nations, "Clearly, Waldheim felt that if the Security Council hid its light too much under a bushel the UN's reputation would suffer—and so would his own" (Berridge 1991, 7).

Despite his managerial style, Waldheim is one of the few Secretaries-General to directly employ Article 99. In 1979, the American Embassy in Iran was stormed and those trapped inside were taken hostage. In what initially appeared to be a visionary move, Waldheim invoked Article 99 for the first time since Hammarskjöld, announcing to the press that he had sent a letter to the Security Council urging them to convene a meeting to deal with this threat to the peace. However, there has been much debate over how explicit this invocation was and whether it truly represented a statement of his desire to be at the forefront of efforts to address the crisis (Baehr and Gordenker 1994). Instead, it has been suggested that his use of Article 99 was a result of pressure from behind the scenes to get the Security Council engaged with the issue and Waldheim's desire for publicity made him more than willing to go along. As will be shown later, he did not have a plan for handling the hostage crisis, so there was no real basis to his initiative in terms of trying to influence what the Security Council should do about the matter.

In relation to the General Assembly, the manner in which Waldheim handled the infamous Resolution 3379 passed in November 1975, which equated Zionism with racism, is illustrative of his managerial tendencies. He did initially attempt to work to sidetrack the resolution. For example, he discussed the issue with the Iranian permanent representative and also called the shah of Iran trying to get them to remove the resolution. When these efforts did not have the desired effect, he did not take a public stance against the resolution. Thus, in discussing Waldheim's approach, several analysts conclude that, had there been a different type of Secretary-General in office—one who was bolder and more creative, it may have been possible to stop this divisive resolution from proceeding (Meisler 1995b; Boudreau 1991).

Inherent strategic position

Although operating from a strategic point within the United Nations, Waldheim did not seize this opportunity to influence member-state representatives. When not traveling, it is true that he was engaged in a range of meetings. Astrachan recounts, "His daily schedule is extended by ambassadors and foreign ministers anxious to cable home that they spent a half-hour discussing the way of the world with the secretary-general" (1974, 13). However, Waldheim did not appear to actively seek out such encounters and, more importantly, he seemed to welcome them primarily for the attention that he received instead of using the meetings to push for his own agenda. In fact, the member-state representatives took far greater advantage of the interactions to influence Waldheim and get information from him instead of the reverse.

Summary style comparison for strategic political position

Waldheim's managerial style is clearly displayed in his lack of use of the potentially influential strategic political position from which a Secretary-General operates. He did not use his strategic political position to press for his ideas on how to handle global security. Instead, Waldheim's record in this area reflects continual deference to the member-states and their representatives.

PUBLIC PRONOUNCEMENTS

Waldheim was very much involved in the activities captured in the public pronouncements category. At first glance, his efforts to encourage a high public profile appear puzzling because this does not match managerial expectations. Managers are expected to largely remain out of the limelight, quietly carrying out their duties. Yet, as Meisler observes, "Waldheim was an active secretary-general; he worked hard, traveled a good deal, communicated with leaders, strove for attention, and blathered to reporters even when he had nothing to say" (1995b, 199). As discussed earlier, however, this behavioral deviation makes sense in light of Waldheim's high need for recognition that is unusual for a manager. He enjoyed publicity and was committed to remaining in a high-status position, which led him to be involved in self-promotion, but, as the following discussion illustrates, his overriding managerial style still shines through in his subservient interactions with the member-states.

Annual report to the General Assembly

Waldheim's handling of the annual report confirms his managerial nature. He generally did not use the report to strongly influence how international peace and security issues should be addressed or to press for a greater role for his office. As Jackson reports, "Unlike Hammarskjold and Thant, Waldheim has not used the introduction to the Annual Report as a vehicle for the promulgation of a doctrine of activism on the part of the Secretary-General" as he preferred instead to give in to the primacy of the Security Council (1978, 240). Thus, overall Waldheim's annual report text provided a straightforward account that did not aim to guide the agenda.

Official representational activities

Although Waldheim did not make use of the influential capabilities of the annual report, he was greatly involved in representing the United Nations. While a manager would not be expected to strive to impress others with how important of an actor he is, Waldheim's behavior does fit with his high need for recognition. However, he did not use these situations to stress his opinion on matters as much as to revel in the spotlight and to make sure that he stayed in office. This meant maintaining a high profile on the international scene, but not presenting much of a message to go along with this presence. When participating in representational activities, he tried to impress others with his importance and enjoyed the attention he received, but did not take advantage of these opportunities to push his ideas.

Like Hammarskjöld, Waldheim often traveled: "The job, for him, seems synonymous with travel. From the first he was on the move and, apart from early September to late December (when the General Assembly is in annual session) he appears hardly to stop. No issue of the monthly *U.N. Chronicle* seems complete without a 'Secretary-General visits six countries' story" (James 1983, 85). While he claimed that he wanted to travel to meet those influencing the "destiny of the world," Finger and Saltzman point out that Waldheim was unable to provide insight into what the leaders who he met with were like (1990, 51). Instead, many analysts emphasize that one of Waldheim's primary attractions to travel was being in the limelight and the potential for pomp and ceremony in his honor. For example, Urquhart relates that Waldheim was invited to the 1973 Paris Conference on the Agreement of Ending the War and Restoring Peace in Vietnam, where he would play no real role and would instead serve as a "sop to international opinion," but he attended anyway simply because "Waldheim aspired to the presidency" (1987, 232) and the feeling of recognition that the event would provide.

When he traveled, Waldheim preferred to go to countries where he was well received. He was very methodical regarding proper protocol and the more he was to be honored the better. This led him to travel often to Africa, where he relished the way he was treated. A UN official notes that, compared to trips to Western Europe, where "the Secretary-General of the United Nations is received like any Minister of Foreign Affairs," he felt he was treated like a "king" in Africa, so he always "returned full of enthusiasm from each of his trips to Africa" (quoted in Cohen and Rosenzweig 1987, 135). Indicative of Waldheim's lack of real engagement in the issues of Africa, during a tour of the continent during a famine "he greeted a mother with a dying baby in her arms by telling her what a lovely child she had" (Bassett 1988, 118). Waldheim's appreciation of ostentatious events as a driving force behind his hectic travel schedule is reflected in his insistence on traveling in style. One interesting demonstration of this point is that he had toilet paper shipped in a diplomatic pouch from New York to London because he believed that the American paper was of better quality (Cohen and Rosenzweig 1987, 135).

Throughout his journeys, Waldheim maintained a cautious approach of not overstepping his bounds out of fear of angering the member-states. James relates, "Especially in view of the exacting nature of this schedule, it would not have been hard even for a skilled diplomat sometimes to give inadvertent offence . . . But this kind of blunder has been very exceptional" (1983, 85). This reflects the fact that, along with the ceremonial advantages, the constant necessities of the re-election campaign seemed to both guide and limit the impact of much of Waldheim's travels. From his first days in office, Waldheim used his ability to travel for self-serving purposes. For example, since China was the only country to oppose his 1971 election—out of a desire for a Secretary-General from a developing country—he quickly traveled to China after his election to bolster his position. He traveled back to China and elsewhere across the globe to secure his re-election chances in 1976 and his "travel program for 1981 left no doubts that he was hell-bent on running for a third term" (Urquhart 1981, 331)—including visits to all five Security Council permanent members.

Overall, Waldheim's travels, while relatively effective for reinforcing his desire for recognition and re-election, were not designed to place him at the right locations to be influential in handling crises. His trips often kept him away from the United Nations and at destinations that he found more personally gratifying or politically advantageous instead of related to influential opportunities. His cautious use of the travel mechanism does not mean that he was precluded from involvement in matters of peace and security: "Waldheim's ability to exercise his good offices does seem to have been assisted by the fact that, partly in consequence of indefatigable traveling, he is generally thought to be reliable. Unexciting, maybe, but reliable" (James 1983, 86). However, as James' observation emphasizes, Waldheim was called upon due to a reputation for quiet consistency and not stressing his own vision.

This point also comes across clearly when Waldheim's record is reviewed for evidence of challenging member-states in his public statements. To an overwhelming degree he stuck to his managerial role and did not speak out against state interests. Even when he would take a stance, Waldheim would quickly back down in the face of state intransigence. Ryan notes that after Waldheim's "early essays at diplomatic leadership earned him a variety of rebukes . . . he recognized that he was safest articulating positions supported by UN consensus" (2001, 32–33). One evaluation of his time in office concludes, "Waldheim was safe. He did not hector. He was nervous about offending members and conflicted with governments only three times" (Armstrong, Lloyd, and Redmond 1996, 110). This point is mirrored by Jackson who relates the same three public stances that "placed him in direct confrontation with governments": the 1972 condemnation of the United States bombing of North Vietnamese dikes, pushing for terrorism to be placed on the 1972 General Assembly agenda, and calling for a cease-fire for Lebanon along with opposing any partition of the state in 1976 (1978, 242). Such limited engagement in challenging the handling of breaches of the peace stands in stark contrast to the high number of directed pronouncements issued by Hammarskjöld and, as detailed in the following chapter, Annan.

Regarding his concern for the 1972 bombings, despite being cited as one of the few clear examples of Waldheim challenging a major power, the statement itself was not all that bold, but rather "a discreet enough statement, as befits a discreet man" (Viorst 1972, 39). The incident has probably garnered more attention based on a strong rebuttal from President Nixon. More importantly, after his stance was rebuffed by Nixon, Waldheim "did not further provoke the great powers," reflecting his "extreme receptivity to national pressures" (Hazzard 1990, 89). Waldheim is credited with the push in 1972 to place terrorism on the General Assembly agenda due to the slaughter of Israeli athletes at the Olympics in Munich, although this only came after a request from West German government officials. He abandoned this effort when Arab and Soviet bloc members expressed their disapproval.

Waldheim did initiate strong public appeals regarding the need to address the conflict in Lebanon. He also called the 1976 Israeli raids on Entebbe a violation of Ugandan sovereignty, but after Israel berated him, he backed away and emphasized "that he was satisfied with the fact that the operation had enabled 104 lives to be saved" (Cohen and Rosenzweig 1987, 126) and generally "said little while the world watched and agonized over Entebbe" (Ryan 2001, 78). Reflecting his equal opportunity sensitivity, Waldheim was also hesitant to support the 1978 Egypt-Israel peace initiative due to the objections of the Soviet and Arab members. Finally, James points out that Waldheim did openly challenge the member-states at the end of his tenure, when he criticized the 1981 Israeli bombing of an Iraqi nuclear reactor, "although here too, given the nature of the act and the identity of the perpetrator, he was on safe ground" (1983, 85).

"Unofficial" representational activities

When dealing with the media, because Waldheim was rarely willing to commit himself to a strong public stance on matters of international peace and security out of fear of offending a particular country, his public performances lacked substance. The publicity mattered more than the message, but this approach failed to win him much support among members of the press. In fact, "[p]erhaps Waldheim's biggest frustration, other than failing to win a third term as secretary general, was his inability to woo the media successfully," even though "[h]e paid great attention to his public image and was always ready to talk to reporters" (Finger and Saltzman 1990, 76). Waldheim held himself up in comparison to Hammarskjöld's prestigious standing and became disheartened that he could not cultivate a similar image. In the end,

> Waldheim worried a great deal about his public image, but his efforts to tackle this problem usually made things worse. He was too anxious to be given credit and tended to be too accessible to the media. He

frequently had to resort to cliches and to bland, noncommittal statements which bored the press. His manner sometimes seemed ingratiating, and he tried too hard with too little to say. (Urquhart 1987, 229)

Although Waldheim's public pronouncements did not earn much press interest or respect, many of the member-states liked what they heard. Despite the fact that he claimed upon his election, "I can tell you right now that I have concrete and firm ideas about the office of the Secretary General and how I am going to deal with it. The United Nations has to be used as an instrument of peace," (quoted in Tanner 1971, 11) he rarely spoke out in a manner that challenged state predominance over international affairs. Instead, as James relates:

> For in his many speeches Waldheim made it abundantly clear that his picture of the world was and remained basically that of the foreign offices of the member States. He was quick off the mark in reminding audiences that the United Nations was not a super-State and that what it could do was limited to what its members could agree upon. He spoke of the Security Council as a safety valve; he urged a pragmatic approach to the United Nations work; he encouraged quiet diplomacy. All this could not but have had the members nodding in approval. (1983, 83)

This stands in stark contrast to Hammarskjöld's use of public pronouncements to push for a greater role for the United Nations and his office.

Summary style comparison for public pronouncements
Linked to his high need for recognition, Waldheim did want to maintain a high profile and sought much publicity, so he used public pronouncements to a greater degree during his tenure than one would expect from a manager. However, truer to his managerial nature, his public pronouncements lacked an influential message and were crafted to avoid challenging the authority and policies of the member-states. On the few occasions where he was critical, he backed down if the member-states expressed displeasure with his comments. While he traveled extensively, his trips were not used for influential means, but were instead guided by his drive for re-election and the degree of recognition that he might receive. Newman summarizes Waldheim's method well when he states, "Kurt Waldheim's approach to the job was high profile but also low key: he was very visible but avoided confrontation with member states and did not use his visibility as leverage to apply pressure upon states" (1998, 52).

PEACEFUL SETTLEMENT OF DISPUTES:
CAUTIOUS USE OF THE LIMELIGHT

Waldheim's record in relation to peacefully resolving breaches of the peace reinforces his managerial approach to the office. This section demonstrates that although he did become actively engaged in working on resolving some conflicts, he undertook a relatively limited number of missions on his own initiative and primarily relied on being assigned a mission before acting. Once engaged in a peaceful settlement effort, he was careful to keep his activities within parameters accepted by the member-states and his efforts were often only "symbolic" (Nachmias 1993, 122). When faced with sensitive security issues he backed down if confronted and he did not seek to take actions that deeply challenged the member-states. While Ryan's analysis details a range of engagements by the Secretary-General in the area of peace and security, he is careful to note that Waldheim was "relentlessly reluctant to act" out of a concern that his actions would undermine member-state support, so his diplomatic efforts generally reflected a "trimming [of] his sails to the will of the majority" (2001, 118, 33).

INDEPENDENTLY INITIATED

Although the closest the United Nations has had to an ideal manager, Jackson explains, "As Secretary-General, Waldheim has not refrained entirely from attempting to play a conflict management role on his own initiative; some important examples of activism do appear on his record" (1978, 241). To support this claim, Jackson cites Waldheim's initiatives toward Vietnam, Ulster, and Korea in the early 1970s, and Lebanon in 1976. Similarly, James argues, "Waldheim has made it clear that if the Council is stymied he will see if he can move things forward" and that "occasionally he has tried to prod the Council into action" (1983, 86). Further examples of such actions, beyond the aforementioned, include personal engagement in the Middle East in the 1970s and limited initiatives in regards to the Pakistan-India conflict.

Despite these instances, in examining Waldheim's independent efforts it becomes clear that there were definite limits to his willingness to undertake such initiatives or to carry out certain missions. For example, Waldheim backed off from his involvement in the Middle East in 1977 when U.S. Secretary of State Cyrus Vance stressed to him that any such actions should be run by the Americans first. Another example is the limited engagement in Africa. This was certainly not due to a lack of insecurity in the region. Some analysts claim that Waldheim was unable address African conflicts despite a desire to do so:

> Waldheim's efforts to alleviate conflict in such areas were stymied because these conflicts were a result of historical forces, exploited by external factors which prolonged and exacerbated them . . . In this context there was little role for the UN or Waldheim in Angola . . . The Horn of Africa . . . was outside the realm of Waldheim's influence. (Newman 1998, 60)

However, a more likely scenario, given Waldheim's personal predilections, is that he was concerned about the ramifications of getting involved in such a politically difficult area. Thus, it was not that the Secretary-General could not act, but that he did not want to act due to the superpower dynamics involved. In addition, he did not want to go against the wishes of the African states, which were not enthusiastic on the whole about the United Nations becoming involved in their affairs at this point. As Meisler notes, "Waldheim was so intent on pleasing African countries that he rarely brought their problems to the U.N." (1995b, 200).

Waldheim was more involved in efforts to resolve the conflict in Cyprus. Jackson argues, "Waldheim's most important involvement as a mediator has been in Cyprus," where he displayed "considerable energy" (1978, 238, 240). While Waldheim did bring the parties together for negotiations, these were largely unsuccessful and did little to enhance his position. Many important negotiations took place outside of the UN setting. In addition, it is important to note that he was more willing to take action and to become directly involved in Cyprus than other areas where he faced a much greater chance of angering the great powers. Nitza Nachmias compares the role of the Secretary-General in Cyprus and the Middle East and concludes for Waldheim: "This could, perhaps, explain why he was more involved in the Cyprus dispute than in the Arab-Israeli conflict, which was in the thick of superpower jousting in the Middle East" (1993, 125).

Another area that merits close attention is the American hostage crisis in Iran in 1979. As mentioned earlier, Waldheim did call for the Security Council to take action on this matter. However, although Waldheim invoked Article 99, he had little success getting the Iranians to attend the Security Council meetings. Without Iranian participation, Waldheim was stuck because "he had no real plan or program to recommend . . . and his initiative was simply lost in subsequent events" (Boudreau 1991, 78). Even more telling, the Secretary-General had to subsequently be coerced by the Americans to travel to Teheran. In Iran, he did not manage to talk with anyone in an influential position and was even chased at one point by an angry Iranian mob, barely escaping unharmed. The way that he handled the crisis revealed his managerial nature, so "[a]t the end of it all he was blamed for timidity" (Urquhart 1987, 324). According to Gertrude Samuels, the handling of the hostage situation presents a clear contrast between the styles of Hammarskjöld and Waldheim. She notes that, considering how Hammarskjöld worked to resolve the American airmen being held hostage in China, "observers here have been wondering whether his [Waldheim's] style is not one reason the Iranian crisis is still with us" (1979, 4).

MANDATED ASSIGNMENTS

The above discussion focused on independently initiated exercises, which Waldheim pursued to a relatively limited degree and with a series of qualifications regarding how truly independent he was willing to be. However, these activities were more the exception than the rule and most of Waldheim's problem-solving activities relied on a mandate:

> Waldheim has not displayed a tendency to undertake conflict manage-
> ment responsibilities without the prior approval of the Security Council
> or General Assembly . . . Generally, Waldheim's conflict management
> missions have been undertaken at the request of the Security Council,
> or in some cases, the Assembly . . . [so] the dependence of the
> Secretary-General's role as a conflict manager on the political organs of
> the U.N. has become increasingly apparent. (Jackson 1978, 240)

This fits with Waldheim's belief that "the secretary-general should negotiate only at the request of the parties to the dispute. Nothing is worse, and nothing would be less wise, than for him to force himself upon a situation" (quoted in Newman 1998, 52). Thus, while Waldheim "was very keen on playing a personal role" in several conflicts, he waited for the principal organs to grant him the opportunity to be involved (Narasimhan 1988, 290). Once engaged, he maintained a strict awareness of the political desires of the member-states and was sure not to stray from the bounds of the mandated assignment.

SUMMARY STYLE COMPARISON FOR PEACEFUL
SETTLEMENT OF DISPUTES

A review of Waldheim's handling of peaceful settlement of disputes shows that he maintained a managerial stance in relation to the member-states. While he was more engaged in independent initiatives than one might expect for an ideal manager, he primarily waited for others to set mandated missions, to guide these mandated efforts, and he carefully limited the forcefulness of any independent or mandated efforts to make sure that he had not "overstepped the limits of accept-able action" (James 1983, 87). Overall, he relied primarily on the guidance of states to determine where and how he should act and was not proactive in seeking chances to provide input on how mandated missions should be carried out or, for the most part, in initiating independent efforts.

UN INTERVENTION: ON THE SIDELINES

For UN intervention, Waldheim's managerial approach again held true to form. During his time in office three peacekeeping operations were established, all in the Middle East. The Second United Nations Emergency Force (UNEF II) both started and ended during his tenure. After the Egyptian request for the withdrawal of the first UNEF operation, the Middle East was beset by war in 1967 and once again in 1973 before the United Nations was able to get UNEF II in place that year. This mission was ended following the peace agreement between Egypt and Israel in 1979. The United Nations Disengagement Observer Force (UNDOF) for the Golan Heights and the United Nations Interim Force in Lebanon (UNIFIL) began in 1974 and 1978 respectively and still supply a buffer zone of separation between these areas and Israel.

Although Secretaries-General cannot independently create a UN force to intervene in an insecure area, they can attempt to influence the development or makeup of such a mission. In Waldheim's case, he was far from the heart of the three peacekeeping operations created under his watch. UNEF II and UNDOF "were largely Kissinger cre-ations" set up with a serious "lack of U.N. input" and UNIFIL "also came out of American diplomacy" instead of at the prompting of the Secretary-General (Meisler 1995b, 198–199). In addition, Waidheim did not push for involvement in regions outside of the Middle East that also could have employed UN forces to help stabilize the situation.

The lack of involvement in shaping UN peacekeeping operations leads Newman to bluntly state, "Waldheim was a tool of Kissinger, not the United Nations" (1998, 55). This was seen in the degree of lati-tude that the Americans possessed in relation to UN peacekeeping missions during Waldheim's time in office. For example, UNEF II was set up following the October 1973 war in the Middle East, but Waldheim allowed the Americans, who wanted to wait until the military situation met their interests instead of issuing an immediate cease-fire, to dictate the timing of UN involvement. In regards to the mandate itself, Kissinger stressed that "our draft finessed the issue of UN auspices by language that could be interpreted as confining the United Nations to convening the conference, not running it; the Secretary-General's participation was expressly limited to the opening phase" (quoted in Newman 1998, 56). Once Waldheim had been used for United States' purposes he was set aside. Nachmias' examination of Waldheim's handling of UNEF II concurs, "Ending the October 1973 Yom Kippur War was essentially a superpower undertaking, and the ensuing peace negotiations were primarily dominated by Secretary of State Henry Kissinger," including the official peace conference at Geneva where Waldheim did not play a significant role (1993, 121–122).

While the shuttle diplomacy used to set up UNDOF "was an extraordinary feat of ingenuity, endurance, and persistence on Kissinger's part," once again Kissinger was the driving force with Waldheim primarily watching from the sidelines (Urquhart 1987, 249). The creation of UNIFIL was also driven by the Americans, with Waldheim accepting rather than shaping the mandate. This caused many operational difficulties because the wording of the mandate did not address underlying differences among members of the Security Council, leaving Waldheim with ambiguous instructions.

In carrying out these peacekeeping operations, Waldheim did not display any drive to use the situation as a platform for influence. His approach centered on catering to the views of the powerful members and making compromises to ensure that no member-state was dissatisfied with his handling of peacekeeping. With the establishment of UNDOF, Waldheim took charge of running the operation: "However, the diplomatic initiative remained in Washington, overshadowing any efforts by the United Nations or the Secretary-General," so his control remained mostly limited to basic administrative details (Nachmias 1993, 122–123). He did travel to Syria in association with the UNDOF mission, but this was simply an ongoing part of the need to renew the mission every six months. In administering UNIFIL, Waldheim was better able to carry "significant authority both locally and in New York with respect to operational peacekeeping matters"; however, "this was largely the result of US pressure," so once again the United States was the primary influential force guiding the mission (Newman 1998, 59). In addition, Waldheim is not noted for having extended the idea of peacekeeping in any meaningful fashion in relation to new or existing missions.

SUMMARY STYLE COMPARISON FOR
UN INTERVENTION

Waldheim was on the sidelines for both the development and implementation of UN peacekeeping operations. He was not engaged in the mandate formulation process and, when running the operations, he did not deviate from his mandated instructions. Thus, for both the creation and the implementation stages of UN intervention, Waldheim maintained a managerial pattern of behavior.

CONCLUSION

As the evidence presented in this chapter illustrates, Waldheim maintained a managerial role as Secretary-General. Instead of making use of the various influential activities available to him in the Secretary-General's toolbox, he acted more as a tool of the member-states. While observers debate the merits of Waldheim's approach, they all agree that he rarely challenged the prerogatives of other actors in the international arena. The opposite held true as he sought to accommodate their wishes in how he ran the operations of the United Nations. As with the visionary Hammarskjöld, these findings confirm the leadership style behavioral expectations. Waldheim's personal characteristics predisposed him to behave in a managerial fashion and, for the vast majority of the time, this is how he handled the office.

The greatest deviation from the managerial style prototype is Waldheim's unusually high need for recognition. However, as the analysis in this chapter has shown, this trait combined with other personal characteristics in a manner that often reinforced his managerial nature. This is shown in the first two sections of the chapter, which detailed Waldheim's background and set the tone for his time as Secretary-General. His desire for the high level of recognition that the Secretary-Generalship would provide drove him to arduously campaign for the office. However, he carefully built each of his campaigns on a managerial platform. The member-states wanted and received a manager in Waldheim and continued to support his re-election efforts based on his managerial record. Similarly, while there has been concern expressed that Waldheim's Nazi past could have been used to pressure him into managerial subservience as Secretary-General, his equal opportunity responsiveness reflected his character. The Nazi historical evidence is important, however, in a different way because it illustrates how Waldheim was willing to do whatever the power in control desired in order to maintain his career.

For his tenure as Secretary-General, Waldheim entered and left with a managerial reputation. He was an agenda implementer, carrying out the instructions of the principal organs instead of attempting to dictate the path of the United Nations. While his aberrant level of need for recognition meant that Waldheim was more involved in voluntary activities, especially in the degree to which he sought media attention and maintained a hectic travel schedule, these activities were mostly hollow. He rarely had a message to provide during these efforts. Instead of pushing for a particular agenda, Waldheim was primarily using these activities to bolster his level of recognition and to ensure his re-election chances. The few contradictory public stances that he took were rebuffed and he responded by downplaying or rescinding his position to placate the complaints of the member-states.

In addition, the Waldheim case illustrates that just because a Secretary-General has a managerial style does not mean that this individual will be a particularly engaged administrator. This questions the idea that unwillingness to challenge member-state prerogatives will translate into attentiveness and efficiency in the administrative realm. With Waldheim, the desire to please led him to cave to state demands in personnel matters. The lesson is that with a manager in office the member-states will largely get what they want, but because this often involves conflicting national interests this does not necessarily translate into an efficiently run organization.

Waldheim also displayed a managerial style in his handling of military interventions by the United Nations. He was not very involved in shaping the mandates of the three peacekeeping operations established while he was in office, leaving much of this effort to Kissinger and the United States. In carrying out peacekeeping mandates, Waldheim provided basic administrative guidance, but did not work to push the boundaries of the missions or to expand his level of influence in the Middle East based on his position running the peacekeeping operations.

Waldheim did not adhere as closely to the managerial Secretary-General expectations in relation to the peaceful settlement of disputes. He was more independently involved in a range of conflict areas than would have been predicted for an ideal manager. His nonmanagerial need for recognition could have pushed him to take advantage of the chances to become enmeshed in these activities that were provided. However, it is vital to recognize that Waldheim's involvement is only striking relative to expectations for a manager and that it was rare for him to independently address a breach of the peace or to try to shape the mandated response. For the great majority of situations, he relied on the mandate of the principal organs to guide where and how he would intervene. In addition, when he did employ these tools, he maintained a very cautious approach and quickly backed away when his activities were challenged.

Overall, Waldheim retained a managerial approach to his involvement in international peace and security. He stressed the predominant place for the member-states in both setting policy and in resolving disruptions of the peace. He was willing to play a role, but primarily only when he was called upon to act. This stands in stark contrast to the visionary approach to the office undertaken by Hammarskjöld. The next chapter presents the final case study to explore whether Annan's behavior also matches his leadership style.

CHAPTER 6

The Strategist: Kofi Annan

The degree of the Secretary-General's involvement will depend to a great extent on his personality and attitude. He can be an interventionist, as Hammarskjöld and Boutros Boutros-Ghali were, or at the other extreme, as in the cases of Kurt Waldheim and Perez de Cuellar, can largely remove himself from day-to-day command and management of operations. The attitude of the current Secretary-General, Kofi Annan, appears to fall somewhere between these two extremes.

(Findlay 2002, 10)

INTRODUCTION

Now that the visionary leadership of Hammarskjöld and the managerial behavior of Waldheim have been detailed, this chapter turns to the only Secretary-General whose content analysis coding results indicate a strategic leadership style, Kofi Annan. A strategist such as Annan should represent a balanced mix between what was observed for Hammarskjöld and Waldheim, but exploring this is somewhat more complicated than in the previous two cases. Part of the difficulty comes from addressing a Secretary-General who is, at the time of writing in December 2005, still in office. The material presented in this chapter thus lacks the historical hindsight available when detailing the actions of Hammarskjöld and Waldheim. The great highs and lows Annan has faced since taking over the office at the beginning of 1997 add to the complexity of the analysis. He was lauded early in his tenure, receiving an early re-election to a second term in June 2001 and a wide range of awards—including joining Hammarskjöld as a Nobel Peace Prize winner later that year. By 2004, stung in particular by accusations of corruption in relation to the Iraq oil-for-food program, Annan had endured what he referred to as an "annus horribilus" and 2005 proved equally trying, to the point where it was questioned whether he would even manage to serve out the remainder of his second term. However, as in the previous cases, this analysis is not looking to pass judgment on Annan's time as Secretary-General. Instead the emphasis is on tracking the connection between his strategic leadership style and how he handled avenues of influence in the area of international peace and security.

The chapter opens by discussing Annan's background as a lifetime Secretariat member, and the related election expectations, which set the stage for his ascension to the Secretary-Generalship. This is followed by a discussion of how others describe Annan's personal characteristics and overarching strategic style, which reinforces the content analysis coding results. The second part of the chapter shifts to an investigation of Annan's time as Secretary-General. The analysis begins by discussing his behavior in general and then moves into a specific examination across the different behavioral categories established in chapter 3. These sections provide evidence that supports the link between Annan's leadership style and his corresponding strategic behavior.

ANNAN: BACKGROUND AND STYLE OVERVIEW

THE ELECTION: RISING FROM WITHIN

While Hammarskjöld and Waldheim transitioned from serving their respective countries to the Secretary-Generalship, Annan rose up through the ranks of the UN bureaucracy—the first office-holder to do so. Annan started with an administrative position in the World Health Organization in 1962 and moved up the ladder, ascending to the head of the United Nations 35 years later. Along the way he worked in a myriad of positions within the United Nations, taking only a brief respite in the mid-1970s for two years to return to Ghana to direct efforts to develop tourism in his home country, and most recently before taking office he served as Under Secretary-General for Peacekeeping Operations.

Since the embattled Boutros-Ghali was the first Secretary-General not to serve a second term, when it came time to choose a replacement in 1996 the search focused on African candidates because it was the region's unofficial turn to hold the post for another five-year period. As usual, power politics played a large part in the selection process. France was particularly active in demanding that the Secretary-General should be a French-speaking African. China also made it clear that a potential candidate from Senegal was not acceptable because his home country had recently established diplomatic relations with Taiwan. After using their veto power to prevent a second term for Boutros-Ghali, the United States also continued to be very active in the selection process. The political differences obfuscated discussion of what personal capabilities the candidates would bring to the office. Matthew Jallow and Opa Ramba comment, "On the final day of the selection process, the air between the French and the Americans was thick with the rejection of each other's choices, thus relegating the qualification of candidates to the background" (1997, 13). Unlike the Americans, who refused to back away from their veto of Boutros-Ghali despite a 14–1 vote, the French finally gave in regarding Annan's selection.

During the selection struggle, the United States often claimed to be open to a range of African candidates, but their "behind-the-scenes manoeuvres" were viewed by some as "bullying tactics" to press for Annan (Ankomah 1997, 36). Boutros-Ghali provides his perspective on the effort to replace him:

> The Clinton administration mentioned no one, apparently fearing its choice would be regarded as America's handpicked puppet. Inside the United Nations, however, everyone knew that the United States candidate was Kofi Annan of Ghana . . . As December began, the African position began to waver. Even as the United States continued to profess a willingness to see any African other than me as secretary-general, it encouraged Ghana to begin openly to promote the U.S. choice, Kofi Annan. (1999, 298, 322)

Annan was a "known quantity" to the Americans from his time in the United Nations (Rieff 1999, 20). In particular, he had recently served as a special representative for Boutros-Ghali to the former Yugoslavia and his careful handling of the situation may have helped him to win him the Secretary-Generalship (Holbrooke 1998). The irony of this occurring is explained by James Traub: "In fact, it was widely believed inside the U.N. that Boutros-Ghali had sent Annan to Yugoslavia in 1995 in the hope of removing a potential competitor as he sought renomination. He wound end up giving his rival a new stage" (1998, 47).

A core aspect of Annan's "known quantity" was the expectation that he would be a less visible and independently active Secretary-General than Boutros-Ghali. The Americans were willing to elevate Annan to the Secretary-Generalship "because he appeared suited to effecting a low profile stewardship of the UN organisation; someone, above all, who would work better as a manager of the institution and not a maker of diplomatic waves . . . As some observers put it at the time, Annan promised to be more secretary than general" (Usborne 1998, 5). Once again, the hope was for a Secretary-General who would be willing to limit his activities and act according to member-state dictates.

Given such political maneuverings and American backing, many believed that Annan would operate as a manager and, potentially, as a puppet of the United States. In a typical statement, one report observes, "A UN official for 30 years, he seemed a gifted bureaucrat, administrator, and diplomat, though not a leader" (Black 1998, 5). However, Annan has not proven to be a manager committed to the whims of the superpower, but instead a Secretary-General with his own mind, albeit one with a constant eye out for the approval or dis-approval of the member-states. To better understand why Annan con-founded the initial managerial predictions, one must turn to his leadership style. His behavior is understandable in light of the content analysis results that indicate he does not possess a managerial leader-ship style, but is instead a strategist.

ANNAN'S STRATEGIC STYLE

As the first Secretary-General to possess a strategic leadership style, it is not surprising that analysts have commented on the divergence between Annan and the previous office-holders. Headlines describing his selection such as "Annan to Bring Change of Style to World Body: Soft-Spoken Bureaucrat is Pragmatic, Well-Liked" (Goshko 1996) highlight the perceived difference. Comments along the lines of Paula Span's "He is in many ways a different character from his predeces-sors," (1998, C1) are also common. Annan is often specifically compared with his immediate predecessor and he has been called the "living opposite of Boutros-Ghali" due to their contrasting styles (Traub 1998, 47). In comparisons that reflect Annan's strategic style, other observers also focus on Boutros-Ghali's arrogance, aloof-ness, contentiousness, and forceful independence versus Annan's mod-esty, accessibility, restraint, and conciliatory skills (e.g., see Crossette 1996; Fröhlich 1997; Meisler 2003; Rieff 1999; Schmemann 2001; Steele 1996; Stewart 1998; Turner 1996; and Williams 1997, 2000).

Annan is often referred to as possessing a "cautious style." For example, Thomas Omestad and Linda Fasulo write, "Avoiding mis-takes and showing respect to everyone have been the hallmarks for Annan's exceptionally cautious style" (1998, 36), and an editorial in the *New York Times* ran with the headline "Kofi Annan's Cautious Style" (1997, A24). Great patience and self-restraint are often mentioned as key aspects of this cautious style. As one report details,

> The first epithet that comes to mind with Kofi Annan is "dignified." There is an unruffled quality to him and everything he does . . . Even when critical he is the epitome of politeness. Never does he lose his cool. A slight shifting of weight from one foot to the other, perhaps, in a moment of high strain, an aide reports, "that's about all the tension you can see." (Cornwell 1998, 3)

Those who have known Annan for a long time echo these sentiments. One colleague, who met Annan in 1965, claims that Annan is always "sober and measured" (Assfaw 1997, 4). In fact, the "rare sightings" of Annan's subtle signs of frustration "tend to be mentioned with proprietary pride, as evidence of the speaker's inside position" (Gourevitch 2003, 61).

With such a "calm and unruffled style of leadership" (de Breadun 2001, 14), Annan is portrayed as willing to sit back and react to circumstances rather than being goaded into action. Instead of seeking the immediate gratification of a bold action, he is described as preferring a great deal of forethought and consultation. Lamin Sise, a colleague of Annan's, comments, "His style is very open, very inclusive. And he is that way with everyone" (quoted in Meisler 2003, 33–34). Overall, he wants to build toward a solid conclusion through carefully considered planning, which is indicative of his "qualities of a long-distance runner with an eye on the distant goal" (Crossette 1998a, 5).

Some question whether Annan's style goes too far in this direction to the detriment of a clearer desire to take decisive action. He is often referred to as "too nice," the implication being that this will lead to him being too compliant, or managerial, as Secretary-General. For example, a profile of Annan notes, "The main charge against him is that he is too nice, and will be too accommodating . . . a kind of 'super-clerk' rather than the strong independent figure needed" (Steele 1996, 4). One diplomat asserts that "Kofi is conflict-averse in all his personal relationships and perhaps more broadly. There's a danger of allowing things to slide because they may involve conflict" (quoted in Traub 1998, 47). Others wonder whether an active United Nations is possible when a Secretary-General with a "quiet, incremental style" is in charge (Handelman 1996, A19) or whether Annan has the "boldness and imagination to lead" (Goshko 1996, A22).

However, Razali Ismail, the Malaysian ambassador to the United Nations and president of the General Assembly when Annan took office, argues, "The appointment of Mr. Kofi Annan as secretary-general may prove to be a watershed for the United Nations" since he has the "style to invigorate the U.N." (1997, 64). This position is echoed by others who point out that, while Annan is a patient and caring individual, he also possesses an underlying strength that separates him from those only willing to act as an acquiescent clerk. For example, one observer claims that it is important not to confuse "Annan's personal amenability with a malleability of principles" (Williams 1997, 22), while another analysis notes, "Under Annan's quiet, soft-spoken demeanor lies a steely determination" (Marquardt and Berger 2000, 65). Annan himself has reacted against the notion that he is too self-restrained and feels that his "studied, low-key style" is not a liability because confrontation is often not necessary to achieve one's goals (Sciolino 1997, 6).

STRATEGIC ALIGNMENT OF PERSONAL CHARACTERISTICS

The previous section established how observers describe Annan's over-arching style in strategic terms. Accounts of his personal characteristics similarly mesh with the content analysis results. To begin with, Annan's score for responsivity is the highest of the seven Secretaries-General and this is a major aspect of his style upon which observers often comment. He is noted as a strong believer in the need to listen to different views and monitor situational cues before settling on a plan of action. For example, Omestad and Fasulo indicate that one of Annan's "lifelong traits" is his "obsession with consultation" (1998, 36). This is supported by one of Annan's professors, and adviser for the debate team, at Macalester College: "He never took a strong, confrontational position before he sought out the other person's viewpoint" (Span 1998, C1). An important part of this responsive nature is his desire to establish consensus on the best way to proceed. In one report, a colleague describes Annan as possessing "instinct . . . to avoid confrontation and seek consensus" (quoted in Cornwell 1998, 3).

Along with sensitivity, responsivity also reflects an important analytical capability component. In this respect, Annan's character is described as combining "attentiveness" with "clarity" (Traub 1998, 50) and the ability to be "patient" yet "wise" (Assfaw 1997, 6) in combination with recognizing "the importance of seeing and understanding the larger picture" (Tessitore 2000, 28). Further along these lines, Annan is noted for his capacity to read a situation with an "almost Zenlike evenhandedness, this ability to see the parts and the whole at the same time" (Bogert 1996, 30). He has also been described as possessing a "keen intellect" (Marquardt and Berger 2000, 63) and a "preternatural instinct" for determining the correct thing to say or do (Maniatis 2001, 45).

Annan also displays a clear need for relationships, a trait on which he scores second highest of all the Secretaries-General. He is noted for his "excellent interpersonal skills" (Fasulo 2004, 19), possessing "legendary geniality" (Steele 1996, 4), and is "widely viewed as amiable with a natural affinity for people" (Forster 1998, 22). When asked how Annan "is establishing his personality within the Organization," Shashi Tharoor, a close aide of the Secretary-General, responded, "He comes across as the person he is—somebody who is warm, who is accessible, who is compassionate, who engages with people on issues directly, who is absolutely on his image" (1999, 9). In the end, as one of the his friends explains, "If Kofi weren't secretary general, you'd call him up and go out for a beer and have a great time" (quoted in Span 1998, C1).

However, as a former colleague notes, "Kofi gets on with everyone, so he won't get on with any thing" (quoted in Mortimer and Lambert 1997, 19). This observation reflects Annan's low emphasis on task completion. When Annan pursues solutions to problems he displays "a draining sensitivity to the moods and psychic needs of others" (Traub 1998, 71) and a deep sense of "compassion" (Ramo 2000, 40). He believes that it is very important to take time to consider the interpersonal needs of others. In addition, virtually every analysis describes Annan as "soft-spoken," both literally and figuratively. One interviewing experience illustrates Annan's speaking style and demeanor:

> Annan is so soft-spoken that though we were sitting next to each other on a couch in his wood-paneled office, I later found that I could barely hear his voice on my tape recorder. He has an elegance that comes less from dress than from equipoise; he barely moves when he speaks, and he never hurries either a gesture or a word. (Traub 1998, 48)

Annan's style of speech matches his temperament, where he is "ever-polite" (Brennock 1999, 10). This relaxed approach translates into a relatively low drive for task accomplishment and greater concern for the feelings of others.

Annan's low emphasis on task completion is a slight deviation from the strategic personal characteristic expectations. A strategist is supposed to possess a balance between a focus on task completion and concern for interpersonal issues, as indicated by a medium level of problem-solving emphasis in table 2.2. In other words, while strategists are not supposed to be as driven to complete tasks at the risk of alienating those they work with, they are supposed to balance wanting to get the job done with the sensitivities of those involved. Annan's low score raises the question of whether he is able to stay focused on the task at hand without being distracted by interpersonal concerns. Given this aberration from the ideal strategic style, it may be that Annan should be thought of as an "interpersonal strategist." Although he matches with the strategic style requirements for all other personal traits, his style may reflect a greater emphasis on interpersonal concerns than one would expect from an ideal strategist.

Annan's low problem-solving emphasis is balanced by a high belief in his ability to have influence, a trait on which he has the highest score out of all of the Secretaries-General. As one observer states, "[N]ever mistake Mr. Annan's gentleness for evasiveness or fear" (Cornwell 1998, 3). Instead, he is recognized as possessing the "courage" (Ramo 2000, 40) to take "decisive action" (Williams 2000, 22). As "above all, an optimist" (Gourevitch 2003, 53), he perceives himself as capable of undertaking actions and does not like to hear pessimistic evaluations of his ability to handle problems. Instead, Annan insists on focusing on the positive possibilities of a situation as part of his personal motivation and belief in ability to make a difference (Tessitore 2000, 55; Traub 1998, 49).

Supranationalism is clearly engrained into Annan's character. He is noted for possessing a "fundamental commitment" to handling international issues on a multilateral basis (Williams 1997, 23). The content analysis results indicate that Annan possesses a similar level of supranationalism as Hammarskjöld, and Annan has cited his predecessor's statement: "it is a question not of a man, but of an institution" as reflecting his own philosophy. William Shawcross supports this claim, noting that Annan "has come to personify . . . the United Nations and its ideals," and displays a "quasi-religious belief in the institution" (2000, 26, 34). This perspective is bolstered by Lt. General Roméo Dallaire, the commander of UN forces in Rwanda, who observes, "I found him to be genuinely, even religiously, dedicated to the founding principles of the UN" (2003, 50).

At the same time, Annan does not have the high level of need for recognition seen for Hammarskjöld and Waldheim. The "modest by nature" (Bogert 1996, 31) Annan is more than willing to adopt a quiet approach and avoid the spotlight when necessary. Pushing for greater recognition is not a part of his character. Instead, he possesses an "utter lack of pretense" and "self-advertisement is contrary to his nature" (Traub 1998, 50, 81). Many observers have noted Annan's lack of ego, including John Ruggie, who worked closely with Annan as an adviser and is often quoted on this issue, including the following claim: "With Kofi it's never about him. His ego's just not involved" (quoted in Gourevitch 2003, 66). Annan often displays his modesty though the use of self-depreciating humor, which he uses to deflect attention from himself. Friends were always impressed by his willingness to downplay his possible achievement of power, including Toni Goodale—who met Annan when they were enrolled in school together in Geneva in the 1970s—who states, "You felt the presence of power without its being overt . . . I used to tease him, 'Oh, Kofi, you'll be secretary general some day.' He'd say, 'Yes, and you're going to be president of the United States.' He'd just joke about it. He'd never say, 'You know, I think you're right' " (quoted in Span 1998, C1).

ANNAN IN ACTION: STRATEGIC BEHAVIOR OVERVIEW

Despite the early doubts over whether he would be able to act in an independent fashion Annan quickly established that he was not content to act simply as a manager, as indicated by a headline in the *Guardian* just two months into his tenure: "Annan Takes Firm Hold of UN Tiller" (Black 1997). John Tessitore captures Annan's level of engagement that went beyond managerial expectations: "If world leaders thought that the even-tempered Annan was going to be a weak leader in world affairs, they were learning very quickly that they had been greatly mistaken" (2000, 78). While Annan has demonstrated his independence and the ability to take a "firm hold" of the United Nations, putting questions over whether he would be a manager reminiscent of Waldheim to rest, he has taken a more cautious approach to the office than a bold visionary such as Hammarskjöld. As one of Annan's aides expresses, "He's not the missionary type" (quoted in Henneberger 2003, 34). Annan has carefully followed the middle path of a strategic Secretary-General, independently pursuing his own ideas, but at the same time seeking the advantageous times and methods to do so.

Patience has been a hallmark of Annan's tenure. Although under pressure at times to move faster, he has "demonstrated remarkable calm under stress. Counseling patience and determination, he frustrated those in search of a quick fix to complex problems" (Ziring, Riggs, and Plano 2005, 155). Annan has followed the approach described early on by a close aide: "Kofi is not planning revolutions. He is going to be scaling back and seeking consensus" (quoted in Ankomah 1997, 37). In doing so, Annan has worked to cultivate relationships to provide him with greater connections, information, and latitude to act. As part of this process, he has aimed to bring together divergent groups and to promote a cohesive atmosphere at the United Nations. In his examination of the beginning of Annan's tenure, Newman reinforces this point: "Kofi Annan's early activities in Office under the theme of 'healing' the discord both within the Organization and between the UN and its sponsors certainly appeared to reflect a more conciliatory approach" (1998, 189).

Annan has sought to be assertive without disrupting relationships. Frederick Barton notes, "He's good, very good, at balancing interests. That's one of his great strengths" (quoted in *CQ Researcher* 2004, 181), which has been a key part of such an approach. This balancing act has been strained at times as Annan holds the unenviable position of being viewed as the choice of the United States, yet still often lacks full U.S. backing for the United Nations. He has simultaneously sought to work closely with the United States to ensure that the United Nations would not lose further support from the organization's highest contributor, while convincing the other countries that he was also capable of representing their interests. This has been an ongoing effort, but one that has been aided by that fact that Annan is "a master of talking politics without politicizing, naming names, or apportioning blame" (Gourevitch 2003, 53), so that he can better work across constituencies.

Annan has regularly reinforced his ability to undertake independent initiatives and has been willing to involve himself in difficult situations. David Usborne titles his profile "The Forceful Peacemaker" based upon the observation that Annan "is not frightened of taking risks" where he deems them necessary (1998, 5), while Meisler similarly notes how "unlike many career bureaucrats, he doesn't shrink from trouble" (2003, 33). However, as one account stresses, Annan's "not a visionary, but a practical man who is a skilled persuader" (Brinkbäumer 2004). Thus, while Annan has been active, he has also maintained a diplomatic approach that has emphasized his ability "to listen thoughtfully and play the conciliator" (Gordon 2005, 43) and he is "known for the subtle push, the deft move, the calculated but gentle blow" (Duke 2003, C1). In this manner, Annan has been very responsive to the situation and needs of others, which has allowed him to carefully monitor relations with those that he is trying to influence.

While noting the bounds of what is politically acceptable, Annan has still worked diligently to address international peace and security. Philip Gourevitch notes how Annan focused on strengthening the United Nations while simultaneously "diminishing its pretensions and ambitions" (2003, 71). As Ian Williams further explains, "While expanding the UN's agenda and trying to carve out an independent role for it, Annan has carefully restrained his ambitions for the organization within pragmatic limits" (2000, 22). This has led some analysts to conclude that Annan has not been sufficiently active. In one statement to this effect, Irving Brecher argues that Annan has not been forceful enough in addressing the conflicts around the world and concludes that "[s]erious questions have to be raised about the quality of leadership at the United Nations" (1999, B3). In a similar vein, David Rieff contends that Annan is "managerial, and managerialism is not enough" since the "secretary-general must offer a vision of the world" (1999, 23, 22).

At the same time, others have compared Annan's tenure to the days of the visionary Hammarskjöld, with Usborne noting, "It is common nowadays to hear him likened to the only other UN leader who inspired common awe, Sweden's Dag Hammarskjold" (1998, 5; for other examples see Fasulo 2004; Shawcross 2000; and Tripoli 1998). Such contrasting analyses are indicative of Annan's strategic style. While Annan is certainly not a thrustful visionary like Hammarskjöld, he is also not a subservient manager like Waldheim, with Meisler arguing "Annan's approach as Secretary-General differs from that of his predecessors. He's a world apart from Kurt Waldheim" (2003, 34). Annan's pattern of behavior is a mixture of the managerial caution exemplified by Waldheim and the independent stance taken by Hammarskjöld. Although Hammarskjöld's complex visionary style limits the contrast with Annan's somewhat, the differences in behavior are present and observable. To support this point, the rest of this chapter provides a detailed examination of Annan's time in office across the behavioral categories established in chapter 3. This analysis is summarized in table 6.1.

Table 6.1 Annan: Strategist in Action

Activity	Ideal Strategist	Annan Behavior
Agenda Setting *Administrative Duties*		
• Supervise Reports	Produce reports reflecting own views; but not as likely to offer independently when seen as politically disadvantageous	Through a series of reform reports and other reports on international peace and security, gradually built up ambitious but pragmatic recommendations through a process of consultation and consensus-building
• Oversee Finances	Involved in budget design; give-and-take over final budget depending on political resistance	Creatively engaged in budgetary matters as encouraged financial commitments to reflect agenda and process priorities; supported through give-and-take approach and acceded when necessary to political constraints
• Shape Administrative Structure	Likely to restructure, but will back away from areas that are too politically volatile; will try to provide for more influence for own office but not to detriment of politically challenging recalcitrant members; will lobby but be willing to make political sacrifices	Major part of reform plans; sought to alter management structure and culture with stress on coordination, efficiency and delegation; reactive to political pressure, but not beyond bounds of what believed was acceptable

• Staffing the Secretariat	Flexible in appointment process, willing to make political sacrifices when under pressure; but seek to have influential compatriots put into place when possible	Did much to appoint individuals that wanted to key positions and sought to balance own weaknesses with appointments; connection to staff generally bolstered morale; at times did not take strong action to address difficult staffing situations or overcome political pressure
Strategic Political Position		
• Representative in Meetings	Will attend meetings, where will be active in listening to different views and determining what avenues for influence exist; unlikely to employ Article 99 unless asked to do so	Worked closely with member-states at UN meetings in a give-and-take process aimed at reaching consensus decisions; at times gave special priority to great powers; encouraged multilateral meetings within the UN where can be a participant; has not invoked Article 99
• Inherent Strategic Position	Will build relationships, gather information, and use position to get ideas into agenda in a give-and-take process; open to others' needs and ideas	Excelled at cultivating strategic connections and information gathering; expanded contacts by working with new constituencies; very open to others' views
Public Pronouncements		
• Annual Report to General Assembly	Express views regarding conflicts, but in guarded tone and unlikely to take on most politically sensitive conflicts; see as good opportunity to float general ideas for reaction	Did use to address security issues, but began with relatively low key reports and built up to more innovative and challenging ideas; then maintained as a platform to reinforce themes and ideas

Continued

Table 6.1 Continued

Activity	Ideal Strategist	Annan Behavior
• Official Representational Activities	Will take advantage of opportunities to express opinions; temper pronouncements according to the situation	Aimed to impress ideas upon others and provided strong official statements when believed necessary or appropriate, but often cautious with controversial wording and approach helped to temper political backlash; traveled extensively in official capacity and used the opportunity to build connections and get message across in manner tailored to situation
• "Unofficial" Representational Activities	Seen as good avenue to get message across, but will temper according to audience and sensitivity of topic	Maintained a concerted public relations effort through statements, intense travel schedule and connections with media that employed creative methods to impart his message to a broad audience; although cautious when expressing opinions that touch on sensitive issues did have notable times where faced backlash for comments
Peaceful Settlement of Disputes		
Independently Initiated	Will undertake such missions, but only after careful consideration to determine receptiveness to action; will listen to views of combatants in helping them work toward a common understanding and solution	Undertook multiple missions but maintained close consultation with UN organs and parties involved to ensure support for involvement; took advantage of opportunities when presented but did not force self into situations; before offering services carefully reviewed situation, gathered information and

Mandated Assignment	Will probe to determine if input for mandate would be accepted; will use own judgment in interpreting mandate and will seek to test bounds of mandate, although will seek to clarify mission and back away if face backlash over activities	determined what actions were acceptable and emphasized a collaborative approach to establishing solutions, including involvement of alternative actors where appropriate Worked with members to provide input for specific mission details; sought clear expectations in mandates to support the mission; maintained close involvement in carrying out missions in a cautious yet creative manner; displayed a pragmatic approach where sensed political possibilities and dangers and acted accordingly
UN Intervention Peacekeeping Missions	Will probe to determine if input for mandate would be accepted; will use own judgment in interpreting mandate, although will seek to clarify mission and back away if face backlash over activities	Worked collaboratively with Security Council to provide input for specific mission details, carefully reviewing the needs of the situation in advance to determine a suitable plan of action, while also developing reforms and plans for the future of peacekeeping; close involvement in carrying out missions in cautious yet creative manner; displayed a pragmatic approach where sensed political possibilities and dangers and acted accordingly, including openness to engagement and cooperation with alternative actors in handling breaches of the peace, with goal of enhancing long-term impact

ANNAN AND INFLUENTIAL ACTIVITIES

AGENDA SETTING: AGENDA MANIPULATOR

In the category of agenda setting, Annan has pursued an active, yet flexible and responsive, approach. Within the administrative realm, he is widely noted for his reform reports. In addition, he used the ability to supervise reports to build up critiques of the UN's approach to handling international peace and security and to offer suggestions for changes as part of an ongoing collaborative process. His efforts to oversee UN finances took into account political necessity and the need to carefully consider new budgetary outlay, while also encouraging member-states to meet their financial obligations, implement budgets that reflected his priorities, and adjust the budget process. The structure, and general management, of the Secretariat was adjusted to meet his desire for greater coordination and collegiality and he worked to place the people that he wanted into key positions. However, he has also limited his plans when facing political pressure.

Annan has used his strategic political position to great advantage. As a representative in meetings, he worked closely in a give-and-take manner to encourage consensus decisions. He excelled at building connections with member-state representatives through informal interactions. He pursued strategic associations beyond the United Nations as well, drawing on new constituencies such as non-governmental organizations (NGOs) and the business community. Throughout all of his interactions, he has displayed an openness to gathering new information and listening to the opinions of others as he formulates his plan of action. In regards to public pronouncements, he gradually produced more innovative and challenging ideas in his annual reports and maintained this as a platform for explaining his views on international peace and security. In presenting statements through both official and unofficial forums, he has aimed to impart a strong message when possible or necessary in his view, but he is most often noted for the soft-spoken tone and cautious approach undertaken when imparting his messages.

ADMINISTRATIVE DUTIES

From the beginning of his tenure, Annan was active in bolstering his position within the United Nations. Given his Secretariat background, Annan was well aware of the influential possibilities of managing administrative affairs. As Secretary-General, his strategic style led how he took advantage of these duties—as Newton Bowles emphasizes it was the combination of "personality and experience" that made Annan a "good manager" (2004, 132)—and he proved to be a focused administrator who applied his acumen to the array of avenues of influence within the reach of his office.

Supervise reports

The use of reports to guide the UN's reform agenda, including many proposals related to international peace and security, is a hallmark of Annan's time as Secretary-General. Because of the great level of detail contained in Annan's reform proposals, specifics will not be closely discussed at this point (see Beigbeder 2000; Bhatta 2000; Burgess and Piper 2005; Laurenti 1997a, 1997b; Martens 2005; Müller 2001; Paepcke 2005; Prins 2005; Thakur 2003, 2005; The Stanley Foundation 2005; and Zedillo 2005). Key reform aspects are touched upon throughout the following sections within the appropriate behavior framework categories, while this section provides an overview of Annan's main reform reports and how the approach he undertook reflected his strategic style.

When he took office, Annan was under pressure to present his reform plans quickly. He was able to counteract some of this demand by presenting a first wave of reforms in March as a "Track One" set of proposals related to changes that fell under the Secretary-General's authority and a promise of extended "Track Two" plans to follow, which were issued that July in *Renewing the United Nations: A Program for Reform*. Indicative of his "dedication to consensus-building" (Rich 2000, 5), Annan wanted additional time and input to help formulate these proposals. The feedback that he received "led the Secretary-General to scale back some dramatic proposals that he had reportedly been considering" (Laurenti 1997b), leading to what has been described as "an ambitious programme, but politically accept-able with a few exceptions" (Beigbeder 2000, 213).

Building out of Annan's initial reform drive, his proposal to hold a special Millennium Summit and Assembly in September 2000 was approved. In March 2000 he issued *We The Peoples: The Role of the United Nations in the Twenty-First Century*—known as the "Millennium Report"—that aimed to put his "personal imprint" (Lynch 2000a, A22) on the agenda for the September meetings and beyond. The report represented "Annan's seminal policy document . . . [that] set out views that gave form to his subsequent public initiatives" (Gordenker 2005, 85) and provided a detailed analysis of how he believed that a range of global problems, including peace and security, should be addressed. Overall, Annan presented a bold report where he was "aware of the controversy" (Lian 2000, 28) that could arise regarding some of his proposals, but one that was designed largely to remain within the bounds of the politically possible as he was "reaching out to all people" in an effort that was both "ambitious and pragmatic" (Bowles 2004, 142). In addition, by setting out his "Millennium Report" well ahead of time, Annan provided plenty of time for feedback and consideration before the meetings occurred.

With his second term underway, Annan launched the next stage of his reform effort with a September 2002 report *Strengthening the United Nations: An Agenda for Further Change*, which was designed for debate in the General Assembly that October. His report not only "reiterated and reinforced" earlier reform efforts (O'Neil and Rees 2005, 199), but was also designed to address new dimensions. As before, the preparation of the report included a wide range of consultation and coordination. Ramesh Thakur, who was closely involved in writing the report, explains that "reactions and suggestions [were] carefully noted" in relation to the draft and briefings provided details to members of the Secretariat and member-state delegations due to the "standing instruction . . . that no one in the UN was to be caught by surprise by the final report" (2003, 50).

In addition, Annan maintained an emphasis on Millennium reform efforts through a series of follow-up reports that provided a road map and reflection on implementation. This set the stage for his March 2005 report *In Larger Freedom: Towards Development, Security and Human Rights for All*. As with the previous efforts, *In Larger Freedom* was established to set the agenda—in this case for the sixtieth anniversary General Assembly and the linked Summit of Heads of State that September. The report fulfilled the five-year Millennium Declaration progress report requested by the General Assembly, but the text moved far beyond a routine report. Simon Chesterman aptly describes how the report was both "broad in scope, seeking to define a new security consensus" and "narrow in detail" (2005, 376), as Annan sought to place his final stamp on the UN reform effort.

As this brief review reveals, Annan carried out a sustained and focused reform effort, with each stage building upon the last. The strategic underpinnings are evident in Annan's motto that "reform is not an event; it is a process" and in references to the "quiet revolution" that he initiated upon taking office. While Annan was proactive in encouraging and arranging the reform process, he also monitored what the acceptable bounds were and sought to build consensus as he gradually extended his plans. As a strategist, "Annan does not see it as his role to tilt at political windmills" (Laurenti, 1997b) and he remained "consciously pragmatic" regarding the scope of his proposals (Martens 2005, 2) as he worked collaboratively to pursue a viable reform plan.

Along with the reform efforts, Annan has used other reports to critique and seek improvements for the UN's handling of international peace and security. A prime example is a report commissioned by the Security Council that was issued in April 1998 titled *The Causes of Conflict and the Promotion of Durable Peace and Sustainable Development in Africa*, which Bowles describes as encompassing "a new kind of presentation: direct, clear in identifying sensitive problems . . . and in balancing international and national responsibility" (2004, 16). Despite serving as the "African" Secretary-General, Annan was willing to take African leaders to task. In the very "candid report," he argued that conflict in Africa was "neither inevitable nor intractable" (Singh 1998, 60) and that Africans must stand up better for themselves to prevent these conflicts instead of continually blaming others for their problems.

Reports in 1999 analyzing UN performance in Bosnia and Rwanda were also very frank. However, the reports widely distributed blame, which helped to temper the political backlash. Urquhart elaborates, "Both are detailed and outspoken to an unusual degree, and both criticize the Secretary-General and the Secretariat, the Security Council, various governments and alliances, and, less vehemently, the local leaders who were responsible for the horrors in the first place" (2000, 21). Annan's report detailing UN involvement in Srebrenica is described as an "extraordinarily candid, self-critical report" presenting a "no-holds-barred 150-page account of bureaucratic failure, vacillation, and political cynicism" (Smyth 1999, 12). For the Rwanda report, also depicted as "an unusually critical retrospective analysis" (Gordenker 2005, 18), Annan commissioned an inquiry to detail the UN's failure to prevent the mass slaughter. He ensured that investigators had unfettered access to documents and individuals involved and unconditionally approved the findings. Shawcross cites these reports as a prime example of "a new culture of openness at the United Nations under Annan" (2000, 408) as he sought to have all information honestly and openly presented so that better decisions could be made in the future.

These critical reports helped to set the groundwork for a broader review of peacekeeping designed to focus on better ensuring future success. In March 2000 Annan announced that a panel of advisers would examine how to make peacekeeping more efficient. The *Report on the Panel on United Nations Peace Operations*, known as the

"Brahimi Report" after panel head Lakhdar Brahimi, was released that August just ahead of the Millennium Summit events in September. Thakur stresses how the panel "looked back on the half-century's experience of peacekeeping in order to bring it into line with the realities of the new century" while also indicating "far-reaching recommendations on improving the efficiency and effectiveness of UN peace operations" (2003, 43). Annan provided a range of follow-up reports that discussed the possibilities and requirements for implementing ideas contained in the Brahimi Report, including a June 2001 report that marked "a significant departure for the UN" because "it was prepared with the help of external management consultants" and included an expert review board in "an attempt to ensure that the views of developing countries were considered" (Findlay 2002, 339).

The pattern of soliciting external expertise continued when Annan established a High-level Panel on Threats, Challenges and Change chaired by Anand Panyarachun, the former prime minister of Thailand, in November 2003. In an effort to "forge a new consensus" on international security (Thakur 2005, 281), the panel was asked to undertake an extensive exploration well beyond peacekeeping to consider the full range of threats to peace and to provide recommendations for strengthening a collective response through the United Nations. Given the scope of this task the panel took until December 2004 to release their report *A More Secure World: Our Shared Responsibility*, which one analyst describes as "of considerable intellectual significance . . . it makes a seminal contribution to the new literature on the twenty-first-century threat environment" (Prins 2005, 374). Annan largely incorporated the panel's proposals within his report *In Larger Freedom*. Overall, as with the broader reform reports, he engaged a range of opinions and gradually built up and expanded the scope of his reporting efforts.

Annan's issue-specific reports to the Security Council are extensive and wide-ranging. In 2004 alone he issued 80 reports to the Security Council, from a January 6 report on the Ivory Coast to a December 31 report on the Congo (see http://www.un.org/Docs/sc/sgrep04.html). Beyond such country-focused documents, Annan has also used reports to expound on improving peace and security more broadly. This is illustrated by a series of reports in 2001. He issued a report in March on protecting civilians in armed conflict; in April he tackled the closure or alteration of peacekeeping missions, and in June he submitted a report jointly to the General Assembly on the prevention of armed conflict.

Oversee finances

With his background experience at the United Nations working on financial concerns—while serving in the Secretariat he even wrote about the importance of the budget for the influential capabilities of the Secretary-General (Annan 1993)—Annan's high level of engagement in budgetary issues is not surprising. Yet, while he sought to influence UN finances to reflect his agenda, he also recognized and scaled back his approach in the face of political constraints. Annan took over in a financially precarious time and his first step was to propose that the United Nations operate under a negative-growth budget for the first time for the 1998–1999 budget cycle. However, he also endeavored to make the money work more effectively. For example, his initial reform efforts targeted cost-cutting possibilities, including making aspects of peacekeeping missions more efficient.

Once the UN's financial situation stabilized, Annan recognized the opportunity to gradually push for greater funding levels. He began referring to a zero growth budget as a "starvation diet" due to the demands that had been added on the organization without additional budget outlay (Pisik 2001, A15). When the 2002–2003 budget fell $75 million short of his request, he resorted to cutbacks in basic Secretarial service (see ST/IC/2002/13) to get his point across, despite some member-state claims that greater efficiency could make up the gap. Annan continually lobbied to support his budget proposals, appealing against cutbacks and targeting increases to support particular programs or staffing needs that he believed were priorities. This included stressing the need for financial backing for reform measures. This is illustrated by how he followed the Brahimi Report with his own report detailing the resource requirements, specified a revised budget to address the priorities established in his 2002 reform plan, and sought a new fund to support the Peacebuilding Commission called for within 2005's *In Larger Freedom*. Overall, Annan has worked to design budgets to better meet his interests, but he has also maintained an approach that balances programmatic desires of various member-states.

The budget process itself has also been targeted by Annan. His 1997 plan called for results-based budgeting where the General Assembly would specify the desired program "outputs," but the Secretary-General would possess "greater responsibility for determining the precise mix of inputs to generate the desired outputs" (Bhatta 2000, 171). The 2002 reform plan further emphasized that the Secretary-General should be provided with the independent capability to shift money to needed areas, instead of relying on further approval.

The report also targeted streamlined and efficient allocation procedures. As Thakur details, "The SG's Report outlines the elements of a
simpler and more rational package that could help to bring ends and
means closer together" (2003, 58).

Along with internal budget management, Annan has focused on
ensuring that the United Nations is properly financially supported.
With the United States being the largest contributor, and thereby
often the largest debtor, this has often meant a focus on American
officials. Annan has cajoled the United States in a "firm but not abrasive" manner (Williams 2000, 24). In his first years in office, whenever
he traveled to Washington he reminded "his hosts (with exquisite
politesse, of course) about the small matter of that unpaid bill"
(Cornwell 1998, 3). This has been an ongoing process, with Annan
engaged in a give-and-take process in an effort to maintain American
financial commitments. For example, in one episode late in his tenure,
the United States opposed approving the normal two-year budget
cycle at the end of 2005 and instead sought a several month stop-gap
budget until the expenditures required for reform proposals could be
factored in. Annan stressed his perspective that the budget should be
adopted in full because the reforms could instead be paid for through
supplemental budgets in 2006 and later canceled a planned December
2005 trip to Asia to remain in New York during negotiations for a
solution.

Annan has also been creatively engaged in seeking other means to
financially bolster the United Nations. For example, in his 1997
reform plan he proposed a Revolving Credit Fund as stopgap relief
until the UN's financial status improved. The private sector has also
been engaged to provide support; most notably with the $1 billion
that Ted Turner pledged to set up the UN Foundation, which has
worked closely with a variety of UN programs to provide funding. His
outreach to private business has also paid off in a more indirect manner. For example, in 1998 American business leaders placed open let-
ters in the *Washington Post* and the *New York Times* that pushed the
American government to pay its dues (Silber 1998a).

Annan has been involved in a great number of appeals for contri-
butions and efforts to bolster peacekeeping funds. The case of Sierra
Leone provides an illustrative example of the complexity of the task.
Annan moved through a series of funding stages in the effort to bring
peace to Sierra Leone, including working on financial details for the
United Nations Observer Mission in Sierra Leone (UNOMISIL)
established in 1998 and the United Nations Mission in Sierra Leone
(UNAMISIL) that followed, reporting on the funding needed to

support expanding the size of the peacekeeping mission, calling for money to fund peace building as force levels were reduced, and guiding the financial backing for the Special Court for Sierra Leone. The extended process for establishing the Special Court is indicative of how Annan strategically approached the funding requirements. To begin with, he tried to counter the Security Council plan to support the court with voluntary contributions and instead "argued for assessments, saying contributions have proven unreliable" (Crossette 2001, A8). Recognizing that the political will was not there for such assessments, he focused on increasing the length of financial commitment before the court would begin operations. Annan also scaled back the size of the court's budget level from the initial planned levels when it became clear that this amount of money could not be raised. In the end, he authorized the establishment of the court in January 2002 without the full funding amount in place. However, Annan remained involved in efforts to keep the court functioning as the voluntary funding levels fell short. This included requesting a special subvention from the General Assembly to support the court through 2005 and encouraging further voluntary pledges to keep the court operating in 2006.

Shape the administrative structure
Annan moved quickly to streamline the Secretariat. By March 1997 he had already eliminated 900 Secretariat staff, close to the 1,000 total that were cut within his first year. However, he was unwilling to push personnel cuts further than he thought necessary: "While Washington demands further reductions in UN staff in its pursuit of 'reform,' the Secretary General says he is down to the bone and any more cuts would be suicidal for UN programmes" (Littlejohns 1999, 14). Thus, Annan's actions could be tied to political pressure, but he saw the process as "much more than simply cutting staff and reducing budgets" (Marquardt and Berger 2000, 69) and instead aimed to turn the drive to limit positions to the benefit of a more efficient organization. With "maximum performance demanded of all staff" (Müller 2001, 110) that remained, Annan also sought to ensure better training and emphasized improving human resources capabilities. Annan's "reform proposals for human resources covers the entire gamut" (Salomons 2003, 130) and were designed to "dovetail" with other aspects of "management overhaul" in order to improve the structure's functioning as a whole (Bhatta 2000, 199). In fact, the journal *Workforce* awarded the United Nations an Optimas Award for Global Outlook in 2000 for its human resources program, citing the important role of Annan's reform efforts (Sunoo 2000).

Annan has also exerted much energy in reshaping the administrative structure, with his efforts often focused on improving efficiency and coordination. Shortly after taking office, he consolidated the Secretariat's "work programme around the five areas that comprise the core missions of the UN," one of which was peace and security (Beigbeder 2000, 212). More generally, as Thakur explains, Annan "also created some new posts and departments and resurrected some old ones" (2003, 42). This included establishing a Senior Management Group to provide support through weekly meetings as a cabinet for the Secretary-General. The new system brought together senior officers in a manner designed to break down "the walls of old fiefs" (Crossette 1998a, 5) and reflected Annan's "inclusive style" (Shawcross 2000, 241). The cabinet members provide a range of ideas and perspectives to the decision-making process and can help sort through the agenda-setting plans. One report describes the setting of a meeting in January 2003: "It is a Wednesday, the day to meet with the cabinet . . . As he enters his conference room, members of the 33-person body are poring over a list of priorities for the year. It is a long list (three pages), an exhaustive one. Of course, Iraq is on that list. But so are scores of other issues and hot spots around the world" (Duke 2003, C1). However, as Elisabeth Lindenmayer, who served as a close adviser in the executive office, explains, Annan solicits information and opinions but retains final say: "He asks us what we think, listens, is silent and thinks, and then he announces clear decisions" (quoted in Brinkbäumer 2004).

Another important addition to the management structure was the first Deputy Secretary-General, a position filled by Canadian Louise Fréchette. The creation of a Deputy Secretary-General post had long been discussed within the United Nations, but had never been carried out. Although having the assistance of a Deputy would leave the Secretary-General freer to pursue "sustained intellectual and organisational leadership" (Mortimer and Lambert 1997, 19), the position can also represent a challenge to the Secretary-General's power and authority. However, the post fit with Annan's strategic view of the organizational structure. Such structural moves reflected Annan's general desire to increase the level of delegation. In his first month in office, Annan "at once ended the extreme centralization of power and information practiced by his predecessor and has delegated authority to those who need it to function well" (Hottelet 1997, 18). While Annan quickly implemented an initial delegation of authority, he gradually pursued further delegation from senior officials on down the managerial ranks in order to ensure that the structure and understanding of this approach had time to be put into place.

Overall, Annan's major push was to alter the management culture of the Secretariat so that it reflected his way of doing things. In other words, Annan implemented a strategic working environment that reflected his style. As such, his conceptualization of managerial culture stressed coordination and collegiality to build a "communications culture within the Secretariat" (Bhatta 2000, 197). He aimed to remove the decision-making burden on single individuals, including himself, within a hierarchical chain of command and, instead, designed a cabinet-style support system along with promoting an administration that was open and welcomed input.

Finally, the oil-for-food scandal is an important issue to discuss in relation to Annan's tenure. The challenges in this area that Annan has faced can be related to his administrative and staffing reactions. The oil-for-food program allowed Iraq to sell oil under UN supervision and use the proceeds to purchase food and other humanitarian supplies for the civilian population in order to help counteract the impact of sanctions on the country, along with contributing to a fund for war reparations and supporting weapons inspections. Questions of impropriety arose in early 2004, including allegations of bribery and mismanagement leveled against UN officials that projected a view of the management under Annan as a culture of corruption rather than communication. Annan was viewed by some as responding too slowly to the oil-for-food accusations; he did not establish an independent inquiry headed by Paul Volcker until April 2004; and critics took this as an indication that he was not taking seriously the structural problems of the United Nations that this issue potentially revealed. Once the investigation was underway, Annan's response time was once again questioned, but he stressed the need for an investigatory process to be carried out before analyzing the results and implementing appropriate actions. Following upon Volcker's reports, Annan announced that steps would be taken to reform management structure and practices, including establishing a new Ethics Office, but the capability of these efforts remains to be seen.

Staffing the secretariat

Upon taking office, Annan moved steadily to assemble the staff that he desired. He surrounded himself with a "loyal circle of aides" based largely on those who had worked with him in the peacekeeping department (Mortimer and Lambert 1997, 19). Annan has used staff appointments throughout his tenure to bolster his potential influence. An illustrative example from late in his tenure is the 2005 appointment of Ibrahim Gambari to Under Secretary-General for Political

Affairs, which was described as a "move seen as advancing" his reform plans and as a "courageous move that would establish his legacy" (Akande 2005, 2). In addition, he has been involved in appointing the heads of other agencies; thereby, "Annan has broadened his small power base with strong appointments to satellite agencies" (Crossette 1998a, 5). In doing so, Annan wanted individuals whose style meshed well with his own. For example, he bypassed Jan Pronk for UN High Commissioner for Refugees because he "felt his style was abrasive," yet mollified the Dutch government by choosing Ruud Lubbers, the former Dutch prime minister (Steele 2001, 17)—although, as discussed below, this choice would backfire as Lubbers was accused of sexual harassment while holding the position.

Annan's early staffing selections were "considered prudent by UN-watchers" (Bhatta 2000, 148) as he brought together "a number of individuals considered as experienced and competent" (Beigbeder 2000, 212). In addition, Annan was willing to acknowledge his limits and aimed to counteract them through the appointments and advice of strong outside experts. David Malone, from the International Peace Academy, observes, "When he became secretary general, he knew that his strength was to be an insider . . . But that was also going to be a weakness. The outsiders have been playing a key role in challenging not only how the U.N. does things, but also how the U.N. thinks about itself" (quoted in Crossette 1999, A1). However, although Annan has generally been "known for making courageous appointments" (Crossette 2003), as noted in a 1999 *New York Times* editorial, when faced with resistance over his choices for certain posts he "has not consistently backed his appointees." Similarly, while Annan has backed his staffers against critiques—for example he publicly defended UN High Commissioner for Human Rights Louise Arbour when U.S. Ambassador Bolton questioned her views on detention and torture—this represented "an unusual instance" of directly criticizing a particular member-state representative (Hoge 2005c, A6).

Annan has at times demonstrated firm resolve in handling personnel matters, with one report claiming, "His management style is easygoing but not loose. Associates say there is never a harsh word or raised voice, yet there is no doubt who is boss" (Hottelet 2001, 11). For example, he set a "benchmark for the managerial and administrative changes he plans" when he "swiftly administered the smack of firm government" by firing two Rwandan war crime tribunal officials who had been reported for being wasteful and incompetent (Black 1997, 18). Yet, as one profile notes, "Annan has always had a reputation for being reluctant to fire employees" (Gordon 2005, 44) and he has preferred to avoid addressing difficult staffing situations. In a revealing account, Romesh Ratnesar reports, "Once, when Ruggie got upset at Annan for not cracking down on recalcitrant staff members, Annan asked Ruggie why he was panicking. 'The only reason I am panicked is because you are not panicked,' Ruggie said. Grinning, Annan responded; 'Why do I need to panic when I have people like you to panic for me?' " (1998, 62).

Particular problem areas have also called into question Annan's control over staffing matters. The oil-for-food allegations regarding management corruption and how Annan addressed the related staffing issues have been particularly problematic. Other individual cases have further highlighted concerns, including the handling of sexual harassment charges against Lubbers that eventually led to his resignation and allegations of abuse of authority and harassment within the Electoral Assistance Division that led to the dismissal of the head of the division Carina Perelli from office in December 2005. Annan's handling of such cases has reinforced the critique that he is often loyal to a fault and "has stood by people who made too many mistakes" (Brinkbäumer 2004). Recent staffing moves involving U.S. nationals and political pressure also raised issues of whether Annan went too far in wooing the American administration. For example, in 2005 it has been suggested that Peter Hansen was not reappointed as the head of the United Nations Relief and Works Agency (UNWRA) due to criticism from the United States and Israel over a perceived pro-Palestinian bias, with one report indicating that Annan told Hansen that "I don't have the political capital with the Americans to keep you" (McGreal 2005, 17). Particularly troubling to some was the statement by Christopher Burnham, "one of a handful of Bush administration supporters hired by the United Nations in recent months" who took over in June 2005 as Under Secretary-General for Management, that his primary loyalty remained to the United States (Lynch 2005, A21). Although Annan rebuked him and Burnham apologized, this still raised questions regarding the staffing practices.

The way that Annan interacted with staff reflected his style and his approach often bolstered staff morale. In contrast to his predecessor, who was perceived in the Secretariat as "haughty and remote" (Bogert 1996, 31), Annan established greater connections with the staff and "morale has gradually improved" as "his team-oriented approach and inclusiveness build support" (Marquardt and Berger 2000, 61–62). A college classmate visiting Annan in New York commented on the "often-interrupted tour," stating, "He knew everybody in the building, high and low, ambassador to doorman" (Span 1998, C1). A security guard noted at the first UN Christmas party organized by Annan that he "had transformed this house and made it feel like home," to which one observer added, "He was referring to the Secretary General's residence. But he could equally well have been speaking of the whole United Nations family" (Usborne 1998, 5).

In more recent times, serious cracks in Secretariat morale have appeared. The oil-for-food backlash has taken its toll. As one of Annan's aides observes, "We're human. It affects morale" (quoted in Gordon 2005, 42). However, a survey conducted in February 2004 for an internal report revealed that Secretariat members were already greatly concerned about potential retribution for reporting misconduct. Investigations into sexual abuse by UN peacekeepers serving in the Congo, and the potential for similar revelations in relation to other missions, have served as an additional major distraction and added to the sense of mismanagement. Secretariat staff have also been on edge regarding their security, especially following the August 2003 bombing of UN headquarters in Baghdad that raised significant concerns regarding management capability of implementing proper security measures. In November 2004, the UN staff union passed a resolution criticizing senior management, who had "eroded the trust of staff." The resolution did support Annan, with the president of the union stressing, "He is in a very difficult job under very difficult circumstances. He is doing his best," but a draft was leaked to the press that indicated an initial consideration of a vote of no confidence (*Australian* 2004, 12).

Despite the external pressure throughout 2004, which Annan confided to friends felt "a bit like a lynching, actually" (quoted in Walker 2005, 10), he was still open to advice on how to improve matters. A key step in that direction came late in 2004 in the form of "the diplomatic equivalent of a substance-abuse intervention" (Gordon 2005, 44), when a small group of friendly experts met with Annan to push him to get back on track. Staffing matters were a focus of the discussion, where the need to shake up his top management personnel as part of an effort to rebuild confidence in the Secretariat and to improve relations with the American government was stressed. Annan did undertake some major changes, including replacing longtime chief of staff Iqbal Riza with Mark Malloch Brown as part of "shedding most of his inner circle" and, in the process, replacing "traditionalists" with more "modernists" (Hoge 2005a, A3). He also extended his efforts to revitalize the Secretariat in his March 2005 reform report that "criticises the efficiency, professional abilities and integrity of the UN Secretariat's present staff in an astonishingly open manner" and asked for approval from the General Assembly for a one-time staff buyout to update and shift staff positions (Martens 2005, 8). At the time of writing, it remains to be seen whether these actions have the desired effect in relation to Annan carrying out his final year in office.

Summary style comparison for administrative duties
Annan's behavior in the area of administrative duties represents a balanced approach. He clearly had an agenda in mind with his guidance of reports and the budget, and his use of such strong and critical reports goes beyond the bounds of expectations for an ideal strategist, but at the same time he proceeded gradually through a process of give-and-take regarding his ideas and took into account political necessities. For administrative structure and staffing concerns, Annan was involved in using his powers to guide these matters, but once again his consideration of political pressures was evident and his approach to structural and staff issues reflected his strategic understanding of how to best run the Secretariat

STRATEGIC POLITICAL POSITION
For Secretaries-General with a strategic leadership style, the strategic political position of the office should be a vital part of their toolbox. This certainly held true for Annan. Information and communication were vital to him as he sought to be continually informed regarding global events. He has been an important player in the United Nations, taking advantage of his position to cajole the member-states to follow his ideas. He carefully developed contacts in both formal and informal settings, devoting much time and energy to cultivating new constituencies. Overall, as one analysis emphasizes, "[i]n contrast with his predecessor, he showed that he would depend more on teamwork within the UN and consultation with regional groups and national delegations" (Beigbeder 2000, 212).

Representative in meetings
Annan made his presence felt in UN meetings. In relation to the General Assembly, one report expressed Annan's sentiments bluntly: "He would also dearly love to bully the Assembly into reorganising its currently chaotic agenda" (*Economist* 1998, 22), but he has worked more carefully to maneuver his ideas. For example he has used his strategic position to good advantage for shepherding his reform plans in the General Assembly—where he encouraged the member-states to support his ideas and to provide him with the basis for future actions.

As part of this process, Annan sought to build a "close and complementary relationship," while countering where he "felt that there was too much encroachment from the General Assembly into his own work . . . so that he could have a freer hand in running the organisation" (Bhatta 2000, 170; 172).

In a give-and-take process that emphasized sharing ideas, Annan has worked in close consultation with the Security Council. Gordenker recounts that Annan "appeared to be fully informed and often a participant in confidential discussions among the Permanent Five of the Security Council" (2005, 92). In the process, he encouraged the members to build consensus and to avoid the deadlocks that paralyze the UN's ability to address breaches of the peace. Annan also holds monthly lunch meetings and other private meetings with Security Council members. In doing so, Annan has walked a fine line. His tendency at times to give special treatment to the five permanent members has caused some difficulties with the rotating members. At one point Canada, Netherlands, and Slovenia expressed their frustration with private meetings that Annan had held with the permanent members. While Annan "took note" of these concerns, he also expressed his belief that there were times where special priority has to be given to the major powers (Trickey 1999, 13). Annan also often used his position to explain reports to the Security Council, thereby further stressing his points. However, as expected for a strategist, he has not directly employed his Article 99 prerogative and there is no evidence of an intention to do so.

Annan has stressed the importance of using the UN's multilateral diplomacy capabilities and appreciates the opportunities that meetings operating under the UN framework provide. He has attended a great number of conferences and special meetings related to peace and security, or sent a message with a representative, to urge progress and multilateral handling of the issue at hand. He engaged member-states with a focus on the cooperative possibilities that these meetings provide to draw together different viewpoints to formulate a plan of action (Reitano 2005). This can be seen in relation to organizing the special Millennium events held in September 2000, where he has been described as undertaking a "catalytic role" (Williams 2000, 22), and the 2005 Summit where Annan "put pressure on member-states not to leave New York empty-handed" (Chesterman 2005, 376).

Inherent strategic position
With information being a vital part of a Secretary-General's strategic position, Annan has emphasized the information-gathering and coordinating capability of his office. He has focused on "the ability to

share information, coordinate operations and communicate" (Marquardt and Berger 2000, 70) and a Strategic Planning Unit was included in reform plans to help gather and use information accordingly. In relation to peace and security, Gordenker details how "the Secretary-General and his staff closely tracked events. They used information from the field missions to underpin instructions and strove to expand their persuasiveness" (2005, 92). Weekly cabinet meetings bolstered this effort, with members participating from around the world via new teleconferencing capabilities. Technology, and its communication-enhancing capability, has been stressed more generally by Annan as part of reform plans for an electronic United Nations. As Bhatta argues, "It is safe to say that these changes would have probably taken place even if Annan had not put so much emphasis on them, but by accepting the utility of this medium, Annan has made it easier for individual agencies to use the technology to its maximum" (2000, 205). The use of technology demonstrated the potential value of the Secretary-General's information in a very different way when it was revealed in early 2004 that the British government had been conducting electronic surveillance on Annan. Although aggravated, he responded with a typically "low key public response" as "he was intent on presenting a calm and knowing outward reaction" (Hoge 2004a, A6)

Outside of the Secretariat, a range of strategic contacts have been actively cultivated by Annan. He has excelled at interacting with member-state representatives on an informal basis. From the beginning of his tenure, the "38th floor, from which he operates, is for the first time in 51 years open to all ambassadors without discrimination" (Ismail 1997, 64). Annan has promoted a wide range of interaction and collaboration around UN headquarters and also reaches out by phone, where, "[o]n any given day, Annan . . . will log over a dozen calls to a pantheon of world leaders" (Maniatis 2001, 44).

The importance of the strategic position for Annan is best illustrated by how this slipped away to some degree as he battled the oil-for-food and other allegations. The opportunity for strategic interaction, and the related influential capability, decreased. One analysis describes the situation as "whittling away at Annan's influence and what used to be his most powerful currency: the amount of time he was allotted for meetings with the world's decision-makers. How long can the secretary general speak; how long is each bilateral meeting . . . who gets how many minutes with whom? The currency is diminishing" (Brinkbäumer 2004). Beyond the more limited chances, questions also arose regarding Annan's ability to use his traditional strategic prowess to take advantage of these opportunities. Throughout her profile of Annan, Meryl Gordon stresses how out of character he seemed. For example, she reports how "Annan's emotions fluctuated visibly" during meetings and observes that the "entire diplomatic community and staffers, it seems, have been swapping stories about how distracted Annan has been" (2005, 43–44).

Social occasions have been another method for Annan to establish and maintain strategic connections. Indicative of this is the title of one profile, "Outside U.N., a Secretary So Social," where Annan is described as "the most sociable, plugged-in United Nations secretary general the city has ever known" (Crossette 2002, B2). Such social interactions allowed him to forge "connections with artists and musicians, Wall Street financiers, publishing executives and, hardly coincidentally, media stars" (Span 1998, C1). The potential influential benefits to be gained through such interactions suggest a "deeper motive" whereby "Annan recognizes the value, as few other U.N. leaders have, of mixing with important people outside politics" (Meisler 2003, 34). However, the pressure of the oil-for-food scandal also limited Annan's desire to socialize and he and his wife greatly cut back on hosting parties and attending events, although he "started to step out again" by spring 2005 (Gordon 2005, 102).

Along with building social connections, Annan developed other new constituencies in the global community through contacts with NGOs and the business community. Strategists like Annan want to gather new information for analysis to determine the best way to manage problem areas and, therefore, see the benefits of extending constituency-building efforts. NGOs were referred to by Annan as "essential partners" with the United Nations for both formulating and executing policy (quoted in Aviel 2005, 159) and he has "kept the welcome mat at his door" for civil society actors (Bowles 2004, 122). In this regard, he was open to NGO feedback from early in his tenure. For example, as part of his initial reform process, a request for NGO input was placed in *Re-Form: The Bulletin of United Nations Reform* (United Nations 1997) and he "proposed that all UN agencies make more effort to draw in the NGOs through increased consultation and participation in the programme development processes" (Bhatta 2000, 172). He also encouraged the creation of a special Millennium event for NGOs, the Millennium Forum held in May 2000, which Douglas Roche refers to as "a watershed moment in moving the world forward to a system of global governance" (1998, 86). Unlike the norm of NGOs holding a parallel conference, by holding the meeting several months before the other Millennium events "it was hoped that civil society would be able to present its views to world leaders more cogently and coherently" (Müller 2001, 158).

Greater connections with the business community have also been actively courted by Annan. He offered UN support for an open global market and connections with business ventures, while these businesses were expected to do their part in promoting more peaceful conditions, especially raising the level of humanitarian concern, in the areas where they operate. A "Global Compact" between the United Nations and world business leaders was established, which set out specific principles that should guide business practices around the globe, and there has since been an ever-increasing degree of interaction between the United Nations and the private sector (Coate 2004; Datta 2000; and McIntosh 2003).

However, while he has supported ties to new constituencies, Annan has maintained his awareness of the needs of different member-states. In relation to international business "his enthusiasm was always tempered by the awareness of those who were not benefiting from the growth and expansion of free markets" (Rieff 1999, 23). He has been equally cautious to stress that he does not see new forms of organization displacing states in the international arena. At the same time, Annan has shown a clear willingness to use his contacts with these groups if that is what it takes to get results. He has been heard by aides to say, "If I can't get the support of governments, then I'll get the support of the people. People move governments" (Crossette 1998a, 5).

Summary Style Comparison for Strategic Political Position
Although his efforts were impaired by difficulties late in his tenure, as a strategic Secretary-General it is not surprising that Annan saw the influential possibilities that come with the strategic political position of the office. He has acted independently to insert his views at meetings and developed contacts in informal settings in order to bolster his influential position. However, both in official meetings and through the contacts that developed around his inherent strategic position, he was willing to listen to others' views and develop plans in a give-and-take process.

PUBLIC PRONOUNCEMENTS
Annan's public pronouncement capabilities led one observer to note, "In Annan the UN has a powerful communicator" (Hottelet 1997, 18). As referenced in chapter 3, the office of the Secretary-General

can be used as a "bully pulpit" and commentators have noted Annan in this regard (e.g., Bhatta 2000, 227; Duke 2003, C1; and Lauria 2001, E2). He has not sought to use his communication capabilities for self-promotion; yet, given his desire to promote the United Nations and to influence governments and public opinion, Annan has displayed a penchant for public promotion of his ideas. In fact, one of Annan's 1997 reforms was to reorganize the UN's main information service, the Department of Public Information, so that greater emphasis could be placed on delivering information to member-states, the media, and NGOs in a more accessible and timely manner.

The way in which Annan expresses himself demonstrates his strategic nature. As detailed earlier, Annan is well known for being soft-spoken, both in terms of the actual volume of his voice and the tone of his public statements. According to Gourevitch, Annan's strategic speaking style works both ways: "Annan can make the vaguest, most innocuous statement sound substantial and profound, and he can deliver his toughest, most challenging arguments without apparent argumentativeness" (2003, 52). He has shied away from conflictual pronouncements and tends to emphasize the positive. Along these lines, he is described as "a man who is reluctant to condemn any member state" (Rieff 1999, 21), while Traub reports, "he speaks fondly of practically everything" (1998, 49).

At the same time, his "diplomatic reserve" should not be confused for "bureaucratic timidity" (Williams 2000, 24). Annan has not been a subservient manager and speaks his mind "when he deems it necessary" (Ramcharan 2002a, 23) and appropriate to the circumstances. While careful to monitor what he says, Annan has not been averse to expressing his opinions where he believes that they can have a well-timed impact and "has challenged nations and individuals with uncomfortable truths (Kennedy 2002, 351). Yet, when he did step forward in this manner, he expressed himself in a "perfectly civil way" (Urquhart in Crossette 1999, A1). Annan often used his pronouncements to emphasize the need to deal with global problems in a multilateral manner. However, Annan's approach, while at times "lofty and idealistic," should not "be interpreted as empty rhetoric" (Marquardt and Berger 2000, 61–62).

Annual report to the General Assembly

Annan's first two annual reports did not stir up any major reaction among the press or member-states, but he gradually built up his ideas and assertiveness in using this tool. In the first two reports he did address issues of peace and security, thus getting his ideas placed into the public debate. In 1997, his report stressed the need to improve the capability of the United Nations in promoting a more peaceful world, but the report was received as a fairly general statement on international peace and the place of the United Nations put forth by a first-time Secretary-General. His 1998 report primarily emphasized the past year's accomplishments in the realm of international security. However, he also appeared to be planting the seeds for future ideas regarding the role of the United Nations in an increasingly interconnected global society: "With terrorism, growing economic instability and poverty, and conflicts round the globe set to dominate the opening of the assembly, Mr. Annan is seeking to map out an agenda for the new millennium" (Silber 1998b, 4).

After gauging the reaction to the first two reports, Annan released a bolder attempt with his 1999 report. The main thrust of Annan's discussion of security issues was that the United Nations needed to directly intervene in the internal affairs of countries where citizens were victims of atrocities. In addition, he called for earlier and better preventive measures to keep such situations from developing in the first place. This notion that there are rights beyond borders that require intervention represented a serious challenge to the sanctity of state sovereignty enshrined in the Charter and coveted by member-states. Needless to say, Annan's controversial stance drew much attention and discussion, which was the desired effect. He had built up to these proposals, so they did not come as a complete surprise and helped to soften the blow, but he still faced uproar as some member-states acted quickly to defend their sovereignty.

Once established in this manner, the annual report remained an important platform for Annan to provide views on international peace and security, although generally not with the major impact of the 1999 report. Instead, he has often used the reports to reinforce key themes and ideas. For example, in 2001, on the heels of the June joint report to the General Assembly and Security Council on prevention of armed conflict mentioned earlier, his annual report once again emphasized the need to shift from reacting to conflicts to preventing them.

Official representational activities

Annan has also strategically taken advantage of official representational activities to try to influence others to follow his ideas. This was clear from his acceptance speech, which led one article headline to proclaim "Annan Shows He's Much More Than 'the U.S. Choice' " and report: "There was a carefully sheathed but nevertheless sharp edge amid the words that Kofi Annan used . . . [F]rom his very first days on the job, Annan is demonstrating that he can both speak out on behalf of all the member-states of the U.N., and, in the appropriate diplomatic language, speak critically of the U.S." (Gwyn 1996, A23). Annan continued to work to impress his ideas upon others while largely limiting the critical backlash. For example, he supported his 1999 annual report with a speech in the General Assembly, which has been referred to as a "landmark address" (Findlay 2002, 327), where he called on the member-states to approve UN intervention in order to protect civilian rights. Reactions to this speech demonstrated that Annan shocked those who had hoped for a managerial head. However, in this speech and others, he was always careful to avoid the phrase humanitarian intervention, "speaking rather of 'intervention' pure and simple . . . In his own speeches the secretary general has been careful to stress that intervention can be of many types" (Tharoor and Daws 2001, 21).

In addition, Annan gradually built up to such proclamations and his good relations with the member-states helped to preclude too critical a reaction. Thus, Urquhart believes that "nobody else could have got away with his speech to the General Assembly on humanitarian intervention" (quoted in Williams 2000, 20). Similarly, when he made a strong statement in 1997 to the Organization of African Unity (OAU) pressing the organization to refuse membership to states where the leaders had taken power by illegal means, the OAU's Secretary-General noted, "That was a bold speech. You are the only one who can make this speech and get out of here without being lynched" (quoted in Meisler 2003, 38).

Annan has continued to take advantage of the stage that the Secretary-General's speech to open a new session of the General Assembly provides. In 2000 he again stressed the need for intervention, so both speeches have been described as "compelling pleas to the international community" (Ramcharan 2002a, 26). His 2002 speech has been cited as an example of how the Secretary-General can be an "influential participant in the legal discourse that infuses much of global politics" (Johnstone 2003, 441). In order to maximize the impact of this speech and ensure that Annan's message was not lost after President Bush spoke, in an unusual move copies were provided to the press in advance. The speech is described by Annan's chief speechwriter as an effort to "put down the marker for multilateralism" (quoted in Duke 2003, C1), although in the process he still "steered a delicate middle course between pleasing the Assembly's antiwar constituency . . . and acknowledging Washington's underlying view"

(Gourevitch 2003, 55). His 2003 speech, at times referred to as the "fork in the road" speech due to Annan's use of the phrase, reflected on the "pain of the previous year, and the breaking of previous consensus" (Prins 2005, 376) and the need to get back on a multilateral track. Again emphasizing the importance of international consensus, and recognizing the need to provide a strong message to stand out in relation to the speech by President Bush that would follow later, in 2004 he "launched a pre-emptive strike with a speech on the rule of law" (Williams 2004, 18).

As Secretary-General, Annan has constantly released official statements expressing his concern or dismay over problems areas, appealing for action, and commending progress and accomplishments (see http://www.un.org/apps/sg/sgstatsarchive.asp). Many of these are routine statements, but they have also been used in creative ways to manipulate the handling of specific breaches of the peace. In doing so, Annan has often been cautious in the wording, but still aims to get his point across clearly. He also has often stepped in when he thinks that his input is vital, but then backed off once his ideas have been imparted.

The use of official statements in relation to Iraq is illustrative. For example, in November 1998 U.S. Secretary of State Madeline Albright had a draft statement on Iraq prepared and faxed to the Secretary-General's office, but, while he was open to ideas from others, Annan insisted that if he was going to make a statement then he needed to do it in his own language and felt that Albright's approach was "too bellicose" (Shawcross 2000, 320). When the bombing campaign against Iraq began in December 1998, the crafting of an official statement was thought out in detail, including requesting three revisions from his speechwriters, because Annan "knew he had to be careful to express his dismay without giving the impression of criticising either Washington or London, or that he was siding with Saddam Hussein in the crisis" (Usborne 1998, 5). Later, with the American-led war in Iraq underway in 2003, "[p]eople the world over were waiting for his big antiwar speech, but he never delivered anything of the kind . . . If anything, he became even more guarded in his own public pronouncements" (Henneberger 2003, 33–34). This included "personally deleting a slightly combative line about how the United Nations would not accept a junior role in Iraq, although it would have been a definite crowd pleaser" for a speech to European leaders (Henneberger 2003, 37).

Annan also sought to limit controversial statements by his staff at times when he thought that they were causing political damage.

For example, Ruggie details Annan's handling of members of the UN Special Commission (UNSCOM) in Iraq: "Whatever differences the secretary general may have had with UNSCOM largely have been matters of style, not substance. On occasion, provocative remarks and indiscretions by UNSCOM personnel have permitted UNSCOM itself to become an issue of contention and the secretary general has consistently sought to curtail them" (1999, A23). When Mary Robinson spoke out as High Commissioner for Human Rights in October 2001 in favor of ending the bombing in Iraq, Annan was described as "livid" because she "broke rank" from his efforts to have the "U.N. speak with one voice" (Maniatis 2001, 47).

Reflective of a strategic Secretary-General who wants to have close interactions with others, Annan has traveled extensively and has used his trips to build connections throughout the world. He made travel an integral part of his Secretary-Generalship from the beginning of his tenure: "The new secretary-general of the United Nations, Kofi Annan, is, as the song says, a 'travellin' man.' Since he took over from Boutros Boutros-Ghali . . . Annan has been in almost constant orbit" (Jane's Information Group 1997, 5). This assertion was based on the fact that, as of May 1997, Annan had already been away from UN headquarters in New York for a third of his time in office. This pattern has continued throughout his tenure, with Annan circulating across the globe (see "Summary of the Secretary-General's Official Travels" at http://www.un.org/News/ossg/sgtrips.htm). Annan's travels were often designed for influential purposes. For example, he was "aggressively globetrotting" in 2005 to lobby for his reform plans and action against the violence in Sudan (Gordon 2005, 102). When traveling, Annan has displayed a strategic approach. For example, during a 1998 visit to the Middle East he was hectored by those who resented the treatment of Israel within the United Nations, but nevertheless he remained a "model of tact and sensitivity" (La Guardia 1998, A10). Yet, his trip still provided him with the opportunity "to tell Israeli leaders things that they would not listen to from others, including the U.S., and the secretary-general took advantage of it" (Williams 1998, 47).

Travel and lobbying efforts have often been focused on American lawmakers. As one report notes, "Never has a U.N. secretary general played the Washington circuit so assiduously" (Omestad and Fasulo 1998, 36). In fact, Annan made visiting the American capital his first traveling priority. In late January 1997, he "made a well-publicized pilgrimage" to Washington to discuss reform proposals and to encourage the Americans to pay their debt to the United Nations (Rieff 1999, 22). He has since visited Washington multiple times, aiming to make connections and to draw the Americans into being more positive contributors to the United Nations—a complicated task "given the fact that the U.S.-UN relationship has been moving between peaks and valleys at an alarming rate" (Smith 2004, 198) across his tenure. As part of this effort he has "notably cultivated" contacts with Congress instead of directing his sole attention toward the executive branch (Gordenker 2005, 98), even explicitly targeting Jesse Helms, one of the largest critics of the United Nations during his time in the Senate.

Although Annan sought to build connections with American law-makers, he maintained a strategic perspective when reacting to their demands. He remained firm on issues that he believed were important, but was willing to make the effort to work toward compromise. Thus, while possessing a clear sense of "political realism," Annan "also has a bottom line" to which he holds firm (Williams 1997, 23). For example, Annan was not willing to continually accept the lack of progress by the United States in paying its dues. He expected his trips and reform efforts to be reciprocated, so when the dues initially still went unpaid, "Annan is said to be disappointed, and one of his aides insisted grimly that 'we will be making fewer trips [to Washington] in the future' " (Rieff 1999, 22).

"Unofficial" representational activities

To ensure that his message is heard, Annan has employed a concerted public relations effort. Press accounts show that he was granting inter-views and expounding on his views as Secretary-General as soon as his selection was announced. He often designed his pronouncements to appeal to a broad audience: "Annan has addressed major initiatives to publics that included, but went well beyond, familiar diplomatic pro-ceedings in UN deliberative organs" (Gordenker 2005 84). He has also published a wide range of articles and opinion pieces (for a selec-tion, see http://www.un.org/News/ossg/sg/stories/articles.asp).

Annan took full advantage of trips to interact with many different groups and people by following a schedule that kept him in constant motion from one event to another. This approach has included appealing directly to the American populace by "barnstorming" across a variety of American cities as "part of a long-term strategy to put constituent pressure on the US Congress and to restore American confidence in the United Nations" (Ruggie, quoted in Lynch 1998, A1). He looked for opportunities "not to meet heads of state but to talk about the need for 'partnership' between the United Nations and business, academia and citizens organizations" because he stressed that the United Nations "must not be aloof" (Dolinsky 1998, A8). Annan was able to use these events to recruit high profile celebrities because he recognized the potential exposure that the United Nations and his ideas could garner when such individuals were encouraged to be involved. This point is stressed by Elaine Lafferty: "Most newspapers and TV networks are closing down their foreign news bureaus . . . At the same time, they are increasing coverage of celebrities and entertainment. So into this new reality comes UN Secretary-General Kofi Annan on a pilgrimage . . . The quest? Celebrities, film producers and sports stars. He hustled and cajoled and persuaded" (1998, 13).

These efforts had an interesting effect, as Annan has "almost improbably . . . become something of a star" himself (Usborne 1998, 5). As one headline reads, "Annan's Stratospheric Profile Gives U.N. a New Cause Celebre" (Crossette 1998b, A6) and, reacting to Holbrooke's observation that "Kofi is the international rock star of diplomacy," Gregory Maniatis agrees that "[r]ock star isn't an exaggeration" (2001, 44). Annan used his status to promote the United Nations in new and creative ways. Along with recruiting celebrities, he appeared with his wife as part of a celebrity couple photo shoot in the February 2003 issue of *Vogue*. He helped to launch a comic book starring Superman and Wonder Woman that explains the dangers of unexploded mines. He has been involved in a wide range of public outreach events, such as presenting a special, interactive BBC World Service lecture, a broadcast town hall meeting event, called "The U.N. Reaches Out to America," after the September 11, 2001 terrorist attacks that drew questions from a range of U.S. cities, and even appeared on the children's television show *Sesame Street* where he mediated an argument over whose turn it was to sing the alphabet song.

Annan's leap in public stature presents an apparent paradox for a strategic Secretary-General with the requisite low need for recognition and "is something of a surprise to many who knew him as a U.N. bureaucrat for more than 20 years" (Reeves 1998, 3C). However, although Annan actively enjoys the social scene and the potential for strategic connections that these situations provide, reflective of his low need for recognition, he only accepted the star-like treatment that arose "resigningly" (Chappell 1998, 136). Those close to Annan emphasize that the publicity is engineered for the good of the United Nations, not out of personal drive for such public exposure (Span 1998, C1).

Public relations require connections with the media and Annan, described as a "media fixture" (Fasulo 2004, 19), has demonstrated a willingness to work closely with the press. He has granted multiple interviews and maintains an open press conference manner. However, when speaking with the press, Annan often judiciously holds his tongue, even when he is clearly opinionated, and responds in a carefully measured manner. If pressed, he will often defer or proceed cautiously. Even after winning the Nobel Peace Prize "the quintessentially diplomatic and carefully spoken Mr. Annan seemed an island of calm, steering well clear of particular criticisms against any one country or policy. Even when he touched on more-contentious topics in an interview . . . the secretary general did it gently, with honey instead of fire" (Lyall 2001, A3). As one profile indicates, this cautious approach extends to personal issues: "His preferred method of deflecting questions about himself is to answer with such remove that you'd swear he was neutral even on the subject of Kofi Annan" (Henneberger 2003, 35).

Creative methods to get a message across to particular audiences while limiting its impact elsewhere have also been employed. In one instance Annan arranged to make "off the cuff" remarks in October 2001, which had actually been carefully crafted in advance, regarding ending the bombing in Iraq to a CNN reporter. This arrangement was designed so the statement would reach most of the world, but would not "play heavily in the U.S. for fear of embarrassing Washington—so there was no press conference or even an announcement to the correspondents on the third floor"; therefore Annan's "statement found its target while producing minimal collateral damage in America" (Maniatis 2001, 47). At the same time, he has seized opportunities to use the press to get his message across when he believes that a more direct, strong statement is necessary. For example, in 2003, "three months after President Bush warned that the United Nations might become irrelevant, the secretary general turned a traditional midsummer news conference into a stump speech on the value of international institutions in general and the United Nations in particular" (Barringer 2003, A16)

Even strategic Secretaries-General are likely to face criticism regarding their public statements. A major example was when, upon Annan's return from the negotiations in Iraq, he mentioned that "I think I can do business" with Saddam Hussein. This comment earned immediate backlash from American lawmakers, but when asked to back off the "Saddam-is-human line" Annan readily agreed (Traub 1998, 74). Annan's comments on Iraq made headlines again when he referred to the war as "illegal" in a September 2004 BBC interview. It is important to note that, as usual in interviews, Annan responded cautiously and only directly used the word "illegal" after the interviewer pushed the term several times in a row. Even then Annan continued to link the issue of legality to "the charter point of view." Analyzing the exchange, another BBC analyst notes how the interviewer "cleverly forced Mr. Annan's hand" so that "the actual word was wrested from him as the final thing he said" (Reynolds 2004). As Hans Blix observes, this was hardly a new point of view: "When Secretary-General Kofi Annan said in the spring of 2003 that he did not find the armed action against Iraq to be 'in conformity with' the UN Charter, not much attention was paid by media and the public" (2004b, 5). Regardless of Annan's intention, as one analysis notes, "Promptly, he joined the ranks of Washington's top political opponents" (Paepcke 2005, 14). Annan's standing among such opponents was not bolstered when he sent out a letter the Sunday before the 2004 American presidential election urging that forces not be sent into the Iraqi city of Fallujah. The letter was viewed by some as an effort to influence the election and, although Annan denies this claim, he now "admits that the Fallujah letter was a mistake" (Gordon 2005, 44). In both cases the backlash that he faced is indicative of how, when a strategist's instincts are off, such statements stand out in stark contrast to his usual approach.

There are other times when Annan's frustrations surfaced, demonstrating how pressure can affect even the most even-tempered individual. Melinda Henneberger reports, "Though he did not shirk his PR duties, he did weary of them, and showed it" at times when dealing with aggravating interviews (2003, 34). The continual questioning regarding aspects of the oil-for-food investigation seemed to particularly weigh on Annan and he has been critical of press coverage of the situation. At his 2005 year-end press conference he lashed out and cut off one reporter that he felt had been out of line. Ironically, this was directed at James Bone, the same reporter who once noted how he preferred Annan's "amiable press conference" which "marked a break with the haughty style of his predecessor" (1996, 9). Earlier that year, Annan provided the widely quoted response "Hell, no" to a question pressing him whether he intended to resign after the release of the March 2005 oil-for-food interim investigative report.

Such outbursts are unusual because Annan has more often employed his sense of humor to deflect difficult situations. For example, the French pushed for a French-speaking Secretary-General and expressed concerns that, while Annan does speak the language, his skills were not viewed as of high enough quality. Annan's response was that from then on he would even speak English with a French accent. As Secretary-General, he has continued to deflate criticism with his wit. As one early report noted, "It is only eight weeks since Kofi

Annan took over as secretary-general of the United Nations and he has already learned to respond with a joke when criticised for not moving quickly enough to reform the world body" (Black 1997, 18). He has also used humor to decrease tension. For example, during a Security Council meeting in January 2000,

> In the only light moment of the day-long debate on a grim subject, he expressed gratitude to Mr. Gore for introducing him effusively. "Thank you Mr. Vice President, or perhaps I should say Mr. President," Mr. Annan said, leaving a long pause before adding "of the Security Council." By council standards, it brought down the house. (Crossette 2000, A3)

In the midst of the oil-for-food investigation, he opened a speech to the UN Correspondents Association "by saying, 'I have resigned.' A stunned silence fell over the assembly. Then Annan grinned and continued, 'resigned myself to having a good time this evening.' " (Walker 2005, 17).

Summary style comparison for public pronouncements
Annan has been extensively engaged with public pronouncements. The level of controversy that some of his pronouncements have produced indicate that he acted beyond a strict understanding of the behavioral expectations for a strategist. However, it is equally clear that he has maintained an overarching strategic approach to his handling of public pronouncements. His initial annual reports did not present much of a challenge to the international community on how global security should be addressed, but his efforts became more innovative and agenda influencing and provided a continued base for supporting his views on international security. His official pronouncements were generally expressed in a noncritical manner, but he also showed that, when he thought it was necessary or appropriate, he was willing to step forward and speak out more forcefully on some issues. Similarly, he cultivated media connections and designed a vibrant public relations presence to reach a broad audience, but was, for the great majority of the time, simultaneously cautious in expressing himself in relation to sensitive areas.

PEACEFUL SETTLEMENT OF DISPUTES: "RELENTLESS YET SOFT-SPOKEN" DIPLOMAT

The reference in the subheading comes from Meisler, who notes Annan's "particular brand of relentless yet soft-spoken diplomacy"

(2003, 33). Annan has been actively engaged in the peaceful settlement of disputes, working on mandated assignments while also undertaking efforts on his own initiative. At the same time, he approached each conflict with a keen sense of political realism and an appreciation for the particular circumstances and needs of the actors involved. An analysis of his first few years in office reflects Annan's carefully developed approach:

> Technically, Annan is the servant of the UN Security Council. In practice, he has slowly expanded his personal diplomacy from one of simply reporting to the Council and executing the Council's directives to the job of actually expressing the will of the United Nations, while avoiding a clash in the UN Security Council. Annan has to be careful not to infuriate the "Big Five" and, at least for the last few years, he has succeeded beyond anyone's expectations. (Jane's Information Group 1999, 2)

Across his tenure, Annan has been willing to offer his services, but he has not forced himself into situations and carefully scopes out the acceptability of his actions before moving forward. His sensitivity has allowed him to be engaged in difficult situations and he has been "praised for his ability to effectively handle the spectrum interests and egos that sabotaged previous negotiations" (Chappell 1998, 136).

The negotiations with Hussein in February 1998, which led to a Memorandum of Understanding that, temporarily at least, forestalled military activity against the Iraqis, have often been highlighted as a major step for a Secretary-General. For example, Traub argues, "It might well have been the most dramatic achievement by a Secretary General since the era of Dag Hammarskjold . . . Some of the people around Annan believe that he 'revealed himself' in Baghdad—that he had begun to act more like a general than a secretary" (1998, 46, 74). However, details of his handling of Iraq reveals how his behavior actually reflects his strategic style—in other words, a bit of a general and a secretary. In addition, Annan's engagement in Iraq demonstrates how the lines between mandated and independently initiated missions often blur for Annan due to his consultative approach to peaceful settlement efforts.

The trip to Iraq was, strictly speaking, not a mandated mission. Although Annan's actions were constrained by the terms of earlier Security Council resolutions, the trip itself was based on the authority of his office. The United States did attempt to get the Security Council to approve written instructions, but this effort failed and Annan was only provided with what has been described as general "oral guidance" that outlined the goals of the mission (Sicherman 1998, 459). Building up to this point, Annan spent many hours conferring with members of the Security Council, as well as Iraqi officials and other foreign leaders, regarding the possibilities of the trip before committing himself (see Krasno and Sutterlin 2003, 122–135). He did not want to rush his involvement in the crisis and refused to undertake the mission until he felt comfortable that he had the necessary support of the Security Council as well as assurances from the Iraqi side that his trip would not be in vain. He used these meetings to cautiously build up an understanding of what would be acceptable to ensure that he would not be the focus of blame for the ongoing problems with Iraq, joking, as he often has, that SG stood for scapegoat instead of Secretary-General in the minds of some. By the end of this process, "he had obtained not only the capacity to negotiate, but also a strong sense of the fundamental issues on which there could be no compromise" (Brehio 1998, 603).

While Annan left for Baghdad with a clear idea of his negotiating boundaries, he also insisted on not being locked into taking over the framework for an agreement that did not provide him with flexibility during the negotiations. For example, he resisted demands that the Iraqis should be forced into unconditional surrender and instead sought a workable compromise acceptable to all parties involved. While in Iraq, Annan maintained contact with other member-states, staying up late at night on the phone with leaders around the globe. Yet, he also showed the capability to read a situation and act in the midst of tense negotiations without such consultations. When he met directly with Hussein, he suggested that the two leaders sit down one-on-one without the interference of their aides based on the notion that if he tried to give Hussein an ultimatum in front of others, he would not accept it, but he would be able to explain in private what was necessary and get Hussein to agree.

Upon his return to UN headquarters, Annan was met with a mixture of ebullience and censure. The leading critics were Republican members of the U.S. Congress, who were upset at both a perceived subcontracting of American foreign policy to the United Nations and the appeasing of a dangerous leader like Hussein. Congressman Gerald Solomon went so far as to call for Annan to be "horse-whipped." Annan drew on humor to try to defuse the assault, responding that in Ghana there is a proverb: "The horse may be mad, but the rider may not be" (quoted in Dolinsky 1998, A8). More broadly, he aimed to counterbalance the criticism and calm the situation by deferring credit for the success of the mission to the support he received.

Although the Memorandum of Understanding did not hold for long, with Operation Desert Fox air raids launched in December 1998, Annan refused to let this disappointment keep him from staying involved in efforts to peacefully resolve the Iraqi situation, although he also bowed to political reality and did not force the issue. As Gourevitch details, "[P]eriodically in 2000 and 2001 Annan sought to revive talks with Iraq to gain the inspectors access. But Iraq stonewalled, and last July [2002] he let the dialogue collapse . . . and nobody was asking Annan to go back to Baghdad, nor did he volunteer" (2003, 56). However, Annan still took advantage of opportunities to act when they were presented. In September 2002, after attending an Arab League meeting where he made contact with the Iraqi foreign minister, he was told that Hussein would allow the weapons inspectors back so he worked with Iraq to compose a letter laying this out, despite the fact that the action was perceived in Washington as "dramatically undercutting America's push for a new Security Council resolution" (Foer 2002, 20). Hope of avoiding a war was further bolstered when the Security Council passed a resolution in November 2002—with Annan "in the background, talking constantly by phone . . . urging patience and endurance in the negotiations" (Gourevitch 2003, 57)—which led to the first UN weapons inspectors in Iraq since 1998, but the effort failed to hold once again and the American-led attack began in March 2003.

Like many of the other Secretaries-General, Annan has also been involved in trying to resolve the Arab-Israeli conflict in the Middle East. His efforts in the region began in a cautious fashion. During a March 1998 trip, even though it came on the heels of his engagement in Iraq, Annan resisted the hope expressed by Palestinian leaders that he would similarly be able to encourage Arab-Israeli peaceful relations. As one report under the headline "Annan Steps Warily Into Middle East Minefield" notes, Annan was "treading a very gentle path . . . Captain Kofi is not going to sail his boat into an iceberg" (Fisk 1998, 17). When questioned before his trip about what he hoped to accomplish, Annan said that he hoped to assist with the peace process, but, in a bow to the great power presence, he did not intend to act as a mediator because the United States already played that role in the region.

However, the trip helped to prime acceptance of Annan's extensive engagement starting in October 2000 when violence disrupted the peace process. Annan stepped in as a key diplomatic player, using what has been described as a "calm persistence that became his trademark" that culminated in a summit held in Egypt (Pubantz and Moore

2003, 130). Indicative of the level of his involvement, one report claims that the summit "might not have happened if not for Annan's efforts" (Farley 2000, A8). At the same time, he was working in close collaboration with the Americans and was willing to defer to political necessity to keep the process moving forward. Following consultation with the United States, EU, and Russia, Annan decided to return to the region in June 2001 to try to capitalize on the opportunity presented by a cease-fire. Despite his efforts to similarly convince the Palestinians and Israelis that this was an opportunity that must be taken advantage of, this trip did not prove to be fruitful. His engagement tailed off as the approach built around collaborative ties with the Americans largely foundered as the Bush administration shifted its policy focus.

The Cyprus conflict is another problem area that has drawn the attention and personal involvement of the Secretaries-General across the years (Nachmias 1993; Newman 2001). Annan also made a concerted attempt to resolve the Turkish-Greek division of the island, carrying out an extended collaborative effort that sought to take advantage of pressing external deadlines as befits his strategic style. Newman observes that Annan's "more down to earth and quiet approach" contrasted with "the rather high-handed approach of Boutros-Ghali" (2001, 144). In his first year in office, Annan promoted talks as part of a process that he believed could gradually gather momentum and lead to an understanding of the mutual trade-offs necessary to reach agreement. After off-and-on talks, it became clear to Annan and his personal envoy to Cyprus Alvaro de Soto "that the principals would continue to talk around the subject until a document was set before them" (Rotberg 2003, 8). A comprehensive approach to resolving the situation, which widely became known as the Annan Plan, was first publicly presented in November 2002. This was just a month before the EU vote on whether to admit Cyprus, which indicated that only the internationally recognized Greek Cypriot section would be accepted unless a peace plan was approved by the spring.

The Annan Plan has been described as "the most comprehensive blueprint to date aimed at resolving the conflict and reuniting the island," although most of the details were not new as the plan built on "previous well-known blueprints" (Heraclides 2004, 38). Through an extended effort to gather the opinions of leaders in the Cypriot camps, the plan was revised several times (see Palley 2005, 275–324 for a detailed breakdown of changes across the different versions), but the process still failed to reach the needed agreement in March 2003. A last push was made with meetings in early 2004 and a final revised plan was presented at the end of March ahead of the accession of Cyprus to the EU on May 1, but in a referendum held that April the Greek Cypriots voted against the plan. Annan has not further pressed the plan after this failure, indicating that it was first necessary for the political will to be in place that would suggest a better chance of success.

Annan also inherited the conflict between India and Pakistan, where he probed for a chance to be involved, but did not force the issue. For example, he offered to act as an intermediary between the two countries when tensions flared after both sides openly tested nuclear weapons in 1998, but hastily added that he did not plan to travel to the region without a clear invitation and hope for positive progress. The next year, when an Indian jet was hijacked and taken to Afghanistan, with suspicions of Pakistani support for the hijacking running high, Annan declined to be involved. As one report details, despite the fact that the hijacking occurred "[a]t a time when Secretary General Kofi Annan is seeking greater authority to intervene in civil conflicts around the world, he has charted a decidedly conservative course in responding . . . leaving mediation to a team of Indian negotiators" (Lynch 1999, A24). The situation was diplomatically explosive and Annan decided that he had little leverage to bring to the crisis.

When Annan traveled to both Pakistan and India in March 2001 as part of a trip to the region he indicated his readiness to use his good offices to support a dialogue between the two countries, but rebuffed Pakistan's pressure to intervene unless India also expressed a willingness to be engaged in the process. Early the next year Annan traveled to Pakistan, Afghanistan, and Iran, but a planned stop in India was cancelled. UN officials claimed that scheduling problems arose, but reports indicated that India spurned Annan's offer to visit to reinforce the unwillingness to have a third party involved in negotiations. He has continued to provide encouragement to keep the peace process moving forward; however, as in other cases, he wanted both sides to be ready to engage in a collaborative process before he would be fully committed to the process as well.

When opportunities arise Annan has moved to involve himself in peaceful settlement efforts, as illustrated by his engagement in Africa, where he has been directly engaged in trying to resolve particular hostilities. One report notes how by 2001 Annan had already traveled to Africa more than any previous Secretary-General and "then returns trying to engage the international community" (Lauria 2001, E2). Although the United Nations was already active in the area with peacekeeping missions, Annan sought to provide additional impetus to bringing peace to the conflict-wracked Great Lakes area by organizing the International Conference on the Great Lakes Region, which held its first summit session in fall 2004. As Annan's special representative Ibrahima Fall emphasizes, "Peacekeeping is temporary . . . This Great Lakes process, on the other hand, is long term" (Fall 2005; see also Traub 2004).

Annan's involvement with a border dispute between Nigeria and Cameroon is a further illustration of his resolve to keep parties engaged in handling their differences in a peaceful manner. He met with the leaders of both countries in 2002 to ensure that they would agree with an upcoming ruling on the dispute by the International Court of Justice. When the court ruled for Cameroon, Nigeria backed out of this agreement and rejected the decision, which led to an increase in tension and concerns over the increasing possibility of violence. Annan quickly invited both presidents to meet with him again and they worked out an agreement to establish a commission under the watch of the United Nations to study ways to resolve the problem. Although the issue has still not been satisfactorily resolved, Annan has continued to meet with both parties to keep the process peacefully on track.

Annan will often wait for the opportune moment to personally intervene. This can be seen in relation to his handling of the Lockerbie bombing suspects. The Libyans had continually refused to release the suspects of a terrorist bombing of a plane that went down in Scotland in 1988. As with many other cases that he inherited, "[w]hen Annan became secretary general of the UN in January 1997, he began to look at how he could address the issue" (Shawcross 2000, 344). Finally, in December 1998, Annan, while already in Africa on a prearranged trip, agreed to add a personal meeting with Muammar Gaddafi to his agenda to try to convince the Libyan leader to release the suspects for an international trial. In this situation, Annan reasoned that failing to act would cause more damage than not agreeing to the meeting. The December trip was not immediately successful, but subsequent contacts—including a controversial letter in February 1999, the text of which was released in August 2000, that conveyed assurances from the British and Americans that the suspects "will not be used to undermine the Libyan regime"—helped to secure Libyan agreement to allow the suspects to undergo a trial at the Hague (quoted in Lynch 2000b, A14).

Conversely, Annan has delayed personally traveling to Zimbabwe in reaction to the government's "Operation Murambatsvina." The operation began in May 2005 and led to evictions and destruction of informal businesses and housing that displaced an estimated 700,000 people

(Wines 2005, A1). Annan first sought to gather information, sending a special envoy on a two-week fact-finding mission. Following the harsh report findings released in July, which were also taken up by the Security Council, President Robert Mugabe invited Annan to come to Zimbabwe. Annan indicated a willingness to do so, although he declined to set a date until he felt that steps were being taken to improve the situation and that details could be worked out to his satisfaction in order to ensure that the trip would be effective. Under Secretary-General for Humanitarian Affairs, Jan Egeland, traveled in his stead that December to further assess the situation.

In another instance, Annan closely followed the situation in Cambodia since the UN-supported rebuilding effort collapsed with the coup by Hun Sen in July 1997. He offered to assist in defusing the ongoing tensions and finding a long-term peaceful solution. A core aspect of discussions has been the establishment of a tribunal to judge crimes against humanity carried out by the Khmer Rouge. By February 2002, Annan grew frustrated by the inability to resolve disputes over the functioning of the tribunal and abandoned the negotiations. After the Cambodian government signaled that it was willing to compromise, Annan indicated that he would be willing to restart the effort if he received a clear mandate with details to guide to process, but his spokesman stressed, "Without that, he will not resume" (quoted in Mydans 2002, A11). The General Assembly provided such a mandate and talks resumed late that year.

Beyond such specific peaceful settlement efforts, Annan has also been engaged in broader efforts to promote a more peaceful international arena. This includes his reform plans, which have targeted the need to address weapons of mass destruction and terrorism. For example, the section on "freedom from fear" in his 2000 report called for a potential major conference to identify ways to eliminate nuclear weapons, while the same section in the 2005 report emphasized the need to deal with weapons of mass destruction and terrorism as a key part of promoting security. Annan has made a concerted effort to promote a multilateral approach to addressing terrorism. In the wake of the 2001 terrorist attacks in the United States, he moved quickly to emphasize that this represented an attack on the world and demonstrated that terrorism was a global threat that should be handled by the international community as a whole. At that point, and ever since, he has encouraged the General Assembly to agree upon a comprehensive convention on terrorism that would include a clear definition of the term.

Annan has also strategically reached out to the other actors, including regional organizations and NGOs, to assist with peaceful settlement. In relation to NGOs,

> Their contact with the affected populations and government leaders gives them a unique perspective on the causes of the conflict and opportunities for its resolution. The Secretary-General can draw upon the NGOs' knowledge to enrich his understanding of a dispute, the parties' motivations and interests, and alternative solutions. (Brehio 1998, 622)

He has also recognized NGOs potential importance in conflict prevention, their lobbying on behalf of global peace—such as the important role they played in formulating the Convention on the Prohibition of the Use, Stockpiling, Production and Transfer of Anti-Personnel Mines—and has encouraged the Security Council to be more receptive to NGO input.

SUMMARY STYLE COMPARISON FOR PEACEFUL SETTLEMENT OF DISPUTES

Given the wide range of peaceful settlement efforts in which Annan has been involved, it is impossible to detail every one. In addition, Annan's consultative approach extends across mandated and independently initiated efforts, where he aimed to keep the protagonists and member-states back at headquarters informed of his actions. Thus, unlike the structure used in the Hammarskjöld and Waldheim chapters, his activities in the previous section were not clearly demarcated into these two categories and, instead, his general approach was tracked across all instances of peaceful settlement. The key examples drawn on for this section illustrate how Annan was closely involved in a range of missions while displaying a pragmatic approach that took into account the political possibilities and pitfalls. In an interview when Annan was awarded the Nobel Peace Prize, Desmond Tutu commented, "He is an outstanding diplomat. He has been able to walk a tightrope, elegantly" (quoted in *Kofi Annan: Center of the Storm*, 2003). Annan worked to ensure support for his efforts and devised solutions through a process of give-and-take in close consultation with the parties involved to try to better ensure that coordination and compromise occurred. While he stepped forward in an active manner to help guide the peaceful settlement of disputes, he also employed a great level of sensitivity to the needs of the parties involved and did not try to impose solutions. He has also sought creative ways in which to improve peaceful settlement efforts through his reform efforts and engagement of other actors, as well as maintaining an emphasis on the multilateral handling of global threats.

UN INTERVENTION: STRATEGICALLY ENGAGED

Annan's UN intervention responsibilities have been much more extensive than those of Hammarskjöld or Waldheim, with 16 peacekeeping operations in the field as of December 2005, so this section does not attempt to provide details on every mission, but instead focuses on a cross-section in order to demonstrate Annan's strategic approach. This analysis highlights his efforts to resolve ongoing peacekeeping missions while continuing to work to create additional missions when new threats to peace and security deem it necessary. In both situations he has demonstrated a clear sense of the political possibilities, as well as dangers, as he shifts from one problem area to another. He has maintained a "pragmatic" approach to peacekeeping operations (Ruggie 1999, A23), but he has also employed creative methods to stay involved in UN intervention efforts and to keep the political process moving along at difficult times.

Despite the assumption that he would quickly have much to say regarding peacekeeping given his previous position as Under Secretary-General for Peacekeeping Operations, Annan took time to develop his proposals regarding UN intervention. One commentary shortly after his election observed, "Annan is keeping his cards close to his chest" on peacekeeping, as he held off on overly "ambitious proposals" (Handelman 1996, A19). Since then, however, Annan has continually built up his plans for how peacekeeping should be handled. As discussed earlier, his reform plans often sought to bolster UN intervention capability, he has been at the forefront of encouraging analysis of peacekeeping operations, has proposed major initiatives that would shift the burden of peacekeeping to cover humanitarian intervention, and, additionally, he presented a five-point action plan to prevent genocide in 2004 (Wagner 2004, 13–14). As the United Nations entered a new millennium of peacekeeping operations, he clearly sought to have an impact on how these missions are carried out. Overall, instead of only involving himself in individual peacekeeping cases as they arrived, he aimed to influence the very basis of peacekeeping rules and functions.

As with peaceful settlement efforts, Annan has shown appreciation for NGO assistance in relation to UN intervention. He has also worked to build strategic connections with other intergovernmental organizations (IGOs) to broaden his base of potential action. Part of his peacekeeping reform plans included increasing the formal relations between the United Nations and regional security organizations. He has broadly stressed the need to build cooperation among different organizations, as well as welcoming intervention by state powers, to better address difficult conflicts. While "[p]ast secretaries-general have been very dubious about such arrangements," Annan was willing to pursue them because he "is a practical man, rather than an ideologist" (Jane's Information Group 1999, 3).

For the creation of new missions, Annan has been willing to allow such alternative actors to step to the forefront of handling certain conflicts. This includes Kosovo and East Timor, where the North Atlantic Treaty Organization (NATO) and Australian-led forces were initially the primary actors engaged in addressing the conflicts. However, Annan carefully monitored both situations and worked to ensure that, in the end, a UN presence was firmly established. In the case of Kosovo, Annan maintained the longer-term perspective that the United Nations could still be a contributing actor in the area as long as the differences between the major powers did not become too inflamed. So instead of simply vociferously criticizing NATO's actions, and feeding the fire of Chinese and Russian complaints, Annan focused on maintaining a UN presence at the end of the NATO bombing campaign. In doing so, Annan had a difficult path to negotiate between stressing the need for Security Council approval so that UN authority was not undermined and ensuring that action was taken to alleviate the conflict. In the end, he employed a "carefully crafted statement" that argued sometimes force was legitimately necessary to achieve peace, thus tacitly supporting NATO actions, but Annan "balanced this, however, by pointing out that under the charter the Security Council should be involved in any decision to resort to the use of force" (Shawcross 2000, 366).

Once the NATO bombing campaign began, Annan strove to ensure that he was engaged in the continuing diplomatic efforts. He continued to press for a peaceful resolution, albeit in a manner that took into account the difficult political situation involved. During this process he was careful to offer both praise and criticism of all parties to try to keep constructive solutions moving forward. Through such engagement, Annan "carefully positioned" himself to "emerge as a key player after all, giving all sides political cover to strike a deal" in a cooperative effort that his spokesperson Fred Eckhard described as ensuring that he stayed "running with the lead pack" while encouraging those involved to move in the same direction toward a joint solution (Fasulo 1999, 6A). Through his machinations, he was able to keep closely involved whereby "the ultimate deal which introduced troops into Kosovo was negotiated in the Security Council, with the secretary-general being given the last word on the operation, even though it was not a UN one" (Jane's Information Group 1999, 3). With the UN Interim Administration Mission in Kosovo (UNMIK) in place, Annan continued to monitor and encourage the peacebuilding process. He met with a variety of the actors involved, including a tour of the area in November 2002, and appealed for violence to not disrupt progress. In 2005, he commissioned a report on the region and determined that the time was right for talks between Serb and the Kosovo Albanian representatives to get underway, with the hope that UN administration could soon be withdrawn.

In East Timor, Annan again encountered difficult political circumstances, but he worked to ensure that action was taken. Early in his tenure he "initiated a more proactive approach" to negotiations aimed at resolving the East Timorese question (Martin 2004, 144). A referendum was held at the end of August 1999, but the East Timorese suffered a brutal retaliation from pro-Indonesian militias when they voted for separation. Instead of insisting on a traditional UN force up front, and risking a slow or possibly even nonexistent reaction, Annan encouraged the creation of a multinational force led by Australia that could have a more immediate impact. He recognized the political exigencies and moved to create a workable short-term solution while heading off potential disruptions to this plan. This included making arrangements while convincing the Indonesians to allow an international force into East Timor. In the documentary *Kofi Annan: Center of the Storm*, Tharoor details Annan's efforts:

> He slept two, three hours a night for a week because of the time differences talking to the Americans, the Brits, various other countries, the Portuguese gearing countries to be ready to intervene and he orchestrated the whole thing to a point where the Indonesians finally made a public request to the UN to intervene and then he pushed through the Security Council an action and got the troops in. (2003)

As this statement illustrates, Annan operated through close consultation so that he did not try to force the United Nations into the situation, but he was still instrumental in encouraging and developing the intervention—labeled the International Force for East Timor (INTERFET)—for authorization by the Security Council.

Once INTERFET had moved into East Timor and established a more stable situation, Annan turned his attention to putting a broader

UN mission into place. The United Nations Transitional Administration in East Timor (UNTAET) was established to guide East Timor to full independence within several years and Annan remained engaged in the process in order to encourage long-term peace and stability. He visited East Timor in early 2000 as the UN mission was in the final stages of taking control and returned to preside over the May 2002 handover to independence, with the country joining the United Nations as the Democratic Republic of Timor-Leste that September. Post-independence, he helped to guide the gradual withdrawal of UN support, arguing that continued UN presence was necessary to consolidate the successful transition, and at the time of writing only the small United Nations Office in Timor-Leste (UNOTIL) is mandated to remain through May 2006.

The engagement of regional organizations or special member-state supported interventions is also on display in relation to UN missions established in Africa during Annan's time in office. In Sierra Leone and the Ivory Coast, Annan welcomed British and French intervention respectively and he courted U.S. engagement in neighboring Liberia. In May 2003, seeking to bolster the United Nations Organization Mission in the Democratic Republic of the Congo (MONUC) in the face of ongoing violence, Annan called for the assistance of all capable countries willing to serve as a "coalition of the willing"—which was answered by the insertion of a French-led multinational force (Astill 2003, 15). Annan has also backed the peacekeeping efforts of the Economic Community of West African States (ECOWAS) and the African Union (AU) in situations where the United Nations was also involved. This included cochairing a donor conference on behalf of the AU in May 2005 to support the organization's operations in the Darfur region of Sudan. Annan has also lobbied for EU and NATO involvement in order to bring more capability to bear on ending the violence in Darfur. Overall, these organizations and actors were not viewed by Annan as challengers to UN missions, but as means to collaboratively address the breaches of the peace in a manner that would have the greatest impact.

Annan has been strategically engaged with the establishment and functioning of UN missions in Africa. His general approach has been to take time to gather information and opinions as to how best to proceed before presenting concrete proposals. Thus, the peacekeeping operations often came on the heels of extended peaceful settlement efforts, with Annan calling for a mission to be established when the situation warranted. The case of the Ivory Coast highlights this process. Annan tracked the peace talks on the Ivory Coast, including personally attending a summit of African leaders held in France in January 2003 that led to a peace deal, and proposed the United Nations Mission in Côte d'Ivorie (MINUCI) that April. When he presented a plan to establish the United Nations Operation in Côte d'Ivorie (UNOCI) to replace MINUCI observers in early 2004, he was careful to connect his support for such a mandate to ensuring that enough progress had been made toward peace in the country.

Annan's engagement with conflict in the Sudan represents a particularly committed effort to promote UN intervention. He paid his first official visit to Sudan in July 2002 and encouraged the ongoing peace process to bring an end to the extended civil war between the north and the south, but the situation grew more complicated in early 2003 as violence also broke out in western region of Darfur. With the two dimensions to address, Annan has not only targeted the use of UN peacekeepers to solidify agreements ending the north-south war, but has also been closely involved in suggesting the need for intervention to address Darfur. For example, he used the ten-year commemoration of the 1994 massacres in Rwanda to highlight the Darfur violence and the need for the international community to respond. He has also returned to Sudan several times, including a highly publicized trip in mid-2004 that coincided with U.S. Secretary of State Colin Powell's visit. He has also pressed the Security Council to take action, "trying in his mild-mannered way to shame the council into action" (Traub 2004) and even asserted himself through "an unaccustomed intervention into a Security Council debate" in September 2004 to indicate his support for a resolution that included a commission to investigate Darfur and to head off a potential Chinese veto (Hoge 2004b, A12).

At the same time, interviews with staff members emphasize that Annan chose not to adopt an inflexible position or attempt to force action, which could have included invoking Article 99, but instead primarily patiently engaged the members of the Security Council in a behind-the-scenes manner to create a collaborative response (Smith 2005). Although the Americans declared that the violence in Darfur was genocide, Annan in a "politically calculated omission" has avoided such terminology (Reeves 2004, 10). He recognized that the Security Council members were divided on whether genocide was occurring and sought for the commission of inquiry to be mandated as a method to overcome the difference of opinion (Smith 2005), although the commission findings released in early 2005 concluded that genocide had not occurred. He also emphasized that the reality of the peacekeeping situation was that the United Nations was not ready to go into Darfur at the height of the genocide concerns. This has led to criticisms by some that he was not pressing for fast enough action, including columnist Nicholas Kristof, who wrote that Annan will be viewed as having "presided ineffectually over the failure to stop genocide, first in Rwanda and then in Sudan" (2004, A15). Finally, as indicated above, in relation to Darfur, Annan has largely relied on supporting AU peacekeeping up to this point.

Once Annan had a peacekeeping plan in place, he used his position to lobby for its implementation. Continuing the discussion of Sudan, building out of the north-south civil war peace accord in January 2005 Annan quickly recommended the establishment of the United Nations Mission in the Sudan (UNMIS) and then, "exasperated over continuing procrastination," called the Security Council members to a closed-door meeting to press for approval (MacAskill 2005, 2). At the same time, he reinforced the need for public and media pressure to bring about action, including meeting with NGOs to determine the best way to focus this pressure. In another instance, in July 2003 when Annan sought American approval for, and involvement in, the United Nations Mission in Liberia (UNMIL), he traveled to Washington to meet with President Bush and on the same trip discussed the situation with members of the Senate.

Once UN operations were established, Annan remained engaged in monitoring and supporting the missions. Maintaining the operations has not been an easy task. For example, the mission in the Congo has been hampered by the aforementioned sexual misconduct scandal, as well as allegations that UN charter flights had been used to smuggle diamonds, violence against members of MONUC, looting of offices, and even a volcano eruption. Yet, Annan has persevered and stepped in to keep the operations functioning. For example, in relation to Sierra Leone, one study emphasizes that, along with the British military intervention, the "on the verge of collapse" mission was "turned around thanks in large measure to extraordinary personal efforts by the UN Secretary-General" (Dobbins et al. 2005, xx).

Annan has also been involved in UN peacekeeping operations that were established before he took office. In these situations he has focused most of his attention on trying to resolve the underlying conflicts so that the missions might be withdrawn. As discussed in the previous section, a prime example is his attempt to overcome the Greek-Turk division in Cyprus, which would have had the added benefit of allowing the United Nations to remove the long-standing peacekeeping mission that remains as a buffer between the two sides. Annan has also been engaged in Africa in an effort to encourage the mandate completion of the United Nations Mission for the Referendum in Western Sahara (MINURSO), which was established in 1991 primarily to monitor the cease-fire between Morocco and the POLISARIO Front and to organize a referendum to decide the future of the disputed territory. However, by the time Annan took office the referendum had still not been held.

The efforts in Western Sahara were largely driven by Annan's special envoy, former U.S. secretary of state James Baker, who worked on resolving the differences from 1997 until resigning in frustration in 2004. However, Annan also personally traveled to the area in 1998 in order to "intensify efforts towards resolving the Western Sahara dispute" (Khalaf 1998, 4). After meeting with both sides, he decided that it was necessary to keep MINURSO at full strength to ensure the best chances of success. However, when disagreements over who would be allowed to vote in the referendum remained unresolved, Annan suspended the referendum yet again. Since then he has periodically issued reports recommending MINURSO's renewal in order to maintain a UN presence, including a February 2002 report presenting four options based on Baker's ideas to the Security Council for overcoming the impasse (Adebajo 2002, 28–29; Shelley 2004, 151–152). The negotiations continue to drag on, with new personal envoy Peter van Walsum declaring the differences between the disputants "quasi-irreconcilable" in October 2005 (UN News Service 2005).

Annan also faced a complicated situation in the Middle East starting in 2000 when Israel withdrew from its position in southern Lebanon. With this aspect of its mandate complete, questions arose regarding the proper role of UNIFIL and there were concerns that the mission might face the burden of increased violence. Initial emphasis was on greatly bolstering UNIFIL or authorizing a new force in order to maintain the peace. Recognizing that the United Nations was approaching overload with its newer operations elsewhere, Annan encouraged the contesting sides to link the pullout to a broader Middle East peace process that would not place the burden on inserting another large UN presence. However, in late April 2000 the Security Council requested that he examine the situation and determine whether the UNIFIL force should be expanded. Annan reacted by deferring on a recommendation until he could gather further information. However, as the Israeli pullout accelerated ahead of schedule in late May, Annan put a plan before the Security Council that called for the expansion of UNIFIL to try to ensure that the situation did not spiral out of control. Once the removal of Israeli troops was confirmed, Annan sought to take advantage of the opportunity and "promptly departed on a week-long trip" to the region "to discuss ways for the United Nations to build on the achievement" (Wren 2000, A16).

As time passed and the feared violence failed to arise, Annan recommended a "prudent approach" that would reduce troops to around the level before the Israeli pullout (S/2001/66). Despite ongoing Lebanese concerns and calls for maintaining a more sizable UN military presence, he continued to encourage further scaled reductions to provide a smaller force to monitor the "blue line" demarcation between Israel and Lebanon. The call for troop reduction was reiterated in early 2002, with the aim getting the force down to 2,000 by the end of the year. Annan's July 2002 report allowed for an extension of the mission, but included a strong criticism of Lebanon because the government had not asserted its authority in the south as continually requested. His January 2003 report sought to maintain the status quo level of a 2,000 strong force due to the continuing hostilities as Annan continued to try to make the "interim" part of UNIFIL's name finally apropos.

SUMMARY STYLE COMPARISON FOR UN INTERVENTION

Annan once again sheds his preelection managerial label with his handling of peacekeeping operations during his time as Secretary-General. He worked with the members of the Security Council to probe for where he could provide ideas for establishing missions and how these operations should be structured. He provided broader input through his reform and other plans designed to guide the direction of UN intervention. He has also remained closely involved in carrying out interventions by the United Nations, including missions that were established before he took office, but has operated in a pragmatic manner, including demonstrating flexibility and openness to alternative actors engaged in helping to address breaches of the peace. Overall, Annan did use his position to try to influence UN peacekeeping efforts, but worked within the confines of the political limitations that he faced as he sought practical solutions.

CONCLUSION

In an interview shown in *Kofi Annan: Center of the Storm*, Annan was asked, "You get the impression that there is a 'Kofi Annan' style." Annan replied, "I know I do things in my own way. I don't know if it's a 'Kofi Annan' style—but it's the way I am" (2003). This analysis has shown that the "Kofi Annan style" is a strategic one and that his behavior while in office reflects that style accordingly. While his actions have generally not pushed the boundaries of the Secretary-Generalship in a forceful, visionary manner, he has attempted to be far more independent and influential than one would expect from a manager. Annan's approach is well captured in one observer's literary analogy: "Annan seems to have adapted to the role so that he appears more like P.G. Wodehouse's butler, Jeeves: the unflappable provider of good advice, quietly put, expressed in a way that observes protocol but makes it clear to all just who is right" (Williams 2000, 21).

As shown across the range of influential categories, Annan's strategic leadership style has translated into the expected behavior throughout his tenure as Secretary-General. From his early reform plans, Annan took hold of the reins of the Secretary-Generalship and worked to mold the United Nations to better fit his style. He used a series of reports to criticize previous efforts to bring about a more peaceful world, while being careful to state that the Secretariat and even his own office share the burden of past failures. With the continued reform efforts and analyses of UN peace operations, Annan continued to gradually push the boundaries in an attempt to influence how global insecurity is addressed by the United Nations, although overall such an extensive set of penetrating reports does seem to stretch beyond the bounds of what one would expect from an ideal manager. After bowing to political necessity and implementing the first negative-growth budget, he has slowly but surely worked to expand the UN budget in a manner that targets the areas that he believes deserve more attention while also seeking to alter the budget process itself. While he has been reactive to political pressure in structure and staffing issues, he also remade the Secretariat through a series of appointments and reorganization measures to create a United Nations that reflects his desire for greater coordination, openness to ideas, and efficiency.

As a strategic Secretary-General, Annan has appreciated and employed his strategic political position within the United Nations. He has worked closely with UN organs and representatives to encourage consensus decisions. He has excelled at building relationships with delegates and other government representatives. At the same time, he has moved beyond the traditional relationships available at the United Nations by cultivating social interactions and linking with NGOs and the business community. From his strategic vantage point, he remained very open to information and ideas. He sits at the point of information flowing in and then out of his office and has attempted to use this position to influence others.

Annan has also been willing to use the public pronouncement tools at his disposal to his advantage. As with the reporting mechanism, Annan's willingness to publicly challenge major, politically important areas is more than an ideal strategist would be expected to pursue. However, he has still been careful to temper his message. Despite several notable examples to the contrary, it is rare for him to be strongly critical when addressing sensitive issues and he carefully monitors what he says. His annual reports gradually became bolder and remain an important statement to support his views on international peace and security. Recognizing the importance of public relations for promoting his ideas and the United Nations, he built up relations with the media and continuously traveled in an effort to get his message across and to build new contacts.

Annan has not shied away from addressing the peaceful settlement of disputes or UN intervention. He has been involved in trying to help resolve conflicts throughout the globe. At the same time, he has been careful to make sure that his role is accepted before becoming engaged. His emphasis has been on carefully listening to the different sides of a disagreement and encouraging the conflicting parties toward a consensus decision. When the use of force has become necessary, Annan has worked with the Security Council to design missions that can properly handle the conflict, drawn in a range of actors to address the violence, and carried out his mandates with an eye toward creating the most stable situation guided by UN involvement over the long term. For long-standing peacekeeping missions, Annan maintained his involvement by trying to guide the conflicts to final settlement and adjusting the missions accordingly.

At the time of writing, Annan is entering the last year of his second, and presumably last, term as Secretary-General, so it remains to be seen whether he will remain on a strategic path, but the indications from his leadership style and behavior across his time on office so far indicate that this is what should be expected. While some observers applaud Annan's tenure, others continue to question his leadership capabilities. Despite Annan's efforts to strategically handle his office, some critics yearn for a more visionary approach, while others view him as already too independent a Secretary-General. Thus, the debate over the role of the Secretary-General continues, and it will be up to Annan's successor to define the next phase for the office.

CHAPTER 7

From Manager to Visionary:
Contrasting the Secretaries-General

Examination of the literature on the influence of the secretary-general forcefully suggests two conclusions about that literature: It is large and growing rapidly, yet there is little in the way of systematic explanation of the behavior of the secretary-general.

(Knight 1970, 594)

INTRODUCTION

Plimpton reports that a tourist once asked, "I know what a secretary is, and I know what a general is, but what on earth is a secretary general?" Plimpton responds, "The answer is not simple" (1966, 58). This study reaches the same conclusion. How the role of Secretary-General has been carried out varies across the tenures of the different office-holders. Some have behaved as a secretary implementing the instructions of the member-states. Others stand out as a general, providing independent, visionary leadership. Occasionally an office-holder balances the two aspects of the job, bringing together a secretarial understanding of the needs of the member-states while still providing a general's independent initiatives.

All three case studies, and the comparative review discussion in this chapter, demonstrate such considerable differences between the Secretaries-General. Dag Hammarskjöld, Kurt Waldheim, and Kofi Annan were shown not only to possess divergent leadership styles, but these styles were also explicitly linked to dissimilar political behavior. The role played by the Secretary-General in addressing breaches of the peace varied greatly, and primarily in the manner expected, across the avenues for influence depending upon whether the managerial Waldheim, strategic Annan, or visionary Hammarskjöld was in charge. This supports the argument that Secretaries-General must be viewed as individuals who bring a personal style to bear on their activities; in other words, the answer to "what is a Secretary-General?" depends upon who holds the office.

For this concluding chapter, the leadership styles and corresponding actions of Hammarskjöld, Waldheim, and Annan are revisited and compared in order to clearly contrast their time as Secretary-General. This analysis includes a comparison of style expectations with the actual behavior of the three Secretaries-General to indicate where variation from the behavioral forecasts occurred and what the potential consequences of these differences might be for the study of other office-holders. The three ideal leadership styles are then reconsidered. The review concludes that the styles are useful organizing tools for building a better understanding of how Secretaries-General behave in office, but a closer examination of personal characteristics is often necessary in order to fully understand their actions. The chapter then moves into a discussion of how the leadership style analysis presented in this study could be integrated with contextual factors in order to provide a more complete understanding of the role played by the Secretary-General in international affairs. The final section presents the future research possibilities that build out of this study.

CONTRASTING HAMMARSKJÖLD, WALDHEIM, AND ANNAN

The content analysis coding results reported in chapter 2 indicate that the seven Secretaries-General clearly varied across their personal characteristics and the corresponding leadership styles. Based on these results, this study focused on the three Secretaries-General who most closely met the criteria of the ideal leadership styles: Waldheim the manager, Annan the strategist, and Hammarskjöld the visionary. The three men clearly possessed divergent views of the office that reflected their personal predilections. Hammarskjöld had a clear vision of global politics guided by international law and collective interests and foresaw a vital role for the United Nations and the Secretary-Generalship in helping to bring this vision to fruition. He was predisposed to step forward with conviction to ensure that his ideas would be followed and that breaches of the peace were handled along the lines that he believed necessary. Conversely, Waldheim believed that his role as Secretary-General was to carry out the wishes of the member-states and not to interfere in their affairs when he was not wanted. Annan's strategic style falls in between. While recognizing the boundaries of acceptable action, he also thought that he had a role to play in working to prod others in the direction that he believed was best and he was not willing to sacrifice the independence of his office or the principles of the United Nations.

The leadership styles that these three Secretaries-General possessed guided how they addressed international peace and security in different manners. Hammarskjöld emphasized his independence and desire to influence events as he stepped to the forefront of handling threats to global security. While some deride Waldheim and others applaud his conduct, depending upon their perception of how a Secretary-General should act, the consensus is clear that he behaved in a managerial manner. Throughout his tenure he followed the demands of the member-states instead of charting his own course in international affairs. Annan, the first strategic Secretary-General, took a different approach. He was attentive to the needs and desires of others, while carefully working to ensure that his views influenced how breaches of the peace were addressed.

These broad behavioral patterns generally hold true across the specific influential activities available to office-holders. The following analysis reviews the actions of the three Secretaries-General in relation to the avenues of influence, which reinforces how the different approaches undertaken reflect their respective leadership styles. At the same time, revisiting the behavioral expectations set out in chapter 3 to see how well these mesh with the actual behavior of Waldheim, Annan, and Hammarskjöld reveals some deviations that indicate the behaviors related to different leadership styles may not be as clear-cut as assumed and shows the behavioral nuances that can occur. Some of these differences may be attributed to the office-holders' styles not exactly matching the ideal types, which will be further explored in the next section, while other deviations indicate that some of the behavioral expectations may need to be reconsidered.

AGENDA SETTING

ADMINISTRATIVE DUTIES

In handling administrative duties, Waldheim did not pursue the opportunities for influence and allowed the member-states to dictate matters. It is difficult to find any point across the four subcategories of administrative duties—supervising reports, overseeing finances, shaping the administrative structure, and staffing the Secretariat—where Waldheim sought to exert his influence. The one minor deviation was that he endeavored to restructure the upper level of the Secretariat early in his tenure, whereas an ideal manager was believed to be unlikely to carry out any restructuring unless told to do so. However, the appointments Waldheim used to fill these slots were still designed to curry political favor. In addition, as noted in chapter 5, his actions do counter any general impression that observers might have that Secretaries-General with a managerial leadership style will be focused on handling administrative affairs. In fact, Waldheim generally ignored the administrative side of his job and often let member-states dictate how Secretariat businesses should be conducted.

Hammarskjöld was involved in all aspects of administrative duties. From the arrangement and content of reports and the budget proposal to independent control over staffing and the structure of the Secretariat, he insisted on doing things his way. Thus, when Hammarskjöld was engaged in administrative duties, his behavior closely matched the visionary expectations across all four categories. However, as discussed in chapter 4, he was particularly involved with administrative issues in his first few years as Secretary-General or when his control was challenged, with the Soviet troika proposal being the prime example, but he largely left the basic administrative details to others later in his tenure as he focused on directly addressing international conflicts. So while no differences occur in relation to the behavior categories, there is some across time variance in terms of level of involvement.

Annan was also engaged in administrative affairs, but he displayed a more gradual approach—acquiescing to political necessities while simultaneously working to build up his influential capabilities through a give-and-take process with the member-states. Annan's conduct solidly matches with expectations for a strategic Secretary-General in three of the four categories. An exception to some degree was in his use of reports. Although strategists are supposed to express themselves through the reporting mechanism, some of Annan's reports stand out as more critical and candid than expected.

Overall, the approach to administration was varied and related to the different leadership styles. Under Waldheim, the Secretariat and its work reflected member-state preferences. Hammarskjöld grasped control of administrative affairs in an iron grip and shaped what occurred to fit his inclinations, creating a top-down approach where he had the final say on matters. Annan worked to create an administration that broke away from a hierarchical approach and instead promoted an open and cooperative environment where his voice remained important, but as one among the many collaboratively considering how to handle situations.

STRATEGIC POLITICAL POSITION

In relation to the Secretary-General's strategic position, which puts office-holders at the official and unofficial crossroads of an array of information and contacts, the three men again display clear differences in their approach. Waldheim was used for the access that his position provided; Hammarskjöld employed the connections to encourage adherence to his ideas; and Annan worked to build wider constituencies than any previous Secretary-General—gathering new information and ideas from others as he proceeded. There is little evidence to suggest that Waldheim generally did more than defer to the member-state representatives at meetings and he explicitly expressed his great willingness to work under the authority of the other UN organs. Similarly, contacts that come from the Secretary-General's inherent strategic position were not used by Waldheim to try to set the agenda or to frame how problems should be addressed, but instead delegates came to him to take away information and to try to influence how his office would address issues. At the same time, although Waldheim was not pursuing the inherent strategic position as an avenue for influence, he does seem to have been more actively engaged in meeting with others through his strategic connections than expected for a manager.

Hammarskjöld used his strategic position to initiate continual contact among the delegates and has been referred to as the chief legislator of the United Nations due to the way that he worked to devise policy. He was involved in many UN meetings, where he would openly express his views on what should be done, and sought to have other deliberations, such as disarmament, brought under UN auspices to ensure that he had a better opportunity to be involved in discussing the subject. He employed his strategic position to assert informal influence where he used middlemen to get his position across. Member-state representatives constantly came in and out of his office and some delegates who fell under Hammarskjöld's sway commented that they felt a conflict of allegiance between their home country and the United Nations. While Hammarskjöld's actions as a representative in meetings mirrored expectations, some deviation from his anticipated use of the inherent strategic position does occur. Where visionaries were presumed to attempt to continually press their ideas on others that they came into contact with, Hammarskjöld engaged in a more subtle use of this avenue for influence. Instead of simply trying to force his views, he used his position to build up working relationships and strategic connections that he could employ to funnel his ideas into UN policy.

As a strategic Secretary-General, interactions with others have been a focal point of Annan's time in office and he has excelled at cultivating strategic connections. He has been open to new ideas and information and expanded the contacts of his office beyond the traditional government representatives to work with new constituencies, from NGOs and the business community to star performers and the general public. In the process he became a desired social guest and worked tirelessly to get his message across to those he came into contact with while at the same time learning about their views. In his formal capacity in meetings, he endeavored to keep the political process moving toward consensus decisions and also encouraged multilateral meetings to be held at the United Nations so he could maintain his strategic presence. While Annan's actions as a representative in meetings matched expectations, his inherent use of the strategic political position is worth a closer look. His behavior here might be considered a "match-plus" since he not only met expectations, but also exceeded them. Strategists are naturally inclined to use these connections as an avenue for influence, but Annan went even further than envisioned in undertaking a great effort to expand his constituencies, meet with new groups and individuals, and engage in near constant interaction with others as he gathered information and ideas.

Waldheim did use his Article 99 powers to bring the American hostages in Iran to the attention of the Security Council, which was unexpected as managers should be the least likely to invoke Article 99. However, he did not offer clear plans for how to handle the situation and the true independence of his effort has been called into question. Thus, this occurrence does not appear to warrant a change in expectations for other managers, although it does serve as a reminder that this power is always available to a Secretary-General and could come into play no matter what style an office-holder possesses. In contrast, Hammarskjöld, the first Secretary-General to call for a meeting under Article 99, did so in order to control the timing and agenda of the Security Council meeting. He built upon this power to guide deliberations and to shape how the United Nations addressed the crisis in the Congo. Annan, as expected, has not displayed any intention of explicitly employing Article 99.

PUBLIC PRONOUNCEMENTS

While Waldheim approached the annual report in the manner expected, providing relatively straightforward accounts that did not provide him with a greater say in how international peace and security should be handled, deviations from an ideal managerial approach do exist for the other two public pronouncements categories. For both official and unofficial public pronouncements he issued many statements, traveled extensively, and generally attempted to promote a high profile for himself. However, the managerial underpinnings of his character come across clearly when the message, or lack thereof, that he used these activities to promote is examined. The best description of Waldheim, as indicated by Newman in chapter 5, is high profile but low key since he avoided making statements that would aggravate the member-states. In the few cases where he did make a condemning statement, he quickly backed away when faced with a negative reaction.

The opposite approach held true for Hammarskjöld. He treated the annual report as a vital forum to expound upon both specific issues of the day and his general vision for the future despite the political controversy that arose from his efforts. All of his annual reports sought to influence the agenda and observers agree that these are a must-read to get a feel for Hammarskjöld's views. The media was seen as a mouthpiece for his message and he worked to control interview sessions so that questions and answers focused on the topics that he wanted to address. He traveled extensively; he especially relished trips to the hot spots of the world so that he could monitor and speak directly to the combatants, and used these opportunities to speak his mind as well. At the same time, Hammarskjöld's complexity shines through as many times his pronouncements displayed a greater sense of the circumstances than anticipated. He did not take advantage of all times and situations to speak out as assumed for a visionary, but instead he avoided public statements when he felt that they might disrupt efforts to resolve problems.

Unlike Waldheim who rarely communicated a controversial opinion, Annan stepped forward and strongly expressed himself when he believed that it was a necessary or appropriate time to try to influence the handling of global affairs. The pattern of being more forceful at times than expected in his reports, as established under the administrative duties category discussion, is repeated across the three categories of public pronouncements. For example, his recurrent message regarding the need for intervention on humanitarian grounds challenged the basic tenet of member-state sovereignty. At the same time, Annan has carefully crafted public pronouncements that are generally nonconfrontational in tone. This can be seen in the way that he has maintained an intense travel and speaking schedule and has been extremely accessible to the media, but he has also carefully monitored what he said in order to avoid offending member-states to the best of his ability.

PEACEFUL SETTLEMENT OF DISPUTES

When tracing the involvement of the Secretaries-General in the peaceful settlement of disputes, disparate patterns of behavior once again emerge. Waldheim handled mandated peaceful settlement missions as anticipated for a manager. However, to some degree he contradicted the projection that a manager would stick with mandated assignments and was unlikely to undertake independently initiated efforts. The number of such endeavors was relatively low, but they were still more than expected for an ideal manager. At the same time, when he undertook such missions he largely carried them out in a managerial fashion and avoided becoming independently involved when faced with politically disadvantageous circumstances.

Hammarskjöld undertook many independently initiated missions and pushed the boundaries of his office's authority. In addition, visionaries should attempt to influence mandates and interpret the needs of the mission when carrying out the assignment, which Hammarskjöld did, but he also went further by insisting that the independent powers of his office remain intact even when operating on a mandated mission. This was most explicitly displayed with his use of the Peking Formula where, even though the missions to China and South Africa were initiated at the request of the General Assembly and the Security Council respectively, he based his actions on the independent authority of the Secretary-Generalship. Thus, similar to the argument made in relation to Annan and his use of inherent strategic position, given the high degree of independence asserted by Hammarskjöld in handling mandated peaceful settlement of disputes this could even be considered a "match-plus" when compared to expectations.

Annan, while displaying a greater willingness to undertake independently initiated missions in comparison to the managerial Waldheim, most of the time did not forthrightly challenge the member-states in the way that Hammarskjöld's methods did. He sought to guide mandates to create clear expectations for his missions and, even when initiating peaceful settlement efforts, maintained a collaborative process in establishing the missions and in seeking resolutions. He was careful to gather a range of information regarding the possibilities for peaceful settlement and what actions would be most suitable before becoming engaged with the problem. When the mission was underway he prodded parties toward an agreement, displayed a pragmatic approach where he worked within the acceptable parameters of a mission, and looked for greater support for his actions, including engagement with alternative actors, before moving forward.

UN INTERVENTION

When the United Nations went beyond peaceful settlement and employed force, the Secretaries-General also handled the situations differently. Based on his vital role in this area, Hammarskjöld has been referred to as the father of peacekeeping. He endeavored to put a personal imprint on the very character of these missions. He stepped in and took over the observation missions established under Lie and shaped them through personnel changes and increased attention to ensure that they were performing in the manner that he desired. For all three new peacekeeping operations set up under his watch, he performed in a visionary manner. He was closely involved from the beginning as he worked to shape the mandates for the missions. Once the mandate was set, he continued to monitor and guide all aspects of the operations to ensure that he could influence their performance to the best of his capabilities. Hammarskjöld did display a complex awareness of global hot spots in his handling of interventions. In relation to the Congo and Lebanon, instead of waiting to react to crises as they emerged, he was aware of a need for action well in advance and set up contingency plans to handle the conflicts.

UN intervention under Waldheim was dominated by the member-states. He showed no inclination to intervene to influence the peace-keeping operations that he inherited. Waldheim watched from the sidelines as others, primarily the Americans, guided the creation of the new peacekeeping missions in the Middle East. In carrying out his duties in implementing the operations, Waldheim ensured that he catered to the views of all those involved and did not undertake independent initiatives to guide the handling of the missions.

By contrast, Annan has pursued a role of strategic middleman in shaping and carrying out peacekeeping operations. He has demonstrated a sense of the political possibilities and limits for UN peace-keeping around the globe. He sought to encourage existing operations toward completion and worked with member-states, in addition to welcoming the participation of alternative forces, for the creation and management of new missions, while also promoting reforms that could guide the future of peacekeeping. His overall approach has once again largely been a gradual one. He carefully studied situations, gathered information and opinions on how to proceed in order to help guarantee support for his plans and to avoid isolating or aggravating particular actors, while maintaining a strong long-term impact for the United Nations in maintaining international peace and security.

VARIATION ACROSS AN ACTIVITY CATEGORY OR LEADERSHIP STYLE

To conclude the comparison of Secretary-General behavior, this section draws out and examines trends exposed across different activities to consider whether there are broader implications for reconsidering behavioral expectations. Within the activity categories some expectations matched closer with the actual behavior displayed by the Secretaries-General than others. The projections for administrative duties matched well, with only Waldheim's minor involvement in shaping the administrative structure and Annan's stronger use of reports deviating from assumptions. The efforts at peaceful settlement of disputes and UN intervention also met expectations, with Waldheim's engagement in independently initiating the peaceful settlement of disputes standing out as the major exception.

The actual behavior under the strategic political position varied from expectations to a greater degree. While Waldheim's use of Article 99 is the only deviation for the Secretary-General as a representative in meetings, some level of variation occurred for all three Secretaries-General in their use of the inherent strategic position. Waldheim was more engaged and Hammarskjöld more collaborative than expected. The strategic Annan even exceeded expectations as he expanded his strategic base and contacts. The greatest level of variation from expectations for any activity category is displayed in the use of public pronouncements. While Waldheim and Hammarskjöld used the annual report as expected, the message of Annan's annual reports, although developed gradually, was more controversial than expected for a strategist. This pattern for Annan continued across official and unofficial representational activities, but there were deviations for the other two office-holders as well in these categories as Waldheim was much more engaged and Hammarskjöld more sensitive in the use of these mechanisms than would have been suggested by their overall style profile.

A theme runs across many of the activity categories in the Secretary-General's toolbox. Both the distinction between voluntary and mandatory activities designed to capture whether a particular tool would be used or not and the expectations for the use of these tools appear to be overly restrictive at times. Specifically, for public pronouncements it was misplaced to expect Waldheim to remain largely silent while Secretary-General. Given the important position of the office in global affairs, it is doubtful that any Secretary-General is going to match the expectations of operating out of the limelight at the beck and call of the member-states. Are there any Secretaries-General who will not travel and give speeches to private groups or give interviews to the press? The focus when examining public pronouncement behavior should not be on the quantity of pronouncements, but on the tone and message of these efforts. While Waldheim was more likely to undertake public pronouncements than expected from a manager, the lack of challenging or substantive messages still reflects a managerial leadership style. Despite the potential link of Hammarskjöld's complexity to his behavioral variation, it may be that the visionary expectations for these activities need to be adjusted as well. While a visionary such as Hammarskjöld should be expected to express strong views in his public pronouncements, in retrospect it seems extreme to expect visionaries to speak out at all times and situations.

As Annan's public pronouncements demonstrate, just because strategists are likely temper their message does not mean that they will maintain a noncritical stance at all times. Sometimes the situation or audience might be receptive to or expect a faultfinding message. In this case the expectations may not be misplaced, but instead not fully investigated. After all, strategists were supposed to adjust pronouncements according to the situation or not offer biased reports when viewed as politically disadvantageous, so there needs to be more of an effort to relate these activities to contextual cues and Annan's perceptions regarding what was politically possible. This indicates that a more careful analysis of his reports and statements is necessary to determine how their release was timed, what reaction occurred, and how—if at all—his public positions were bolstered or altered accordingly.

Overall, the distinction between official and unofficial public pronouncements, while analytically useful in demarcating aspects of the framework, turned out to be much more problematic in practical terms when tracking the actual influential efforts of the Secretaries-General. The hope was to use official-unofficial dichotomy as part of capturing the broader voluntary versus mandatory expectations. However, this latter distinction was not as valuable as expected and seems to have led to an artificial separation of material into two categories. This was found in particular for Secretary-General travel. For coherence of presentation in the case chapters, the discussion of Waldheim's travel was combined under the official pronouncements category, while for Hammarskjöld it was only presented under unofficial pronouncements. Although the discussion of Annan's official trips to visit government officials was divided from his outreach to the public, this made presentation of his travel more awkward overall. In the future, it will probably be more useful to just consider the range of statements, speeches, writing, travel, and so on that an office-holder provides as one collection to best gauge the effort put forth to use these as avenues of influence. The annual report holds such a distinctive position that it still seems advantageous to keep this as a separate public pronouncement category.

The inherent strategic political position appears to be even more a part of a Secretary-General's activities than expected and the way that office-holders employ this tool may also need to be reconsidered. In hindsight, despite the emphasis in the chapter 3 description of the importance of Secretary-General's inherent strategic position and the range of informal contacts that this provides, the behavioral expectations did not fully take into account the central place this activity could have across different types of office-holders. Although it was emphasized when the framework of influential activities was established that the strategic position aspects were only "voluntary" in the sense of whether a Secretary-General would take advantage of the position to be influential, and the analysis showed that Waldheim stayed true to his managerial roots by not using his inherent strategic position to try to influence those with whom he came into contact, his level of engagement in the inherent strategic position still raises questions about the presentation of managerial expectations for this tool. In other words, the day-to-day interactions in which a Secretary-General can be engaged is simply a natural part of the job that any office-holder will perform and needs to be factored into the analysis of all Secretaries-General to a greater degree than expected even for managers.

It remains to be seen whether it was Hammarskjöld's complex nature that led him to work in conjunction with others from this strategic position, thus blurring the lines somewhat between visionary and strategist, or whether all visionaries will engage in more of a give-and-take process instead of trying to use their position to force their views upon others. Similarly, it is unclear if Annan's efforts to extend his strategic position is a unique event or if other strategists would behave in a similar manner. For example, has the increase in communication capabilities or the rise in importance of new groups on the international scene led to these opportunities that Annan is reacting to, or would a strategist in earlier times also have pursued such strategic connections? More generally, it may be that Annan's expansion of the strategic position shows that analysts need to consider a broader range of potential strategic connections that any Secretary-General could pursue in the future.

Looking at peaceful settlement behavior, it appears once again to be the case that the boundaries of the ideal role of different types of

Secretary-General should be reconsidered. For independent initiatives, the managerial expectations should be upgraded. Even an ideal manager should not be expected to remain fairly inactive in relation to these activities. In other words, while it would expected for managers to be relatively less involved or forceful in independent peaceful settlement than a strategist or a visionary, they will still undertake such missions. In addition, even a visionary requires some guidance and does not possess the power to impose solutions on others, so this aspect of the behavioral expectations was overemphasized.

Finally, the case study research revealed particular contrasts connected to leadership style differences that deserve greater emphasis when examining the shaping of the administrative structure or staffing the Secretariat. Although Gordenker's observation regarding administrative structure being linked to "personal style" was noted in chapter 3, this was not fully extended to the behavioral expectations. Attempts by both Annan and Hammarskjöld to reshape the administrative structure not only reflected efforts to increase their chances to be influential, but also more generally the structure itself mirrored their styles. Hammarskjöld imposed a hierarchical structure where he operated from the top, while Annan reacted against this type of setup by emphasizing a structure that reflected a more collegial and coordinated atmosphere with greater delegation. Previous work has shown that the advisory systems of national level leaders can be related to leadership style (Hermann 1994, 1995a; Hermann and Preston 1994; Preston and Hermann 2004), so these ideas could be explored further in relation to the Secretary-General.

In the area of Secretariat staffing, different leadership styles also seem to relate to the level of staff morale. Waldheim largely undermined morale because, with his greater focus on the interests of the member-states, he was not representing Secretariat concerns and he also did not build a connection with the staff. Annan and Hammarskjöld both tended to bolster morale to a greater degree, but in different manners. Although Hammarskjöld initiated his office with an extended effort to personally meet staff members throughout headquarters, he soon grew more distant from such day-to-day interactions and led more by example and through protecting the independence of the Secretariat. Annan worked more to bolster morale by building connections within the organization, although in the latter years of his tenure morale suffered as his office came under increasing pressure and questions were raised regarding how well he was able to extend his support beyond his senior associates to bolster all levels of staff. It will be interesting to explore what impact other Secretaries-General with similar styles had on morale.

A REEXAMINATION OF THE LEADERSHIP STYLE IDEAL TYPES

Since the three styles were derived from the debate over Secretary-General leadership, one of the benefits of examining these in detail is to determine how well these ideal categories capture the leadership styles and behavioral predispositions of the office-holders. Despite the overall linkage displayed between the visionary, managerial, and strategic leadership styles and the political behavior of the related Secretaries-General as they addressed international peace and security, both the office-holders' personal characteristics and their subsequent behavior did deviate in places. The ideal types were useful for organizing the research on how the Secretaries-General behave and clearly capture important dimensions for the study of office-holder behavior. However, the results also indicate that for a finer-tuned understanding of the behavioral predilections of a Secretary-General analysts must be careful to closely examine the underlying personal characteristics and not rely on the overall leadership style alone.

In Hammarskjöld's case, he was more responsive than an ideal visionary Secretary-General. Out of the seven Secretaries-General, Hammarskjöld possessed both the highest level of self-confidence and conceptual complexity, the underlying components of the responsivity measure. This combination limits his responsivity score to some degree, but he can still be categorized as a complex visionary. This means that he was much more contextually aware than an ideal visionary and undertook detailed analysis of issues in order to discern the best strategies to cope with them. However, given his otherwise overwhelmingly visionary character, once he had determined what he viewed as the correct way to handle a problem, he would fully focus his efforts in that direction and strenuously defend his actions. The Congo provides an illustrative example. Hammarskjöld displayed a keen early awareness that the Congo could develop into an explosive situation and carefully monitored conditions to determine when and what types of action were required. Once he ascertained what he believed should be done, he explicitly used Article 99 for the first time ever by a Secretary-General in order to guide the timing and debate in the Security Council, where he worked to shape the mandate. Once the mandate was set, he did refer to the Security Council for guidance when problems arose, yet he largely continued to control all aspects of the mission and refused to alter UN involvement despite facing a high degree of political backlash.

Due to Waldheim's high need for recognition, he could be categorized as a high profile manager. The impact of this side of his character is most closely seen in relation to public pronouncements. Although Waldheim maintained a subservient tone and message in his pronouncements, he did actively pursue publicity and a high profile in a manner that does not mesh with an ideal manager. The analysis suggests that his high profile nature might also have impacted on his use of the strategic position. For example he was more engaged in meetings with member-state representatives due to the level of attention that this provided and this might help to explain the unexpected invocation of Article 99. In addition, his general lack of concern for administrative affairs may be connected to the limited exposure that such activities provide and, as the subtitle "cautious use of the limelight" indicated, his engagement in peaceful settlement may have moved somewhat beyond managerial expectations due to the publicity that these efforts provided.

Annan's primary deviation from the strategic profile in regards to problem-solving emphasis does not appear to have significantly altered his behavior from the strategic expectations. Thus, unlike in the chapters on Hammarskjöld and Waldheim, the impact of the deviating trait was not traced across the analysis. To begin with, the deviation is more minor than that of the other two Secretaries-General, with a shift from an expected medium score to a low score on the trait. In addition, remember from the discussion in chapter 2 that problem-solving emphasis was the most debated personal trait. It may be that the assumed medium level of problem-solving emphasis that was established for the strategic leadership style was misplaced and Annan's greater emphasis on interpersonal concerns is the norm for a strategic Secretary-General. That being said, the potential implications of Annan being what could be termed an interpersonal strategist have led some observers to question whether his concern for the feelings of others impeded his ability to complete tasks more efficiently. From the analysis carried out in this study, the interpersonal emphasis might in particular be linked to issues raised regarding Annan's handling of staffing matters, such as the noted tendency to remain loyal and delay action when others argued for the need to move forward more quickly.

It should be noted that when unexpected behavior occurred the Secretaries-General did not stray too far from their predominant behavior pattern. By considering the style expectations as operating along a continuum, from managerial to strategic to visionary, it is clear that the office-holders almost never shifted more than one style category away. In other words, a manager might act more like a strategist, but not a visionary, and a visionary might tend toward a strategic behavior but will not shift all the way to a managerial approach.

The only potential exception to this rule is Waldheim's use of Article 99, which could be linked to a visionary manner of acting since strategists are also not likely to use this power unless encouraged to do so. In all other cases, both Waldheim and Hammarskjöld's behaviors do not deviate further than the expectations that reflect a more strategic way of handling matters.

These shifts make sense in light of the leadership style scores for each office-holder. Waldheim's second highest leadership style score is a 48.98 for the strategic style, in comparison to his 41.90 for the visionary style. Conversely, Hammarskjöld's 45.74 for the strategic style outranks his low score of 38.13 for the managerial style. However, this pattern does not hold true for Annan. Since a strategist sits in the middle of the continuum it is obviously only possible to shift one place along, either up to reflect a more visionary approach or down toward a managerial behavior. For Annan, his behavioral variations often contained a more visionary streak than expected. Yet, his score of 44.88 for the visionary style falls well behind his high score of 61.11 for the managerial style, so such behavioral shifts occur in the opposite direction from what would be expected. This may indicate that, as discussed previously, the root of the variation is not in a move to a more visionary way of operating, but is actually a result of misplaced assumptions regarding a strategist in action.

For the remaining four office-holders coded and briefly discussed in chapter 2, none match the personal characteristic pattern of a strategic Secretary-General, but there are several examples of the other two leadership styles. Perez de Cuellar does not possess any trait matches with the visionary style profile, so it is not surprising that he registers the lowest score among the office-holders for this style. While he does receive a medium level score for the strategic style, his score of 59.25 identifies him as a manager. When looking at his personal traits, this becomes even clearer as no strong deviations from the managerial style stand out. Although he does possess a medium level of problem-solving emphasis instead of a low level, his relatively low scores on belief that can influence and supranationalism tilt his overall style away from the strategist and over to the managerial side. Boutros-Ghali also clearly registers with one leadership style, in this case the visionary style. Just as the managerial Perez de Cuellar did not possess any visionary traits, Boutros-Ghali's personal characteristics do not overlap with the managerial style. His shared strategic traits, and only a medium high level of problem-solving emphasis, provide him with a 56.59 for the strategic style, but the differentiating characteristics of need for recognition, need for relationships and responsivity move him to the visionary style.

Lie's predominant leadership style is also visionary, but, unlike Hammarskjöld and Boutros-Ghali, his score of 53.62 is not high, although this does clearly stand out in comparison to his low 40.05 for the managerial style and 42.50 for the strategic style. This is due to an interesting aberration in his personal traits, a low emphasis on problem solving, which brings down his visionary score. For belief that can influence, need for relationships, and need for recognition Lie scores in the mid- to upper 40's and ranks fourth relative to the other office-holders. However, for the other three characteristics, Lie falls at the extremes when compared to his compatriots. The visionary aspect of his style is driven by the lowest score for responsivity and the highest score for supranationalism, but this is counteracted by the lowest level of problem-solving emphasis. In the end, Lie appears to be an interpersonal visionary, which suggests operating as a visionary, but in a manner more open to the feelings of others than otherwise expected.

The true outlier is Thant, who has an interesting character profile that does not fit cleanly into any of the three ideal leadership style types due to a complicated mixture of personal traits. He scores highest on the managerial style, but only receives a 49.13, which is just below the mean score of 50. He scores even lower on the other two styles, with a 41.13 for visionary and a 34.77 on strategist. For five of the six personal characteristics he has low scores where he ranks last or next to last among the Secretaries-General. The only high scoring trait is problem-solving emphasis, so a major defining characteristic appears to be his focus on completing tasks over interpersonal concerns. Looking at this in terms of the ideal leadership styles, he possesses two traits that distinguish him as a manager, low belief that he can influence what happens and supranationalism, and one trait, low need for recognition, which matches with a managerial or a strategic profile. However, he also possesses three demarcating visionary characteristics with a low level of responsivity and need for relationships and a high level of problem-solving emphasis. Overall, Thant is hard to categorize in any of the existing styles and the best that can be said about his character is that he is not responsive to the context and does not need to build relationships, but instead is driven mostly by carrying out tasks and is willing to do so behind the scenes without recognition. However, this is not backed by a corresponding belief in his ability to be influential or a feeling of supranationalism.

Thant's case notwithstanding, the three ideal types do appear to be useful for categorizing and examining the Secretaries-General. These styles provide an overarching sense of the behavior guidelines expected in most cases. The long-standing discussion among observers that contrasts these styles appears to be validated. However, it is also clear that at times these are too simplistic of labels and in order to fully comprehend a particular Secretary-General's behavior it is also necessary to have an understanding of the individual traits that underlie the leadership style.

RELATING LEADERSHIP STYLE TO CONTEXTUAL FACTORS

The focus of this study has been on leadership style. Yet, as stressed in the discussion of the Secretary-General as an individual in chapter 2, this emphasis should not be interpreted as an assertion that contextual factors are not important when studying the behavior of an office-holder. In order to fully address the role played by the Secretary-General in global affairs, both personal and contextual variables should be considered. If it is true that the "main factors in the development of the office of the secretary-general have been the incumbents' personalities and the political climate in which they worked" (Urquhart 1995, 23), then complete analyses of the Secretary-General must take both factors into account. The focus on leadership style in this study was in part a reaction to the underemphasis and lack of understanding of the repercussions of this factor for a Secretary-General's political behavior. Now that it has been demonstrated both that leadership style can be studied in detail for the Secretary-General and that it is an important factor for understanding the actions of office-holders, the discussion turns to considering how this work might be integrated with contextual factors. The overarching theme of this deliberation is that the leadership style of a Secretary-General guides how individual office-holders will address contextual factors. In particular, the varying degrees of sensitivity to contextual factors across the leadership styles means that the office-holders deal with constraints in different manners.

In exploring this argument, the following section begins by revisiting the dispute over environment versus leadership style that was touched upon in chapter 2. Given the results of this study, the position taken is that debates over the relative weight of contextual versus personal variables should be put aside in favor of considering the interrelation of these factors. This discussion raises the related issues of how Secretaries-General can change the context within which they operate, how well office-holders match with their environment, and how integrating contextual factors could better illuminate the level of influence that a Secretary-General has on the handling of global security. The discussion then moves from such general considerations to a more specific examination of how leaders with visionary, managerial, or strategic styles could be studied in relation to environmental constraints. This is followed by an initial consideration of how the interaction between leadership style and context could be related to the roles played by Waldheim, Hammarskjöld, and Annan and how this discussion can be built upon and examined in future work.

HOW MIGHT LEADERSHIP STYLE AND CONTEXT RELATE?

When considering how leadership style and context could be related, core questions include the following: are contextual considerations or leadership style the predominant factors for determining how Secretaries-General behave? Is it possible to move away from this type of either-or argument to better understand how leadership style and context interrelate with one another to guide behavioral predilections? Is it more important to focus on whether the situational requirements and style match instead of clash? Are the variables weighted differently depending upon whether the focus is on what the individuals attempt to do instead of the actual impact of their actions? This section refers to all of these questions and poses some initial thoughts that can serve as the basis for further consideration.

As explained in chapter 2, much of the literature on the Secretary-General emphasizes the importance of contextual variables. A brief look at the arguments of James (1985, 1993) further illustrates such an approach. James initially focused on the importance of organizational structure over other factors, where he states, "My theme is that what any secretary-general can do is chiefly a function of the nature of his organisation" (1985, 31) and he later argues for the impact of the global setting. Although, like the work of Newman and Rivlin discussed in chapter 2, James admits, "This is not to deny that personality affects the way any job is executed, thus each Secretary-General will have his own style," his argument revolves around the limiting influence of international impediments:

> There is still appreciable scope for worthwhile independent action by the Secretary-General. One does well, however, to recognize that the

limits to the effectiveness of that action are set not by the personal or legal credentials of the office-holder, but by the character or the international system within which he has his political being. (1993, 37)

James and Rivlin's work in 1993 comes from an edited volume where the analytical focus is on the importance of context. Rivlin and Gordenker's *The Challenging Role of the UN Secretary-General* is the product of a 1991 conference where experts gathered to discuss how the shift in the global political climate would impact the Secretary-General's role. The core theme throughout the text is that the Secretary-General "can at times exercise political initiative . . . Yet, the Secretary-General functions within a framework of legal and political constraints that both limit his activities and offer opportunities for leadership" (1993, ix). As a later chapter explains, "This view is not intended to denigrate the importance of personal characteristics of the Secretary-General and his assistants, but rather to place those personal attributes in an institutional context" (Forsythe 1993, 212). However, as with much of the work that preceded it, this emphasis on contextual factors, with only a fleeting mention of personal characteristics, has left the study of the Secretary-General largely bereft of a clear understanding of the relative importance of these factors. This study has helped to address the lack of attention paid to personal characteristics and could provide a basis for exploring the claims made by some analysts for the predominance of contextual factors.

Based on the relevance of leadership style demonstrated in the study, however, instead of focusing energies on treating personal qualities and context as competing explanatory variables, examining their interaction is likely to be a more productive avenue of research. Courtney Smith emphasizes this perspective when he argues that it is "more fruitful to consider the interplay between the personal attributes of the secretary-general and the environment in which the UN was forced to operate" (2003, 146; see also Smith 2006, 94–99). Others also emphasize making room for both contextual and personal variables, but place the stress on the personal side of the equation. For example, Donald Blaisdell reports,

> But even with the same "givens," the discretion enjoyed by a secretary-general, coupled with the shifts in the structure of power and influence of the organization, results in one incumbent of the office reacting in one way to a given crisis while another reacts quite differently. In both cases the office is the same, likewise its Charter position and authority, political support, and oath of office. The difference is in the style, or mode of operation, of the incumbents. (1966, 120)

Such approaches linking personal characteristics and context will likely provide the greatest understanding of the behavior of the Secretaries-General. Given the strong findings shown for the impact of leadership style when one separates this variable from contextual issues, it is hard to believe that personal characteristics will be a subservient factor when reintegrated with the study of contextual factors. For the Secretary-General, only careful exploration and comparison in the future will tell, but it is the interrelation of style and environment that will probably provide the greatest explanatory value.

One interesting extension of this idea is that what a Secretary-General is like and how they subsequently interact with their surroundings could change contextual factors. As Zacher explains, "This means that the Secretaries-General by their handling of the problems presented to them have changed those aspects of the international environment . . . which most crucially determined the activities and effectiveness of their office" (1966, 731). As the Secretaries-General carry out their jobs, they may change their context and, thereby, help to shape the environment that they, and their successors, work within.

It may also hold true that an important factor to consider is whether the leadership style of a particular Secretary-General matches or clashes with the times. If the international environment is conducive to the behavioral tendencies of a particular Secretary-General, then that individual will have greater latitude for action along the lines that they desire. The notion of leader-situation match is hardly a new idea confined to the Secretary-General. Studies of leadership have emphasized this connection and debated the degree to which match is an important issue. As David Winter (1987) reviews, scholars have long disagreed over whether leaders' characteristics should be considered separately or if the focus on leadership should be the match between leaders and the situation or their followers. As with other literature that explores the interaction of personal traits and situation, efforts should be made to use the research done on the Secretary-General to help to address this debate. That such similar arguments occur across work in other fields shows the nexus of greater dialogue between work on Secretary-General and the broader literature on political leadership that ought to exist.

The idea of styles meshing or clashing with the situation relates to the potential impact that a Secretary-General might have on global politics. While a Secretary-General may maintain a set pattern of behavior, at certain times office-holders may find that their actions will have a greater impact due to the environment being more welcoming to their type of approach. As outlined in this book's introduction, the focus of this study has been on what the Secretaries-General *attempt* to do, not on the *impact* of their actions. It was argued that influence is a two-step process. The first step is how and the degree to which a Secretary-General seeks to be an influential actor, while the second step is whether these efforts play an important part in guiding how the United Nations and international society in general addresses issues. This study provides a much better understanding of the first step, without which comprehension of the second step will be incomplete. In other words, until one knows what Secretaries-General will attempt to do, it is difficult to determine what kind of impact they will have on global politics. However, for a fuller understanding of the role of the Secretary-General in international affairs, it is necessary to move beyond explaining what drives the efforts of various office-holders to a consideration of the impact of their behavior on international events.

MANAGERS, STRATEGISTS, AND VISIONARIES AND THEIR UNDERSTANDING OF CONTEXTUAL FACTORS

How can the differences in style between visionaries, managers, and strategists be explicitly related to contextual factors to provide a clearer understanding of the role played by a Secretary-General? Directly addressing the leadership style-context connection demonstrates the potential utility of the three leadership styles specified in the study. The interrelation of leadership style and the environment in which a leader acts is hardly a new consideration. Previous work on leadership style has pointed to this dimension. For example, in an article on international decision making and the importance of leadership, Hermann and Joe Hagan stress that whether leaders identify constraints and how they react to them is an important part of understanding the overlap between style and environment and conclude, "To chart the shape of any future world, we need to be able to demarcate which leaders and leadership groups will become more caught up in the flow of events, and thus perceive external forces as limiting their parameters for action, and which will instead challenge the international constraints they see in their path" (1998, 135). In fact, sensitivity to environmental constraints as a core part of leadership style, and the effect that this has on leaders' political behavior, has been an important theme throughout much of Hermann's work (for a summary presentation of leadership style as a function of responsiveness to constraints, along with other factors, see Hermann et al. 2001, 95 and Hermann 2003a, 185).

This notion of variation in how leaders define and react to contextual constraints is well captured by the three leadership styles presented in this study. As noted in chapter 3, managers are constraint respecters, visionaries are constraint challengers, while strategists are constraint accommodators. This way of approaching leadership style when considering leaders' responses to constraints has also been noted by Jonathan Keller (2005a, 2005b), who similarly emphasizes the differences between constraint respecters and constraint challengers. In relation to the Secretary-General, the situation is very important for managers. They do not want to challenge constraints, so their behavior revolves around finding out what they are expected to do and then carrying out their duty. Strategists also carefully monitor the environment. They are primed to react to situational cues but, unlike managers, they aim to work around constraints so they try to determine what avenues of influence exist that can be taken advantage of as well as when they need to downplay efforts to challenge constraints. The core idea of the strategic style is that there will be an interplay between the Secretary-General's ideas and what the environment will allow that guides their behavior. For visionaries the situation is not as important for determining what they will try to do. They are the most likely to challenge constraints and their opinions regarding how to address problems should predominate. Since they are less responsive, they will take their ideas on how to handle issues and will push ahead with them without recognizing situational imperatives that could steer their efforts.

This study also provides a basis for considering how variation across the leadership styles could be linked to the impact of the Secretaries-General. When considering the three ideal styles, prospective links between the type of behavior displayed and the potential for influence may be proposed. Managers are the least likely to attempt to be influential. Their style predisposes them to be deferential to the wishes of the member-states. Thus, managerial Secretaries-General should have the least impact across their tenures out of the three types since this primarily relies on how they handle tasks provided by others. While they will not usually independently seek to have a great bearing on the world scene, if such a role is accepted and encouraged by the global community, a managerial Secretary-General could still have an important effect on international relations. Yet, since a manager's efforts will not translate into more than what the member-states want, it is unlikely that they will meet the hopes of those who desire a leader to guide the organization to an expanded role in handling breaches of the peace.

On the other hand, visionaries will seek to have a major impact in the international arena. This can work well when their approach meshes with individual state interests. Visionaries possess a style that predisposes them to challenge constraints, so they are also the most capable of having an impact despite an uninviting situation since such an approach may also be necessary for overcoming intransigence on the part of some member-states. However, their zeal for playing a consequential role can also be their downfall. When a visionary's approach does not fit with what the member-states desire from the Secretary-General, they are likely to face political resistance that will frustrate their efforts. A strong, independent Secretary-General seeking greater involvement by the United Nations in global affairs is far more likely than a manager to clash with the member-states over how to handle issues. Without the support of the member-states, over time the utility of the office can be undermined and, despite continued efforts by the visionary Secretary-General, the level of impact will likely decrease.

The reason that many observers have called for a strategic Secretary-General is that they believe such a leader will be able to avoid the pitfalls faced by managers and visionaries. By pursuing a more balanced approach that is proactive, while sensitive to the situation, strategists should be able to maintain a steady impact on global affairs. Strategists will be good at identifying when and where to operate as an influential Secretary-General, but they will not be inclined to push their way through situational impediments in order to ensure that they guide how problem areas are addressed. Therefore, their short-term direct impact might decrease when the environment does not welcome an active Secretary-General, but they will continue to focus on long-term impact and gradually insert themselves into handling issues.

The retort by supporters of a visionary Secretary-General is that this is not enough. In a world full of states clinging to their sovereignty, only a fully independent Secretary-General with the interests of the United Nations at the forefront will succeed in changing the way that global security is addressed. Those arguing for a managerial Secretary-General counter that, given the realities of international relations dominated by anarchy and national interest, the best to aim for is to maintain a functional United Nations on the scene to ameliorate the situation since any leader more forceful than a manager will simply raise the ire of the member-states. The member-states will determine when the time is right for things to change and the manager needs to be there to assist with the process. Then again, Winter has shown that the performance of U.S. presidents is not necessarily linked to how well they fit with the situation and what the public wants. In fact, he found that "among American presidents it appears that the greatest presidents were those who were least congruent with the followers of their society," (1987, 201) so the connection between traits and situation is a complicated issue.

In the end, it may turn out that a blend of the different types over the years will work best for the long-run significance of the Secretary-Generalship and the United Nations in international politics. Visionaries can break down barriers to greater UN involvement. Then managers can lull aggravated member-states back into rebuilding relationships with the organization. Strategists could move into this situation to continue to prod the status of the United Nations forward to the point that visionaries can come back in for the next bold step and so on.

CONTEXTUAL ISSUES: AN INITIAL LOOK AT WALDHEIM, HAMMARSKJÖLD, AND ANNAN

Moving beyond such observations in the abstract, this section provides an initial consideration of how leadership style and contextual factors might be connected for the three Secretaries-General examined in this study. Looking at the record of Waldheim, it appears that his time in office was context-driven. This leads Newman to claim that Waldheim "must be seen in the context of the general condition of the United Nations, and the environment which did not afford a prominent role to the Organization . . . Thus, any assessment of Waldheim as Secretary-General must be framed in the light of the restrictions imposed upon the Office by the environment (1998, 52). However, this should not automatically lead to the conclusion that Waldheim's style was not of consequence. Instead, it is likely *because* of his style that contextual factors were so important. His managerial style may have promoted this kind of interaction with the environment and led to behavior that is clearly less assertive than that displayed by Hammarskjöld or Annan. Thus, it has been suggested that if a different type of individual held the office in the 1970s then there might have been a changed outcome. For example, Meisler argues, "At a time when the rest of the U.N. behaved badly, Waldheim never made up for it by trying like Dag Hammarskjöld to assume the role of a moral force" (1995b, 188). Finger and Saltzman echo this point: "The real question is whether other conflicts might have been prevented or stopped by a dynamic secretary general, with a sense of mission . . . Perhaps the time was not ripe. Still, one must feel regret that to our knowledge no major effort was made by Waldheim to help resolve these issues" (1990, 64–65).

The explanation of Waldheim's lack of independent efforts might, of course, be a double negative. In other words, it may be a case of a managerial Secretary-General who was not predisposed to use his office to have an impact on global affairs operating within an environment that did not provide many opportunities or encouragement to do so in any case. Along these lines, Cohen and Rosenzweig note, "Kurt Waldheim's role corresponds, in fact, to the organizational and political decline," and while "[t]his has been a long process," Waldheim was also clearly "part of the problem" (1987, 131). Similarly, other observers also acknowledge that Waldheim did little to challenge the member-states and argue, "This was, firstly, because Waldheim was spared the types of controversies that faced Lie and Hammarskjöld" but that this can also be tied to his approach to the office (Armstrong, Lloyd, and Redmond 1996, 110). With Waldheim's managerial leadership style established, further detailed study of situational constraints could be related to this style in order to better examine how these factors interacted to guide his behavior and general lack of impact.

Since Hammarskjöld is more conceptually complex than an ideal visionary, his behavior does not always mesh as well with the constraint challenging overview described. However, many observers still note the power of his personality and argue for the predominance of his style for understanding his reign as Secretary-General. Wallensteen asks a key question that relates to this point: "Who, then, was Secretary-General Hammarskjöld? What made him so unique? Did he have creative qualities, or was he shaped by the global political conditions that prevailed in his day?" (1995, 3). He answers, "It was not at all self-evident that the UN Secretary-General would achieve the position that Dag Hammarskjöld attained. He created his own role and it grew over time . . . The reason why Dag Hammarskjöld achieved his unique position must be sought primarily in his personality, and not only in the circumstances that surrounded him" (1995, 41–42). Many analyses concur with the assessment that Hammarskjöld's personal characteristics were an important factor for his time in office and this stress on the personal side has led some to conclude that Hammarskjöld was a unique individual whose visionary spark for the United Nations might never be recaptured. As Lippman succinctly stated, "No one knows today who can come after Hammarskjöld, and there are many signs that he is in fact irreplaceable" (1961, 548).

More recently, Jones acknowledges that "[m]ore than forty years after Hammarskjöld's death, people at the UN who are confronted with difficult situations still ask: 'If Hammarskjöld were here today, what would he do?'" (2005, 195–196).

At other times the match between Hammarskjöld and the context within which he operated as Secretary-General has been emphasized. These observers acknowledge Hammarskjöld's visionary style, but they also point out that the great strides that occurred under him might be due to his approach meshing well with how the situation was primed. Along these lines, Heller indicates that international affairs at the time provided a "vacuum" into which "a new secretary-general might become the key to useful political action. Dag Hammarskjöld could not have arrived at a more opportune time" as "it took an activist internationalist such as Dag Hammarskjöld to probe the farthest limits of UN authority and the 'elasticity' of the Charter" (2001, xv, 148). Edward Johnson provides an interesting argument that the British government largely supported Hammarskjöld's activist political role because it matched with their national interests at the time, but grew wary when his actions did not fit with their interests and, more broadly, worried that his "recasting of the powers of the Secretary-General might create difficulties for the future" if his successors' personal capabilities meant that they were not suited to properly employ these powers (2003, 95).

Still other analysts seem to argue that it was not just a match between personal traits and situation that explains Hammarskjöld's role, but instead they place the accent on the welcoming environment with which he was greeted. In other words, if these circumstances had not existed then even Hammarskjöld would not have been able to overcome barriers to being an influential Secretary-General. James and Newman once again point to the importance of context. James acknowledges that Hammarskjöld was a "brilliant man," but argues that he flourished because he was able "to take advantage of the unusual conjunction of circumstances" (1983, 93). Newman indicates that Hammarskjöld's success was at least in part due to his efforts, but concludes that "a large element of Hammarskjöld's success was fortuitous and dependent upon a certain alignment of circumstances . . . Above all, Hammarskjöld should be seen in the context of institutional shifts which were in turn a reflection of systemic trends" (1998, 47, 49).

So where does all of this leave the legacy of Hammarskjöld as Secretary-General? Was it his visionary style that led to one of the most remarkable tenures of a Secretary-General? Would his record be diminished if the circumstances had been different? If the environment had not been welcoming to his endeavors would he have been unable to overcome the barriers? Many views have been expressed. This study supports the arguments that Hammarskjöld possessed a visionary style, so at the very least it appears that his record is based on the interaction between his style and the conflicts that he addressed, but it is only with a more detailed understanding of contextual factors that can be explicitly related to the role he played that a clearer picture of his tenure will develop.

With the inherent interaction between individual and situation at the heart of the strategic style, it is important to consider how contextual factors could be more explicitly drawn into the study of Annan's tenure to provide greater insight into what he tried to do and how the impact of these efforts varied. In a sense, strategists should always seek to "match" with the times in that they monitor the environment and adjust their moves accordingly. The material presented on Annan in this study does point to a range of ways in which he read and reacted to contextual cues along such strategic lines. However, as stressed at the beginning of the chapter on Annan, it is also clear that the early part of his time in office were marked by great highs, but he encountered serious struggles in the latter part of his tenure. How might his strategic character provide insight?

To begin with, it might be that a shift in contextual constraints takes away the advantage of a strategist. In other words, perhaps a strategic approach is not the "silver bullet" answer for the Secretary-Generalship for all situations. Certain difficulties could, for example, undermine the ability of a strategist to maintain the balance that is key to this approach. In Annan's case, he has faced a continual challenge of harmonizing the demands of the United States with other member-states. He had been largely noted for his balancing ability in this regard. For example, one analysis concludes, "Although Annan appreciates the need to win the United States' support, he is careful to emphasize the global nature of the UN" (Marquardt and Berger 2000, 65), while another observes that Annan "showed that he would search for practical solutions to the Organization's problems and, although he owed his election to US insistence, that he had 188 masters, not just one" (Beigbeder 2000, 212). However, this task became increasingly complicated following the American-led invasion of Iraq in March 2003. As one report indicates, "Annan admits his job has grown more difficult . . . In jobs like these, he says, it's important to be able to keep your balance. But these days he manages that less and less frequently" (Brinkbäumer 2004). This speaks to the issue of how well a strategic balance can be maintained in a strongly divided United Nations.

In addition, since strategists are so in tune with environmental cues, when these turn sour it could undermine a strategic approach. As stressed earlier, strategists operate as constraint accommodators, but what if the constraints cannot be accommodated? It may be that Annan became paralyzed in the face of such strong constraints. Another emphasis for strategists is on building relationships, but what happens when they lose those connections? One study stresses this in relation to Annan's engagement in the Middle East peace process: "Annan's inability to maintain a strong personal bond of mutual trust and confidence with the American president—in contrast to his relationship with president Clinton—had undercut the UN role" (Pubantz and Moore 2003, 140). This is speaking only to the Middle East, but a similar dynamic has clear implications across a range of peace and security issues and could reflect Brinkbäumer's (2004) observation, noted in chapter 6, regarding Annan's decreased influential "currency" linked to his relationships and related meetings. This remains especially problematic at a time when Annan faces great backlash from American conservative politicians and commentators (see Price 2005; Traub 2005; and Williams 2005). Strategists are best at probing for openings to take action, not reacting to attacks, so many questions have been raised regarding Annan's ability to respond to such challenges.

Another consideration is that Annan wore down and, therefore, was behaving in an uncharacteristic manner. As a strategist so tuned in to environmental cues, it may be that in the face of continual pressure he became overwhelmed and frustrated by the negative feedback he was receiving. In other words, as opposed to the ideas presented above that a strategic approach does not work in certain environments, it may be instead that the struggles were due to Annan not operating with his strategic instincts in place. This suggestion is supported in profiles by Henneberger and Gordon. Henneberger notes how the process began with the American invasion of Iraq: "Since then, Annan has at times seemed uncharacteristically unsure of himself, and oddly distracted" (2003, 33). Gordon stresses a similar point in quoting a "prominent diplomat" as stating, "Kofi seemed disturbed, bothered, unfocused" (2005, 44). Further along these lines, Gordon emphasizes, "The multiple crises have changed him . . . [F]or a man renowned for his personal charm and ability to remain calm under pressure, Annan came across as wary and abrupt . . . The overall impression he left was that of a man at the center of a maelstrom, coping by the hour" to the point that "Annan seemed to have lost his once-vaunted political instincts" (2005, 43–44). These descriptions do not capture a strategist planning how to use the situation to his advantage, but an individual just trying to cope with overly pressing short-term demands.

This initial overview indicates how further research on the Secretary-General might benefit from incorporating contextual factors alongside personal qualities. This study represents a useful step forward in understanding this relationship because the personal traits dimension is now much better specified and understood. However, much work remains before these findings can be properly integrated with contextual factors. While, as this study has illustrated, each Secretary-General is armed with a similar toolbox of activities, the situations that they face while employing these tools can vary widely. This had led observers to make comments such as "Of course, no two holders of the office ever face exactly or even approximately the same conditions" (Blaisdell 1966, 120). Rikhye concurs, stating, "Each [Secretary-General] has had opportunities for action, but situations and their environments were different" (1991, 71). Yet, just because office-holders have faced varying circumstances at different times does not mean that certain general contextual commonalities cannot be compared. Even if individual office-holders deal with varying specific circumstances, as long as common factors that categorize their experiences can be determined it will be possible to explore the impact of these shared contextual concerns across the Secretaries-General and in relation to their personal characteristics.

Progress can be made by recognizing those areas where there is no variation across proposed situational variables. While these factors may have an impact on the operation of Secretary-Generalship, as long as different behaviors are displayed under similar circumstances it is necessary to focus on other contextual possibilities. Observers often note the constraining consequences of the United Nations operating in an international system made up of self-interested sovereign states. For example, Barros cautions that studies of the Secretary-General must not "avoid the harsh fact that the politics of the world community, as mirrored in the politics of the world organization, are the politics of sovereign states, and especially the politics of the Great Powers" (1983, 34). However, in order to pursue a better understanding of the behavioral variation among Secretaries-General, it is necessary to move from stressing such broad concerns and to focus efforts on a more nuanced understanding of how situational factors can be tied to the differences between the actions of the office-holders.

Specifying and comparing contextual variables will also allow competing claims for the effects of similar factors to be explored. For example, there has been much emphasis placed on the constraints faced by the Secretaries-General due to the Cold War political conflict between the great powers. However, when these claims are examined it is unclear exactly what impact should be expected as assertions regarding the effect of Cold War politics at times conflict with one another. Jakobson (1974) argues that detente in the 1970s limited opportunities for the Secretary-General to act since greater coopera-tion between East and West increased the authority of the Security Council. Boudreau agrees that the 1970s detente led to a "general relaxation in international tension" but indicates instead that conflicts were placed more beyond the control of the Secretary-General because "most of the important negotiations during the period . . . occurred outside the United Nations" (1991, 78). Alternatively, Hazzard views the early 1970s as a time of "great opportunities to a new Secretary-General" to step forward into a more cooperative environment and bolster the role of the Secretary-General and the United Nations (1990, 72). Tharoor argues that the Cold War environment in general "provided a nimble diplomat with room for manoeuvre between two irreconcilables," but Boutros-Ghali and Annan instead faced the limi-tations of an "era of one single dominant member" (2005, 153). Such contrasting claims regarding environmental impact could be explored more closely in conjunction with personal differences between the Secretaries-General.

FURTHER AVENUES FOR FUTURE RESEARCH

Beyond addressing the connection between leadership style and con-textual factors, there are other potential avenues for further research that build out of this study. The research could be expanded to detail the behavior of the other UN Secretaries-General and to encompass issues beyond international peace and security. The use of other lead-ership measurement techniques or approaches to individual differ-ences could provide a broader understanding of what drives office-holders' behavior. The importance of the background of the office-holders, both personal and professional, could also be studied in order to gain a better grasp of what shapes the behavior of the Secretaries-General. Change across time is another area that this study has largely left untapped. Secretaries-General could be closely exam-ined to see if their leadership styles or political behavior vary in a sig-nificant manner across the years. Finally, broader comparative groups, including leaders of other international organizations or even national level leaders, could be incorporated.

EXTEND ANALYSIS OF BEHAVIOR TO ALL OF THE UN SECRETARIES-GENERAL

One step for further research would be to investigate the Secretaries-General whose behavior was not examined in this study in the same manner as Hammarskjöld, Waldheim, and Annan in order to provide a comparable base of information across all of the office-holders. The leadership style profiles were established for Lie, Thant, Perez de Cuellar, and Boutros-Ghali in chapter 2, and reexamined in this chapter, but detailed study of their political behavior is necessary to complete the analysis. Incorporating the four remaining Secretaries-General would allow for comparison between office-holders with the same leadership styles to determine how similarly these individuals behaved. Further study would also provide a chance to explore the behavioral implications when a Secretary-General does not fit cleanly within the ideal leadership categories. In particular, it would be interesting to see how Thant's mix of personal characteristics manifested in his political behavior.

EXPAND THE BEHAVIORAL ANALYSIS

Given the breadth of behavioral categories employed in this study it was not possible to closely address all of the relevant material across a Secretary-General's tenure, so future research could focus a more intense effort on examining behavior in a particular area. The case studies in this book provided an overview across the range of activities and supporting illustrative examples in order to explore how well the behavioral pattern matched the leadership styles for each Secretary-General. However, each area in itself, if covered in depth, has the potential for forming the basis of a separate study.

Another approach would be to extend the analysis performed in this study to issue areas beyond international peace and security. Performing such an analysis was considered, but, as Gordenker emphasizes in relation to his work, "a study of the Secretary-General's total role in the organization . . . was too large a subject for one book" (1967, vii). The area of international peace and security was selected because, as stressed in the introduction to this book, this is one of the primary and pressing objectives of the United Nations. Furthermore, it was recognized that this has been an issue where

Secretaries-General have focused much personal attention and effort. Since this study examines the link between leadership style and political behavior, it was decided to select an area where much activity would be available for analyzing the connection. However, exploring the Secretary-General's responsibilities in relation to other global issues would be a worthwhile task. It may be the case that significant variation in the level of involvement or methods used to address these issues exist and can be related to the different leadership styles possessed by office-holders.

ALTERNATIVE MEASURES FOR LEADERSHIP QUALITIES

Along with extending the behavior side of the study, the research could also be expanded by employing alternative measures of leadership qualities. This study relied on measurements adopted from Hermann since these related well to the traits supported through a survey of the literature on the Secretary-General. Although the descriptive accounts set out in the case studies provide solid support for the content analysis results, alternative measurement techniques could be used to produce personal characteristic and leadership style scores that could be compared. In addition, other measurement schemes, such as operational code or cognitive mapping, could be employed to create a more extensive leadership profile and to provide new insights into the Secretary-General. Alternatively, the study of individual differences could shift to a broader consideration of other factors, such as personal values, that Secretaries-General bring to bear in their handling of the office.

IMPORTANCE OF A SECRETARY-GENERAL'S BACKGROUND?

Although an oft-mentioned topic in biographies of political leaders, including those on the Secretaries-General, this study has largely skirted a discussion of the importance of an individual's background. Factors such as personal experiences, professional training, and cultural upbringing are all potentially important for understanding the character of the Secretaries-General. To a large degree, however, such background was not explicitly incorporated into the study because these factors were viewed as shaping the office-holders' leadership styles. In other words, the life experiences of the Secretaries-General might help to mold their style so background factors, although not directly explored in detail, were captured indirectly through the study of leadership style. That being said, research on the background of a Secretary-General could still be an illuminating step to take. An exploration of how, and more specifically in what ways, different personal backgrounds and cultures shaped the individuals who became Secretary-General could be linked to the research in this study. For example, in Herzstein's study of Waldheim, he emphasizes "events that appeared to have molded Kurt Waldheim's character and career" since he believes "that if we can understand where he came from, we can better understand how he arrived at his destination" (1988, 10). Due to its prevalence in analyses of Waldheim, the study did address his Nazi past and argued that this highlighted his managerial nature. However, a closer examination of whether this style was really already in place or if the Nazi experience helped shape the subsequent style that he brought to the United Nations years later could be employed.

Claims such as Herzstein's could be seized upon and applied to any of the Secretaries-General in an effort to better understand the individual behind the office. For example, in the case of Annan this could mean exploring the implications of his being the first Secretary-General to serve in the UN Secretariat for most of his career. Did his strategic style develop due to his long tenure within the organization? Despite being the "African" Secretary-General, Annan spent much of his life in the Western world, from his college days in Minnesota to the years in Geneva or New York serving the United Nations. Was it this mingling of cultures and experiences that helped guide the development of a strategic nature? Or are all these questions misplaced and would analysis uncover that he actually left Ghana with the personal traits that underlie his leadership style today already in place? These, and other similar questions across the different office-holders, could be illuminated with a better understanding of the impact of their backgrounds.

CHANGE ACROSS TIME

The issue of what shaped the leadership styles of the Secretaries-General just detailed raises another complicated issue. To what degree have the Secretaries-General changed across time? This study has largely maintained a static focus, but a cross-time analysis of leadership style and political behavior would add depth to the existing findings. There are several ways that the issue could be addressed. First, research on how the leadership styles of the Secretaries-General have altered over time could be carried out. Changes in leadership style could be explored either within their time as Secretary-General or across different leadership positions that they have held. Second, shifts across the behavioral indicators could be traced to better understand the reasons that these occurred across an office-holder's tenure. Can these be linked to a corresponding change in style, a contextual change, or some combination of these factors?

In relation to whether the leadership styles of the individuals varied according to different leadership positions that they have held, for example, analysis could focus on whether Annan also displayed a strategic leadership style when he held other posts in the United Nations. Similarly, did Hammarskjöld's unexpected visionary behavior as Secretary-General correspond to a shift in his leadership style, or did he previously possess such a style in the Swedish bureaucracy and the switch to the global arena provided a stage for him to fully display his visionary potential? In a different direction, Waldheim's managerial leadership style as Secretary-General could be contrasted with his time afterward in office as president of Austria to see if he possessed a different style when he moved into the national political arena.

A change in leadership style of a particular Secretary-General may also provide insight into their time in office. Whereas the previous discussion of Annan's difficulties in the latter stages of his tenure revolved around insights that his strategic style might provide and the notion that he struggled to maintain his strategic instincts in the face of great pressure, Gordon's assertion that the "multiple crises have changed him" (2005, 43) might need to be reframed. Instead of the context impacting on Annan to such a degree, it may be that what really changed was his leadership style. In other words, the "uncharacteristic" behavior that was noted may not be so uncharacteristic after all if Annan no longer possessed a strategic leadership style. Of course, it could also be a combination of shifting style alongside altered context that provides the greatest explanatory capability. With cross-time leadership style analysis, the shifts in leadership style could be combined with changes in behavior to see whether they correspond. Where such a connection does not appear, the contextual implications could be examined more closely.

The actions of Hammarskjöld provide an additional consideration from this perspective. For the first several years of his tenure he focused on administrative affairs, but later turned his attention primarily to resolving conflicts throughout the world. The argument made in chapter 5 was that he initially focused his visionary energies on solidifying his place within the UN hierarchy and, once this was set, he looked to move from this position of strength to handling breaches of the peace. However, it may be that his visionary style grew in strength over time, which explains the shift in behavioral emphasis. Alternatively, a more limited number of conflicts early in his tenure may mean that he just had not had a chance to show his visionary streak outside the United Nations to such a degree. This would mesh with Deryck Thorpe's claim that "the first year of his secretaryship was to be spent largely in administrative work. Fortunately, nations were living in relative peace with each other, and there was no immediate crisis or threat to world peace which demanded his urgent attention" (1969, 71; see also Henderson 1969, 23). Competing ideas such as these could be explored with the proper cross-time data in place.

EXTENSION TO DIFFERENT FORUMS

The approach developed in this study, along with future research based on the dimensions outlined above, would be useful for studying the leaders of other international organizations. The debate over the type of leadership that a UN Secretary-General should aim to provide is reflected in scholarship on the heads of other international organizations and analysts have similarly argued for the importance of personal factors. For example, in the study of the Commonwealth referenced in chapter 2, Akinrinade observes that "the question whether the Secretariat's role should be wholly supportive of and reactive to the mandates of governments, or whether it should also include a more activist approach, was never really resolved" and argues that a primary factor in determining which role the Commonwealth Secretary-General played was the personal traits of the leader (1992, 64–65). Along similar lines, as also mentioned in chapter 2, the first Secretary-General of the League of Nations, Drummond, has been compared to the head of the International Labour Organization (ILO) at the same time, Thomas. Since they "had obviously different personalities" (Newman 1998, 15) there is interest in how the League of Nations might have been shaped in a different manner if the visionary Thomas was in charge instead of the more managerially oriented Drummond (for example, see Alexandrowitz 1962; Barros 1979; and Cox, 1969). However, there have been no efforts to explicitly measure the leadership style profiles of these leaders to demonstrate the supposed impact on their performance.

Other scholars have explored the heads of organizations within the UN System, such as Michael Schechter's (1987, 1988) examination of World Bank presidents and heads of the United Nations

Educational, Scientific, and Cultural Organization (UNESCO) and the United Nations Development Programme (UNDP), which included consideration of "activist" versus "pragmatist" leadership. In another study, Yves Beigbeder (1997) compares a sample of "activist" heads of Specialized Agencies such as the ILO, World Health Organization (WHO), and United Nations Children's Fund (UNICEF). The methods presented in this study could be used to examine whether more activist leadership reflects a visionary leadership style. In an earlier study, Arthur Holcombe (1962) looked at Specialized Agency heads in comparison to the Secretary-General. Interestingly, he argues,

> On the whole, they have struck a good balance. Most of the Directors-General have found that if they outdistance their governing bodies too far, they doom themselves to ineffectiveness. But they have also learned the equally important lesson that if they provide no policy leadership at all, they doom their organization to sterility. In this ability to strike the correct balance between initiative and withdrawal, between determined leadership and sensitivity to the needs and demands of the member nations, lies the key to a successful international executive in the United Nations family. (Holcombe 1962, 34)

This descriptive account sounds much like the approach that should be taken by a strategic Secretary-General. Thus, it would be interesting to explore whether such behavioral tendencies could be related to the heads of Specialized Agencies possessing strategic leadership styles.

Content analysis of leaders' personal traits could also be incorporated into studies of heads of organizations outside of the UN System, such as the Secretary-General of the North Atlantic Treaty Organization (NATO) (for recent work on the NATO Secretary-General, see Hendrickson 2002, 2004a, 2004b, 2006). For example, claims have been made such as "This official has, through the personalities of the successive incumbents, become politically significant" (Fox and Fox 1967, 261). Similarly, the approach taken by Robert Jordan, where his focus is "not of structure but of individuals and the impact of their personalities and vision on international events . . . The desire is to go beyond an analysis of NATO as a political system, or as a military coalition, in order to portray the secretaries-general as individuals within that system" (1979, 1, 18) could be bolstered with such measurement techniques. Extending content analysis coding to other international organizations allows for not only addressing the leadership issues in those organizations, but also to expand the

database of leaders of international organizations for comparative purposes. Research has already moved in this direction by relating the
leadership styles of the UN Secretaries-General and the European
Union Commission presidents, which established that these leaders
could be studied along the same personal and behavioral dimensions
despite hailing from different organizations (Kille and Scully 2003).

UN Secretaries-General could also be analyzed alongside national
level leaders. Hermann's research has led to the compilation of a database of political leaders using similar measurement requirements that
could be used for these purposes. Such analysis would provide a better understanding of the similarities and differences between individuals who hold leadership posts and types of leadership styles that exist
across a range of forms of political organization, as well as how these
styles can be linked to political behavior. This study should not be
considered as an isolated effort to closer examine the UN Secretary-
General, but instead as a piece in the continuing broader research
effort to better understand the place of leaders in political organizations. The work done in the foreign policy realm on national leaders
has informed the analytic possibilities for the head of the United
Nations, but this research exchange should be a two-way street.
Information gained from research on the Secretary-General can be
related back to those scholars working on national level leaders to
inform their work. Such an interchange of ideas moves us closer to the
broader end goal of a generalized understanding of political leadership that can guide studies across all levels.

CONCLUSION

This study has shown that leadership style does matter when studying
the political behavior of the UN Secretaries-General. The visionary
Hammarskjöld, managerial Waldheim and strategic Annan display
clear variation across their efforts to manage international peace and
security largely in the manner that was projected. With the three ideal
leadership style types and behavioral expectations analyzed, a much
better understanding of how office-holders should attempt to handle
global security has been established. As stressed earlier in the conclusion, one important caveat is that when a Secretary-General's personal
characteristics do not match with the leadership style pattern this can
lead to corresponding behavioral differences that do not mesh with
the general expectations for the style. Thus, the results of this study
suggest that, along with the overarching leadership style, it is often
necessary to carefully examine the separate personal characteristics of

office-holders in order to better understand their political behavior. In addition, the expected behavior for Secretaries-General with different leadership styles has been honed through comparison with the actual behavior of Hammarskjöld, Waldheim, and Annan.

In the years since Knight's 1970 review of scholarship related to the influence of the Secretary-General, many further studies of this office have been carried out, but his basic criticism set out in the opening quote of this chapter remains applicable. Previous studies of the Secretary-General, while generally interesting and informative, have often lacked the kind of analytical clarity required to closely examine and compare how office-holders attempt to be influential players in international affairs. This study represents another effort to spur more systematic study of the Secretary-General. In the process, this study answered doubts regarding both the possibility of measuring and demonstrating the importance of personal qualities for the study of the Secretary-General. In addition, the study also endeavored to organize the literature on the Secretary-General in relation to both leadership qualities and influential behavior. The case studies of Hammarskjöld, Waldheim, and Annan provide a wealth of information that should be of use to those interested in these office-holders regardless of their perspective on the approach employed in this study. Beyond the information that this study provides on the Secretary-General, it is hoped that this work will also assist with the continuing dialogue between scholars interested in leadership across all forms of political organization.

At the same time, much work remains to be done in order to better comprehend the role that the Secretary-General plays on the world stage. A range of possible routes have been presented that will allow future studies to build upon the foundation set down by this research, including an emphasis on examining contextual factors alongside personal characteristics in order to create a fuller understanding of the role played by office-holders. This book opened by stressing the potential importance of the Secretary-General in helping to handle global problems, but to truly gauge and understand the place of office-holders both the leadership style of the individuals and the environment in which they operate must be addressed. By detailing and explaining the impact of leadership style on attempts by Secretaries-General to influence how international peace and security is addressed, the research in this book represents a useful step in that direction.

APPENDIX

ARTICLES IN THE UN CHARTER RELATED TO THE SECRETARY-GENERAL

Article 7

1. There are established as the principal organs of the United Nations: a General Assembly, a Security Council, an Economic and Social Council, a Trusteeship Council, an International Court of Justice, and a Secretariat.
2. Such subsidiary organs as may be found necessary may be established in accordance with the present Charter.

Article 97

The Secretariat shall comprise a Secretary-General and such staff as the Organization may require. The Secretary-General shall be appointed by the General Assembly upon the recommendation of the Security Council. He shall be the chief administrative officer of the Organization.

Article 98

The Secretary-General shall act in that capacity in all meetings of the General Assembly, of the Security Council, of the Economic and Social Council, and of the Trusteeship Council, and shall perform such other functions as are entrusted to him by these organs. The Secretary-General shall make an annual report to the General Assembly on the work of the Organization.

Article 99

The Secretary-General may bring to the attention of the Security Council any matter which in his opinion may threaten the maintenance of international peace and security.

Article 100

1. In the performance of their duties the Secretary-General and the staff shall not seek or receive instructions from any government or from any other authority external to the Organization. They shall refrain from any action which might reflect on their position as international officials responsible only to the Organization.
2. Each Member of the United Nations undertakes to respect the exclusively international character of the responsibilities of the Secretary-General and the staff and not to seek to influence them in the discharge of their responsibilities.

Article 101

1. The staff shall be appointed by the Secretary-General under regulations established by the General Assembly.
2. Appropriate staffs shall be permanently assigned to the Economic and Social Council, the Trusteeship Council, and, as required, to other organs of the United Nations. These staffs shall form a part of the Secretariat.
3. The paramount consideration in the employment of the staff and in the determination of the conditions of service shall be the necessity of securing the highest standards of efficiency, competence, and integrity. Due regard shall be paid to the importance of recruiting the staff on as wide a geographical basis as possible.

NOTES

CHAPTER 2 THE SECRETARY-GENERALSHIP: THE INDIVIDUAL BEHIND THE OFFICE

1. Support for this section comes from a review of analysts who provide insight into the personal characteristics of the Secretary-General, in particular are Claude (1993), Cordovez (1987), Fosdick (1972), Goodrich (1962), Gordenker (1967, 1972, 2005), Narasimhan (1988), Pechota (1972), Ramcharan (1990a), Rikhye (1991), Rivlin (1993), Rovine (1970), Skjelsbaek (1991), (UNA-USA) United Nations Association of the United States of America (1986), Urquhart and Childers (1996), and Young (1967).

2. For a general overview of political psychology in foreign policy, see Levy (2003) and Rosati (1995, 2000). For a broader consideration of political psychology and the range of issues addressed from this scholarly perspective, see Cottam et al. (2004), Hermann (2004, 1986), McDermott (2004), Sears, Huddy, and Jervis (2003), Kuklinski (2002), Monroe (2002), Renshon and Duckitt (2000), Montero (1997), Catellani (1996), Iyengar and McGuire (1993), Barner-Barry and Rosenwein (1985), and Knutson (1973).

3. For work that provides for the comparison of different measurement schemes see Post (2003), Valenty and Feldman (2002), Feldman and Valenty (2001), Young and Schafer (1998), Snare (1992), Winter et al. (1991), and Winter and Stewart (1977).

4. Rubenzer and Faschingbauer (2004) provide one way to get around this limitation. They had experts fill out a personality test for the office-holders and compiled the comparative data for all 43 presidents. Also see Lyons (1997), who employs the Myers-Briggs Type Indicator to analyze presidential personality. More generally, the U.S. presidency has been the target of a range of psychological analyses. Noted examples include the work of Barber (1992), George (1980, 1988; George and George 1998), Greenstein (1982, 1987, 1994, 2003, 2004), and Renshon (1993, 1995, 1996a, 1996b, 2004, 2005). For an overview of how psychological principles can be applied to the study of the president, see Goethals (2005).

5. Crichlow (2005, 2002, 1998), Keller (2005a, 2005b), Marfleet and Miller (2005), Steinberg (2005), Walker (2004, 2003, 2000), Cairo (2004), Thies (2004), Shaw (2003), Preston (2001, 1997),

Schafer (2000, 1999), Walker and Schafer (2000), Marfleet (2000), Preston and 't Hart (1999), Walker, Schafer, and Young (1999, 1998), Kaarbo and Hermann (1998), Satterfield (1998), Kaarbo (1997), and Kowert (1996); for an overview of earlier work see Winter (2003a, 2003b, 1992) and McDermott (2004).

6. For example, see Andrew Cordier and Wilder Foote's (1969–1975), and for later volumes Cordier and Max Harrelson (1976–1977), collection *The Public Papers of the Secretaries-General of the United Nations,* which they view as an invaluable source for those interested in the Secretaries-General and the importance of the office to the United Nations. More recently, Charles Hill (2003) has edited *The Papers of United Nations Secretary-General Boutros Boutros-Ghali.*

7. Evidence supporting the reliability and validity of Hermann's leadership trait analysis is provided in Hermann (1980b, 1987b, 1999, 2003a). Intercoder reliability scores for the personal characteristics have averaged greater than .85 across multiple studies (Kaarbo and Hermann 1998). For the specific data employed in this study, intercoder reliability scores once again were greater than .85 for all of the personal characteristics (Kille and Scully 2003). Dille and Young (2000) provide careful analysis of the reliability and validity of Hermann's conceptual complexity trait. Keller (2005a) also provides a review of the reliability and validity tests that have been performed to support Hermann's content analysis approach.

8. It should be noted that the author was aware of Hermann's characteristics in advance of the survey of the work done on the Secretary-General, but this careful literature review did not reveal additional characteristics that would necessitate the development of new coding mechanisms.

9. The United Nations maintains these official documents under the SG/SM (for Secretary-General/Statements) label. Older SG/SM documents are available at the Dag Hammarskjöld library at UN headquarters in New York, while recent press conferences are available at http://www.un.org.

10. The coding was performed with the assistance of the KWIC Concordance computer program (Hermann, 1987a). The program goes through each response in alphabetical order and highlights one word at a time, within the surrounding ten words in order to provide context for coding. The coder must then decide whether the word indicates a particular personal characteristic. If the word does not reflect any of the characteristics then the coder moves on to the next word. If the word does capture a characteristic then the coder marks that word as such before moving on. At the end of the response, the program tallies all of the times that a personal characteristic was noted and how it was coded. For example, if there were six self-references and the coder noted that three of these represented self-confidence and three did not represent self-confidence then the final result would be 3/6 for a score of .50.

All coding decisions are left to the human coder with this program. Future studies will be able to take advantage of recently developed fully automated methods, which allows for quicker analysis of a larger amount of data (Young 1996, 2000, 2001; Dille and Young 2000; Schafer 2003; and see http://www.socialscienceautomation.com).

11. Expressed as a formula: Managerial style = 2 × (Responsivity+Need for Relationships)+(100−Belief That Can Influence)+(100−Need for Recognition)+(100−Supranationalism)+(100− Problem-Solving Emphasis); Strategic Style = 2 ×(Responsivity+Belief That Can Influence+Need for Relationships+Supranationalism)+Problem-Solving Emphasis+(100−Need for Recognition); Visionary Style = 2 ×(Belief That Can Influence+Need for Recognition+ Supranationalism+Problem-Solving Emphasis)+(100−Responsivity)+ (100−Need for Relationships).

BIBLIOGRAPHY

Adebajo, Adekeye. 2002. *Selling Out the Sahara: The Tragic Tale of the Referendum.* Occasional Paper Series, Institute for African Development. Ithaca, NY: Cornell University.

Afulezi, Uju Nkwocha, and Ugochukwu Uju Afulezi, eds. 2002. *African and Africa-Related Nobel Prize Winners: Portraitures in Excellence.* Lanham, MD: University Press of America.

Ahman, Sven. 1958. "Mr. Hammarskjöld's Not-So-Quiet Diplomacy." *Reporter* 19: 9–13.

Akande, Laolu. 2005. "Why Annan Named African Gambari Top UN Political Chief." *New York Amsterdam News* 96: 2.

Akinrinade, Olusola. 1992. "The Commonwealth and its Secretariat: An Essay on Leadership and Influence in an International Organization." *Quarterly Journal of Administration* 26: 62–86.

Alexandrowicz, Charles H. 1962. "The Secretary-General of the United Nations." *International and Comparative Law Quarterly* 11: 1109–1130.

Alleyne, Mark D. 2003. *Global Lies? Propaganda, the UN and World Order.* New York: Palgrave Macmillan.

Ameri, Houshang. 1996. *Politics of Staffing the United Nations Secretariat.* New York: Peter Lang.

Ankomah, Baffour. 1997. "Kofi Annan in the Hot Seat: What Sort of UN Secretary General Will the Ghanian Be?" *New African* 349: 36–37.

Annan, Kofi. 1993. "The Secretary-General and the UN Budget." In *The Challenging Role of the UN Secretary-General: Making "The Most Impossible Job in the World" Possible*, edited by Benjamin Rivlin and Leon Gordenker. Westport, CT: Praeger.

———. 2001. "Dag Hammarskjöld and the 21st Century." *Development Dialogue* 1: 3–14.

Annan, Nane. 2000. *The United Nations: Come Along With Me!* New York: American Forum for Global Education.

Armitage, Richard L. 1994. "Bend the U.N. to Our Will." *New York Times*, February 24.

Armstrong, David, Lorna Lloyd, and John Redmond. 1996. *From Versailles to Maastricht: International Organisation in the Twentieth Century.* New York: St. Martin's.

Ascoli, Max. 1965. "On Reading Hammarskjöld." *The Reporter*, May 20, 37–40.

Ask, Sten, and Anna Mark-Jungkvist, eds. 2005. *The Adventure of Peace: Dag Hammarskjöld and the Future of the UN*. New York: Palgrave Macmillan.

Assfaw, Berihun. 1997. "Kofi Annan, Fit to Be King." *New African* 349: 4–5.

Astill, James. 2003. "French Offer Relief Force For Congo Emergency." *Guardian*, May 14.

Astrachan, Anthony. 1974. "Waldheim: Learning the Uses of Limited Power." *Saturday Review* 1: 13–14.

Aulén, Gustaf. 1969. *Dag Hammarskjöld's White Book: An Analysis of Markings*. Philadelphia: Fortress.

Australian. 2004. "UN Staff in Revolt Over Top Brass." November 22.

Aviel, JoAnn Fagot. 2005. "NGOs and International Affairs." In *Multilateral Diplomacy and the United Nations Today*, 2nd ed., edited by James P. Muldoon, Joann Fagot Aviel, Richard Reitano, and Earl Sullivan. Boulder, CO: Westview.

Baehr, Peter R., and Leon Gordenker. 1994. *The United Nations in the 1990s*, 2nd ed. New York: St. Martin's.

Bailey, Sydney D. 1962. "The 'Troika' and the Future of the UN." *International Conciliation* 538: 3–64.

———. 1964. *The Secretariat of the United Nations*, rev. ed. New York: Praeger.

———. 1966. "The United Nations Secretariat." In *The Evolution of International Organizations*, edited by Evan Luard. New York: Praeger.

———. 1988. *The Procedure of the UN Security Council*, 2nd ed. Oxford: Clarendon.

Baratta, Joseph P. 1991. "The Secretary-General: Should His Role Be Abolished?" In *A New World Order: Can it Bring Security to the World's People? Essays on Restructuring the United Nations*, edited by Walter Hoffman. Washington, DC: World Federalist Association.

Barber, James David. 1992. *The Presidential Character: Predicting Performance in the White House*, 4th ed. Englewood Cliffs, NY: Prentice Hall.

Barner-Barry, Carol, and Robert Rosenwein. 1985. *Psychological Perspectives on Politics*. Englewood Cliffs, NJ: Prentice Hall.

Barnes, Roger. 1982. "Tenure and Independence in the United Nations International Civil Service." *New York University Journal of International Law and Politics* 14: 767–782.

Barringer, Felicity. 2003. "Annan Warns of World 'Crisis.' " *New York Times*, July 30.

Barros, James. 1969. *Betrayal From Within: Joesph Avenol, Secretary-General of the League of Nations, 1933–1940*. New Haven, CT: Yale University Press.

———. 1972. "A More Powerful Secretary-General for the United Nations?" *American Journal of International Law* 66: 81–84.

———. 1977. "Pearson or Lie: The Politics of the Secretary-General's Selection, 1946." *Canadian Journal of Political Science* 10: 65–92.

———. 1979. *Office Without Power: Secretary-General Sir Eric Drummond 1919–1933*. Oxford: Clarendon.

———. 1983. "The Importance of Secretaries-General of the United Nations." In *Dag Hammarskjöld Revisited: The UN Secretary-General as a Force in World Politics*, edited by Robert S. Jordan. Durham, NC: Carolina Academic Press.

———. 1989. *Trygve Lie and the Cold War: The UN Secretary-General Pursues Peace, 1946–1953*. DeKalb: Northern Illinois University Press.

Bassett, Richard. 1988. *Waldheim and Austria*. London: Viking.

Beigbeder, Yves. 1987. *Management Problems in United Nations Organizations: Reform or Decline?* London: Pinter.

———. 1988. *Threats to the International Civil Service*. London: Pinter.

———. 1997. *The Internal Management of United Nations Organizations: The Long Quest for Reform*. New York: St. Martin's.

———. 2000. "The United Nations Secretariat: Reform in Progress." In *The United Nations at the Millennium: The Principal Organs*, edited by Paul Taylor and A.J.R. Groom. New York: Continuum.

———. 2003. "Fraud, Corruption, and United Nations Culture." In *Rethinking International Organizations: Pathology and Promise*, edited by Dennis Dijkzeul and Yves Beigbeder. New York: Bergham.

Bennett, A. LeRoy, and James K. Oliver. 2002. *International Organizations: Principles and Issues*, 7th ed. Englewood Cliffs, NJ: Prentice Hall.

Berdal, Mats. 2005. "The UN's Unnecessary Crisis." *Survival* 47: 7–32.

Berridge, G.R. 1991. *Return to the UN: UN Diplomacy in Regional Conflicts*. London: Macmillan.

Beskow, Bo. 1969. *Dag Hammarskjöld: Strictly Personal*. Garden City, NY: Doubleday.

Bhatta, Gambhir. 2000. *Reforms at the United Nations: Contextualising the Annan Agenda*. Singapore: Singapore University Press.

Black, Ian. 1997. "Annan Takes Firm Hold of UN Tiller." *Guardian*, November 28.

———. 1998. "Annan, the Inconvenient Man of Peace." *Guardian*, November 16.

Blaisdell, Donald C. 1966. *International Organization*. New York: Ronald Press Company.

Blix, Hans. 2004a. *Disarming Iraq*. New York: Pantheon.

———. 2004b. "The Use of Force in the International Community." Hersch Lauterpacht Memorial Lectures, Lauterpacht Centre for International Law, University of Cambridge, Cambridge, UK, November 22, http://lcil.law.cam.ac.uk/lectures/hersch_lectures_2004.php.

Bogert, Carroll. 1996. "The Peacemaker." *Newsweek* 128: 30–31.

Bolton, John R. 1999. "Kofi Annan's Power Grab." *World Today* 5: 13–14.

Bone, James. 1996. "Annan Promises to Streamline the UN for 21st-century Role." *Times*, December 19.

Boudreau, Thomas E. 1991. *Sheathing the Sword: The U.N. Secretary-General and the Prevention of International Conflict*. Westport, CT: Greenwood.

Bourloyannis, M. Christiane. 1990. "Fact-Finding by the Secretary-General of the United Nations." *New York University Journal of International Law and Politics* 22: 641–669.

Boutros-Ghali, Boutros. 1999. *Unvanquished: A U.S.-U.N. Saga*. New York: Random House.

Bowett, Derek W. 1982. "Tenure, Fixed Term, Secondment from Governments: The United Nations Civil Service and the European Civil Service Compared." *New York University Journal of International Law and Politics* 14: 799–805.

Bowles, Newton R. 2004. *The Diplomacy of Hope: The United Nations Since the Cold War*. London: I.B. Tauris.

Bozeman, Barry, and Hal G. Rainey. 1998. "Organizational Rules and the 'Bureaucratic Personality.'" *American Journal of Political Science* 42: 163–189.

Brecher, Irving. 1999. "Leadership Crisis at the UN." *Montreal Gazette*, September 6.

Brehio, Alys. 1998. "Good Offices of the Secretary-General as Preventive Measures." *New York University Journal of International Law and Politics* 30: 589–643.

Brennock, Mark. 1999. "Talking of Peace But With Conflict on His Mind." *Irish Times*, January 23.

Bring, Ove. 2003. "Dag Hammarskjöld and the Issue of Humanitarian Intervention." In *Nordic Cosmopolitanism: Essays in International Law for Martti Koskenniemi*, edited by Jarna Petman and Jan Klabbers. Leiden: Martinus Nijhoff.

Brinkbäumer, Klaus. 2004. "The Campaign Against Kofi." *Der Spiegel*, December 7, http://www.spiegel.de/international/spiegel/0,1518,331280,00.html.

Buckley, William F. Jr. 1974. *United Nations Journal: A Delegate's Odyssey*. New York: G.P. Putnam's Sons.

Bunche, Ralph J. 1965. "The United Nations Operation in the Congo." In *The Quest for Peace: The Dag Hammarskjöld Memorial Lecture*s, edited by Andrew W. Cordier and Wilder Foote. New York: Columbia University Press.

Burgess, J. Peter, and Robert Piper, eds. 2005. "Report of the High-Level Panel on Threats, Challenges and Change." Special section, *Security Dialogue* 36.

Bustelo, Mara R. and Philip Alston, eds. 1991. *Whose New World Order? What Role for the United Nations*. Sydney: Federation.

Butler, Richard. 2000. *Saddam Defiant: The Threat of Weapons of Mass Destruction and the Crisis of Global Security*. London: Weidenfeld and Nicolson.

Búza, László. 1962. "The Position of the Secretary-General of the United Nations in International Law." In *Questions of International Law*, edited by László Búza, Gyula Hajdú, and György Haraszti. Budapest: Hungarian's Lawyers' Association.

Cairo, Michael F. 2004. "The 'Operational Code' of the Bush Administration: Leadership Perceptions and Foreign Policy Making." In *A Noble Calling: Character and the George H.W. Bush Presidency*, edited by William Levantrosser and Rosanna Perotti. Westport, CT: Praeger.

Caminos, Hugo, and Roberto Lavelle. 1989. "New Departures in the Exercise of Inherent Powers by the UN and OAS Secretaries-General: The Central American Situation." *American Journal of International Law* 83: 395–402.

Carnegie Endowment for International Peace. 1950. *The United Nations Secretariat*. UN Study No. 4. New York: Carnegie Endowment for International Peace.

Catellani, Patrizia. 1996. "Political Psychology." In *Applied Social Psychology*, edited by Gün R. Semin and Klaus Fiedler. Thousand Oaks, CA: Sage.

Chai, F.Y. 1981. "A View From the UN Secretariat." In *Paths to Peace: The UN Security Council and Its Presidency*, edited by Davidson Nicol. New York: Pergamon.

Chappell, Kevin. 1998. "One-On-One With UN Secretary-General Kofi Annan." *Ebony* 13: 136.

Chesterman, Simon. 2005. "Great Expectations: UN Reform and the Role of the Secretary-General." *Security Dialogue* 36: 375–377.

Chinmoy, Sri. 2002. *Kofi Annan: Cynosure-Eyes*. Jamaica, NY: Agni.

Claude, Inis L. 1971. *Swords Into Plowshares: The Problems and Progress of International Organization*, 4th ed. New York: Random House.

———. 1993. "Reflections on the Role of the UN Secretary-General." In *The Challenging Role of the Secretary-General: Making "The Most Impossible Job in the World" Possible*, edited by Benjamin Rivlin and Leon Gordenker. Westport, CT: Praeger.

Coate, Roger A. 2004. "Civil Society as a Force for Peace." *International Journal of Peace Studies* 9: 57–86.

Cohen, Bernard, and Luc Rosenzweig. 1987. *Waldheim*. New York: Adama.

Commission to Study the Organization of Peace. 1962. *The UN Secretary-General: His Role in World Politics*. Fourteenth report. New York.

Conforti, Benedetto. 2005. *The Law and Practice of the United Nations*, 3rd ed. The Hague: Kluwer Law International.

Cordier, Andrew W. 1961. "The Role of the Secretary-General." In *Annual Review of United Nations Affairs, 1960–1961*, edited by Richard N. Swift. Dobbs Ferry, NY: Oceana.

———. 1962. "Hammarskjold's Legacy to the U.N." *New York Times Magazine*, September 16, 31, 76, 79, 80, 82.

———. 1967. "Motivations and Methods of Dag Hammarskjold." In *Paths to World Order*, edited by Andrew W. Cordier and Kenneth Maxwell. New York: Columbia University Press.

Cordier, Andrew W., and Max Harrelson, eds. 1976–1977. *Public Papers of the Secretaries-General of the United Nations, Vol. VII: U Thant, 1965–1967; Vol. VIII: U Thant, 1968–1971*. New York: Columbia University Press.

Cordier, Andrew W., and Wilder Foote, eds. 1965. *The Quest for Peace: The Dag Hammarskjöld Memorial Lectures.* New York: Columbia University Press.

———, eds. 1969. *Public Papers of the Secretaries-General of the United Nations. Vol. I: Trygve Lie.* New York: Columbia University Press.

———, eds. 1969–1975. *Public Papers of the Secretaries-General of the United Nations. Vol. II: Dag Hammarskjöld, 1953–1956; Vol. III: Dag Hammarskjöld, 1956–1957; Vol. IV: Dag Hammarskjöld, 1958–1960; Vol. V: Dag Hammarskjöld, 1960–61.* New York: Columbia University Press.

Cordovez, Diego. 1987. "Strengthening United Nations Diplomacy for Peace: The Role for the Secretary-General." In *The United Nations and the Maintenance of International Peace and Security,* by UNITAR. Dordrecht: Martinus Nijhoff.

Cornwell, Rupert. 1998. "Mr. Good Guy's Burden." *Independent,* February 22.

Cottam, Martha, Beth Dietz-Uhler, Elena Mastors, and Thomas Preston. 2004. *Introduction to Political Psychology.* Mahwah, NJ: Lawrence Erlbaum.

Cox, Robert W. 1969. "The Executive Head: An Essay on Leadership in International Organization." *International Organization* 23: 205–230.

Cox, Robert W., and Harold K. Jacobson. 1973. *The Anatomy of Influence: Decision Making in International Organization.* New Haven, CT: Yale University Press.

CQ Researcher. 2004. "Kofi Annan's U.N. Balancing Act." 14: 181.

Crichlow, Scott. 1998. "Idealism or Pragmatism? An Operational Code Analysis of Yitzakh Rabin and Shimon Peres." *Political Psychology* 19: 683–706.

———. 2002. "Legislators' Personality Traits and Congressional Support for Free Trade." *Journal of Conflict Resolution* 46: 693–711.

———. 2005. "Psychological Influences on the Policy Choices of Secretaries of State and Foreign Ministers." *Cooperation and Conflict* 40: 179–205.

Crossette, Barbara. 1996. "Salesman For Unity Kofi Atta Annan." *New York Times,* December 14.

———. 1998a. "Annan Makes His Bid to Make His Job Count." *New York Times,* March 8.

———. 1998b. "Annan's Stratospheric Profile Gives U.N. a New Cause Celebre." *New York Times,* June 14.

———. 1999. "Kofi Annan Unsettles People, As He Believes U.N. Should Do." *New York Times,* December 30.

———. 2000. "Gore Presides Over Rare Security Council Debate on AIDS." *New York Times,* January 11.

———. 2001. "Support for War Crimes Court is Fading, Sierra Leone Fears." *New York Times,* April 17.

———. 2002. "Outside U.N., A Secretary So Social." *New York Times,* May 30.

———. 2003. "Sixteen Wise People and the Future of the U.N." *UN Wire,* December 1, http://www.theatlantic.com/foreign/unwire/crossette 2003–12–01.htm.

Curtis, Gerald L. 1964. "The United Nations Observer Group in Lebanon." *International Organization* 18: 738–765.

Dallaire, Roméo. 2003. *Shake Hands With the Devil: The Failure of Humanity in Rwanda*. Toronto: Random House Canada.

Datta, Reema. 2000. "Business, the U.N., and the Millennium: Where Are We?" *Interdependent* 25: 12–13.

Davies, Michael D.V. 2002. *The Administration of International Organizations: Top Down and Bottom Up*. Aldershot: Ashgate.

Dayal, Rajeshwar. 1976. *Mission for Hammarskjold: The Congo Crisis*. Princeton, NJ: Princeton University Press.

de Breadun, Deaglan. 2001. "World Civil Servant With Quiet Authority." *Irish Times*, June 29.

de Cooker, Chris, ed. 1990. *International Administration: Law and Management Practices in International Organizations*. Dordrecht: Martinus Nijhoff.

Dille, Brian. 2000. "The Prepared and Spontaneous Remarks of Presidents Reagan and Bush: A Validity Comparison for At-a-Distance Measurements." *Political Psychology* 21: 573–585.

Dille, Brian, and Michael D. Young. 2000. "The Conceptual Complexity of Presidents Carter and Clinton: An Automated Content Analysis of Temporal Stability and Source Bias." *Political Psychology* 21: 587–596.

Dobbins, James, Seth G. Jones, Keith Crane, Andrew Rathmell, Brett Steele, Richard Teltschik, and Anga Timilsina. 2005. *The UN's Role in Nation-Building: From Congo to Iraq*. Santa Monica, CA: RAND.

Docking, Tim. 2001. *Peacekeeping in Africa*. United States Institute of Peace Special Report 66. Washington, DC: United States Institute of Peace.

Dodd, Clement. 2004. *Disaccord on Cyprus: The UN Plan and After*, 2nd ed. Huntington, UK: Eothen.

Dolinsky, Lewis. 1998. "Wide-Ranging Interview With Kofi Annan on S.F. Visit." *San Francisco Chronicle*, April 20.

Donald, Dominick. 2002. "Neutrality, Impartiality and UN Peacekeeping at the Beginning of the 21st Century." *International Peacekeeping* 9: 21–38.

Dorn, A. Walter. 1995. "Keeping Watch for Peace: Fact-Finding by the United Nations Secretary-General." In *United Nations Reform: Looking Ahead After Fifty Years*, edited by Eric Fawcett and Hanna Newcombe. Toronto, Ontario: Science for Peace.

———. 2004. "Early and Late Warning by the UN Secretary-General of Threats to the Peace: Article 99 Revisited." In *Conflict Prevention from Rhetoric to Reality, Volume 1: Organizations and Institutions*, edited by Albrecht Schnabel and David Carment. Lanham, MD: Lexington.

Draper, Theodore. 1960. "Ordeal of the UN: Khrushchev, Hammarskjold and the Congo." *The New Leader* (November): 3–35.

Duke, Lynne. 2003. "Thinking Globally: Kofi Annan Reminds the World That the United Nations Has a Bully Pulpit, Too." *Washington Post*, January 30.

Duodu, Cameron. 2001. "A Man With Whom it is Difficult to Quarrel." *New African* 401: 40–41.

Economist. 1998. "Reforming the United Nations: Pope Kofi's Unruly Flock." 348: 19–22.

Eichelberger, Clark M. 1970. *UN: The First Twenty-Five Years.* New York: Harper and Row.

Elarby, Nabil. 1970. *The Legal Framework of the Secretary-General's Diplomatic Role in the Settlement of Disputes.* New York: New York University Press.

———. 1987. "The Office of the Secretary-General and the Maintenance of International Peace and Security." In *The United Nations and the Maintenance of International Peace and Security*, by UNITAR. Dordrecht: Martinus Nijhoff.

Eliasson, Jan, and Peter Wallensteen. 2005. "Preventive Diplomacy." In *The Adventure of Peace: Dag Hammarskjöld and the Future of the UN*, edited by Sten Ask and Anna Mark-Jungkvist. New York: Palgrave Macmillan.

Fall, Ibrahima. 2005. "Great Lakes: Interview With Ibrahima Fall, Special Representative of the UN Secretary-General." Interview by Integrated Regional Information Networks, March 31, http://www.irinnews.org/report.asp?ReportID=46433&SelectRegion=Great_Lakes&SelectCountry=GREAT%20LAKES

Farley, Maggie. 2000. "U.N. Chief's Effort to Earn Israeli Trust Helped Bring About the Summit." *Los Angeles Times*, October 17.

———. 2004. "With Eye Toward Legacy, Annan Grasps for Order." *Los Angeles Times*, September 21.

Fasulo, Linda. 1999. "U.N. Chief Knows Peace in Kosovo is Not Up to Him: Annan Has Very Little Leverage, but He May Still Play a Vital Role." *USA Today*, May 21.

———. 2004. *An Insider's Guide to the UN.* New Haven, CT: Yale University Press.

Feldman, Ofer, and Linda O. Valenty, eds. 2001. *Profiling Political Leaders: Cross-Cultural Studies of Personality and Behavior.* Westport, CT: Praeger.

Fenton, Neil. 2004. *Understanding the UN Security Council: Coercion or Consent.* Aldershot: Ashgate.

Findlay, Trevor. 2002. *The Use of Force in UN Peace Operations.* Oxford: Oxford University Press.

Finger, Seymour Maxwell, and John F. Mungo. 1975. "The Politics of Staffing the United Nations Secretariat." *Orbis* 19: 117–145.

Finger, Seymour Maxwell, and Arnold A. Saltzman. 1990. *Bending With the Winds: Kurt Waldheim and the United Nations.* New York: Praeger.

Finkelstein, Lawrence S. 1988. "The Political Role of the Director-General of UNESCO." In *Politics in the United Nations System*, edited by Lawrence S. Finkelstein. Durham, NC: Duke University Press.

Fisk, Robert. 1998. "Annan Steps Warily into Middle East Minefield." *Independent*, March 21.

Foer, Franklin. 2002. "Turtle Dove: How Kofi Annan Fooled the Bushies." *New Republic* 227: 20–23.

Foote, Wilder, ed. 1962. *Servant of Peace: A Selection of the Speeches and Statements of Dag Hammarskjöld*. New York: Harper and Row.

Forster, Gwynne. 1998. "Kofi Annan: Soldier of Peace." *Crisis* 105: 21–22.

Forsythe, David P. 1993. "The UN Secretary-General and Human Rights: The Question of Leadership in a Changing Context." In *The Challenging Role of the UN Secretary-General: Making "The Most Impossible Job in the World" Possible*, edited by Benjamin Rivlin and Leon Gordenker. Westport, CT: Praeger.

Fosdick, Raymond B. 1972. *The League and the United Nations After Fifty Years: The Six Secretaries-General*. Newtown, CY: Raymond B. Fosdick.

Fox, William T.R., and Annette B. Fox. 1967. *NATO and the Range of American Choice*. New York: Columbia University Press.

Franck, Thomas M. 1984. "Finding a Voice: How the Secretary-General Makes Himself Heard in the Councils of the United Nations." In *Essays in International Law in Honour of Judge Manfred Lachs*, edited by Jerzy Makarcyzk. The Hague: Martinus Nijhoff.

———. 1985. *Nation Against Nation: What Happened to the U.N. Dream and What the U.S. Can Do about It*. New York: Oxford University Press.

———. 1987a. "The Role and Future Prospects of the Secretary-General." In *The Adaptation of Structures and Methods at the United Nations*, edited by Daniel Bardonnet. Dordrecht: Martinus Nijhoff.

———. 1987b. "The Prerogative Powers of the Secretary-General." In *Public International Law and the Future World Order*, edited by Joseph Jude Norton. Littleton, CO: Fred B. Rothman & Co.

———. 1995a. "The Secretary-General's Role in Conflict Resolution: Past, Present and Pure Conjecture." *European Journal of International Law* 6: 360–387.

———. 1995b. *Fairness in International Law and Institutions*. Oxford: Clarendon.

Franck, Thomas M., and Georg Nolte. 1993. "The Good Offices Function of the UN Secretary-General." In *United Nations, Divided World: The UN's Roles in International Relations*, edited by Adam Roberts and Benedict Kingsbury, 2nd ed. Oxford: Clarendon.

Fröhlich, Manuel. 1997. "Der Alte und der Neue UNO-Generalsekretar." *Aussenpolitik* 48: 301–309.

———. 2002. "A Fully Integrated Vision: Politics and the Arts in the Dag Hammarskjöld-Barbara Hepworth Correspondence." *Development Dialogue* 1: 17–57.

———. 2005a. "Hammarskjöld and His Legacy." In *United Nations and Global Security*, edited by Magnus Lundgren and Henrik Holmquist. Stockholm: United Nations Association of Sweden.

———. 2005b. "The Quest for a Political Philosophy of World Organisation." In *The Adventure of Peace: Dag Hammarskjöld and the*

Future of the UN, edited by Sten Ask and Anna Mark-Jungkvist. New York: Palgrave Macmillan.

Garrison, Jean A., ed. 2003. "Foreign Policy Analysis in 20/20: A Symposium." Special symposium, *International Studies Review* 5: 155–202.

Gavshon, Arthur L. 1962. *The Mysterious Death of Dag Hammarskjold*. New York: Walker and Company.

George, Alexander L. 1980. *Presidential Decisionmaking in Foreign Policy: The Effective Use of Information and Advice*. Boulder, CO: Westview.

———. 1988. "The President and the Management of Foreign Policy: Styles and Models." In *The Domestic Sources of American Foreign Policy: Insights and Evidence*, edited by Charles W. Kegley, Jr. and Eugene R. Wittkopf. New York: St. Martin's.

George, Alexander L., and Juliette L. George. 1998. *Presidential Personality and Performance*. Boulder, CO: Westview.

Gibbs, David N. 1993. "Dag Hammarskjöld, the United Nations, and the Congo Crisis of 1960–1: A Reinterpretation." *Journal of Modern African Studies* 31: 163–174.

———. 2000. "The United Nations, International Peacekeeping and the Question of 'Impartiality': Revisiting the Congo Operation of 1960." *The Journal of Modern African Studies* 38: 359–382.

Gillett, Nicholas. 1970. *Dag Hammarskjöld*. London: Heron.

Gisselquist, Rachel M. 2002. *To Rid the Scourge of War: UN Peace Operations and Today's Crises*. Cambridge, MA: World Peace Foundation.

Glennon, Michael J. 2005. "Idealism at the U.N." *Policy Review* 129: 3–14.

Goethals, George R. 2005. "Presidential Leadership." *Annual Review of Psychology* 56: 545–570.

Goodrich, Leland M. 1962. "The Political Role of the Secretary-General." *International Organization* 16: 720–735.

———. 1974. "Hammarskjold, the UN and the Office of the Secretary-General." *International Organization* 28: 467–483.

Goodrich, Leland M., Edward Hambro, and Anne P. Simons. 1969. *The Charter of the United Nations: Commentary and Documents*, 3rd ed. New York: Columbia University Press.

Goodwin, Geoffrey L. 1961. "The Political Role of the United Nations: Some British Views." *International Organization* 15: 581–602.

Gordenker, Leon. 1960. "Policy Making and Secretariat Influence in the UN General Assembly: The Case of Public Information." *American Political Science Review* 54: 359–373.

———. 1967. *The UN Secretary-General and the Maintenance of Peace*. New York: Columbia University Press.

———. 1969. "Conor Cruise O'Brien and the Truth About the United Nations." *International Organization* 23: 897–913.

———. 1972. "The Secretary-General." In *The United Nations: Past, Present, and Future*, edited by James Barros. New York: Free Press.

———. 1993. "The UN Secretary-Generalship: Limits, Potentials and Leadership." In *The Challenging Role of the Secretary-General: Making*

"The Most Impossible Job in the World" Possible, edited by Benjamin Rivlin and Leon Gordenker. Westport, CT: Praeger.

———. 1996. *The UN Tangle: Policy Formation, Reform, and Reorganization*. Cambridge, MA: World Peace Foundation.

———. 2005. *The UN Secretary-General and Secretariat*. New York: Routledge.

Gordenker, Leon, and Paul R. Saunders. 1978. "Organization Theory and International Organization." In *International Organization*, edited by Paul Taylor and A.J.R. Groom. London: Printer.

Gordon, Meryl. 2005. "No Peace for Kofi: A Father's Burden." *New York Magazine* 38: 40–45, 102.

Goshko, John M. 1996. "Annan to Bring Change of Style to World Body; Soft-Spoken Bureaucrat Is Pragmatic, Well-Liked." *Washington Post*, December 14.

Goulding, Marrack. 2003. *Peacemonger*. Baltimore, MD: Johns Hopkins University Press.

———. 2004. "The UN Secretary-General." In *The UN Security Council: From the Cold War to the 21st Century*, edited by David M. Malone. Boulder, CO: Lynne Rienner.

Gourevitch, Philip. 1998. "The Genocide Fax." *New Yorker* 74: 42–46.

———. 2003. "The Optimist: Kofi Annan's U.N. Has Never Been More Important and More Imperiled." *New Yorker* 79: 50–73.

Grahm, Norman A., and Robert S. Jordan, eds. 1980. *The International Civil Service: Changing Role and Concepts*. New York: Pergamon.

Greenstein, Fred I. 1982. *The Hidden-Hand Presidency: Eisenhower as Leader*. New York: Basic Books.

———. 1987. *Personality and Politics: Problems of Evidence, Inference and Conceptualization*. Princeton, NJ: Princeton University Press.

———. 1994. "The Two Leadership Styles of William Jefferson Clinton." *Political Psychology* 15: 351–361.

———. 2003. "The Leadership Style of George W. Bush." In *The George W. Bush Presidency: An Early Assessment*, edited by Fred I. Greenstein. Baltimore, MD: Johns Hopkins Press.

———. 2004. *The Presidential Difference: Leadership Style from FDR to George W. Bush*, 2nd ed. Princeton, NJ: Princeton University Press.

Gross, Ken. 1986. "His Nazi Past Rises to Haunt Former U.N. Chief Kurt Waldheim." *People Weekly* 25: 49–51.

Guéhenno, Jean-Marie. 2005. "The Peacekeeper." In *The Adventure of Peace: Dag Hammarskjöld and the Future of the UN*, edited by Sten Ask and Anna Mark-Jungkvist. New York: Palgrave Macmillan.

Gurstein, Michael, and Josef Klee. 1996. "Towards a Management Renewal of the United Nations—Parts I and II." *Public Administration and Development* 16: 43–56, 111–122.

Gwyn, Richard. 1996. "Annan Shows He's Much More Than 'the U.S. Choice.'" *Toronto Star*, December 27.

Haas, Ernst B. 1964. *Beyond the Nation-State: Functionalism and International Organization*. Stanford, CA: Stanford University Press.

Halper, Stefan. 1998. "UNreformed: Kofi Annan is Subtle, Canny—And a Threat to U.S. Interests." *National Review* 50: 36–38.

Hammarskjöld, Dag. 1953. "The United Nations and the Political Scientist." *American Political Science Review* 47: 975–979.

———. 1964. *Markings.* Translated by W.H. Auden and Leif Sjöberg. New York: Alfred Knopf.

Han, Henry H. 1988. "The U.N. Secretary-General's Treaty Depositary Function: Legal Implications." *Brooklyn Journal of International Law* 14: 549–572.

Handelman, Stephen. 1996. "U.N. Veteran Tackles 'Most Impossible Job' Kofi Annan Knows He'll Have a Rocky Ride as Secretary-General." *Toronto Star*, December 23.

Hannay, David. 1996. "Anyone For a Roller-Coaster?" *World Today* 52: 48–49.

Hazzard, Shirley. 1989a. "Reflections: Breaking Faith—I." *New Yorker* 65: 63–99.

———. 1989b. "Reflections: Breaking Faith—II." *New Yorker* 65: 74–96.

———. 1990. *Countenance of Truth: The United Nations and the Waldheim Case.* New York: Viking.

Heller, Peter R. 2001. *The United Nations Under Dag Hammarskjöld, 1953–1961.* Lanham, MD: Scarecrow.

Helms, Jesse. 1996. "Saving the United Nations: A Challenge to the Next Secretary-General." *Foreign Affairs* 75: 2–7.

Henderson, James L. 1969. *Hammarskjöld: Servant of a World Unborn.* London: Methuen Educational Limited.

Hendrickson, Ryan C. 2002. "NATO's Secretary General Javier Solana and the Kosovo Crisis." *Journal of International Relations and Development* 5: 240–257.

———. 2004a. "Leadership at NATO: Secretary General Manfred Woerner and the Crisis in Bosnia." *Journal of Strategic Studies* 27: 508–527.

———. 2004b. "NATO's Secretary-General and the Use of Force: Willy Claes and Operation Deliberate Force." *Armed Forces and Society* 31: 95–117.

———. 2006. *Diplomacy and War at NATO: The Secretary General and Military Action After the Cold War.* Columbia, MO: University of Missouri Press.

Henneberger, Melinda. 2003. "Weight of the World." *Newsweek* 141: 33–37.

Heraclides, Alexis. 2004. "The Cyprus Problem: An Open and Shut Case? Probing the Greek-Cypriot Rejection of the Annan Plan." *Cyprus Review* 16: 37–54.

Hermann, Margaret G. 1974. "Leader Personality and Foreign Policy Behavior." In *Comparing Foreign Policies: Theories, Findings, and Methods,* edited by James N. Rosenau. New York: Halsted.

———. 1976. "When Leader Personality Will Affect Foreign Policy: Some Propositions." In *In Search of Global Patterns,* edited by James N. Rosenau. New York: Free Press.

————, ed. 1977. *A Psychological Examination of Political Leaders*. New York: Free Press.

————. 1978. "Effects of Personal Characteristics of Political Leaders on Foreign Policy." In *Why Nations Act: Theoretical Perspectives for Comparative Foreign Policy Studies*, edited by Maurice A. East, Stephen A. Salmore, and Charles F. Hermann. Beverly Hills, CA: Sage.

————. 1980a. "Explaining Foreign Policy Behavior Using the Personal Characteristics of Political Leaders." *International Studies Quarterly* 24: 7–46.

————. 1980b. "Assessing the Personalities of Soviet Politburo Members." *Personality and Social Psychology Bulletin* 6: 332–352.

————. 1983. "Assessing Personality at a Distance: A Profile of Ronald Reagan." *Mershon Center Quarterly Report* 7: 1–8.

————. 1984. "Personality and Foreign Policy Decision Making: A Study of 53 Heads of Government." In *Foreign Policy Decision Making: Perception, Cognition, and Artificial Intelligence*, edited by Donald A. Sylvan and Steve Chan. New York: Praeger.

————, ed. 1986. *Political Psychology*. San Francisco: Jossey-Bass.

————. 1987a. *Handbook for Assessing Personal Characteristics and Foreign Policy Orientations of Political Leaders*. Mershon Occasional Paper, Mershon Center for International Security Studies. Columbus, OH: Ohio State University.

————. 1987b. "Foreign Policy Role Orientations and the Quality of Foreign Policy Decisions." In *Role Theory and Foreign Policy Analysis*, edited by Stephen G. Walker. Durham, NC: Duke University Press.

————. 1987c. "Assessing the Foreign Policy Role Orientations of Sub-Saharan African Leaders." In *Role Theory and Foreign Policy Analysis*, edited by Stephen G. Walker. Durham, NC: Duke University Press.

————. 1988. "Syria's Hafez Al-Assad." In *Leadership and Negotiation: A New Look at the Middle East*, edited by Barbara Kellerman and Jeffrey Z. Rubin. Westport, CT: Praeger.

————. 1993. "Leaders and Foreign Policy Decision-Making." In *Diplomacy, Force, and Leadership: Essays in Honor of Alexander George*, edited by Dan Caldwell and Timothy McKeown. Boulder, CO: Westview.

————. 1994. "Presidential Leadership Style, Advisory Systems, and Policy Making: Bill Clinton's Administration After Seven Months." *Political Psychology* 15: 363–374.

————. 1995a. "Advice and Advisers in the Clinton Presidency: The Impact of Leadership Style." In *The Clinton Presidency: Campaigning, Governing, and the Psychology of Leadership*, edited by Stanley A. Renshon. Boulder, CO: Westview.

————. 1995b. "Leaders, Leadership, and Flexibility: Influences on Heads of Government as Negotiators and Mediators." *Annals of the American Academy of Political and Social Science* 542: 148–167.

————. 1999. *Assessing Leadership Style: A Trait Analysis*. Hilliard, OH: Social Science Automation, Inc.

Hermann, Margaret G. ed. 2001. "Leaders, Groups, and Coalitions: Understanding the People and Processes in Foreign Policymaking." Special issue, *International Studies Review* 3.

———. 2003a. "Assessing Leadership Style: Trait Analysis." In *The Psychological Assessment of Political Leaders*, edited by Jerrold M. Post. Ann Arbor, MI: University of Michigan Press.

———. 2003b. "William Jefferson Clinton's Leadership Style." In *The Psychological Assessment of Political Leaders*, edited by Jerrold M. Post. Ann Arbor, MI: University of Michigan Press.

———. 2003c. "Saddam Hussein's Leadership Style." In *The Psychological Assessment of Political Leaders*, edited by Jerrold M. Post. Ann Arbor, MI: University of Michigan Press.

———, ed. 2004. *Advances in Political Psychology, Volume 1*. Amsterdam: Elsevier.

Hermann, Margaret G., and Charles F. Hermann. 1989. "Who Makes Foreign Policy Decisions and How: An Empirical Inquiry." *International Studies Quarterly* 33: 361–387.

Hermann, Margaret G., and Charles W. Kegley, Jr. 1995. "Rethinking Democracy and International Peace: Perspectives from Political Psychology." *International Studies Quarterly* 39: 511–533.

Hermann, Margaret G., and Joe D. Hagan. 1998. "International Decision Making: Leadership Matters." *Foreign Policy* 110: 124–135.

Hermann, Margaret G., and Thomas Preston. 1994. "Presidents, Advisers, and Foreign Policy: The Effect of Leadership Style on Executive Arrangements." *Political Psychology* 15: 75–96.

Hermann, Margaret G., Thomas Preston, Baghat Korany, and Timothy M. Shaw. 2001. "Who Leads Matters: The Effects of Powerful Individuals." *International Studies Review* 3: 83–131.

Hershey, Burnett. 1961a. "Dag Hammarskjold: A Personal Portrait." *Look* 25: 140.

———. 1961b. *Soldier of Peace: Dag Hammarskjold*. Chicago: Britannica Books.

Herzstein, Robert E. 1988. *Waldheim: The Missing Years*. New York: William Morrow.

Higgins, Rosalyn. 1970. *United Nations Peacekeeping 1946–1967: Documents and Commentary*. London: Oxford University Press.

Hill, Charles, ed. 2003. *The Papers of United Nations Secretary-General Boutros Boutros-Ghali*. New Haven, CT: Yale University Press.

Hoffman, Stanley. 1957. "Sisyphus and the Avalanche: The United Nations, Egypt, and Hungary." *International Organization* 11: 446–469.

———. 1962. "In Search of a Thread: The UN in the Congo Labyrinth." *International Organization* 16: 331–361.

Hoge, Warren. 2004a. "On Bugging News, Annan Had Low-Key Reaction to Old Practice." *New York Times*, February 28.

———. 2004b. "Authority is Approved for Sanctions Against Sudan." *New York Times*, September 19.

———. 2005a. "U.N. Is Transforming Itself, but Into What Is Unclear." *New York Times*, February 28.

———. 2005b. "Clash By Diplomats at U.N. Over Reform Bares Divisions." *New York Times*, September 10.

———. 2005c. "Annan Defends U.N. Official Who Chided U.S." *New York Times*, December 9.

Holbrooke, Richard. 1998. *To End a War*. New York: Random House.

———. 2004. "Kofi Annan: Problem Solver." *Time* 163: 59.

Holcombe, Arthur N. 1962. *The UN Secretary General His Role in World Politics*. Fourteenth Report of the Commission to Study the Organization of Peace. New York.

Hoole, Francis W. 1976. "The Appointment of Executive Heads in UN Treaty-based Organizations." *International Organization* 30: 91–108.

Hotchkiss, Ron. 1988. "The Most Impossible Job on Earth." *Canada and the World* 54: 18–20.

Hottelet, Richard C. 1997. "Reforming the UN: A High Wire Act for Annan." *Christian Science Monitor* 89: 18.

———. 2001. "The UN's Soft-Spoken Champion." *Christian Science Monitor* 94: 11.

Hudson, Valerie M. 2005. "Foreign Policy Analysis: Actor-Specific Theory and the Ground of International Relations." *Foreign Policy Analysis* 1: 1–30.

Hudson, Valerie M., and Christopher S. Vore. 1995. "Foreign Policy Analysis Yesterday, Today, and Tomorrow." *Mershon International Studies Review* 39: 209–238.

Hume, Cameron R. 1994. *The United Nations, Iran, and Iraq: How Peacemaking Changed*. Bloomington, IN: Indiana University Press.

———. 1995. "The Secretary-General's Representatives." *SAIS Review* 15: 75–90.

Independent Working Group on the Future of the United Nations. 1995. *The United Nations in its Second Half-Century*. New York: Ford Foundation.

Ismail, Razili. 1997. "Reformer Kofi Annan: He has the Experience and the Style to Invigorate the U.N." *Asiaweek*, March 14, 64.

Iyengar, Shanto, and William J. McGuire, eds. 1993. *Explorations in Political Psychology*. Durham, NC: Duke University Press.

Jackson, Elmore. 1957. "The Developing Role of the Secretary-General." *International Organization* 16: 431–445.

Jackson, William D. 1978. "The Political Role of the Secretary-General Under U Thant and Kurt Waldheim: Development or Decline?" *World Affairs* 140: 230–244.

Jakobson, Max. 1974. "Detente Nourishes a New U.N." *Saturday Review* 1: 10–14.

———. 1991. "Filling the World's Most Impossible Job." *World Monitor* 4: 24–33.

———. 1998. *Finland in the New Europe*. Westport, CT: Praeger.

Jallow, Matthew, and Opa Ramba. 1997. "Will Kofi Annan Be Allowed to Succeed?" *African Profiles USA*. February: 11–15.

James, Alan. 1983. "Kurt Waldheim: Diplomats' Diplomat." In *The Year Book of World Affairs, Volume 37.* Boulder, CO: Westview.

———. 1985. "The Secretary-General: A Comparative Perspective." In *Diplomacy at the UN*, edited by G.R. Berridge and A. Jennings. New York: St. Martin's.

———. 1993. "The Secretary-General as an Independent Political Actor." In *The Challenging Role of the Secretary-General: Making "The Most Impossible Job in the World" Possible*, edited by Benjamin Rivlin and Leon Gordenker. Westport, CT: Praeger.

———. 1995. "UN Peace-keeping: Recent Developments and Current Problems." In *The United Nations in the New World Order: The World Organisation at Fifty*, edited by Dimitris Bourantonis and Jarrod Weiner. New York: St. Martin's.

Jane's Information Group. 1997. "Annan in Orbit." *Foreign Report*, May 6.

———. 1999. "Saving the UN: Its Secretary-General Has a Secret Plan Which Works." *Foreign Report*, September 16.

Jensen, Erik. 1985. "The Secretary-General's Use of Good Offices and the Question of Bahrain." *Millennium* 14: 335–348.

Johnson, Edward. 2003. "The British and the 1960 Soviet Attack on the Office of the United Nations Secretary-General." *Diplomacy and Statecraft* 14: 79–102.

Johnstone, Ian. 2003. "The Role of the UN Secretary-General: The Power of Persuasion Based on Law." *Global Governance* 9: 441–458.

Jonah, James O.C. 1982. "Independence and Integrity of the International Civil Service: The Role of Executive Heads and the Role of States." *New York University Journal of International Law and Politics* 14: 841–859.

———. 2005. "An Independent International Civil Service." In *The Adventure of Peace: Dag Hammarskjöld and the Future of the UN*, edited by Sten Ask and Anna Mark-Jungkvist. New York: Palgrave Macmillan.

Jones, Dorothy V. 1994. "The Example of Dag Hammarskjöld: Style and Effectiveness at the UN." *The Christian Century* 111: 1047–1050.

———. 2004. "The World Outlook of Dag Hammarskjöld." In *Ethics and Statecraft: The Moral Dimension of International Affairs*, 2nd ed., edited by Cathal J. Nolan. Westport, CT: Praeger.

———. 2005. "International Leadership and Charisma." In *The Adventure of Peace: Dag Hammarskjöld and the Future of the UN*, edited by Sten Ask and Anna Mark-Jungkvist. New York: Palgrave Macmillan.

Jordan, Robert S. 1979. *Political Leadership in NATO: A Study in Multinational Diplomacy.* Boulder, CO: Westview.

———. 1981. "What Happened to Our International Civil Service? The Case of the United Nations." *Public Administration Review* 41: 236–245.

———, ed. 1983. *Dag Hammarskjöld Revisited: The Secretary-General as a Force in World Politics.* Durham, NC: Carolina Academic Press.

———. 1988. "Truly Independent Bureaucracies: Real or Imagined?" In *Politics in the United Nations System*, edited by Lawrence S. Finkelstein. Durham, NC: Duke University Press.

Kaarbo, Juliet. 1997. "Prime Minster Leadership Styles in Foreign Policy Decision-Making: A Framework for Research." *Political Psychology* 18: 553–581.

Kaarbo, Juliet, and Margaret Hermann. 1998. "Leadership Styles of Prime Ministers: How Individual Differences Affect the Foreign Policymaking Process." *Leadership Quarterly* 9: 243–263.

Kaas, Harold Munthe. 1998. "A Reformed UN by the Year 2000?" *Internasjonal Politikk* 56: 539–555.

Kanninen, Tapio. 1995. *Leadership and Reform: The Secretary-General and the UN Financial Crisis of the Late 1980s.* The Hague: Kluwer Law International.

———. 2001. "Recent Initiatives By the Secretary-General and the UN System in Strengthening Conflict Prevention Activities." *International Journal on Minority and Group Rights* 8: 39–43.

Karns, Margaret P., and Karen A. Mingst. 2004. *International Organizations: The Politics and Processes of Global Governance.* Boulder, CO: Lynne Rienner.

Kaufmann, Johan. 1980. *United Nations Decision Making.* Rockville, MD: Sijthoff and Noordhoff.

Kay, David A. 1966. "Secondment in the United Nations Secretariat: An Alternative View." *International Organization* 20: 63–75.

Kelen, Emery. 1966. *Hammarskjöld.* New York: G. P. Putnam's Sons.

———, ed. 1968. *Hammarskjöld: The Political Man.* New York: Funk and Wagnalls.

Keller, Jonathan W. 2005a. "Leadership Style, Regime Type, and Foreign Policy Crisis Behavior." *International Studies Quarterly* 49: 205–231.

———. 2005b. "Constraint Respecters, Constraint Challengers, and Crisis Decision Making in Democracies: A Case Study Analysis of Kennedy versus Reagan." *Political Psychology* 26: 835–867.

Kelly, Peter J., ed. 1999. *United Nations Secretaries General: A Bibliography With Indexes.* Huntington, NY: Nova Science.

Kennedy, Caroline. 2002. "Profile in Courage Award 2002: Secretary-General Kofi Annan." In *Profiles in Courage for Our Time.* New York: Hyperion.

Kenworthy, Leonard S. 1988. "Dag Hammarskjold: World Peacemaker." In *Twelve Trailblazers of World Community.* Grand Rapids, MI: Four Corners.

Khalaf, Roula. 1998. "Annan In Drive to Resolve Sahara Dispute." *Financial Times,* November 9.

Khan, Rahmatullah. 1965. "Judicial Control of the UN Secretary-General's Discretionary Powers in Personnel Matters." *International Studies* 7: 279–310.

Kille, Kent J., and Roger M. Scully. 2003. "Executive Heads and the Role of Intergovernmental Organizations: Expansionist Leadership in the United Nations and the European Union." *Political Psychology* 24: 175–198.

Kirsch, Robert. 2002. "The Peacemaker: An Interview with UN Under-Secretary General Alvaro de Soto." *Fletcher Forum of World Affairs* 26: 83–89.

Knight, Jonathan. 1970. "On the Influence of the Secretary-General: Can We Know What it Is?" *International Organization* 24: 594–600.

Knutson, Jeanne N., ed. 1973. *Handbook of Political Psychology.* San Francisco: Jossey-Bass.

Kofi Annan: Center of the Storm. 2003. Produced by David Grubin and Sarah Colt. New York: PBS Home Video. Videocassette.

Kowert, Paul A. 1996. "Where Does the Buck Stop? Assessing the Impact of Presidential Personality." *Political Psychology* 17: 421–452.

Kowert, Paul A., and Margaret G. Hermann. 1997. "Who Takes Risks? Daring and Caution in Foreign Policy Making." *Journal of Conflict Resolution* 41: 611–637.

Krasno, Jean E. 2003. "The Group of Friends of the Secretary-General: A Useful Leveraging Tool." In *Leveraging for Success in United Nations Peace Operations,* edited by Jean E. Krasno, Bradd C. Hayes, and Donald C.F. Daniel. Westport, CT: Praeger.

———, ed. 2004. *The United Nations: Confronting the Challenges of a Global Society.* Boulder, CO: Lynne Rienner.

Krasno, Jean E., and James S. Sutterlin. 2003. *The United Nations and Iraq: Defanging the Viper.* Westport, CT: Praeger.

Kristof, Nicholas D. 2004. "Reign of Terror." *New York Times,* September 11.

Kuklinski, James H., ed. 2002. *Thinking About Political Psychology.* Cambridge: Cambridge University Press.

Kunz, Josef L. 1946. "The Legal Position of the Secretary General of the United Nations." *American Journal of International Law* 40: 786–792.

———. 1958. "The Secretary General on the Role of the United Nations." *American Journal of International Law* 52: 300–304.

La Guardia, Anton. 1998. "Israeli Speaker Subjects Annan to Anti-UN Rant." *Ottawa Citizen,* March 26.

Lafferty, Elaine. 1998. "Annan Targets Celebrities In Campaign For Survival of UN." *Irish Times,* April 25.

Langrod, Georges. 1963. *The International Civil Service: Its Origins, Its Nature, Its Evolution.* Dobbs Ferry, NY: Oceana.

Lash, Joseph P. 1961. *Dag Hammarskjold: Custodian of the Brushfire Peace.* Garden City, NJ: Doubleday.

———. 1962. "Dag Hammarskjöld's Conception of His Office." *International Organization* 16: 542–566.

Laurenti, Jeffrey. 1997a. "Kofi Annan's U.N. Reform Measures to Do More with Less: UNA-USA Assessment of the 'Track One' Initiatives." United Nations Association of the United States of America, March, http://www.unausa.org/site/pp.asp?c=fvKRI8MPJpF&b=475017.

———. 1997b. "A Critical Assessment of the Secretary-General's 'Track Two' Reform Program." United Nations Association of the United States of America, July, http://www.unausa.org/site/pp.asp?c= fvKRI8MPJpF&b= 475015.

Lauria, Joe. 2001. "Kofi Annan: Letting the World Hear Africa's Troubled Voice." *Boston Globe*, April 22.

Lavalle, Roberto. 1991. "The 'Inherent' Powers of the UN Secretary-General in the Political Sphere: A Legal Analysis." *Netherlands International Law Review* 37: 22–36.

Lentner, Howard H. 1965a. "The Diplomacy of the United Nations Secretary-General." *Western Political Quarterly* 18: 531–550.

———. 1965b. "The Political Responsibility and Accountability of the United Nations Secretary-General." *The Journal of Politics* 24: 839–860.

Levine, Israel E. 1962. *Champion of World Peace: Dag Hammarskjold*. New York: Julian Messner.

Levy, Jack. 2003. "Political Psychology and Foreign Policy." In *Oxford Handbook of Political Psychology*, edited by David O. Sears, Leonie Huddy, and Robert Jervis. Oxford: Oxford University Press.

Lians, Wang. 2000. "Annan's Millennium Dream." *Beijing Review* 43: 27–28.

Lie, Trygve. 1948. "Trygve Lie Appraises the Future of the U.N." *New York Times Magazine*, May 9, 10.

Lippman, Walter. 1961. "Dag Hammarskjöld: United Nations Pioneer." *International Organization* 15:547–548.

Little, Marie-Noëlle, ed. 2001. *The Poet and the Diplomat: The Correspondence of Dag Hammarskjöld and Alexis Ledger*. Syracuse, NY: Syracuse University Press.

———. 2002. "Travelers in Two Worlds: Dag Hammarskjöld and Alexis Leger." *Development Dialogue* 1: 59–79.

Littlejohns, Michael. 1999. "Annan Expected to Ride Out Storm Over Iraq and Other Problems as UN Honeymoon Period Ends." *Irish Times*, January 22.

Loescher, Gil. 2001. *The UNHCR and World Politics*. Oxford: Oxford University Press.

Loveday, Alexander. 1956. *Reflections on International Administration*. Oxford: Clarendon.

Luard, Evan. 1994. *The United Nations: How It Works and What it Does*, 2nd ed. New York: St. Martin's.

Luck, Edward C. 2005. "How Not to Reform the United Nations." *Global Governance* 11: 407–414.

Lyall, Sarah. 2001. "In Nobel Talk, Annan Sees Each Human Life as the Prize." *New York Times*, December 10.

Lynch, Colum. 1998. "Annan Crusades to Rebuild US Support for UN." *Boston Globe*, July 10.

———. 1999. "U.N. Spurns Request To Talk to Hijackers; Annan Limits Role in Hostage Crisis." *Washington Post*, December 29.

———. 2000a. "Annan Seeks Debate on U.N. Future in 'Millennium Report.' " *Washington Post*, April 4.

Lynch, Colum. 2000b. "U.N. Assured Gadhafi in Pan Am 103 Case." *Washington Post*, August 26.

———. 2005. "At the U.N., a Growing Republican Presence." *Washington Post*, July 21.

Lyons, Michael. 1997. "Presidential Character Revisited." *Political Psychology* 18: 791–811.

MacAskill, Ewen. 2005. "Britain Backs UN Sanctions After Losing Patience in Sudan Crisis." *Guardian*, March 8.

MacPherson, Myra. 1980. "Waldheim." *Washington Post*, January 18.

Mango, Anthony. 1988. "The Role of the Secretariats of International Institutions." In *International Institutions at Work*, edited by Paul Taylor and A.J.R. Groom. London: Pinter.

Maniatis, Gregory A. 2001. "On Top of the World." *New York Magazine* 34: 42–47.

Marfleet, B. Gregory. 2000. "The Operational Code of John F. Kennedy During the Cuban Missile Crisis: A Comparison of Public and Private Sources." *Political Psychology* 23: 545–558.

Marfleet, B. Gregory, and Colleen Miller. 2005. "Failure After 1441: Bush and Chirac in the UN Security Council." *Foreign Policy Analysis* 1: 333–360.

Marquardt, Michael J., and Nancy O. Berger. 2000. "Kofi Annan: Leading the United Nations into the Twenty-First Century." In *Global Leaders for the Twenty First Century*. Albany, NY: State University of New York Press.

Martens, Jens. 2005. *"In Larger Freedom": The Report of the UN Secretary-General for the Millennium+5 Summit 2005*. Berlin: Friedrich Ebert Foundation.

Martin, Ian. 2004. "International Intervention in East Timor." In *Humanitarian Intervention and International Relations*, edited by Jennifer M. Walsh. Oxford: Oxford University Press.

Martin, Ian, and Alexander Mayer-Rich. 2005. "The United Nations and East Timor: From Self-Determination to State-Building." *International Peacekeeping* 12: 125–145.

Mathiason, John R. 1997. "Who Controls the Machine, Revisited: Command and Control in the United Nations Reform Effort." *Public Administration and Development* 17: 387–397.

Maxwell, Simon. 2005. "How to Help Reform Multilateral Institutions: An Eight-Step Program for More Effective Collective Action." *Global Governance* 11: 415–424.

Mayer, Ann M. 1974. *Dag Hammarskjold: The Peacemaker*. Mankato, MN: Creative Education.

McDermott, Anthony. 1998. "UN Reform: A Task to Test the Patience of Sisyphus." *Security Dialogue* 29: 119–120.

McDermott, Rose. 2004. *Political Psychology in International Relations*. Ann Arbor, MI: University of Michigan Press.

McGreal, Chris. 2005. "Bush Forces UN Refugee Chief to Go." *Guardian*, January 20.

McIntosh, Malcolm, ed. 2003. "The United Nations Global Compact." Special issue, *Journal of Corporate Citizenship* 11.

McLaren, Robert I. 1980. *Civil Servants and Public Policy: A Comparative Study of International Secretariats*. Waterloo, Ontario: Wilfrid Laurier University Press.

Meisler, Stanley. 1995a. "Dateline U.N.: A New Hammarskjöld?" *Foreign Policy* 98: 180–197.

———. 1995b. *United Nations: The First Fifty Years*. New York: Atlantic Monthly Press.

———. 2003. "Man in the Middle: Travels With Kofi Annan." *Smithsonian* 33: 32–39.

Meron, Theodor. 1977. *The United Nations Secretariat: The Rules and the Practice*. Lexington, MA: Lexington.

———. 1982. "The Role of the Executive Heads." *New York University Journal of International Law and Politics* 14: 861–869.

———. 1991. " 'Exclusive Preserves' and the New Soviet Policy Toward the UN Secretariat." *American Journal of International Law* 85: 322–329.

Miller, Paul David. 1993. *Leadership in a Transnational World: The Challenge of Keeping the Peace*. Cambridge, MA: Institute for Foreign Policy Analysis.

Miller, Richard I. 1961. *Dag Hammarskjold and Crisis Diplomacy*. New York: Oceana.

Miron, David. 1982. "Tenure, Fixed Term Appointments and Secondment in the United Nations." *New York University Journal of International Law and Politics* 14: 783–798.

Monroe, Kristen R., ed. 2002. *Political Psychology*. Mahwah, NJ: Lawrence Erlbaum.

Montero, Maritza. 1997. "Political Psychology: A Critical Perspective." In *Critical Psychology: An Introduction*, edited by Dennis Fox and Isaac Prilleltensky. Thousand Oaks, CA: Sage.

Montgomery, Elizabeth Rider. 1973. *Dag Hammarskjold: Peacemaker for the U.N.* Champaign, IL: Garrard.

Morgenthau, Hans J. 1963. "The New Secretary-General." *Commentary* 35: 62–65.

———. 1965. "The U.N. of Dag Hammarskjold is Dead." *New York Times*, March 14.

Mortimer, Edward, and Richard Lambert. 1997. "Unraveling the UN." *Financial Times*, October 17.

Mouritzen, Hans. 1990. *The International Civil Service, A Study of Bureaucracy: International Organizations*. Hants, UK: Aldershot.

Müller, Joachim, ed. 2001. *Reforming the United Nations: The Quiet Revolution*. The Hague: Kluwer Law International.

Murthy, C.S.R. 1995. "The Role of the UN Secretary-General Since the End of the Cold War." *Indian Journal of International Law* 35: 181–196.

Mydans, Seth. 2002. "Cambodia and U.N. Break an Icy Silence on Khmer Rouge Trials." *New York Times*, September 1.

Nachmias, Nitza. 1993. "The Role of the Secretary-General in the Israeli-Arab and the Cyprus Disputes." In *The Challenging Role of the Secretary-General: Making "The Most Impossible Job in the World" Possible*, edited by Benjamin Rivlin and Leon Gordenker. Westport, CT: Praeger.

Narasimhan, C.V. 1962. "Administrative Changes in the Secretariat." In *Annual Review of United Nations Affairs, 1961–1962*, edited by Richard N. Swift. Dobbs Ferry, NY: Oceana.

———. 1988. *The United Nations: An Inside View*. New Delhi: Vikas.

Nayar, M.G. Kaldaharan. 1974. "Dag Hammarskjöld and U Thant—The Evolution of Their Office." *Case Western Reserve Journal of International Law* 7: 36–83.

Newman, Edward. 1998. *The UN Secretary-General From the Cold War to the New Era: A Global Peace and Security Mandate?* New York: St. Martin's.

———. 2001. "The Most Impossible Job in the World: The Secretary-General and Cyprus." In *The Work of the UN in Cyprus: Promoting Peace and Development*, edited by Oliver P. Richmond and James Ker-Lindsay. New York: Palgrave.

New York Times. 1971. "The New U.N. Secretary General: Kurt Waldheim." December 22.

———. 1997. "Kofi Annan's Cautious Style." February 12.

———. 1999. "A Turn for the Better at the U.N." January 3.

Newsweek. 1972. "United Nations: The New S-G." 79: 24.

Nicholas, H.G. 1975. *The United Nations As a Political Institution*, 5th ed. Oxford: Oxford University Press.

Nielsson, Gunnar P. 1994. *Mediation Under Crisis Conditions: The U.N. Secretary-General and the Falkland-Malvinas Islands Crisis*. Washington, DC: Pew Charitable Trust.

Norden, Eric. 1965. "The Strange Death of Dag Hammarskjöld." *Fact* 2: 3–11.

Nossiter, Bernard D. 1981. "Waldheim Moves to End Deadlock." *New York Times*, December 4.

———. 1988. " 'Our' Waldheim." *Nation* 246: 256.

O'Brien, Connor Cruise. 1962. *To Katanga and Back*. London: Hutchison & Co.

———. 1986. "The Very Model of a Secretary-General." *Times Literary Supplement*, January 17.

O'Flaherty, Michael. 2004. "Sierra Leone's Peace Process: The Role of the Human Rights Community." *Human Rights Quarterly* 266: 29–62.

Odio-Benito, Elizabeth. 2005. "No Peace Without Justice." In *The Adventure of Peace: Dag Hammarskjöld and the Future of the UN*, edited by Sten Ask and Anna Mark-Jungkvist. New York: Palgrave Macmillan.

Omestad, Thomas, and Linda Fasulo. 1998. "Behind the Serenity of the U.N.'s Annan." *U.S. News & World Report*, March 9, 36.

O'Neill, John T., and Nicholas Rees. 2005. *United Nations Peacekeeping in the Post-Cold War Era*. New York: Routledge.

Paepcke, Henrike. 2005. *Another U.N. Secretary-General Soon Decapitated?* DIAS Analysis 14. Duesseldorf: Duesseldorf Institute for Foreign and Security Policy.

Palley, Claire. 2005. *An International Relations Debacle: The UN Secretary-General's Mission of Good Offices in Cyprus 1999–2004.* Oxford: Hart.

Palumbo, Michael. 1988. *The Waldheim Files: Myth and Reality.* London: Faber and Faber.

Paquette, Laure. 2002. "An Individual and a Group of Nations: Dag Hammarskjöld, UN Secretary-General." In *Strategies of Individuals: How Individuals Make Extraordinary Changes to Organizations or Society.* New York: Nova Science.

Parker, Joakim E. 1992. "Electing the U.N. Secretary-General After the Cold War." *Hastings Law Journal* 44: 161–84.

Parsons, Jim. 1996. "Minnesota Winters Helped Educate New U.N. Leader." *Star Tribune,* December 14.

Pasternack, Scott. 1994. "The Role of the Secretary-General in Helping to Prevent Civil War." *New York University Journal of International Law and Politics* 26: 701–759.

Paulsell, William O. 1990. "Dag Hammarskjöld." In *Tough Minds, Tender Hearts: Six Prophets of Social Justice.* New York: Paulist.

Pearson, Lester B., and Robert W. Reford. 1961. "Dag Hammarskjold: Strength for Peace." *International Journal* 17: 1–6.

Pechota, Vratislav. 1972. "The Quiet Approach: A Study of the Good Offices Exercised by the United Nations Secretary-General in the Cause of Peace." In *Dispute Settlement Through the United Nations,* edited by K. Venkata Raman. Dobbs Ferry, NY: UNITAR-Oceana.

Peck, Connie. 2004. "Special Representatives of the Secretary-General." In *The UN Security Council: From the Cold War to the 21st Century,* edited by David M. Malone. Boulder, CO: Lynne Rienner.

Phelan, Edward J. 1949. *Yes and Albert Thomas.* New York: Columbia University Press.

Picco, Giandomenico. 1994. "The U.N. and the Use of Force: Leave the Secretary-General Out of it." *Foreign Affairs* 73: 14–18.

———. 1999. *Man Without a Gun: One Diplomat's Secret Struggle to Free the Hostages, Fight Terrorism, and End a War.* New York: Times Books.

Pisik, Betsy. 2001. "War on Terrorism, Afghanistan Post Straining U.N.'s Annual Budget." *Washington Times,* December 19.

Pitt, David, and Thomas G. Weiss, eds. 1986. *The Nature of United Nations Bureaucracies.* Boulder, CO: Westview.

Plimpton, Francis T.P. 1966. "Everyone Knows What a Secretary Is, And What a General Is, But What is a Secretary General?" *New York Times Magazine,* November 27, 58, 59, 142, 144, 146–149.

Post, Jerrold M., ed. 2003. *The Psychological Assessment of Political Leaders: With Profiles of Saddam Hussein and Bill Clinton.* Ann Arbor, MI: University of Michigan Press.

Post, Jerrold M. 2004. *Leaders and Their Followers in a Dangerous World: The Psychology of Political Behavior*. Ithaca, NY: Cornell University Press.

Prantl, Jochen, and Jean E. Krasno. 2004. "Informal Groups of Member States." In *The United Nations: Confronting the Challenges of a Global Society*, edited by Jean E. Krasno. Boulder, CO: Lynne Rienner.

Preparatory Commission of the United Nations Report. 1945. UN Document PC/20, 23 December.

Preston, Thomas. 1997. "Following the Leader: The Impact of U.S. Presidential Style Upon Group Dynamics, Structure and Decision." In *Beyond Groupthink: Group Decision Making in Foreign Policy*, edited by Paul't Hart, Eric Stern, and Bengt Sundelius. Ann Arbor, MI: University of Michigan Press.

———. 2001. *The President and His Inner Circle: Leadership Style and the Advisory Process in Foreign Affairs*. New York: Columbia University Press.

Preston, Thomas, and Paul't Hart. 1999. "Understanding and Evaluating Bureaucratic Politics: The Nexus between Political Leaders and Advisory Systems." *Political Psychology* 20: 49–98.

Preston, Thomas, and Margaret G. Hermann. 2004. "Presidential Leadership Style and the Foreign Policy Advisory Process." In *The Domestic Sources of American Foreign Policy: Insights and Evidence*, 4th ed., edited by Eugene R. Wittkopf and James M. McCormick. Lanham, MD: Rowman and Littlefield.

Price, Richard M., and Mark W. Zacher. 2004. *The United Nations and Global Security*. New York: Palgrave Macmillan.

Price, Stuart. 2005. "Knives Out for Kofi Annan." *New African* 436: 32.

Prins, Gwyn. 2005. "Lord Castlereagh's Return: The Significance of Kofi Annan's High Level Panel on Threats, Challenges and Change." *International Affairs* 81: 373–391.

Pubantz, Jerry, and John Allphin Moore, Jr. 2003. "Best of Times, Worst of Times: The Fortunes of the United Nations in the Middle East." *Alternatives: Turkish Journal of International Relations* 2: 122–145.

Pyman, T.A. 1961. "The United Nations Secretary-Generalship: A Review of Its Status, Functions, and Role." *Australian Outlook* 15: 240–259.

Ramcharan, Bertram G. 1982. "The Good Offices of the United Nations Secretary-General in the Field of Human Rights." *American Journal of International Law* 76: 130–141.

———. 1983. *Humanitarian Good Offices in International Law: The Good Offices of the United Nations Secretary-General in the Field of Human Rights*. Dordrecht: Martinus Nijhoff.

———. 1990a. "The Office of the United Nations Secretary-General." *Dalhousie Law Journal* 13: 742–757.

———. 1990b. "The History, Role and Organization of the 'Cabinet' of the United Nations Secretary-General." *Nordic Journal of International Law* 59: 103–116.

———. 1991. "Innovations in the Office of the United Nations Secretary-General." In *The International Law and Practice of Early-Warning and*

Preventive Diplomacy: The Emerging Global Watch. Dordrecht: Martinus Nijhoff.

———. 2001. "Good Offices, Preventive Action and Peacemaking by the United Nations Secretary-General." In *International Human Rights Monitoring Mechanisms: Essays in Honor of Jakob Th. Möller*, edited by Gudmundur Alfredsson, Jonas Grimheden, Bertram G. Ramcharan, and Alfred de Zayas. The Hague: Martinus Nijhoff.

———. 2002a. "The Protection Role of the United Nations Secretary-General." In *The United Nations High Commissioner for Human Rights*. The Hague: Martinus Nijhoff.

———. 2002b. "The Secretary-General and Human Security: Good Offices and Preventive Action." In *Human Rights and Human Security*. The Hague: Martinus Nijhoff.

Ramo, Joshua C. 2000. "The Five Virtues of Kofi Annan." *Time* 156: 35–42.

Ranshoffen-Wertheimer, Egon F. 1945. *The International Secretariat: A Great Experiment in International Administration*. Washington, DC: Carnegie Endowment for International Peace.

Ratner, Steven R. 1995. *The New UN Peacekeeping: Building Peace in Lands of Conflict After the Cold War*. New York: St. Martin's.

Ratnesar, Romesh. 1998. "A Star Turn for the Peace Broker." *Time* 151: 61–62.

Reeves, Eric. 2004. "Too Little, Too Late: Colin Powell's Visit to Darfur Only Highlights the United States' Inaction." *In These Times*, August 9.

Reeves, Richard. 1998. "Annan is Living Up to Great Task." *Buffalo News*, April 25.

Reitano, Richard. 2005. "Multilateral Diplomacy, Summits, and the United Nations." In *Multilateral Diplomacy and the United Nations Today*, 2nd ed., edited by James P. Muldoon, Joann Fagot Aviel, Richard Reitano, and Earl Sullivan. Boulder, CO: Westview.

Renshon, Stanley A., ed. 1993. *The Political Psychology of the Gulf War: Leaders, Publics, and the Process of Conflict*. Pittsburgh, PA: University of Pittsburgh Press.

———, ed. 1995. *The Clinton Presidency: Campaigning, Governing, and the Psychology of Leadership*. Boulder, CO: Westview.

———. 1996a. *High Hopes: The Clinton Presidency and the Politics of Ambition*. New York: New York University Press.

———. 1996b. *The Psychological Assessment of Presidential Candidates*. New York: New York University Press.

———. 2004. *In His Father's Shadow: The Transformation of George W. Bush*. New York: Palgrave Macmillan.

———. 2005. "Presidential Address: George W. Bush's Cowboy Politics— An Inquiry." *Political Psychology* 26: 585–614.

Renshon, Stanley A., and John Duckitt, eds. 2000. *Political Psychology: Cultural and Crosscultural Foundations*. New York: New York University Press.

Renshon, Stanley A., and Deborah Welch Larson, eds. 2003. *Good Judgment in Foreign Policy: Theory and Application*. Lanham, MD: Rowman and Littlefield.

Reymond, Henri, and Sidney Mailick. 1985. *International Personnel Policies and Practices.* New York: Praeger.

Reynolds, Paul. 2004. "Choice of Words Matter." *BBC News Online*, September 16, http://news.bbc.co.uk/2/hi/middle_east/3661976.stm.

Rich, Mari. 2000. "Kofi Annan." *Current Biography* 61: 3–9.

Rieff, David. 1999. "Up the Organization: The Successful Failures of Kofi Annan." *New Republic* 220: 19–23.

Rikhye, Indar Jit. 1983. "Hammarskjöld and Peacekeeping." In *Dag Hammarskjöld Revisited: The Secretary-General as a Force in World Politics*, edited by Robert S. Jordan. Durham, NC: Carolina Academic Press.

———. 1991. "Critical Elements in Determining the Suitability of Conflict Settlement Efforts by the United Nations Secretary-General." In *Timing the De-Escalation of International Conflicts*, edited by Louis Kriesberg and Stuart J. Thorson. Syracuse, NY: Syracuse University Press.

———. 1993. *Military Adviser to the Secretary-General: U.N. Peacekeeping and the Congo Crisis.* New York: St. Martin's.

Rivlin, Benjamin. 1993. "The Changing International Climate and the Secretary-General." In *The Challenging Role of the Secretary-General: Making "The Most Impossible Job in the World" Possible*, edited by Benjamin Rivlin and Leon Gordenker. Westport, CT: Praeger.

———. 1995. "The UN Secretary-Generalship at Fifty." In *The United Nations in the New World Order: The World Organization at Fifty*, edited by Dimitris Bourantonis and Jarrod Wiener. New York: St. Martin's.

———. 1996. "Boutros-Ghali's Ordeal: Leading the United Nations in an Age of Uncertainty." In *A United Nations for the Twenty-First Century. Peace, Security, and Development*, edited by Dimitris Bourantonis and Marios Evriviades. The Hague: Kluwer Law International.

———. 1997. "Leadership in the UN, 1997: The Secretary-General and the U.S.—A Symbiotic Relationship Under Stress." *International Journal* 52: 197–218.

Rivlin, Benjamin, and Leon Gordenker, eds. 1993. *The Challenging Role of the Secretary-General: Making "The Most Impossible Job in the World" Possible.* Westport, CT: Praeger.

Roche, Douglas R. 1998. "An Agenda for the 'People's Millennium Assembly.' " *Medicine, Conflict and Survival* 4: 86–96.

Rosati, Jerel A. 1995. "A Cognitive Approach to the Study of Foreign Policy." In *Foreign Policy Analysis: Continuity and Change in Its Second Generation*, edited by Laura Neack, Jeanne A.K. Hey, and Patrick J. Haney. Englewood Cliffs, NJ: Prentice Hall.

———. 2000. "The Power of Human Cognition in the Study of World Politics." *International Studies Review* 2: 45–75.

Rosenau, James N. 1992. *The United Nations in a Turbulent World.* Boulder, CO: Lynne Rienner.

Rosett, Claudia. 2005. "Kofi Annan's Silence: Blame Game." *New Republic* 232: 17–19.

Rösiö, Bengt. 1993. "The Ndola Crash and the Death of Dag Hammarskjöld." *Journal of Modern African Studies* 31: 661–671.

Rotberg, Robert I. 2003. *Cyprus After Annan: Next Steps Toward a Solution.* World Peace Foundation Report 37. Cambridge, MA: World Peace Foundation.

Rovine, Arthur W. 1970. *The First Fifty Years: The Secretary-General in World Politics 1920–1970.* Leyden: A. W. Sijthoff.

Rubenzer, Steven J., and Thomas R. Faschingbauer. 2004. *Personality, Character, and Leadership in the White House: Psychologists Assess the Presidents.* Washington, DC: Brassey's.

Ruggie, John G. 1999. "Kofi Annan's Goals on Iraq." *Washington Post,* January 18.

Rusk, Dean. 1965. "The First Twenty-Five Years of The United Nations: San Francisco to the 1970s." In *The Quest for Peace: The Dag Hammarskjöld Memorial Lectures,* edited by Andrew W. Cordier and Wilder Foote. New York: Columbia University Press.

Russell, Ruth B. 1958. *A History of the United Nations Charter: The Role of the United States, 1940–1945.* Washington, DC: Brookings.

Ryan, James Daniel. 2001. *The United Nations Under Kurt Waldheim, 1972–1981.* Lanham, MD: Scarecrow.

Ryan, Stephen. 2000. *The United Nations and International Politics.* New York: St. Martin's.

Sabosan, Jeffrey G. 1974. "Politics and Spirituality: A Study of Dag Hammarskjold." *Cithara* 14: 3–12.

Saksena, K.P. 1978. "Hammarskjold and the Congo Crisis: A Review." *India Quarterly* 34: 193–210.

Salomons, Dirk. 2003. "Good Intentions to Naught: The Pathology of Human Resources Management at the United Nations." In *Rethinking International Organizations: Pathology and Promise,* edited by Dennis Dijkzeul and Yves Beigbeder. New York: Bergham.

Saltman, Jack. 1988. *Kurt Waldheim: A Case to Answer.* London: Robson.

Samuels, Gertrude. 1979. "Waldheim's Style." *The New Leader* 62: 3–4.

Sarooshi, Danesh. 1999. *The United Nations and the Development of Collective Security: The Delegation by the UN Security Council of its Chapter VII Powers.* Oxford: Clarendon.

Satterfield, Jason M. 1998. "Cognitive-Affective States Predict Military and Political Aggression and Risk Taking: A Content Analysis of Churchill, Hitler, Roosevelt, and Stalin." *Journal of Conflict Resolution* 42: 667–690.

Schachter, Oscar. 1962. "Dag Hammarskjold and the Relation of Law to Politics." *American Journal of International Law* 56: 1–32.

———. 1983. "The International Civil Servant: Neutrality and Responsibility" In *Dag Hammarskjöld Revisited: The Secretary-General as a Force in World Politics,* edited by Robert S. Jordan. Durham, NC: Carolina Academic Press.

Schafer, Mark 1999. "Explaining Groupthink: Do the Psychological Characteristics of the Leader Matter?" *International Interactions* 25: 1–31.

Schachter, Oscar. 2000. "Issues in Assessing Psychological Characteristics at a Distance: An Introduction to the Symposium." *Political Psychology* 21: 511–527.

———. 2003. "Science, Empiricism, and Tolerance in the Study of Foreign Policymaking." *International Studies Review* 5: 171–177.

Schafer, Mark, and Scott Crichlow. 2000. "Bill Clinton's Operational Code: Assessing Source Material Bias." *Political Psychology* 21: 559–571.

Schechter, Michael G. 1987. "Leadership in International Organizations: Systemic, Organizational and Personality Factors." *Review of International Studies* 13: 197–220.

———. 1988. "The Political Roles of Recent World Bank Presidents." In *Politics in the United Nations System*, edited by Lawrence S. Finkelstein. Durham, NC: Duke University Press.

Schlesinger, Stephen C. 2003. *Act of Creation: The Founding of the United Nations*. Boulder, CO: Westview.

Schmemann, Serge. 1998. "Annan Is Stern But Friendly On Israel Visit." *New York Times*, March 25.

———. 2001. "U.N.'s Candid Reshaper: Kofi Atta Annan." *New York Times*, October 13.

Schwebel, Stephen M. 1951. "The Origins and Development of Article 99 of the Charter: The Powers of the Secretary-General of the U.N." *British Yearbook of International Law* 28: 371–382.

———. 1952. *The Secretary-General of the United Nations: His Political Powers and Practice*. New York: Greenwood.

———. 1972. "A More Powerful Secretary-General for the United Nations?" *American Journal of International Law Proceedings* 66: 78–89.

Sciolino, Elaine. 1997. "Despite Critics, New U.N. Chief Keeps His Style." *New York Times*, February 9.

Sears, David O., Leonie Huddy, and Robert Jervis. 2003. *Oxford Handbook of Political Psychology*. Oxford: Oxford University Press.

Settel, T.S. 1966. *The Light and the Rock: The Vision of Dag Hammarskjöld*. New York: E.P. Dutton.

Shaw, Eric D. 2003. "Saddam Hussein: Political Psychological Profiling Results Relevant to His Possession, Use, and Possible Transfer of Weapons of Mass Destruction (WMD) to Terrorist Groups." *Studies in Conflict & Terrorism* 26: 347–364.

Shawcross, William. 2000. *Deliver Us From Evil: Peacekeepers, Warlords and a World of Endless Conflict*. New York: Simon and Schuster.

Sheikh, Ahmed. 1970. "The Dynamics of the Role of Secretary-General in Divided Counsels on U.N. Peace-Keeping." *Political Science Review* 9: 237–257.

Sheldon, Richard N. 1987. *Dag Hammarskjöld*. New York: Chelsea House.

Shelley, Toby. 2004. *Endgame in the Western Sahara: What Future for Africa's Last Colony?* London: Zed.

Shimura, Hisako. 2001. "The Role of the UN Secretariat in Organizing Peacekeeping." In *United Nations Peacekeeping Operations: Ad Hoc*

Missions, Permanent Engagements, edited by Ramesh Thakur and Albrecht Schnabel. New York: United Nations University Press.

Sicherman, Harvey. 1998. "The Containment of America." *Orbis* 42: 453–463.

Silber, Laura. 1998a. "UN Reformer Looks for New Friends in World of Business." *Financial Times*, March 17.

———. 1998b. "UN Chief Seeks Role for Millennium." *Financial Times*, September 21.

Simma, Bruno. 2002. *The Charter of the United Nations: A Commentary*, 2nd ed. Oxford: Oxford University Press.

Simon, Charlie M. 1967. *Dag Hammarskjöld*. New York: E.P. Dutton.

Singh, Amarnath. 1998. "Annan Wags Finger At Africa." *Financial Mail*, April 24.

Skidelsky, Lord. 2005. "Dag Hammarskjöld's Assumptions and the Future of the UN." In *The Adventure of Peace: Dag Hammarskjöld and the Future of the UN*, edited by Sten Ask and Anna Mark-Jungkvist. New York: Palgrave Macmillan.

Skjelsbaek, Kjell. 1991. "The UN Secretary-General and the Mediation of International Disputes." *Journal of Peace Research* 28: 99–115.

Slim, Mongi. 1965. "Dag Hammarskjöld's Quest for Peace." In *The Quest for Peace: The Dag Hammarskjöld Memorial Lectures*, edited by Andrew W. Cordier and Wilder Foote. New York: Columbia University Press.

Smith, Bradford. 1964. "Dag Hammarskjöld: Peace by Juridical Sanction." In *Men of Peace*. Philadelphia: J.B. Lippincott.

Smith, Courtney B. 2003. "More Secretary or General? Effective Leadership at the United Nations." *International Politics* 40: 137–147.

———. 2004. "The Politics of U.S.-UN Reengagement: Achieving Gains in a Hostile Environment." *International Studies Perspectives* 5: 197–215.

———. 2005. "Politics and Values at the United Nations: Kofi Annan's Balancing Act." Working paper for *The UN Secretary-General as a Moral Authority: Ethics and Religion in International Leadership*.

———. 2006. *Politics and Process at the United Nations: The Global Dance*. Boulder, CO: Lynne Rienner.

Smith, Michael G., and Moreen Dee. 2003. *Peacekeeping in East Timor: The Path to Independence*. Boulder, CO: Lynne Rienner.

Smyth, Patrick. 1999. "Annan Accepts UN Must Carry Blame For Serb Atrocities at Srebrenica." *Irish Times*, December 7.

Snare, Charles E. 1992. "Applying Personality Theory to Foreign Policy Behavior: Evaluating Three Methods of Assessment." In *Political Psychology and Foreign Policy*, edited by Eric Singer and Valerie Hudson. Boulder, CO: Westview.

Snow, C.P. 1966. "Dag Hammarskjöld." In *Variety of Men*. New York: Charles Scribner's Sons.

Soderberg, Nancy E. 2005. "The Role of the UN in an Age of US Hegemony." In *The Adventure of Peace: Dag Hammarskjöld and the Future of the UN*, edited by Sten Ask and Anna Mark-Jungkvist. New York: Palgrave Macmillan.

Söderberg, Sten. 1967. *Hammarskjöld: A Pictorial Biography*. New York: Viking.

Sözen, Ahmet. 2004. "A Model of Power-Sharing in Cyprus: From the 1959 London-Zurich Agreements to the Annan Plan." *Turkish Studies* 5: 61–77.

Span, Paula. 1998. "The U.N.'s Man of Peace; For Kofi Annan, The World's Burdens Are Not Too Much to Bear." *Washington Post*, February 28.

Srivastava, Padma. 1969. *UN and Peaceful Co-Existence: The Role of the United Nations in Peaceful Co-Existence as Conceived and Promoted by its Secretaries-General*. Delhi: Universal.

The Stanley Foundation. 1991. *The United Nations: Structure and Leadership for a New Era*. Report of the Twenty-Second United Nations Issues Conference, February 22–24.

———. 1996. *The United Nations and the Twenty–First Century: The Imperative for Change*. Report of the Thirty-First United Nations of the Next Decade Conference, June 16–21.

———. 1997. *Making UN Reform Work: Improving Member State-Secretariat Relations*. Report of the Twenty-Eighth United Nations Issues Conference, February 21–23.

———. 2004. *Updating the United Nations to Confront 21st Century Threats: The Challenge to the High-Level Panel*. Report of the Thirty-Ninth Conference on the United Nations of the Next Decade, June 11–16.

———. 2005. *Toward "Larger Freedom."* Report of the Fortieth Conference on the United Nations of the Next Decade, June 17–22.

Steele, Jonathan. 1996. "Profile: A Peace of the Action." *Guardian*, December 30.

———. 2001. "UN Rebuffs British Reforms." *Guardian*, January 6.

Stein, Eric. 1962. "Mr. Hammarskjold, The Charter Law and the Future Role of the United Nations Secretary General." *American Journal of International Law* 56: 9–32.

Steinberg, Blema S. 2005. "Indira Gandhi: The Relationship Between Personality Profile and Leadership Style." *Political Psychology* 26: 755–789.

Stephan, Maria J. 2004. "The Case for Peacekeeping in the Occupied Palestinian Territories." *International Peacekeeping* 11: 248–270.

Stewart, Cameron. 1998. "The Peacemaker." *Australian*, February 24.

Stewart, Philip D., Margaret G. Hermann, and Charles F. Hermann. 1989. "Modeling the 1973 Soviet Decision to Support Egypt." *American Political Science Review* 83: 35–59.

Stolpe, Sven. 1966. *Dag Hammarskjöld: A Spiritual Portrait*. New York: Charles Scribner's Sons.

Sunoo, Brenda Paik. 2000. "Around the World in HR Ways." *Workforce* 79: 54–58.

Sutterlin, James S. 1993. "United Nations Decision-Making: Future for the Security Council and the Secretary-General." In *Collective Security in a Changing World*, edited by Thomas G. Weiss. London: Lynne Rienner.

———. 2003. *The United Nations and the Maintenance of International Security: A Challenge to Be Met*, 2nd ed. Westport, CT: Praeger.

Sylvester, Christine. 1980. "UN Elites: Perspectives on Peace." *Journal of Peace Research* 17: 305–323.

Szasz, Paul C. 1991. "The Role of the U.N. Secretary-General: Some Legal Aspects." *New York University Journal of International Law and Politics* 24: 161–198.

Tanner, Henry. 1971. "Security Council Names Waldheim to Succeed Thant." *New York Times*, December 22.

Tavernier, Paul. 1993. "The UN Secretary-General: Attitudes and Latitudes." In *The Iran-Iraq War: The Politics of Aggression*, edited by Farhang Rajaee. Gainesville, FL: University Press of Florida.

Taylor, Paul, Sam Daws, and Ute Adamczick-Gertes. 1997. *Documents on the Reform of the United Nations*. Aldershot: Dartmouth.

Tessitore, John. 2000. *Kofi Annan: The Peacekeeper*. New York: Franklin Watts.

Thakur, Ramesh. 2003. "Reforming the United Nations: Changing With and For the Times." *International Peacekeeping* 10: 40–61.

———. 2004. "United Nations Security Council Reform." *African Security Review* 13:67–74.

———. 2005. "A Shared Responsibility for a More Secure World." *Global Governance* 11: 281–289.

Thakur, Ramesh, and Albrecht Schnabel, eds. 2003. *Conflict Prevention: The Secretary-General's Report—The Way Forward*. Tokyo: United Nations University Press.

Thant, U. 1965. "Looking Ahead." In *The Quest for Peace: The Dag Hammarskjöld Memorial Lectures*, edited by Andrew W. Cordier and Wilder Foote. New York: Columbia University Press.

Tharoor, Shashi. 1999. "Image of the United Nations." Interview by Michael Littlejohns, with Barbara Crossette and Ian Williams, *World Chronicle*, no. 760 (October 20): 1–12.

———. 2005. "The Role of the Secretary-General." In *The Adventure of Peace: Dag Hammarskjöld and the Future of the UN*, edited by Sten Ask and Anna Mark-Jungkvist. New York: Palgrave Macmillan.

Tharoor, Shashi, and Sam Daws. 2001. "Humanitarian Intervention: Getting Past the Reefs." *World Policy Journal* 18: 21–30.

Thelin, Bengt. 2002. "Dag Hammarskjöld—Nature, Landscape, Literature." *Development Dialogue* 1: 81–90.

Thies, Cameron G. 2004. "Individuals, Institutions, and Inflation: Conceptual Complexity, Central Bank Independence, and the Asian Crisis." *International Studies Quarterly* 48: 579–602.

Thorpe, Deryck. 1969. *Hammarskjold: Man of Peace*. Ilfacombe, Devon: Arthur H. Stockwell.

Townley, Ralph. 1968. *The United Nations: A View From Within*. New York: Charles Scribner's Sons.

Trachtenberg, Larry. 1982. "Dag Hammarskjöld as Leader: A Problem of Definition." *International Journal* 37: 613–635.

Trachtenberg, Larry. 1983. "A Bibliographic Essay on Dag Hammarskjöld." In *Dag Hammarskjöld Revisited: The UN Secretary-General as a Force in World Politics*, edited by Robert S. Jordan. Durham, NC: Carolina Academic Press.

Traub, James. 1998. "Kofi Annan's Next Test." *New York Times Magazine*, March 28, 44–50, 62, 71, 74, and 80–81.

———. 2004. "Traveling With Kofi Annan." *Slate*, November 22, http://slate.msn.com/id/ 2110040/.

———. 2005. "The Security Council's Role: Off-Target." *New Republic* 232: 14–17.

Trickey, Mike. 1999. "Two-tier UN Not Likely to Change: Axworthy Gets Little Satisfaction After Questioning Annan About Council Inequality." *Gazette*, October 1.

Tripoli, John S. 1998. "Kofi Annan's Clever Footwork Keeps Him In On Every Deal." *Sunday Telegraph*, December 6.

Turner, Craig. 1996. "Diplomat from Ghana is Picked to Head UN." *Los Angeles Times*, December 14.

———. 1998. "U.N. Chief Gets Starring Role." *Los Angeles Times*, April 22.

UN Chronicle. 1991. "Dag Hammarskjöld: 'Virtuoso of Multilateral Diplomacy.' " 28: 74–75.

———. 1996. "Kofi Annan: The International Civil Servant." 33: 5–8.

UN News Service. 2005. "Positions of Key Players in Western Sahara Quasi-Irreconcilable, Says UN Envoy." October 17. http://www.un.org/apps/news/storyAr.asp?NewsID=16260 &Cr=western&Cr1=sahara&Kw1= walsum&Kw2=&Kw3=.

United Nations. 1997. *Re-Form: The Bulletin of United Nations Reform.* No. 2.

United Nations Association of the United States of America. 1986. *Leadership at the United Nations: The Roles of the Secretary-General and the Member States.* New York: United Nations Association of the United States of America.

———. 2001. *The Preparedness Gap: Making Peace Operations Work in the 21st Century.* New York: United Nations Association of the United States of America.

Urquhart, Brian. 1972. *Hammarskjold.* New York: Alfred A. Knopf.

———. 1981. "International Peace and Security: Thoughts on the Twentieth Anniversary of Dag Hammarskjöld's Death." *Foreign Affairs* 60: 1–16.

———. 1983. "Dag Hammarskjöld: The Private Person in a Very Public Office." In *Dag Hammarskjöld Revisited: The Secretary-General as a Force in World Politics*, edited by Robert S. Jordan. Durham, NC: Carolina Academic Press.

———. 1985. "Die Rolle des Generalsekretars." *Aussenpolitik* 36: 254–260.

———. 1987. *A Life in Peace and War.* New York: Harper and Row.

———. 1995. "Selecting the World's CEO: Remembering the Secretaries-General." *Foreign Affairs* 74: 21–26.

———. 1996. "The Role of the Secretary-General." In *U.S. Foreign Policy and the United Nations System*, edited by Charles William Maynes and Richard S. Williamson. New York: W.W. Norton.

————. 1998. "The Evolution of the Secretary-General." In *The Dumbarton Oaks Conversations and the United Nations, 1944–1994*, edited by Ernest R. May and Angeliki E. Laiou. Washington, DC: Dumbarton Oaks Research Library and Collection.

————. 2000. "In The Name of Humanity." *New York Review of Books* 47: 19–22.

————. 2002. "Dag Hammarskjöld: A Leader in the Field of Culture." *Development Dialogue* 1: 15–16.

————. 2005. "The Secretary-General: Why Dag Hammarskjöld?" In *The Adventure of Peace: Dag Hammarskjöld and the Future of the UN*, edited by Sten Ask and Anna Mark-Jungkvist. New York: Palgrave Macmillan.

Urquhart, Brian, and Erskine Childers. 1990. *A World in Need of Leadership: Tomorrow's United Nations.* Uppsala, Sweden: Dag Hammarskjöld Foundation.

————. 1992. *Towards a More Effective United Nations.* Uppsala, Sweden: Dag Hammarskjöld Foundation.

————. 1994. *Renewing the United Nations System.* Uppsala, Sweden: Dag Hammarskjöld Foundation.

————. 1996. *A World in Need of Leadership: Tomorrow's United Nations, A Fresh Appraisal.* Uppsala, Sweden: Dag Hammarskjöld Foundation.

Usborne, David. 1998. "The Forceful Peacemaker: Kofi Annan, United Nations Secretary General." *Independent*, December 19.

Valenty, Linda O., and Ofer Feldman, eds. 2002. *Political Leadership for the New Century: Personality and Behavior Among American Leaders.* Westport, CT: Praeger.

Van Boven, Theo. 1991. "The Role of the United Nations Secretariat in the Area of Human Rights." *New York University Journal of International Law* 24: 69–107.

Van Dusen, Henry P. 1964. *Dag Hammarskjöld: The Statesman and His Faith.* New York: Harper and Row.

————. 1967. "Dag Hammarskjold: The Inner Person." In *Paths to World Order*, edited by Andrew W. Cordier and Kenneth L. Maxwell. New York: Columbia University Press.

Vance, Cyrus R., and David A. Hamburg. 1997. *Pathfinders for Peace: A Report to the UN Secretary-General on the Role of Special Representatives and Personal Envoys.* New York: Carnegie Corporation.

Viorst, Milton. 1972. "Kurt Waldheim: Embattled Peacemaker." *Saturday Review* 55: 39–44.

Virally, Michael. 1958. "The Political Role of the Secretary-General of the United Nations." *Annuaire Francais de Droit International* IV: 369–399.

Wagner, Cynthia G. 2004. "Preventing Genocide: Plan For Averting Humanitarian Crises is Outlined by UN Secretary-General." *Futurist* 38: 13–14.

Waldheim, Kurt. 1983. "Dag Hammarskjöld and the Office of United Nations Secretary-General." In *Dag Hammarskjöld Revisited: The UN Secretary-General as a Force in World Politics*, edited by Robert S. Jordan. Durham, NC: Carolina Academic Press.

Walker, Martin. 2005. "Bush v. Annan: Taming the United Nations." *World Policy Journal* 22: 9–18.

Walker, Stephen G. 1990. "The Evolution of Operational Code Analysis." *Political Psychology* 11: 403–418.

———. 2000. "Assessing Psychological Characteristics at a Distance: Symposium Lessons and Future Research Directions." *Political Psychology* 21: 597–602.

———. 2003. "Operational Code Analysis as a Scientific Research Program: A Cautionary Tale." In *Progress in International Relations Theory: Appraising the Field*, edited by Colin Elman and Miriam Fendius Elman. Cambridge, MA: MIT Press.

———. 2004. "Role Identities and the Operational Code of Political Leaders." In *Advances in Political Psychology, Volume 1*, edited by Margaret G. Hermann. Amsterdam: Elsevier.

Walker, Stephen G., Mark Schafer, and Michael D. Young. 1998. "Systematic Procedures for Operational Code Analysis: Measuring and Modeling Jimmy Carter's Operational Code." *International Studies Quarterly* 42: 175–190.

———. 1999. "Presidential Operational Codes and Foreign Policy Conflicts in the Post-Cold War World." *Journal of Conflict Resolution* 43: 610–625.

Walker, Stephen G., and Mark Schafer. 2000. "The Political Universe of Lyndon B. Johnson and His Advisors: Diagnostic and Strategic Propensities in Their Operational Codes." *Political Psychology* 21: 529–543.

Wallensteen, Peter. 1995. *Dag Hammarskjöld*. Stockholm: Swedish Institute.

———. 2005. "A Room of Quiet." Interview by Florence Sperling. *Encounter*, Australian Broadcasting Corporation, April 10.

Waltz, Kenneth N. 1959. *Man, the State, and War: A Theoretical Analysis*. New York: Colombia University Press.

Waters, Maurice, ed. 1967. *The United Nations: International Organization and Administration*. New York: Macmillan.

Weintraub, Walter. 1986. "Personality Profiles of American Presidents as Revealed in Their Public Statements: The Presidential News Conferences of Jimmy Carter and Ronald Reagan." *Political Psychology* 7: 285–295.

Weiss, Thomas G. 1998. "Humanitarian Shell Games: Whither UN Reform?" *Security Dialogue* 29: 9–23.

———. 2000. "The Politics of Humanitarian Ideas." *Security Dialogue* 31: 11–23.

Weiss, Thomas G., David P. Forsythe, and Roger A. Coate. 2004. *The United Nations and Changing World Politics*, 4th ed. Boulder, CO: Westview.

Weiss, Thomas G., and Karen E. Young. 2005. "Compromise and Credibility: Security Council Reform?" *Security Dialogue* 36: 131–154.

White, Nigel D. 1997. *Keeping the Peace: The United Nations and the Maintenance of International Peace and Security*, 2nd ed. Manchester: Manchester University Press.

———. 2001. "Commentary on the Report of the Panel on United Nations Peace Operations (The Brahimi Report)." *Journal of Conflict and Security Law* 6: 127–146.

Whittaker, David J. 1997. *United Nations in the Contemporary World*. London: Routledge.

Wiener, Jarrod. 1995. "Leadership, the United Nations, and the New World Order." In *The United Nations in the New World Order*, edited by Dimitris Bourantonis and Jarrod Wiener. London: Macmillan.

Wilenski, Peter. 1991. "Reforming the United Nations for the Post-Cold War Era." In *Whose New World Order: What Role for the United Nations*, edited by Mara R. Bustelo and Philip Alston. Sydney: Federation.

Wilkinson, Philip. 2000. "Sharpening the Weapons of Peace: Peace Support Operations and Complex Emergencies." *International Peacekeeping* 7: 63–79.

Williams, David C. 1958. "Dag Hammarskjold: Lonely Leader of the U.N." *Progressive* 22: 22–24.

Williams, Ian. 1997. "Helms's Coffee for Kofi." *Nation* 264: 21–24.

———. 1998. "Balancing Double Standards at the U.N." *Washington Report on Middle East Affairs* 17: 47, 91.

———. 2000. "Kofi Annan: A 'Moral Voice' " *Nation* 270: 20–24.

———. 2004. "Kofi Annan Speech on Rule of Law Preempts Bush, Israeli Addresses to U.N." *Washington Report on Middle East Affairs* 23: 18–20.

———. 2005. "The Right's Assault on Kofi Annan." *Nation* 280: 13–16.

Winchmore, Charles. 1965. "The Secretariat: Retrospect and Prospect." *International Organization* 19: 622–639.

Wines, Michael. 2005. "In Zimbabwe, Homeless Belie Leader's Claim." *New York Times*, November 13.

Winter, David G. 1987. "Leader Appeal, Leader Performance, and the Motive Profiles of Leaders and Followers: A Study of American Presidents and Elections." *Journal of Personality and Social Psychology* 52: 196–202.

———. 1990. "Measuring Personality at a Distance: Development of an Integrated System for Scoring Motives in Running Text." In *Perspectives in Personality: Approaches to Understanding Lives*, edited by Abigail J. Stewart, J.M. Healey, Jr., and D.J. Ozer. London: Jessica Kingsley.

———. 1992. "Personality and Foreign Policy: Historical Overview." In *Political Psychology and Foreign Policy*, edited by Eric Singer and Valerie Hudson. Boulder, CO: Westview.

———. 2003a. "Assessing Leaders' Personalities: A Historical Survey of Academic Research Studies." In *The Psychological Assessment of Political Leaders*, edited by Jerrold M. Post. Ann Arbor, MI: University of Michigan Press.

———. 2003b. "Personality and Political Behavior." In *Oxford Handbook of Political Psychology*, edited by David O. Sears, Leonie Huddy, and Robert Jervis. Oxford: Oxford University Press.

Winter, David G., and Abigail J. Stewart. 1977. "Content Analysis as a Technique for Assessing Political Leaders." In *A Psychological Examination of Political Leaders*, edited by Margaret G. Hermann. New York: Free Press.

298 ✦ BIBLIOGRAPHY

Winter, David G., Margaret G. Hermann, Walter Weintraub, and Stephen G. Walker. 1991. "The Personalities of Bush and Gorbachev Measured at a Distance: Procedures, Portraits, and Policy." *Political Psychology* 12: 215–245.

Wren, Christopher S. 2000. "UN Says Israel Pullout Complete." *Gazette*, June 17.

Xing, Qu. 2005. "International Negotiator: Mission Beijing." In *The Adventure of Peace: Dag Hammarskjöld and the Future of the UN*, edited by Sten Ask and Anna Mark-Jungkvist. New York: Palgrave Macmillan.

Yandon, Yahspal. 1968. "UNEF, the Secretary-General, and International Diplomacy in the Third Arab-Israeli War." *International Organization* 22: 529–556.

Yoder, Amos. 1996. *The Evolution of the United Nations System*, 3rd ed. Washington, DC: Taylor and Francis.

Yost, Jack. 1991. "The Secretary-General: Should His Role Be Enhanced?" In *A New World Order: Can It Bring Security to the World's People?* edited by Walter Hoffman. Washington, DC: World Federalist Association.

Young, Michael D. 1996. "Cognitive Mapping Meets Semantic Networks." *Journal of Conflict Resolution* 40: 395–414.

———. 2000. "Automating Assessment at a Distance." *Political Psychologist* 5: 17–23.

———. 2001. "Building WorldView(s) with Profiler+." In *Progress in Communication Sciences: Vol. 17. Applications of Computer Content Analysis*, edited by George A. Barnett (series editor) and Mark D. West (volume editor). Westport, CT: Ablex.

Young, Michael D., and Mark Schafer. 1998. "Is There a Method in Our Madness? Ways of Assessing Cognition in International Relations." *Mershon International Studies Review* 42: 63–96.

Young, Oran. 1967. *The Intermediaries: Third Parties in International Crises.* Princeton, NJ: Princeton University Press.

———. 1991. "Political Leadership and Regime Formation: On the Development of Institutions in International Society." *International Organization* 45: 281–308.

Zacher, Mark W. 1966. "The Secretary-General and the United Nations' Function of Peaceful Settlement." *International Organization* 20: 724–749.

———. 1969. "The Secretary-General: Some Comments on Recent Research." *International Organization* 23: 932–950.

———. 1970. *Dag Hammarskjold's United Nations.* New York: Columbia University Press.

———. 1983. "Hammarskjöld's Conception of the United Nations' Role in World Politics." In *Dag Hammarskjöld Revisited: The Secretary-General as a Force in World Politics*, edited by Robert S. Jordan. Durham, NC: Carolina Academic Press.

Zedillo, Ernesto, ed. 2005. *Reforming the United Nations for Peace and Security: Proceedings of a Workshop to Analyze the Report of the High-Level Panel on Threats, Challenges and Change*. New Haven, CT: Yale Center for the Study of Globalization.

Ziring, Lawrence, Robert E. Riggs, and Jack C. Plano. 2005. *The United Nations: International Organization and World Politics*, 4th ed. Belmont, CA: Thomas Wadsworth.

INDEX

(Please note that page numbers in *italics* indicate an end note.)